James Pitman.

Alphabets and Reading

"Reading maketh a full man; conference a ready man; and writing an exact man."

Francis Bacon

Alphabets and Reading

THE INITIAL TEACHING ALPHABET

by
Sir James Pitman, K.B.E., *and* John St. John

Pitman Publishing Corporation
New York   London   Toronto

First Published 1969

PITMAN PUBLISHING CORPORATION
20 East 46th Street, New York, N.Y. 10017

SIR ISAAC PITMAN AND SONS LTD.
Pitman House, Parker Street, Kingsway, London, W.C.2
P.O. Box 6038, Portal Street, Nairobi, Kenya

SIR ISAAC PITMAN (AUST.) PTY. LTD.
Pitman House, Bouverie Street, Carlton, Victoria 3053, Australia

PITMAN PUBLISHING CORPORATION (S.A.) PTY. LTD.
P.O. Box 7721, Johannesburg, Transvaal, S. Africa

SIR ISAAC PITMAN (CANADA) LTD.
Pitman House, 381–383 Church Street, Toronto, 3

THE COPP CLARK PUBLISHING COMPANY
517 Wellington Street, Toronto, 2B

Library of Congress Catalog Card
Number 74–79457

Printed in Great Britain by Western Printing Services Ltd, Bristol
F9–(G. 3571)

Introduction

As ITS TITLE IMPLIES, this book is not merely an apologia for my own initial teaching alphabet. While I hope it will come to be recognized as the definitive work on the structure and uses of i.t.a., the book's scope and purpose are more ambitious. Much of the first half is devoted to establishing the theoretical and historical justification for a special teaching medium and to showing that i.t.a., far from being an isolated invention, comes with a long pedigree of earlier reformed and teaching alphabets behind it. Since the time of the first Elizabethans, when our present spelling began to solidify and came to be regarded as sacrosanct, teachers and men of letters have tried out numerous ways of overcoming the difficulties inherent in an inadequate alphabet and of rationalizing spelling. My hope is that my own attempt will be assessed against the perspective of four centuries of wrestling with a problem that has provoked the intellects of men such as Benjamin Franklin, Walter Skeat, Daniel Jones, and Bernard Shaw, to mention but a few. There was also my grandfather, Sir Isaac Pitman, who devoted the greater part of his life to Fonotypy (see Chapter 6) as well as Fonography, his system of shorthand.

In other chapters will be found an interpretation of the subtle but as yet poorly understood psychological and conceptual processes involved in reading and writing, together with an analysis of the *methods* used to teach the skill and an attempt to explain and resolve the conflicts among the teachers these give rise to. Apart from one lengthy footnote, I have eschewed the temptation to propound my own personal views on teaching methods, because I am concerned not with a method of teaching but with a teaching *medium* that is applicable to all methods. On the other hand, throughout the book I have not hesitated to advocate the importance of linguistic competence: for me, the learning of reading and language are inseparable.

Although this book confidently pleads a case, it is, I trust, sufficiently well documented and rigorously argued not to be dismissed as a polemic. There is no sin in advocating one's opinions on education strongly, provided they are held honestly; if I had not done so in the past, i.t.a. might by now have joined many other forgotten, untried or only half-tried innovations. Of course teachers cannot be blamed for being chary of proposed changes in long-established practice or for being soured by what appear to be the naïve enthusiasms of the reformer: only too often has education been influenced by fashion or some gimmicky pseudo-psychological approach. But it is equally true that education suffers from vested interests alarmed at the prospect of reputations being questioned and lecture notes scrapped; from prejudice masquerading as down-to-earth, commonsensical "experience" or, more cunningly, as enlightened, open-minded "neutrality;" from dogmas and assumptions that have never been tested. There is no guarantee that good new ideas in education will spread spontaneously. Theory and evidence have to be reinforced by persuasion and argument.

The audience envisaged for this book is therefore primarily the teachers and the educationists. Their verdict (or the children's?) will be decisive and will carry the day whereas the dry-as-dust, albeit impressive statistics of the researcher provide no more than one of the factors on which a teacher's decision is based. Even so, most of the chapters are well within the competence of the layman, though if he skips the series of extracts from teachers' opinions in Chapters 10 and 11, he will not lose the thread of the book's argument; similarly he may wish to hurry past the descriptions of some of the earlier alphabets (pages 76–105) and to avoid the appendixes and the detailed explanations of the i.t.a. characters (pages 131–9).

It may be wondered why this book was not published earlier. The reason for the delay was partly in order to be able to include a summary of the main i.t.a. research findings (Chapter 9) together with a few, carefully pondered criticisms of what seem to me to be severe and quite unnecessary faults in the research design—despite its overall commendations. Delay was also necessary to accumulate sufficient experience of using the new alphabet before various conclusions could be drawn and/or confirmed. Now that i.t.a. is established in more than 10,000 schools in various parts of the world and i.t.a. readers are available from over 70 publishers, it seems a good moment to survey and consolidate what we have learned. Similarly, I believe it would now be a mistake if the i.t.a. characters or spellings were to be tampered with; in course of time research will perhaps be undertaken, as explained in Chapter 13, and this may lead to some minor changes, but for a decade or two the new alphabet should be left alone and allowed an unimpeded chance to establish itself and generate its own set of attitudes. Meanwhile, i.t.a. is there for all to use without charge, royalty, or restriction. What is left of the absolute copyright has been passed to The i.t.a. Foundation[1] so that it has the power to ensure worldwide conformity to the characters and spellings and to advise and approve any proposals for researches into possible improvements.

Many people have contributed to the early experiments with i.t.a., to the research, and to the contents of this book. In particular I wish to thank the numerous head and assistant teachers who have essayed i.t.a. in their classrooms, several of whose experiences are recorded in Chapters 10, 11 and 12. I acknowledge gratefully the financial help from H.M. Government; the Ford Foundation; the Fund for the Advancement of Education; the Grant Foundation (with the Educational Records Bureau) of New York; the late W. Howard Samuel; Associated Television; Boots Pure Drug Co. Ltd.; Equity and Law Assurance Society Ltd.; and Sir Isaac Pitman & Sons Ltd. Special thanks are also due to London University Institute of Education and the National Foundation for Educational Research for accepting my proposal for the research described in Chapter 9 and those who supported it including Lord Eccles, then Minister of Education; Percy Wilson, H.M. Chief Inspector; Sir William Alexander, Secretary of the Association of Education Committees; Sir Ronald Gould, Secretary of the National Union of Teachers; Walter James, Editor of *The Times Educational Supplement*; Maurice Harrison and other Directors of Education; Dr. Horace King, now Speaker in the House, and numerous of my Parliamentary colleagues.

I am indebted to all those from whose works I have quoted; among them

[1] 154 Southampton Row, London, W.C.1; the American i.t.a. Foundation has premises at Hofstra University, New York.

are Dr. Joyce Morris; the National Foundation for Educational Research in England and Wales; Dr. John Downing; Professor M. D. Vernon; the Cambridge University Press; Penguin Books; *Punch*.

I owe a particular debt to Dr. John Downing and his colleagues who were employed to carry out the research; to Dr. A. Mazurkiewicz, Dr. Ben Wood, Dr. H. Tanyzer, Dr. R. Block, and others in the United States.

Among the many in Britain who have helped with advice and information I must mention the names of Professor David Abercrombie, Lionel Elvin and Dr. W. Wall. Finally, I must express gratitude to my secretaries, Miss Betty Blissett and Miss Dorothy Nordon; and to Miss M. Donaldson, George Hartfield, David Dickson, and the printers for having coped with exceptional demands on their technical skill.

JAMES PITMAN

Author's Note

THIS BOOK IS the product of lengthy and genuine collaboration. Lack of time made it necessary for me to seek a partner in Mr. John St. John, an experienced and professional author. For the most part the ideas are mine, but the words are his; he also undertook much of the research. I do, however, accept responsibility for all that is printed here—the words as well as the ideas.

JAMES PITMAN

Contents

Line Illustrations in Text

Illustrations

Tables

Some Definitions

A letter (Latin *littera*) is a single general concept—as Ay, Bee, See: Alpha, Beta, Gamma: Aleph, Beth, etc. Each letter needs to have its own name (Latin *nomen*) but it has also its own *figura*, or indeed *figurae*, the **character** or characters which are attached to that concept, e.g. in the English alphabet A, a, *a*, and in the Greek Alphabet A and α. Each letter (and its characters) has, or at least ought to have, only one *potestas*—the value of the pure sound or diphthong (called **phonemes***) which is to be conveyed by the shape of that character or those characters. In a **reading** system one moves from the character to the phoneme (*decoding*); in a **writing** system the direction is the reverse (*spelling*). In the course of time the English language has come so to abuse the words *letter*, *character*, and *sound* (and the words *reading* and *spelling*) that confusion can be avoided only by reverting to the precise thought and usage of the Romans. **Letter** is a generalization; **character** is a particular shape; **phoneme** is a particular pure sound or diphthong. Each character and each phoneme ought to have its own distinct **name**. **Reading** is from character to phoneme; **spelling** is from phoneme (whether accurately related or not) to character; **printing** is any mechanical production of characters; **writing** is hand-writing any character; **verbal communication** is the assembly of words into meaningful messages, whether those words be printed, (hand)written, or spoken; **listening** is the auditory counterpart to **reading, speaking** to **writing**.

*See also footnote on page 41 about diaphones.

Part I

I   Backward Readers:
the submerged sixth

I n round figures at least one out of every six school-leavers in England and Wales is a backward reader. They are unable to read in the sense that most people understand the term. Universal literacy is a comparatively modern ideal; official recognition of the need for minimum standards was not promulgated until the Education Act of 1870, but in the "affluent," science-conscious 1960s the bleak statistics of the current reading problem come as a shock. The ability to read fluently is so fundamental that a failure rate of one in six suggests the existence of a flaw in our entire system of education.

It was the need for remedial classes among the Army intake in the 1939–45 war that first drew public attention to the problem, but its full extent became clear only in 1948 when the Ministry of Education tested 3,400 15-year-olds drawn from the whole of England and Wales, to discover that 1·4 per cent were classified as "illiterate"; 4·3 per cent as "semi-literate"; and 24·4 per cent as "backward"—making a percentage of 30·1 who were backward or worse.[1,2]

A new test was devised for the 1948 survey by Dr. A. F. Watts and Professor P. E. Vernon in order to "assess ability to read silently for comprehension." It does more than test the pupils' skill at decoding or

[1] *Standards of Reading 1948-1956*, p. 3, H.M.S.O., 1957. For a full description of post-war reading surveys also see *Reading Ability*. H.M.S.O., 1950 and *Progress in Reading*. H.M.S.O., 1966.

[2] 10–11-year-olds were also tested according to score ranges adapted to their age: of these 3·8 per cent were classified as illiterate or semi-literate and 17·7 per cent as backward.

3

"barking out" the sound of words; it also finds out if the meaning of the words has been grasped. Thirty-five questions have to be answered within a ten-minute time limit. For each answer the pupil has to choose the right answer from five given words. The questions become progressively harder: the early ones demand the ability to read and understand what can be expected of most 11-year-olds, but the last few questions might well tax grammar school boys and girls of fifteen, as indeed was intended. Definitions of illiterate, semi-literate, backward, superior, and so on are inevitably arbitrary and relative. One way of defining the three lowest categories is to say that the *illiterate* are unable to recognize and name correctly all the characters in the alphabet; compared with the *semi-literate* who can name all the characters and also read a few simple words; and the *backward* who can recognize many of the common words and can decipher others with concentrated effort, but who do not—and do not expect to—understand what they read while reading it. For the 1948 survey the test scores were divided into six categories—

TABLE I

Watts-Vernon test score ranges and percentages
for fifteen-year-olds in the 1948 survey

Pupils aged fifteen

Description	Test score range	Percentage
Superior	35–31	8·6
Average +	30–23	34·2
Average −	22–18	27·1
Backward	17–9	24·4
Semi-literate	8–3	4·3
Illiterate	2–0	1·4

Comparisons were made with pre-war "reading age" norms which, when equated with the Watts-Vernon scores, give the arbitrary categories a more realistic definition—

Illiterate (aged 15 and over) are those whose reading age is less than 7 years;

Semi-literate (aged 15 and over) are those whose reading age is 7 years or greater but less than 9 years;

Backward (aged 15 and over) are those whose reading age is 9 years or greater but less than 12 years.

The dividing line between backward and average minus falls therefore at

4

a reading age of 12. Even a reading age of 15 provides no reasons for satisfaction, particularly because the categories were assessed, if anything, too leniently: in arriving at the average reading ages, all levels of children were included, among them the 20–30 per cent of future illiterate, semi-literate, and backward children, and therefore the absolute standards implied were correspondingly poorer. The average itself is dragged down by the low standards that prevailed in the past and were tolerated.

The conclusions of the 1948 survey were couched in cautious language, particularly as the pre-war surveys were not directly comparable, being limited to particular localities. In 1952, 1956, and 1961, however, the Watts-Vernon test was used again in further national surveys, though with an improved sampling design. These surveys can be compared—

TABLE II

Comparisons between national reading surveys undertaken
in 1948, 1952, 1956, and 1961

Pupils aged fifteen

Description	Test score range	Percentages			
		1948	1952	1956	1961[1]
Superior	35–31	9	9	9	18
Average +	30–23	34	39	43	48
Average –	22–18	27	22	23	17
Backward	17–9	24 ⎫	25 ⎫	21 ⎫	15 ⎫
Semi-literate	8–3	5 ⎬ 30	4 ⎬ 30	4 ⎬ 25	2 ⎬ 17
Illiterate	2–0	1 ⎭	1 ⎭	0 ⎭	0 ⎭

It will be seen that there has been, on the face of it, a considerable improvement, though there is, understandably, a tendency among educationists and teachers, complacently, to exaggerate it. The findings also appeared in the Newsom Committee's Report[2] in the form of comparative *average* scores for Modern schools (*Table III*).

The report talked of a "success story" and commented—

A test score which even fourteen years ago would have been good enough to put boys or girls well into the above-average category would today put them firmly into the below-average group. Over the intervening years the general level of performance has risen.[3]

[1] These figures were supplied to me personally by the Minister for Education and Science in a letter dated 5 April 1967; they correct an earlier set given in reply to my Parliamentary question.
[2] *Half Our Future*, a report of the Central Advisory Council for Education (England), p. 185, H.M.S.O., 1963.   [3] Ibid., p. 5, §8.

TABLE III

Average reading scores in Modern schools for pupils aged 14 years, 8 months
1948, 1952, 1956, and 1961

	Average score	Gain in months (7 months = 1 point)
1948	18·0	—
1952	18·4	3
1956	18·9	6
1961	21·3	23

But the committee cautiously matched optimism with a warning—

These are figures in which teachers may well take pride. But they are not the whole story, and the part which they conceal is the part with which we are especially concerned. Roughly a quarter of the Modern school population aged fifteen have a reading age of thirteen years or less. One in seven Modern schools, largely for social reasons, has a median reading age which is fourteen months below the median reading age for all Modern schools. This chapter is largely concerned with these minorities whose numbers at present leave school without reaching an acceptable fifteen-year-old degree of literacy, and then rapidly forget much of what they did learn at school through sheer lack of use.[1]

Moreover, research carried out by Dr. Joyce Morris in Kent with 714 children (born in 1946) in junior schools showed that approximately 16 per cent—

. . . were still struggling with infant primers after two years in junior classes[2] and about a quarter of them were tackling books originally designed for first-year juniors. A year later, the percentage at the primer stage had been reduced to 3, but about 15 and 23 per cent were engaged on books normally considered suitable for first- and second-year juniors respectively.

The progress of these Kent children was followed to the end of their schooldays when it was found that—

. . . only one out of every eight children managed to achieve normal competence by the age of 14 plus, whereas over half the sample remained in the categories of reading ability defined by the Ministry as "backward" or "semi-literate," and their oral performance when attempting to read simple books might be described as a mere "barking at print." Thus, even in Kent where

[1] Ibid., pp. 119–20, §334.
[2] After more than four years at school! (*author*)

standards are above the national average, the prognosis for second-year juniors who have made little headway with reading is very unfavourable.[1]

The improvement shown by the decline from 30 to 17 per cent of backward readers and worse is not really so very dramatic when it is remembered that it refers to the most elementary and fundamental of educational skills; moreover, it can be almost certainly accounted for by the recovery from the dislocation caused by the war and the steady departure of the "evacuee" generations, by higher standards of teaching, better textbooks, more remedial classes, the introduction of television, and so on. Conditions in the schools are likely to continue to improve, and there will one day, I hope, be a serious and permanent reduction in the size of classes; all this may, in time, lead to a further drop in the percentage of backward readers, but there are no grounds for prophesying that it will continue to fall by virtue of the "inevitability of gradualness" or some such law until (by the turn of the century perhaps?) backward reading disappears. No amount of improvement in conditions is likely by itself to reduce the current percentage radically or get anywhere near eliminating it.

There is no reason, no justification for self-congratulation or complacency. The percentages of illiterate and semi-literate are small—though they amount to some 16,000 individual children—but there is no burking the 17 per cent who are still labelled backward—i.e. 136,000 children a *year*. In the United States the situation is, if anything, worse, although it is difficult to make accurate comparisons between the two countries. The U.S. National Council of Teachers of English "estimates that 4 million elementary school pupils have reading disabilities. Other reports indicate that reading is a handicap for 25 per cent to 35 per cent of all high school students and that our nation has a minimum of 8 million adult functional illiterates. We are required to introduce remedial reading instruction in elementary school, beginning in the second grade, and to continue it through high school and college and university."[2] For the whole English-speaking world the annual output of backward readers must amount to at least 1,020,000 children a *year* (out of an annual intake of 6 million).[3] A

---

[1] *How Far can Reading Backwardness be Attributed to School Conditions?* A paper included in the proceedings of a conference on Recent Research and Development in the Teaching of Reading, St. Hilda's College, Oxford, 30 July 1964.

[2] From a paper by Albert J. Mazurkiewicz, presented at the Twenty-ninth Educational Conference sponsored by the Educational Records Bureau, New York City, 30 October 1964.

[3] See *Current School Enrolment Figures.* UNESCO, 1962. The figure does not include English-speaking children in Africa, India, etc.

7

very small proportion cannot read because they are severely under-developed mentally or they suffer from the results of a brain injury or some other rare deficiency (see Chapter 3), but we are justified in assuming that nearly all the backward readers and probably most of the semi-literate and illiterate are capable of verbal communication in the field of sound and are inherently capable of reading effectively. To think otherwise is to assume that 17 per cent of the population are mentally sub-normal! The question cannot be evaded: why is it that in the case of one out of six children we still fail to teach them to read?

The price of backward reading

It is very difficult, if not impossible, for anyone capable of reading and comprehending the sentences in this book to project him- or herself into the mind of a backward reader. The term embraces a wide span of standards, from someone who is scarcely able to make out the instructions on how to heat a tin of soup to someone who can just manage to read most of the words in a football report in an evening newspaper. But in every type of backward reader the effort of deciphering is usually so arduous that little attention or energy is left for comprehension or enjoyment, and in practice the attempt to read is for the most part avoided. Sentences, even when short and simple, seldom appear as meaningful units. A hint of what this can feel like may be gathered if we interpret the word "backward" literally and read a sentence like this—

TAHT DNA DAER NAC EW TAHT EURT SI TI
WAL FO TRUOC A NI EVORP DLUOC EW
EW TAHT REGANAM LOOHCS A OT RO
. . . TUB DAER OT ELBA DEEDNI ERA

but we very soon tire and after several pages we would very likely lose the thread of meaning and therefore lay the passage aside—just as the backward reader after ten minutes tosses aside his barely started thriller and reaches for the illustrated story, or a horror comic with its simple bubble captions, or turns on the T.V. switch.

The essence of being able to read "properly" is that it is fluent and effortless—apart from the occasional unfamiliar word. A textbook on physical chemistry is of course harder going than the latest thriller, but the hardness lies in understanding the author's arguments and

8

thoughts, and not in decoding the visual symbols we call words, a process we are virtually unaware of. As in the case of typewriting, swimming, or riding a bicycle, once the skill of reading has been acquired it is never lost; even after disuse for a long period of years the basic skill may be rusty and need polishing, but it will still be there. Once children have mastered the essentials of reading, there is no backsliding and there is normally a progressive improvement and extension of vocabulary. On the other hand, children who leave school as backward readers are all too likely to find that what little skill they have acquired soon deteriorates and, like the poor snail in the fable, they slither back down the wall up which they have climbed so laboriously. By then they may well have become resigned, without quite knowing it, to their handicap, because years earlier—maybe when they were seven or eight years old—their acceptance of not expecting to read had already taken root. The seeds of the trouble were probably planted even earlier, at five or six years old, when the mind was baffled and frustrated during an early encounter with printed words.

As soon as the quicker among their contemporaries in the junior school are able to read and reading becomes more necessary, a backward reader starts to sink to the bottom third of the class and soon becomes a candidate for the "C" and "D" streams. It is then, at the age of eight or nine if not earlier, that he begins to stop trying at his lessons, and soon he tries even less, the classical way-out from blaming oneself for failing. This familiar pattern is not necessarily because a backward reader lacks intelligence. It is merely because he cannot read—which, as we shall see later, is something altogether different. In so far as he is able with the passage of time and much effort to catch up on his reading, he also catches up on his other school subjects and is dubbed a "late developer" instead of what he basically is: a "late reader."

Failure to learn to read effectively is nowadays, though only to a small extent, overcome by remedial reading classes, but unfortunately in most cases the handicap persists throughout the child's school career. The normal expansion of vocabulary is impeded, muddled and impoverished speech is a common symptom, and inevitably the child's attainment in most subjects at the secondary school suffers. The experience of learning to read in itself nourishes the growth of a young mind and hastens its general perceptual development; once mastered, reading fosters the burgeoning powers of reasoning, but from most of this the backward reader is unable to benefit. Instead, his intellectual powers are stunted. As the

9

child gets older, adjustment to the frustration of failing to read, and therefore to the largely fruitless years at school, leads to recognizable stresses, though their form will depend on other elements in his personality structure. Truancy is common, though by no means all truants are backward readers, nor are all backward readers truants—if they were the gaps in the classroom would be all too obvious! It can easily be imagined how the truanting backward reader of thirteen or fourteen seeks consolation in aggressive indifference, in the self-protecting myth that "reading don't matter," that it is the big, grown-up world outside school that counts. The school truant has already set himself against Authority: he has to make himself scarce during the daytime and finds himself enmeshed in excuses and lies.

Truancy frequently appears in the case histories of maladjusted children or juvenile delinquents and so does a poor school record which is likely to disguise backward reading, though it is not always specifically mentioned. It may well be true that this stems from the same personality and behavioural traits that are associated with the maladjustment and/or delinquency but there are, I believe, reasons also to draw the opposite inference: that backward reading can be an influential factor in the formation of maladjustment or delinquency. Arthur I. Gates, of Columbia University, writes—

> In conclusion, it may be said that personality maladjustment is frequently found to coexist with reading disability. The more serious the reading retardation, the greater is the probability that maladjustment also exists. My estimate is that among cases of very marked specific reading disability, about 75 per cent will show personality maladjustment. Of these, the personality maladjustment is the cause of the reading defect in a quarter of the cases and an accompaniment or result in three-quarters.[1]

The following three (admittedly severe) cases from a remedial teacher's records demonstrate what failure to read can lead to—and also how the maladjustment can be eased—

Michael, aged nine, was totally illiterate. Before the court for stealing from a cinema manager's office; always in trouble at school for being unco-operative and a trouble-maker. An intelligent boy (I.Q. = 119), sensitive and withdrawn, but very skilful with his hands. It took a long time to make friends with him, but once this had been accomplished he quickly learned to read

[1] "The Role of Personality Maladjustment in Reading Disability." *The Journal of Genetic Psychology*, pp. 82–83, Vol. 59, Provincetown, Massachusetts, U.S.A., 1941.

and eventually could spell well and took a delight in demonstrating this. Behaviour at school improved, so did his relationships with teachers and children alike, and he changed from a rather sullen, unhappy little boy into a cheerful, friendly one. He kept in touch for some time after he ceased coming for remedial lessons; at fourteen he became a school prefect and stayed on at school to take several GCE subjects.

John, aged ten, was in trouble at school for stealing, but the police had not been informed; his general behaviour was bad and he was spoken of as a bully. A poor reader, he was thought by the school to be very dull. Parents over-ambitious and nagging. After two terms of remedial classes his reading improved—and so did his self-confidence. He entered a technical modern school where he made good progress towards his eventual goal of becoming an engineer's draughtsman.

Joan, aged twenty-one, was illiterate. Referred by psychiatrist at the National Hospital which she was attending as an out-patient for various psychosomatic symptoms. It was thought that her symptoms were due to the anxiety and sense of inferiority she felt at being a non-reader. She worked in a factory and had quite a lot of responsibility, including signing forms she could not read and also, for a short period, dealing with the lunch order book. To begin with, lessons were occupied in teaching her to write "sausage and mash," "egg on chips," etc., a process which amused and delighted her. Later she progressed to ordinary reading and after about nine months she achieved her life's ambition: to be able to read her horoscope in the Sunday papers and also the names of the greyhounds on dog race cards instead of, as in the past, "choosing her fancy" by its number. Her physical symptoms disappeared and she ceased to attend hospital.

It would be wrong to give too much importance to this aspect of the failure to read and, as with truants, it does not necessarily follow that every backward reader ends up in the courts or a psychiatric clinic, yet I must emphasize that backward reading is often linked with truancy, maladjustment, delinquency and other behavioural and emotional disturbances; that a backward reader can but find it difficult to integrate himself with a society that is so dependent on the printed and written word. Of course, many backward readers do manage to adjust themselves somehow. They get by. But, unless they are particularly skilled with their hands, or they are very lucky, they perforce occupy the lowest paid jobs. As adults, their reading may improve slightly through their own efforts but one suspects they seldom manage more than the short sentences and paragraphs of the mass circulation newspapers and women's magazines. They join the hard core of the "admass." The research has not been attempted, but we have no reason for believing that the total percentage for backward, semi-literate, and illiterate is any lower for adults than the 17 per cent for school-leavers. There are indications as well as good reasons for suspecting it may be higher.

Quite apart from the limitations on the individual, backward reading on the present huge scale is a national liability. Its cost in unhappiness must be vast. With the increasingly complex know-how demanded by modern techniques, it must reduce industrial efficiency and productivity. In some respects it is even more hampering than was complete illiteracy in the nineteenth century. Despite the broadening and informative qualities of television, the failure of so many to read and write effectively obstructs the creation of a well-informed electorate and weakens the values that make a democratic society effective.

Once the size of the problem has been appreciated, its consequences are only too obvious. Notwithstanding the improvement since the war, it remains a challenge to all concerned with education. Not that the teaching profession, as a whole, has been satisfied. I doubt if any other subject in the curriculum has been given so much thought or led to so much discussion. Many are convinced that the fault lies in the use of wrong teaching methods. Others maintain that the causes of backward reading have to be sought outside the classroom—in the pupils' home background, medical and psychological history, etc. All these and various other explanations are potentially valid and are often applicable, either alone or more frequently in conjunction, to particular pupils or particular schools or areas. They will be discussed in the next two chapters but, first, it is logical and necessary to say something about what is entailed in learning to read and about the detailed nature of the reading process.

2 Essentials of the Reading Process

TOO LITTLE IS KNOWN about the psychological processes concerned for me to attempt to provide a precise, definitive, textbook description of what occurs when a person reads. A documented account of the researches into the subject would occupy too many pages and would also be out of place, particularly as the specialist literature is already voluminous and there are several excellent summaries (listed in the Bibliography). Instead, I shall outline what seem to me to be the essentials of the reading process and of the various methods of instilling it, drawing attention to those features that are most germane to the argument of this book, which is not primarily about psychological processes or teaching methods but about the need for a new teaching medium—and this is something quite different.

It used to be believed that reading is a purely mechanical process but it is now recognized that it depends on a delicate complex of physiological skills and psychological faculties which, despite much investigation, are as yet understood, if at all, only imperfectly. In any attempt to describe or understand how it is that meaning is extracted from printed or written alphabetic symbols we are concerned not merely with seeing and hearing but also with visual perception and auditory perception—the psychological processes by which the brain recognizes and digests the messages from the eyes and ears; the speech centres of the brain are also involved, as is memory and past experience and the whole gamut of mental processes embodied in comprehension. It is not surprising that there is no simple or generally agreed explanation of how the art of reading is first learned by young children, or that the methods of teaching them have for long been the subject of dispute among educationists. The various studies of the subject undertaken during this century are said to run into five figures.

It is difficult for adults to realize the complexity and challenge that face a child who starts learning to read—

> Coming to see how letters are parts of words which in turn make up sentences is a mental feat as complex as anything which the reader is going to attempt in the whole of his literate life. . . . The child's new task of seeing how speech can leave its tracks on paper calls for revolutionary perceptual adjustments to be made as well as the equally revolutionary intellectual adjustments enforced by the graphic symbols.[1]

Reading is an extension of listening, just as writing is of speaking, though all four processes are interlinked; reading is the skill of decoding and comprehending the printed equivalent of words and sentences that for the most part can be already understood when spoken. R. A. Wilson in *The Miraculous Birth of Language*,[2] describing the connection, wrote—

> The oral language is still the actual language, since it is the direct expression of the time movement of thought. The written language consists in the transference of this sound language to a spatial representation, to preserve it from the evanescence of time.

In the same way as an understanding of speech follows on from observing objects and actions in a variety of situations and from listening to and remembering a running commentary of associated vocal sounds, so must reading in its early stages follow on from the child's "aural" linguistic knowledge and ability. Unless the child is deaf, an already elaborate skill in handling words, as a listener if not also as a speaker, is an essential pre-condition. The vocal-auditory element in reading persists in the most experienced adult reader and is especially strong in children. They can be seen to "mouth" words silently to themselves when reading, particularly when they meet a word that causes difficulty. Auditory ability supplements the visual perception of the word and, indeed, partners visual ability and helps the reader to discriminate one seen word from another. It also enables the reader to make up for the inevitable deficiencies of the printed code of communication compared with the spoken code,

[1] A. R. MacKinnon: *How DO Children Learn to Read?* pp. 17, 22; The Copp Clark Publishing Co. Ltd., Toronto, 1959.
[2] p. 185: Dent, London, 1942.

such as the lack of stress on certain words and of the "expression," accent, and overtones conveyed by the living voice; even if italic characters or capitals are employed, it is the reader who, understanding the convention, adds the necessary emphasis, surprise, irony, or whatever else is indicated. If in the midst of this paragraph I write: "On a fine winter's day when their breakfast was done all the boys were disposed to enjoy some good fun: Sam sprightly observed it is just half-past eight and there is more time for play when breakfast is late," the reader is unlikely to anticipate any metre or rhyme because no departure is made from the continuous pattern of prose; but most readers, unless their visual element is abnormally dominant, will at once have picked up the metre and rhyme, demonstrating that even "silent" reading touches off speech patterns which, in turn, give rise to sensations that are essentially auditory. If this was not so, the reading of poetry to oneself would lose much of its pleasure. Similarly, if the reader counts carefully the number of *f*s in this sentence—

These functional fuses are the result of scientific investigation combined with the fruit of long experience,

he will probably (unless he knows the trick) have made them come to less than six, which is the correct number. Most people miss the *f*s in the two *of*s, because they hear the word as *ov*, because their reading is auditory as well as visual.[1]

This blending of visual and auditory elements pervades the whole reading process and enables one to arrive at this three-cornered conception—

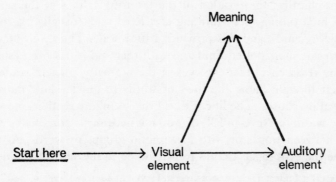

[1] When reading the *Hansard* report of a speech I had listened to in Parliament the day before, I used to find it impossible not to slow down to the pace of the speaker and to "hear" his very words. In the case of the late Sir Winston Churchill, notwithstanding the delay of many years

Because speech historically, and in the individual's own experience, preceded reading, the words as they are seen and perceived (the visual element) are more likely than not to be linked with the brain's memory store of spoken symbols (the auditory element) and be interpreted and decoded with its aid. To put it another way: meaningful recognition of words relates their visual appearance as printed symbols to their spoken sounds and to the reader's general linguistic experience and know-how.

Admittedly this is only a schematic and oversimplified conception but it conveys the essence of the (alphabetic) reading process, certainly in those learning to read, though with the experienced reader and particularly in connection with advanced conceptual associations—a mathematical abstraction of a relationship like π is an extreme example—the auditory element plays such a subordinate part that it is scarcely even vestigial and it is difficult to think of reading except in terms of a *direct* link between the visual symbol and meaning.

EYE FIXATIONS AND THE GRASPING OF MEANING

The grasping of meaning is, after all, the purpose of reading. Studies of the movements of the eyes as they pass over the lines of words, the initial stage in the reading process, show that in an efficient reader they have been well conditioned for this purpose. Investigators have built various apparatus to record and measure eye-movements; if a beam of light is reflected on to the cornea and then from the cornea through a camera lens on to a moving film, it is possible to depict the movements photographically; the position of the beam of light is at the same time broken by a tuning-fork vibrating at a fixed rate—usually 25, 30, or 50 times per second—and this provides a time scale. The result on the film is a series of short dotted lines and with their aid it has been established by many researchers that the eyes of the normally efficient reader travel from left to right along the lines of words in quick, short movements, separated by pauses. The line is thus broken up into sections more or less equal in width (or "eye-fulls") that do not necessarily correspond with the spaces between words or with meaningful groups of words. At the end of a line the eyes make a rapid return sweep to the start of the next line.

and the fact that I might not have been present, I still slow down and seem to "hear" his voice. Further examples of this type of vestigial carry-over from the auditory element to the visual will be found in *Learning to Read*, an address I gave to the Royal Society of Arts, *Journal of the Royal Society of Arts*, Vol. 109, pp. 149–80, London, 1961.

The pauses are termed "fixations," their width, the number of fixations per line, and their duration varying considerably from reader to reader and with the degree of familiarity, difficulty, and interest of the material being read. An average reader uses about four fixations for a line of type set in a book like this; a fast reader may reduce this to only two and a slow reader may increase it to as many as ten.

As the eyes do not travel continuously along the line, these researches show that the practised reader does not proceed from character to character, but that at each fixation the reader recognizes complete words or groups of words. This has been confirmed by another apparatus that exposes characters, words, or sentences for very short periods—e.g. one-fiftieth of a second. Experiments with this apparatus again make it clear that when the material being read is simple or the ideas it expresses are familiar, the widths between fixations increase and their duration decreases —and vice versa. This implies that the reader proceeds along the line just as fast as he has become habituated to grasp the meaning. As this is the object of reading, he merely looks at the groups of words in each eye-full long enough to pick up sufficient clues to recognize them and in this he is greatly aided by the context, structure, and sense of the whole sentence, so that the meaning of words and phrases is fused into ideas inherent in the whole sentence. Often he partially anticipates the words' message and sometimes even reads what he expects to see instead of what is actually printed, overlooking misprints or the omission of whole words. His grasping of the words' meaning is also fused with the concurrent processes of reflecting on, evaluating, and clarifying—in short, thinking and feeling about what is being communicated.

What happens during each fixation, the more detailed mechanisms of recognizing words, differs considerably from person to person; the beginner certainly tackles words differently from the older child or adult reader. Experience enlarges the memory store of visual symbols for words and syllables and, when met repeatedly, words and whole phrases can be recognized and comprehended almost instantaneously. The words need not be recognized individually or in detail, the general configuration of a group of words usually being enough to arouse their auditory image and comprehension. It is only when the mature reader is faced with an unfamiliar or very difficult word or sentence construction that the processes of recognition are likely to resemble those of the beginner. Clues are sought in the context but the reader also has to fall back on examining the

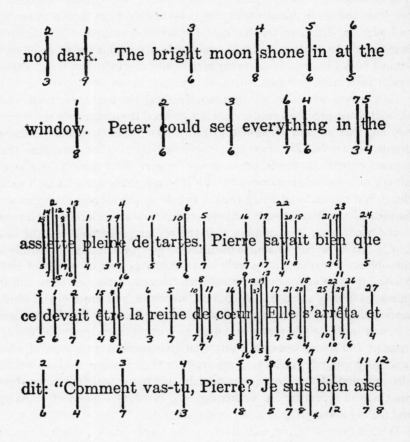

Figure 1. Eye movements of the same student reading passages in English and French; like a child learning to read its mother tongue, the uneven density of eye movements required by the French passage reflect words that cause most difficulty. The vertical lines indicate the central position of each fixation area; the serial numbers above the lines record the order of pauses; those beneath the lines record the duration of the fixation in twenty-fifths of a second. (From *A Laboratory Study of the Reading of Modern Languages* by G. T. Buswell. The MacMillan Co., New York, 1927, pp. 24–5.)

word's shape, syllables, and characters, and to use his linguistic experience of other words and similar syllables—and the sounds they represent—to obtain the sound of the word that is unfamiliar. He may or may not know what it means but, subject to the vagaries of pronunciation, he can hear the sound in his head or if necessary speak it out loud. It is a process involving both analysis and synthesis: the word shapes are broken down into syllables, converted into the sounds of speech, and built up again as a complete word. He reacts with electronic rapidity to each unfamiliar challenge—in the same way as a good tennis player uses his experience of thousands of strokes to return a difficult ball, though he may never previously have been faced with precisely the same combination of spin, height, speed, direction, and so on.[1]

TWO BASIC METHODS OF TEACHING

The child in the course of learning to read likewise has to learn how to perform this skill of analysis and synthesis. This will enable him to tackle unfamiliar words independently and to add to his memory store of visual symbols (and his own spoken vocabulary). Many words, though, particularly in the first weeks of learning to read, he acquires by straightforward memorizing and, empirically, by noticing the link between the appearance of printed words and the spoken equivalents and/or the meanings—the similarity with learning how to understand speech is obvious (e.g., the association of the sounds *cup* and *spoon* with the familiar objects on the tray of the high-chair is paralleled by the association of the two printed words—and their spoken sounds—with pictures of a cup and spoon in a reading primer).

These processes are reflected in the two basic groups of teaching methods: (1) the phonic methods; (2) the look-and-say methods. Nowadays the majority of teachers take something from both and purists of either school are rare, but the emphasis given to each shows wide variations, especially during the early stages of learning, and it is in any case simpler to begin by summarizing their characteristics separately.

The methods grouped under the heading "phonic" succeeded the old

[1] The speed with which the word "Poppolington" can be read is evidence of this alphabetic skill. I invented this artificial word in order to prove to shorthand writers that the skills of analyzing words and synthesizing forms may become ingrained when taking down shorthand dictation; it shows also that similarly basic alphabetic skills are employed in the reverse direction of reading.

alphabetic method which was almost universal from early Greek and Roman days to the end of the Middle Ages, and persisted until the childhood of many who are now adults. It was assumed that by repeating the familiar characters *c-a-t spells cat*, etc., the child would sense the pronunciation of the three elements of the word and learn to recognize its visual form. After practice with two-character combinations—*at, it, ot*—the child graduated to three-, four-, and five-character combinations—*at, hat, sat, that*, and so on. Actual reading was not begun until proficiency was reached in these exercises, and even then the emphasis was on recognition of new words rather than on the extraction of meaning. Numerous devices were used to alleviate the tedium, such as characters printed on coloured bricks, or pictures of words beginning with each character (*a* for *a*pple); in the eighteenth century one enterprising teacher even had the idea of making gingerbread characters which the child was allowed to consume once he had learned them.

The obvious weakness of the method was that the names of the characters by no means always indicate a word's pronunciation. Unless the teacher departed from the usual nomenclature, she found herself in many cases (as in *sea-ay-tee*) giving a wholly misleading direction to the child (who was expected to read *cat*). Thus in the present-day use of the phonic method the name of the character is replaced by its sound. When the child has been taught to recognize the characters and associate them with what is thought to be their commonest sound (e.g. *apple* rather than *able, autumn, aisle, arm*, etc.) he is then taught to identify and pronounce the characters in simple words: e.g., *a* says *ă* as in *apple*; *b* says *buh* as in *bat*; *c* says *cuh* as in *cat*; and so on. By means of graded exercises the child next learns to blend the sounds of characters into short words and syllables, into words of increasing length, and into phrases and sentences. The phonic method has undergone many revisions, but its essence can be summarized as follows—

The first essential is to acquire a mastery of the elements of printed and spoken words and of their two-way relationship: their characters singly and in sequence as syllables and the sounds these represent are the starting-point.

By learning how these elements of sight and sound are related, and then are combined or blended into larger units—analysis and synthesis—the child is said to acquire accuracy in recognizing print. He is taught how to attack printed words that are unfamiliar by relating their syllables to words that are already known.

The child is taught to rely on the basic alphabetic nature of the language and becomes familiar with its system and structure.

The phonic methods have been objected to for many reasons, the standard criticisms being that (1) the child is subjected to too much tedious drilling with characters and sounds, with the result that he tends merely to "bark out" the words; (2) skill in the mechanics of reading is gained at the expense of understanding what is read; (3) words are not taught as wholes, nor are phrases and sentences grasped as meaningful units of language; (4) character- and even word-analysis is too difficult for many children, particularly at an early mental age, and they do not understand what they are doing; (5) preoccupation with the deciphering process prevents much reading in the early stages and therefore the child becomes bored and develops an early antipathy towards reading; (6) reading primers have to be restricted to very simple and uninteresting words, only to words that are recognizable by such an attack and with a minimum of very common words, such as *the, all, was, one,* and *to,* that cannot be taught by the phonic method; (7) undue concentration on the sound of words leads to the formation of slow reading habits in later life; (8) reliance on the slow attack based on intellectual response hampers the development of a rapid attack based on an instinctive response—which is what the efficient reader must cultivate.

Many improvements have been incorporated in the phonic methods, such as the earlier introduction of sentences, greater emphasis on meaning, the use of pictures linked directly with the sounds, and so on, but the essentials and the approach have remained distinct from those of the other group of basic methods: "look-and-say."[1] Comenius (1657) is often given credit for having first advocated this kind of method, but its use did not become widespread until the advent of the "activity" methods of teaching so much favoured in recent years. In a suggested conformity with the Gestalt hypothesis of psychology, look-and-say methods are based on the assumption that children more readily perceive a word as a whole unit rather than as a collection of discrete characters. Any kind of alphabetic analysis is spurned and, from the outset, great emphasis is placed on meaning, pictures often accompanying each concept, word, and sentence

---

[1] Often termed the "global" or "whole word" method.

and activities being devised to associate the appearance of the word or sentence with real objects and situations. Summarized, the essentials of look-and-say are—

The starting-point is the whole word. Once a small number of words have been learned, these are expanded into simple but meaningful sentences.

A direct link is formed between the visual pattern of a whole word and its meaning and, if regretfully, with its spoken equivalent.

Attention is therefore predominantly focused on the visual element in the reading process to the virtual exclusion of the auditory element, with the aim of strengthening the link between printed word and meaning. Reliance is placed on automatic skills rather than on intellectual analysis.

Later, when a large number of whole words are familiar, attention is directed, in turn, to syllables, but the extent to which words are analyzed (e.g. *postcard*, *post*, *card*) varies considerably.

What are known as the "phrase" method, the "whole sentence" method, and the "story" method are really extensions of look-and-say, the starting-points being larger units and an even stronger stress being laid on meaning and context and on complete "units of thought." Awareness of the sounds of words, though inescapable, is often considered to hamper the connection between print-pattern and meaning. Silent reading is the aim; reading aloud is deprecated. The pupil's attention is directed to the recurrence of printed words in a group of short, simple phrases or sentences and by means of various exercises these become so familiar as symbols for meaning that they can be recognized and understood at sight.

The look-and-say group, like the phonic method, is open to obvious criticism: (1) left-to-right reading of each word is developed, if at all, as a subsidiary habit—a right-to-left habit may equally become established and cause difficulty later on; (2) the child is apt merely to memorize words and "read" them when they are not present—this leads to guessing instead of reading and to using words in a meaningless way: he reads the words he knows and guesses in terms of context at those that are unfamiliar; (3) because he is dependent upon didactic teaching for every addition to his vocabulary, his reading must be restricted artificially; (4) the number of words he can write is correspondingly restricted; (5) he is denied the means of independent attack on words not encountered before; (6) there is no awareness of the basic alphabetic structure of the language—it is tantamount to saying that learning to read Chinese is not impeded by its thousands of ideographs and that alphabetic writing has no benefits for the learner.

The objections to look-and-say may be more, or may be less, numerous than the objections to the pure phonic methods but this is, to my mind, irrelevant; the objections to both are equally decisive and convincing. In fact neither group, by itself, is intellectually acceptable nor is in practice satisfactory. This is borne out by numerous research projects. In the words of Dr. F. J. Schonell:[1] "In general, research studies have served to show not that any particular method, effectively used, has complete superiority in every aspect of reading over any other method, but that *each method or major aspect of reading instruction that has been developed over the decades makes its own contribution to the teaching of reading*" [his italics], though Schonell very rightly qualifies this by adding that "this only holds good provided that factors of age, intelligence, motivation, books used and language background of the pupils are favourable." As a result of criticism and discovery of weaknesses not only have many changes and adaptations been made in the application of both the basic methods, but each has become greatly diversified.

ECLECTIC METHODS

As remarked already, the majority of teachers nowadays take something from each of the basic methods and adopt what is therefore an eclectic method.[2] Differences of opinion, deep as they are, occur mainly over the timing and stage in a child's development at which the various teaching procedures should be introduced. It is also true that a given method or timing of method may not be equally suited to all children: in some the visual element appears to be dominant and they possess strong visual memories so that they tend to see things as wholes; compared with others whose auditory element is dominant and whose minds are better able to retain sound rather than word patterns, or those whose minds are given to

[1] *The Psychology and Teaching of Reading*, pp. 91–92. Oliver and Boyd, London, 1961 (fourth edition).

[2] J. P. Daniels and H. Diack in their *Royal Road Readers*, for example, developed what they aptly called the "phonic word method." It was "based on the idea that material for teaching reading ought to be designed so as to give the child in as easy a manner as possible insight into the nature of letters. In the scheme the child does not learn the letters in isolation but functioning in words." *In Spite of the Alphabet*, p. 113, G. Hunter Diack. Chatto & Windus, London, 1965.

establishing relationships, so that early on they seek to generalize from the particular—having, for example, mastered *and*, *hand*, *had*, they find it easy to learn *band*, *bad*, *dad*. The first group are more likely to benefit by exploring a predominantly look-and-say method and the second group will benefit more from a phonic method. Some specialists have asserted that phonic methods should be used with only the more intelligent children; others say that intelligent children require little phonic teaching because they will discover the principles of phonetic blending for themselves.

The whole word approach of look-and-say is frequently preferred during the early stages, but it is also widely believed that sooner or later a child must be able to analyze both the shapes and sounds of syllables and words, to recognize analogous syllables in other words, to know how to break them down and build them up. In this way a store of "habituated" syllables is collected, but to get this far some training in phonics can scarcely be avoided. The need for the child to surmount this barrier between the early and later stages of learning to read has been described succinctly by Professor M. D. Vernon:[1] a child begins by—

> ... becoming familiar with the sounds and meanings associated with a small number of printed shapes of whole words. In particular, he can learn that printed symbols do represent the words which he uses in speech, just as a pattern of lines on a page represents an object with which he is familiar in his ordinary everyday life. It seems essential that he should reach this stage before trying to proceed further. But it is also certain that he will never learn to read efficiently until he *has* proceeded further. The non-reader and the child with severe reading disability have not progressed any further.

Repetitive practices in order to "bed down" the associations between print and sound, and also between print and meaning, allied with practice in spotting and making constructive use of correspondences between words with related syllables, can therefore be considered to be the core of the learning process. This, I believe, applies to all children whether they are taught supposedly by phonics or look-and-say or by any of their combinations. To attach importance to the skills of immediate recognition and effortless recall and to the need for facility in attacking unfamiliar words does not—and should not—entail overlooking the parallel importance of being able to make use of the secondary clues offered by the

---

[1] *Backwardness in Reading*, p. 188. Cambridge University Press, 1960.

context, to anticipate sequences of ideas, and so on. As we have seen, effective reading means going beyond the recognition of individual words, so that the meaning of the whole sentence is grasped, so that eventually reading becomes increasingly effortless and rapid.

Both the basic methods and the mixed methods are well catered for in every country by their own reading primers, arranged in graded series. Much discussion has taken place over what should be included in the beginners' vocabularies, over which words should be introduced first, and how to achieve a balance of words that will teach essentials and yet can be happily assimilated by the child—as we have seen, with both the basic methods vocabularies need to be restricted artificially and not merely by the limits of the child's expected comprehension. Good use is made of illustrations which establish the situational context in which the printed words have their meaning, just as real life establishes the context in which spoken words are learned.

Reading aloud is an inescapable requirement in the organization of a reading class; it is the simplest and virtually the only method of finding out if the child is in fact beginning to read—not necessarily with understanding—and of deciding how he needs most help. It is perhaps as well that reading aloud is a self-limiting activity, particularly when the class is large, because its value can be overestimated and too much of it can lay down habits that inhibit "silent" reading. It is generally[1] thought advisable also to introduce practice in writing at an early stage. Though the ability to read is acquired earlier, the two go hand-in-hand, and progress made in one contributes to progress in the other. The act of forming or tracing a syllable or word and of recognizing that its shape is similar, if not identical with a word the child has read, helps him to associate this with the word's meaning. Before writing a word the child is likely to say it to himself—or at least think it—and therefore, because writing is the obverse analagous process to reading, the bridge between reading and speech is strengthened in the child's mind. The kinaesthetic processes employed in writing, the use of finger muscles to form characters and words, appear to reinforce and supplement perception through both the visual and auditory channels.[2] Teachers who attach importance to writing in the early stages tend to lay

[1] In teaching the deaf large cut-out wooden characters are hidden in a paper bag and the child is asked to find the matching character by feeling for it. For children with normal hearing it may also be helpful to inculcate an awareness by all three senses of the character's shape, if not also the character-sound relationship.

[2] Some teachers from the very beginning use writing as the means of teaching reading.

greater emphasis on the phonic element in a mixed method, compared with those who favour concentrating first on reading.

IMPORTANCE OF LINGUISTIC ABILITY

To offset this very condensed and theoretical summary of teaching methods, it is salutary to think in terms of an actual classroom smelling of chalk-dust and alive with the murmurings of five- and six-year-olds intent (intermittently) on their reading primers or writing books, each with his or her discrete personality, attitudes, background, and problems. The most efficacious combination of methods will lose much of its power unless the teacher knows how to be patient, unless she understands each child's special difficulties, and possesses the gifts of conveying confidence and communicating with immature minds. It is necessary to add another truism: the finest methods and the most sympathetic teacher will fail, or at any rate be far less effective, unless the children—or rather each child— are ready to be taught. Before he begins to learn reading systematically he must have reached what educationists describe as a state of "reading readiness". No one disputes the importance of ensuring that the child feels he is being successful at every stage or that early feelings of failure can severely impede progress, but definitions of reading readiness vary, some experts believing that systematic reading instruction should be postponed until a mental age of $6\frac{1}{2}$ years has been reached.[1] Of greater validity, in my own view, is the achievement of a certain minimum linguistic ability—a "linguistic readiness". It is not always easy to detect a linguistically inadequate child because he can mislead us when responding to the speech of others and even when answering questions. He creates the impression that he is linguistically competent when listening, but while he may appear to understand the essentials of a particular item of communication, it is the secondary clues—from the other speaker's gestures, facial expression, tone of voice, and above all the situation in which the communication is made—that convey to him the essential minimum of meaning (e.g. a child—or a dog—told off for helping himself to an unauthorized piece of chocolate understands that he has been naughty, though he may have but little understanding of the words the irate grown-up is speaking).

[1] In America the practice in many kindergartens would seem to have the force of dogma: no child is deemed "reading ready" until this age and the teacher's function is limited to ensuring that reading readiness is achieved by the proper time.

This is not the place to discuss the processes by which a child learns to listen and speak but it is safe to maintain that most linguistically inadequate children come from homes that do not provide them with enough experiences and opportunities to establish the necessary generalizations and concepts to which words can be related, because the parents confine the child to a very restricted environment and/or they themselves are linguistically backward. They thus neglect a parent's obligation to exploit the opportunities that daily life presents to teach generalizations and language. Nor do they talk to their children at levels they can progressively understand; nor read them stories; nor listen patiently to childish prattle and to the children's tentative and improving efforts to convey their own news and the lively imaginings of childhood; nor correct the mistakes of baby-talk and, later, of syntax and grammar. This kind of deficient home background has been well described by B. Bernstein[1] and by an American author, Charles E. Silberman, who writes[2] that in the typically deficient household "adults speak in short sentences, if indeed they speak at all, and when they give orders to the child, it is usually in monosyllables —'get this,' 'bring that.' The child has never been obliged to listen to several lengthy sentences spoken consecutively. And the speech he does hear tends to be of a very simple sort from the standpoint of grammar and syntax. In school, the middle-class teacher who rambles on for several sentences might just as well be talking another language. The non-verbal atmosphere of the home also means that lower-class children have a limited perception of the world about them: they do not know that objects have names (table, wall, book), or that the same object may have several names (an apple is fruit, red, round, juicy). They also have very little concept of size or time."

A child coming from a home such as this is unlikely to be ready to start learning to read, but whatever the criteria of reading readiness, the infant teacher has to use her own judgement to decide when each child is ready for his first reading primer. Nowadays many teachers prepare for this moment or test its arrival with the help of various language activities that increase concepts, vocabulary, and a general command of sentences. When systematic instruction in reading has actually begun, this, in itself, will—and should—continue to foster the child's linguistic ability. One activity reinforces and partners the other.

[1] "Some Sociological Determinants of Perception." *The British Journal of Sociology*, Vol. 9, London, 1958.
[2] "Give Slum Children a Chance." *Harper's*, Vol. 228, No. 1368, New York, May 1964.

A cardinal supposition of this book is that very often this linguistic element in the reading process is either overlooked or its importance is underrated. This is true not only when assessing reading readiness, but also when considering teaching methods. In particular, I hope to demonstrate that it is unrealistic and likely to be unproductive if a study either of process or methods is attempted without relating both to the actual language concerned and thus to its medium, that is to say its alphabet and spelling. A recognition and a probing, rigorous knowledge of all the linguistic factors involved when reading the English language can, I believe, confirm what teachers have in varying degrees discovered for themselves: that the controversy between the two basic schools of teaching is unreal and comes of failing to ask root questions, of being too concerned with what are really secondary problems; that the conflict can be resolved to produce a natural alliance—a combination of teaching techniques that nurtures an unwarped, all-round expansion of the young growing mind.

THREE POPULAR SCAPEGOATS

When searching for reasons for the high rate of backwardness in reading, it is only too easy to imagine that you have at last discovered the longed-for explanation and panacea, and to create what, in my view, are largely scapegoats. Three examples emerge from the topics discussed in this chapter alone:

1. *The "wrong" method.* The widespread and successful amalgamation of methods in itself suggests that alleged flaws in either of the two main rival methods are apt to be misconstrued. The sheer quantity of research into means of assessing and improving methods of teaching makes it difficult to hope that they can be further improved except marginally. Nevertheless, so-called new methods, which are no more than variants of older ones, appear regularly.

2. *The "wrong" kind of reading primers.* There is a tendency to attach so much importance to the character of reading primers, to the vocabulary and story-content (in relationship to the child's environment), to the quality of their illustrations, to the precise size of type and even to the colour of the paper, that possible faults in other components of the teaching/learning process are largely ignored. Every ten years or so primers

which had previously been hailed as the latest, revolutionary, perfect product of research are held to be not merely old-fashioned but ill-conceived in the opinion of the authors and promoters of the newest publications, compiled as the result of yet more elaborate word counts or of researches in the grammatical and semantic structure of the language. . . . The established rival primers are heaped with most, if not all, of the blame for the continuing poor results.

3. *The "wrong" kind of teachers.* Two recent very high level U.S. reports[1] reveal this trait—

> There are understandable reasons why some reading instruction is not good. The *main* [my italics] reason is the shortage of good teachers which is a plague that affects the teaching in all educational institutions, be they schools, colleges, or universities.

These words echo other despairing pleas made over the years on both sides of the Atlantic: if only the quality of the recruits to the teaching profession could be raised; if only the lecturers in the training colleges could have a more fundamental understanding of their subject; if only the teachers would apply what they have learned once they take charge in their own classrooms—then all would be well.

Of course the nature of the method of teaching and of the reading primers is relevant and it is scarcely necessary to re-emphasize the importance of having teachers of the highest quality, but no amount of further improvements of these three elements is likely to bring about the necessary dramatic reduction in the percentage of backward readers. But before elaborating this proposition further it is necessary to examine some of the other, well-established, and for the most part non-pedagogic theories that account for serious failure in reading as well as for backwardness. The implications of these theories are in many respects relevant to my own suggested solution to the problem and, in the same way as psychiatry has thrown light on the workings of the healthy as well as the sick mind, what little we know of the processes of reading is entangled with the study of the failure to acquire them.

[1] *The Torch Lighters* by Mary C. Austin; foreword by Dean Francis Keppel. Harvard, Cambridge, Massachusetts, 1961. *Learning to Read: a Report of a Conference of Reading Experts,* with a foreword by James B. Conant. Educational Testing Service, Princeton, New Jersey, 1962. The extract quoted comes from pp. 3–4 of the majority report in this second publication.

3   Theories of Reading Failure

A BATTERY OF INGENIOUS TECHNIQUES has been perfected by researchers into the nature and possible causes of reading disability and backwardness. In addition to the series of tests described in Chapter 1 to assess standards in relation to mental and chronological age, Burt, Schonell, Watts, Vernon, Gates, Betts, and others have devised diagnostic tests that provide evidence of characteristic errors made by backward readers and a scale of measurement for such psychological facilities and skills as word recognition, auditory and visual perception, memory span, associative learning, etc. Research into reading has been influenced by the growing knowledge of child development and of the nature of the general learning processes but, while investigations of individual cases are frequently recorded—especially for the purposes of remedial teaching—much of the research is entangled almost inextricably with enquiries into the merits of different teaching methods. The frequency of a certain type of error made by a group of pupils may, for example, in part result from whether the emphasis is on phonics or look-and-say and thus from the vocabulary chosen for the reading primers—one primer may include short words only with plenty of related sounds and syllables, compared with another primer that concentrates on words with unmistakable variations in length and appearance.

Educationists customarily complain of the unscientific basis of many of the studies of reading failure and the lack of adequate controls; in an often quoted paragraph W. S. Gray,[1] the eminent American expert, wrote—

[1] "Reading." *Encyclopedia of Educational Research*, edited by Walter Scott Monroe, p. 966. Macmillan, New York, 1960.

Unfortunately, much of the scientific work relating to reading has been fragmentary in character. As pointed out by various writers, the investigator frequently attacks an isolated problem, completes his study of it, and suggests that he will continue his research at some later time but often fails to do so. In the second place, there is far too little co-ordination of effort among research workers in the field of reading. . . .

Many others, including teachers, have cast doubt on the value of much of the research: to quote from the U.S. report[1] mentioned at the end of the last chapter—

While almost all respondents had suggestions regarding future research in reading, nevertheless many were highly critical of past research and the way it is being utilized currently. One respondent stated categorically that: "nothing new has been done in the field of reading in the last twenty years." . . . an additional comment was made that most teachers would continue to ignore research findings even if they were made more readily available and more easily digestible . . . most classroom teachers had "closed minds" about research and, regardless of the validity of its results, would continue to teach as they had been teaching, without reference to new methods and ideas.

It is relevant also to add the conclusion of Professor M. D. Vernon[2]—

. . . in spite of the numerous studies which have been made in recent years of reading backwardness, its incidence, causes and cure, there was still little reliable information as to the actual nature of this disability and its fundamental causes. This appeared to be due at least in part to the use of unsatisfactory techniques of investigation. In particular, the tendency has been to select and compare groups of normal and backward readers, and to attempt to isolate the factors which are associated with the latter group as a whole, but not with the former. Often the degree of backwardness has not been suitably measured; seldom has its exact nature been investigated in individual cases—that is to say, what exactly it is that each backward reader is unable to do or has failed to learn.

These strictures notwithstanding, no one would dispute the reliability and high quality of many of the research studies nor can we afford to underrate their importance. An analysis of the leading investigations will be found in several of the books that are listed in the Bibliography, but for the purposes of my argument and to provide a perspective for

[1] *The Torch Lighters*, pp. 68–69.
[2] "Specific Dyslexia." *The British Journal of Educational Psychology*, Vol. XXXII, June 1962, p. 143.

my own suggestions I shall limit myself to a summary of—
  (1) observable, characteristic errors made by backward readers;
  (2) a selection of individual, psychological and/or environmental factors associated with backwardness;
  (3) psychological and perceptual weaknesses believed to be responsible for backwardness.

This tripartite classification does, I suggest, help to systematize the unwieldy congestion of incomparable material, but these three groupings must not be thought of as being rigidly divided, for it is often as difficult to separate a symptom from a factor that may help to cause it as it is easy to mistake one for the other.

(1) *Observable characteristic errors made by backward readers*

The individual pupil seldom displays a single, overriding type of error; in nearly all cases a complex of persistent errors is noted which may or may not be related. The following are some of the commonest found among backward readers and also, but in diminishing degrees, among children who learn to read without abnormal difficulty. They are looked for and counted when making individual diagnoses and have been analyzed in investigations by researchers such as Ilg and Ames, Gates, Daniels and Diack, Burt, Schonell, the two Vernons, Monroe, Hildreth, and very many others—

Confusion between reversible ("mirror") characters—*b* and *d*.
Confusion between characters of similar shape—*n* and *h*.
Word ("mirror") reversals—*saw* for *was*.
Transposition of characters—*gril* for *girl*.
Substitution of a wrong single character—*some* for *same*.
Substitution of a wrong general appearance—*securely* for *scarcely*.
Recognition of part of a word and guessing the rest of it.
Omission of a sound—*bind* for *blind*.
Addition of a sound—*cart* for *cat*.
Confusion between similar sounds—*but* for *bud*.
Confusion over vowels—*dig* for *dug*.
Incorrect phonetic rendering of phonetically simple words—saying *read* (the verb) for *red*.
Failing to relate *The* with *the*; *A* with *a*.

Attacking words phonically character by character and misreading "irregular" words—*onky* for *once*.

Incorrect reading of beginning of word.

Incorrect reading of middle of word.

Incorrect reading of end of word.

Confusion over order of characters.

Over-reliance on context, leading to substitution of a wrong meaning— *palace* for *castle*.

Failure to make use of contextual clues.

(2) *Individual, psychological, and/or environmental factors associated with backwardness*

Backward readers are not all of a type. As many possible reasons are put forward to explain the condition as there are variations in the degree of its severity. There is an immense difference between those who are merely slower or comprehend a little less than others in the same chronological age group and the very few who suffer from the relatively rare alexias—the term given to severe types of disability that make the individual more or less incapable of mastering the processes of reading. In between these two extremes come a multitude of recognized types and degrees of backwardness, different both in nature and origin, though their characteristics may in many respects be similar or overlap.

A school's neighbourhood environment as well as the type of school— Public, grammar, secondary modern, technical; urban or rural—has been shown to affect its average reading standard: schools that serve slum and "problem" areas with bad social conditions have significantly poorer results. According to the Newsom Report on secondary education: " . . . the average reading age of the fourth-year pupils in the problem area schools was eight months lower than the average for modern schools generally. In the schools in slums it was nine months lower still—seventeen months in all."[1] But poor standards of reading can be found also among individual pupils in the most expensive private preparatory schools and among pupils coming from the most privileged sections of the community, though admittedly their average standard tends to be much higher and with the small classes and closer individual supervision customary in a preparatory school remedial measures are more likely to be applied—even

---

[1] *Half our Future*, §65, p. 24.

though they are sometimes not effectual and the pupils are seldom able to make up all the ground lost.[1]

Strictly speaking, each case of backward reading is different from any other. It is unique. The frequency of any of the persistent errors listed above can often be related to overt personal symptoms such as exaggerated lip movements in silent reading, holding the book at an abnormal distance from the eyes, failure to enunciate certain syllables, or low levels of comprehension. Provided it is recognized that both errors and symptoms to some extent reflect the difficulty of the material being read, they can be usefully considered together with information about the child's medical and family history, to provide clues to what is responsible for the backwardness. But seldom is a cut-and-dried explanation possible. In fact it is misleading to think in terms of causes of backwardness; instead, it is safer to think merely of factors *associated* with backwardness, of which several may be present and one may be dominant. Some specialists divide these into predisposing factors and causative factors; a division can also be made between factors that are either predominantly individual or predominantly environmental in origin. Classifications can, however, lead to misleading oversimplification and in the ensuing summary of factors associated with backward reading they have purposely been applied very loosely—

Low intelligence is generally accepted to be a handicap and likely to be associated with backwardness in reading—as it is with backwardness in comprehending speech—but children with I.Q.s of 80 to 70 and even lower can and do learn to read and communicate reasonably well, though probably with less than average efficiency; equally many children with relatively high I.Q.s—and even very high I.Q.s—may for some reason be very backward readers or, occasionally, fail completely.

Brain injuries, developmental failures in localized areas of the cerebral cortex, and, in particular, lack of dominance by the major over the minor cerebral hemisphere. This relatively rare, possibly congenital, condition is obscure and difficult to diagnose but it tends also to be related to speech defects; to left-handedness or ambidexterity; or to a combination of being right-handed and left-eyed or left-handed and right-eyed.

---

[1] For example, the failure rate in the Common Entrance examination to Public schools is high and there is reason to believe that the cause of many of the failures lies in the boys' lack of confidence in tackling the printed word and their lack of effortless skill and fluency in reading.

It is worth noting that whereas plenty of excellent readers are left-handed, this can make writing—and therefore reading—more difficult (unless left-handed writing is actively encouraged as indeed it ought to be).

Emotional or personality disorders, resulting from temperamental defects and/or faulty upbringing. These symptoms may themselves entirely or in part stem from the inability to read, the sense of failure and inferiority leading to apathy and resistance to the effort of learning, but emotional or personality disorders can also be the apparently primary factor. Whatever their origin, they inhibit learning; for example, the hyper-active, restless childs finds it difficult to concentrate and apply himself, unless his occasional effort is rewarded by immediate success; so does the child who has been over-protected or spoiled; similarly, the child who has been pressed too hard by parents or teacher becomes tense and anxious and therefore finds his achievement insufficient and reading difficult. In some cases of maladjustment there is a resentment to Authority as represented by the teacher; in others failure to read may be the child's unconscious way of attracting attention to himself or of punishing his parents for having denied him their affection. A disturbed child may also escape from his problems into a world of fantasy, thus avoiding the reality of the classroom and the demands of his reading primer. There are other possible situations that inhibit reading, yet it must not be thought that every maladjusted or emotionally disturbed child is automatically a backward reader—or vice versa.

Poor home background (frequently related to maladjustment), in particular the type of home with an impoverished linguistic background (see Chapter 2, page 27), or in which reading is not encouraged and the child is given no practice.

Mental immaturity or retardation. One of the possible features of reading *un*-readiness (see Chapter 2), and thought by some specialists to manifest itself in a parallel delayed development of visual and auditory perception.

Hearing defects. Deafness is very obviously a dominant factor, but minor defects in hearing acuity, particularly losses in the higher frequencies, can also prevent children from learning to listen and thus to read. These often go undetected and the child has to try to hear and read words that he cannot properly discriminate as sounds.

Speech defects may result from defective hearing, in which case they may also be associated with backward reading. In a few children whose hearing is normal, speech defects, poor articulation, and backwardness in reading may all be related to the same inability to understand words or to make auditory discriminations between certain sounds— e.g., between *might have* and *might of*, *f* and *th*, *r* and *w*, *s* and *sh*.

Ocular defects, if severe and undetected, obviously retard reading. Minor defects can lead to mistaking *m* for *n* or guessing at words or to eyestrain and fatigue that impede effort. Blurred characters normally become clear when the defect is corrected by glasses, but bad habits and the sense of anxiety connected with reading may persist. On the other hand, many children learn to read despite imperfect sight. Inefficient eye-fixations, such as regressions towards the beginning of lines, may result from an ocular defect, but they are more likely to be a symptom rather than a cause of backward reading.

(3) *Psychological and perceptual weaknesses*

It will be noticed that many of the errors (or symptoms) and individual factors listed above can be distinguished according to whether they involve the visual or auditory channels or a combination of the two. In some instances a shortcoming in certain other intrinsic psychological and/or perceptual faculties may be indicated. Many backward readers are subject to one or more of the following basic weaknesses, each of which can inhibit the essential processes of reading. Some suggest that these weaknesses have a general effect, but often they seem to be absent in subjects other than reading—

Poor *visual* perception and discrimination, memory and imagery— resulting in failure to distinguish and analyze *shapes* of characters, syllables, and words when printed.

Poor *auditory* perception and discrimination, memory and imagery— resulting in failure to distinguish and analyze *sounds* of characters, syllables, and words when spoken.

Deficiency in the ability to perceive direction and order—resulting in character and word reversals.

Inability to associate shapes with sounds; to organize and co-ordinate visual and auditory elements—resulting in failure to build up a systematic knowledge of sounds and to blend sounds with whole words (a failure which creates the barrier between the early and later stages of learning to read, described in the previous chapter).

Professor M. D. Vernon, recognized as one of the greatest authorities on reading disabilities, expresses doubts about the existence of any primary innate defect in the ability to hear discrete sounds (provided hearing acuity is normal) but she describes this failure to analyze and associate word shapes and sounds as the "one universal characteristic of non-readers suffering from specific reading disability."[1] She also writes that—

> ... the fundamental and basic characteristic of reading disability appears to be cognitive confusion and lack of system. Why even quite an intelligent child should fail to realize that there is a complete and invariable correspondence between printed letter shapes and phonetic units remains a mystery which ... has not yet been solved. It must be attributed to a failure in analyzing, abstraction and generalization, but one which, typically, is confined to linguistics.[2]

My purpose is to unravel this mystery. It exists only because of the isolation of most of the researches into reading disability from the language, from its alphabet and spelling. The central failure, as Professor Vernon remarks, "is confined to linguistics," but is she correct in saying that "there is a complete and invariable correspondence between printed letter shapes and phonetic units"? In fact, earlier in the same book[3] she writes—

> ... unfortunately in the English language the relationships between sounds and visual percepts vary considerably from word to word. .... Thus even when the child has realized the importance of differentiating and attending to the phonetic sounds, he is set a formidable task in memorizing these differences.

On another page, when summarizing the four essentials which the backward reader fails to understand, she states[4]—

> When the printed letter units and the spoken phonetic units have been analyzed out from the word wholes in which they are combined, they can be associated together in such a manner that visual perception of the letters calls forth certain speech patterns, and hence the corresponding auditory sensations. But the associations, although invariable and consistent for any particular word, are often arbitrary and unsystematic as between different words. Therefore although there are certain rules determining which sounds should be given to certain word and letter shapes, these rules are neither logical nor universally operative.

[1] *Backwardness in Reading*, p. 74. Cambridge University Press, 1960.
[2] Ibid., p. 71.   [3] Ibid., p. 39.   [4] Ibid., p. 187.

Professor Vernon first wrongly assumes (see pages 50–3 *infra*) both an invariable and consistent association for any particular word she then recognizes the difficulty, but nevertheless for some reason does not draw the inevitable conclusion: that the child is expected to take on a task that is formidable for all and for some impossible: to analyze what is scarcely analyzable, to conjure abstractions and generalizations from a printed medium whose associations are in fact neither invariable nor consistent and thus doubly irrational. Would it not be truer to say that the child is perplexed precisely because of his innate ability to reason, to analyze, abstract, and generalize?

Research into reading disabilities has enabled help to be given to a minority of specific cases, and it has extended our knowledge in many ways, but as yet it has not succeeded in providing a convincing explanation—or even a series of explanations—of the fundamental reason why so many end up as backward readers. One or more of the predisposing and causative factors may always be present but in the majority of cases of backwardness they are almost certainly of secondary relevance only—*so far as reading is concerned*. They too are apt to become scapegoats. Even if we add to all these factors weaknesses in methods of teaching, flaws in the quality of reading primers, indifferent standards of teaching, and the effects of some classes that are too large, of some poor school buildings and equipment—to make a grand total of harmful, hindering influences—only part of the high percentage of backwardness is, to my mind, accounted for. If every child could be taught by teachers of the highest quality, using the finest reading primers and the most enlightened, subtle amalgam of existing teaching methods in the finest imaginable school buildings, and if at the same time everything possible were done to alleviate all predisposing and causative factors, it would no doubt lead to a noticeable reduction in the percentage, but not to its elimination. To think otherwise is to fall into the error of mistaking the solution of parts of a problem for the solution of the whole problem. It is as fallacious as believing that the invention of a new teaching method or, say, the earlier diagnosis of poor eyesight obviates the need for smaller classes! A parallel can be drawn with the campaign to eliminate an infectious disease like tuberculosis: improved nutrition, higher standards of nursing, the artificial deflation of the lung and other forms of surgical interference did much to prolong life, but the dramatic fall in the T.B. death rate came only with the discovery of the right kinds of antibiotics.

Can it perhaps be that most of the researches into reading have overlooked, or at any rate neglected, the largest factor of all?—one, what is more, that is capable of acting as an energizer to all the other suggested factors, that enhances their significance. As well as attempting to reduce these factors might it not be at least equally useful—and very much easier —to eliminate for the beginner the avoidable difficulties inherent in what is read?

4   Structure of English Spelling

ALPHABETIC WRITING is, essentially, a visual codi-
fication of speech. Its sequence of characters enables a relationship to be
established between words that are written or printed and words that are
spoken, between the visual capacities of the reader and his auditory/oral
capacities. Even the most inefficient alphabet has obvious advantages over
other forms of graphic communication such as the cumbersome system
of Chinese ideographs in which each written or printed symbol depicts
but a single object or idea and is connected with only the equivalent
spoken word, thus requiring the memorizing of as many as possible
Chinese characters out of a total said to reach 45,000—there are in fact
several different Chinese languages that share the same ideographs. By
comparison the memorizing of the 26 letters of the roman alphabet is
an infinitesimal task, but in the case of the English language the connection
between the visual symbols and spoken words is unfortunately very
imperfect and misleading. The true alphabetic principle is applied only
partially. It has been calculated that the direct visual-to-sound relationship
fails to operate over about a quarter of the words in the language—though
some maintain the proportion is much higher. We do not write as we speak,
nor do we speak as we write. Unlike, say, Finnish, Italian or Spanish
most English printed words are not spelled[1] as they are pronounced. They
represent sounds which we would be horrified to utter. We spell for the
eye and hand rather than for the ear and tongue.

[1] Perhaps I should write "spelt"? *The Oxford English Dictionary* permits either!

No one is likely to dispute that English spelling is difficult and illogical. The spelling bee has long been an Anglo-Saxon institution. *Enough, plough, borough, through, cough, et al.*, are well-known anomalies and even looked upon with affection and treasured as harmless eccentricities, and anyone misguided enough to advocate the need for spelling reform is liable to be dubbed as a pettifogging crank. As will be emphasized and explained at greater length in a later chapter, this book is not a plea for a permanent or universal spelling reform; on the other hand the starting premise for its central argument is that, while the alphabetic principle may be largely abused and ignored by the literate, it is particularly beneficial during the learning stages; and that therefore the problem of how best to teach English-speaking children to read (or adults from other countries to learn English) is inextricably bound up with the question of *when* the inconsistences and illogicalities of English spelling should be presented to the learner. It is necessary therefore to examine these with some precision.

THE SEVENTEEN MISSING CHARACTERS

Speech makes use of a variety of sounds which to the trained ear of a phonetician are as readily distinguishable as notes of the scale in music and the timbre of the different musical instruments. The acoustically distinguishable "speech-sounds" of the human voice are grouped into families called "phonemes,"[1] each of which has a characteristic acoustic form. A word may contain one or several phonemes which can therefore be defined as the smallest semantically functional units of sound that can be identified in an act of speech—e.g. in the word *but* there are three phonemes and in the word *ought* there are only two. A language can exist on relatively few phonemes and the number employed differs in different languages—Polynesian manages with as few as 12; the people of Thailand make use of 39 (and an alphabet of 46 characters). The number of phonemes required differs also in different pronunciations of the same language: e.g. if you rhyme *food* with *good*, you make use of one less phoneme than if you distinguish *full* from *fool*.

---

[1] The term "phoneme" needs qualification. The whole question of the relationship between the phonemes on which a language can be said to be based and the infinite variations in the number of phonemes and how they are used by individuals who share that language is dealt with at length in Chapter 7. "Phoneme" is so frequently misemployed that it is now too late to disentangle it from the correct term "diaphone." This embraces in a single sound classification all those different phonemes from which a listener is able to identify and comprehend a word in however many regional and individual pronunciations it may be spoken.

This question cannot be usefully discussed in the abstract but only in terms of a living language. In the case of a language such as English with its variety of contrasting pronunciations one has to make a choice—or choices—between them. For the purpose of this part of the book the reader is asked to assume that I am writing in terms of what can be termed a generally accepted pronunciation but which in fact no one actually speaks. Where in one regional pronunciation two phonemes are employed (e.g. the Scots *tern* and *turn*) compared with another (e.g. Southern English) that employs only one for the same two words, the more discriminating pronunciation has been chosen.

Opinions among the experts have differed over the precise number of phonemes recognized in acceptably spoken English. It depends on the principles behind the analysis, on whether or not certain diphthongs are considered as one sound or as a combination of two. The absolute minimum number is 32, but this involves disregarding all the diphthongs, whether vowel diphthongs (as in *die*) or consonantal diphthongs (as in *jam*), and representing them by their two constituent characters. To produce a fully phonetic system in which each sound in the English (UK) language is represented by a single character, no less than 79 graphic units are employed—52 for vowels and 27 for consonants.[1] A practical working relationship can, however, be achieved on the basis of a classification of no more than 40 sounds. This conclusion is supported by, among many others, the eminent American authority, Godfrey Dewey,[2] who has stated—

> The large experience of Pitmanic shorthand has demonstrated, I think conclusivly, that 40 sounds ... represent the extreme minimum with which strictly fonetic writing of English may be achievd. By *strictly* I refer to no particular degree of precision but to strict adherence to the principle: one sign for each sound, one sound for each sign.

Unfortunately, unlike the system of shorthand invented by my grandfather, the roman alphabet has not 40 but only 26 letters with which to express this practical minimum of 40 phonemes. There are too few characters to match the sounds of English speech. The actual deficiency amounts not to 14 (40–26) but 17 letters because 3 of the roman letters—*c*, *q*, and *x*—are redundant in that they gratuitously repeat the sounds

---

[1] *See The Shorter Oxford English Dictionary*, p. xxii. Oxford University Press, 1965.

[2] *Relativ Frequency of English Speech Sounds*, p. 124 (printed in fonetic print alfabet). Harvard University Press, Cambridge, Massachusetts; and Sir Isaac Pitman & Sons Ltd., London, 1923. Other inventors of shorthand systems have equally accepted the 40-sound analysis.

symbolized by other letters or combinations of letters, e.g. *cat, kitten*; *quay, key*; *fox, locks*. The 17 missing characters are made up of 6 consonant sounds: *thin, this, ship, vision, sing, church*; and 11 vowel sounds: *father* (counting the *a* in *at* as the normal value of the character), *ape, autumn, feed, fine* (counting the *i* in *fin* as the normal value), *cope* (counting the *o* in *cop* as the normal value), *cute* (counting the *u* in *cut* as the normal value), *out, oil, look, food*. In default of enough characters, we get round the difficulty by such devices as using two or more letters in combination to create digraphs (*th, ng, oi, oo, eigh, ough*, etc.) or by making one letter serve for several phonemes as with the traditional five vowels—

a — *fat, fated, father, what, water, any*
e — *me, met, pretty, Derby* (*the English town*)
i — *fin, final, concertina, meringue*
o — *hover, lover, rover, mover, choir, wolf, women*
u — *pun, puny, full, rule, busy, bury*

The characters for the consonants as well as for the vowels represent a miscellany of sounds. In fact none of them can be counted on to behave reliably, in that they do not represent invariably the same phoneme. As digraphs represent phonemes and do not possess the separate sound values of the monographic characters of which they are made up, it is reasonable to consider digraphs as behaving as single characters. Taking all these combinations into account, this means that a child learning to read has to become familiar not with an alphabet of 26 letters but of many, many more. The extra burdens carried by certain letters also face a child at a very early stage with the following kind of problem: first he learns the values of *t* and of *h* in the words *not her*; when the *n* is changed to *m* and the words are joined together, to make *mother*, he is told that *t* and *h* have shed their old sounds and now together represent a different sound but he is then faced with *shorthand*. The same is true of *mishap*: *bishop*; *ochre*: *such*; and of many other instances.

Entwined with the confusion and ambiguity caused by the lack of 17 characters are the numerous inconsistencies and phonetically arbitrary spellings introduced by borrowings from older languages and by the whims of early lexicographers and printers (see Chapter 5). Whatever the causes, their combined effect is to produce at least several hundred different ways of representing the 40 phonemes. The great Victorian spelling reformer, A. J. Ellis, arrived at a total of 658 different ways (based on 42 phonemes) and his findings have been substantiated by many other researchers. Dr. Godfrey Dewey, for example, working on a basis of 41 phonemes, has identified 507 different ways of representing them.[1] Both of these tables included, in the words of Ellis, "only . . . cases of digraphs which consist entirely of vowels or entirely of consonants, excluding those which are partly made up of consonants and partly of vowels."[2] Furthermore neither of them takes account of the variations of most of the letters (e.g. the characters A, a, *a*, etc.—see pages 50–53) which in turn present the beginner with yet more difficulties. Thus it was that Sir James Murray, who spent thirty-six years in charge of the compilation of *The Oxford English Dictionary*, went on record[3] to deplore " . . . the waste of national resources incurred in the attempt to make child after child commit to memory the 20,000 contradictory facts of English spelling."

Two broad classifications emerge from this maze of inconsistency, the first disrupting the process of learning to read, the second the process of learning to spell—

1. *Falsely implied relationships*

In these the same character or the same group of two or more characters represents a variety of phonemes; the words look as if they should sound the same but in fact they do not. In *go*, *do*, *so*, *one*, *once*, *women*, and the other examples on page 43 the *single* character *o* implies a false common relationship; in *leaf*, *great*, *bread*, *heart*, *earth*, *sergeant*, and *guinea*, seven traps are set for the reader by the digraph *ea*. It is not difficult to discover equally misleading trigraphs, tetragraphs, etc., and there are even many pairs of words that look identical but are pronounced differently such as: *row* (quarrel), *row* (a boat); *wound* (injure), *wound* (coiled); *sewer* (one who sews), *sewer* (drain); *read* (infinitive), *read* (past tense); *live* (verb), *live* (adjective).[4]

---

[1] *English heterografy or How we spel!* Lake Placid Club Education Foundation, N.Y. Revised edition, 1963.

[2] *A Plea for Phonetic Spelling*, p. 28. Fred Pitman, Phonetic Depôt, London, 1848.

[3] Speaking at a meeting of the Philological Society, 20 May 1881, held at University College, London.

[4] A cumbersome but exact description of these pairs of words is "homotypic heterophones." They can be compared with 750 or so "homotypic homophones" which, though identical in sound as well as appearance, yet possess different meanings that can be determined only from their context, e.g.: *bark* (dog), *bark* (tree); *page* (of book), *page* (attendant); *spoke* (speech), *spoke* (wheel); *box* (container), *box* (tree), *box* (fight). The three-letter word *set* has so many homotypic homophones with so many meanings that it occupies more than two-and-a-half very large pages of *The Shorter Oxford English Dictionary*.

The extent and complexity of the falsely implied relationships is demonstrated in *Table IV* (turn to Appendix I). It is divided into three sections: *Table IV* (*i*) contains examples of all the words I can find in each of which the same single character (monograph) represents a different phoneme—the total comes to 131. Note that not one of the 26 characters consistently represents one phoneme only. In *Table IV* (*ii*) will be found a small selection of misleading digraphs and in *Table IV* (*iii*) an even smaller selection of misleading trigraphs. As we have just seen, the characters that make up digraphs, trigraphs, etc. can also in certain other words represent not one phoneme but two or more—in *Tables IV* (*ii and iii*) this form of misrepresentation is shown separately: thus in *leaf, great, bread, heart, earth, sergeant, guinea,* the *ea* is a digraph that represents seven different single phonemes, but in *reality, idea, rearm, reavow, ocean,* the same two consecutive characters represent five other quite different disparate *pairs* of phonemes—a total of twelve traps for the reader. Similarly the trigraph *ana* represents nine different series of phonemes: *canal, canalize, canary, banal, banana, Ghana, manager,* and, in two of its pronunciations, *manana.*

Even more complex are the characters in the tetragraph combinations such as *eight* and *sleight,* or *plague, ague, blague, league,* or in the pentagraph *oughe* which, insofar as the mute *e* is considered to be attached to the *ough* and not to the *d,* in *ploughed* represents one phoneme only, but in *coughed, roughed,* or *hiccoughed* it represents a series of two disparate pairs of phonemes.

2. *Falsely implied dis-relationships*

This is the second main classification; in these groups of words the same phoneme is represented by a variety of characters or digraphs; the words look as if they must be different from each other, whereas in fact they share a common factor of pronunciation.

The most celebrated example is the sound common to *I* and *eye* which can be spelt in twenty-seven different ways: *aisle, assegai, McKay, ayes; seismic, height, eying, eye; I, phial, ice, indict, lie, sign, maligned, high, sighed, island, isle; choir; beguiling, guide, buy, guyed; sty, dye, style.* If we add the words containing the mute *h* as in *rheinberry, rhino, rhinestone,* and *rhyme, rhyming,* the total becomes thirty-two.

It is easy to think of others such as *Caesar, quay, these, me, seen, tea,*

45

chief, seize, fatigue, machine, people, suite; chauffeur, most, yeoman, sew, boat, show, foe, go, brooch, folk, whole, soul, bureau, mauve; straight, halfpenny, make, fail, hay, great, eight, eh!, cabaret, fete, veil, deign, gaol, gauge. Belonging to this category is another large selection of homophones —the heterotypic homophones like: *pair, pear; dew, due; meat, meet; pause, paws; right, write, rite.* Rather than labour the point further, these falsely implied dis-relationships can also be tabulated to show that they amount to no less than 793 (*Table V*, Appendix I).

The Victorians were fond of using ridicule to demonstrate the absurdities of English spelling. In a letter addressed to my grandfather, in his capacity as editor of the *Phonotypic Journal*, a Dr. William Gregory, Professor of Chemistry at the University of Edinburgh, made use of the endless varieties of spelling which are feasible and often quite as logical and as capable of general acceptance as accepted spellings. Here is a short sample from it with the words from which the sounds have been borrowed printed beneath each line in smaller print—

Professor Gregory's "Lebtor"

Tough	**thea**	**Ea**diter	**auph**		**thie**	**Foughnotipick**
(thr)ough	(t)ea	(h)ead	(l)aur(el)	(ne)ph(ew)	(gr)ie(f)	(th)ough

Jolonal : Syrhh,—Eye		obzerve	**yew**	**proepeaux**	**two**	**introwduice**		
(c)olon(el) (m)yrrh	eye	z(eal)	yew	(d)oe (b)eaux	two	(kn)ow (j)uice		

ay	**nue**	**sissedem**	ov	**righting,**	**bigh**	**whitch**	**ue**	**eckspres**
(m)ay	(s)ue	(m)issed	v(ie)	right	(h)igh	(w)itch	(h)ue	(p)ecks

oanly	**theigh**	**sowneds**	**anned**	**knot**	**thee**	orthoggrafey	**oph**
(l)oan	(L.)eigh	(cr)owned	(f)anned	knot	thee	(d)ogger(el) (barl)ey	(Ste)ph(en)

they	**wurds;**	**butt**	**Igh**	**phthink**		**ugh**	**gow**	**to fare inn**
(k)ey	(c)urds	butt	(s)igh	(apo)phth(egm)		(H)ugh	(kn)ow	to are inn

cheighnjing	**owr**	**thyme-onird**	alfahbeat,		**aned**	**ading**	**sew**
(w)eigh	(c)ow	thyme (b)ird	(Hann)ah (sw)eat		(h)a(v)e	(h)ad	sew

The lumbering, waggish joke still makes its point. Equally telling is A. J. Ellis's hilarious calculation[1] of the number of ways in which you can spell the word *scissors*. Basing his calculation on the phonetic rendering, *siserz*, he listed the following varieties—

[1] *A Plea for Phonetic Spelling*, pp. 32–33.

6 for initial S, namely 3, (*ps, s, sw,*) which we represent by S^1,
and 3, (*c, sc, sch,*) which we represent by S^2.
16 for medial I, namely 6, (*au, o, oa, oi, u, ui,*) = I^1,
and 10 (*e, ea, eau, ee, ei, eo, i, ia, ie, y,*) = I^2.
7 for medial Z, namely 5, (*s, ss, sw, z, zz,*) = Z^1,
and 2 (*c, sc,*) = Z^2.
22 for E in a final syllable, namely 8, (*a, ae, ai, ay, oi, u, ue, o,*) = E^1,
9, (*æ, e, ea, ei, eo, ie, œ, y, i,*) = E^2,
3 (*a-e, -e, -i*) = E^3 (meaning by *-e* a postponed *e*, as in *sabre* = *saber*),
and 2 (e-e, i-e,) = E^4.
7 for final R, namely 5, (*r, rr, rrh, rt, rps,*) = R^1,
and 2 (*re, rre,*) = R^2.
and 7 for final Z, namely 5, (*ds, s, se, z, zz,*) = Z^1,
and 2, (*se, ze,*) = Z^2.

Ellis then worked out the total of possible combinations and arrived at this permutation—

$S^1IZ^1ER^1Z^1$	giving	$3 \times 16 \times 5 \times 22 \times 5 \times 5 =$	132,000 forms.
$S^1IZ^1E^1RZ^1$	,,	$3 \times 16 \times 5 \times 8 \times 7 \times 5 =$	67,200 ,,
$S^1IZ^1E^2RZ^1$	,,	$3 \times 16 \times 5 \times 9 \times 7 \times 5 =$	75,600 ,,
$S^1IZ^1E^2R^1Z^2$	,,	$3 \times 16 \times 5 \times 9 \times 5 \times 2 =$	21,600 ,,
$S^1IZ^1E^3R^1Z^1$	,,	$3 \times 16 \times 5 \times 3 \times 5 \times 5 =$	18,000 ,,
$S^1IZ^1E^4R^1Z^1$	,,	$3 \times 16 \times 5 \times 2 \times 5 \times 5 =$	12,000 ,,
$S^1IZ^2E^2RZ^1$	,,	$3 \times 16 \times 2 \times 9 \times 7 \times 5 =$	30,240 ,,
$S^1IZ^2E^2R^1Z^2$	,,	$3 \times 16 \times 2 \times 9 \times 5 \times 2 =$	8,640 ,,
$S^2I^2Z^1ER^1Z^1$	,,	$3 \times 10 \times 5 \times 22 \times 5 \times 5 =$	82,500 ,,
$S^2I^2Z^1E^1RZ^1$	,,	$3 \times 10 \times 5 \times 8 \times 7 \times 5 =$	42,000 ,,
$S^2I^2Z^1E^2RZ^1$	,,	$3 \times 10 \times 5 \times 9 \times 7 \times 5 =$	47,250 ,,
$S^2I^2Z^1E^2R^1Z^2$	,,	$3 \times 10 \times 5 \times 9 \times 5 \times 2 =$	13,500 ,,
$S^2I^2Z^1E^3R^1Z^1$	,,	$3 \times 10 \times 5 \times 3 \times 5 \times 5 =$	11,250 ,,
$S^2I^2Z^1E^4R^1Z^1$	,,	$3 \times 10 \times 5 \times 2 \times 5 \times 5 =$	7,500 ,,
$S^2I^2Z^2E^2RZ^1$	,,	$3 \times 10 \times 2 \times 9 \times 7 \times 5 =$	18,900 ,,
$S^2I^2Z^2E^2R^1Z^2$	,,	$3 \times 10 \times 2 \times 9 \times 5 \times 2 =$	5,400 ,,
$S^2I^2Z^2E^4R^1Z^1$	,,	$3 \times 10 \times 2 \times 2 \times 5 \times 5 =$	3,000 ,,

The grand total shows that *scissors* can be spelled in no less than 596,580 ways.

INCONSISTENT SPELLING OF THE COMMONEST WORDS

It would be simple to fill many more pages with the iniquities of English spelling, to draw attention to the mute characters in words like *knot, scene, lamb, gnaw, hymn,* and *build* or to list words with alternate spellings, but I hope I have included enough to convince anyone who may not previously have thought much about the subject that the pages over which their eyes skim so effortlessly and efficiently are in fact fraught with inconsistency and illogic, that there is a sizable divergence between hearing and reading, between the language of the ear and the language of the eye; that no Englishman can tell how to pronounce a word in his mother tongue if he has only seen that word written and not heard and memorized it; that no Englishman can tell how to spell a word which he has only heard spoken and never seen written. It is not surprising that the English Universities Press's publication *Teach Yourself to Spell* includes a list of 7,800 English words that are "frequently misspelt."[1] Of particular relevance to the child, however, (or the foreigner) learning to read English is that illogical spellings occur with more than average frequency among the commonest words in the language. In an analysis of 3,000 basic words P. R. Hanna and J. T. Moore (jun.) showed that 20 per cent could be said to have irregular spellings.[2] Dr. Axel Wijk in a recent book[3] concluded that the number of irregular spellings in the language amounts to less than 10 per cent of the total vocabulary but that 15 to 20 per cent of the running words on an average page normally display irregular spellings. From a calculation I made myself, based on figures in Dewey's *Relativ Frequency of English Speech Sounds*,[4] it would appear that only 26·5 per cent of the commonest words are likely to cause no difficulty, while 39·25 per cent present the new reader with very serious difficulty (see page 140). So much depends on one's definition of "regular" and "irregular." By means of ingenious rule-making Wijk manages to eliminate whole families of words that in my view and that of many linguistic experts are unassailably *ir*regular. If a complex spelling happens often enough, Wijk decides to "regularize" it, stating: ". . . the vast majority of English words do in fact follow certain regular patterns in their orthography."[5] He arrives at his percentages by frankly abandoning "strict adherence to the phonetic principle and allow[ing], on the one hand, certain symbols to represent

[1] *Mensa*, the exclusive society of top brains, whose members are claimed to score higher than 98 per cent of the population in a standard intelligence test and to be "verbally skilled people of considerable insight," recently issued a handout that spoke of: "thrashing out their *differencies*"; "the *principle* Mensa tenet"; the many "*proffessors*" in Mensa's ranks; and its "completely *independant* journal."—Reprinted in *The Times*: 4 November 1963.

[2] "Spelling: from Spoken Word to Written Symbol." *Elementary School Journal*, Vol. 53, No. 6, pp. 329-37. University of Chicago, U.S.A., Feb., 1953.

[3] *Regularized English*, p. 46. Almqvist & Wiksell, Stockholm, 1959.

[4] See footnote on p. 42.

[5] *Regularized English*, p. 45 (see note 3 above).

more than one sound, and, on the other hand, certain sounds to be represented by more than one symbol, sometimes by as many as half-a-dozen. . . ."[1] To give but two examples, this means accepting as "regular" falsely implied dis-relationships in words like *matron, make, vain, vein, straight, Gaelic, they* or like *bishop, mission, conscience, special, pension, nation, ocean, appreciable*.

In many systems of teaching reading steps are taken to eliminate some of the more irregular words until later. By careful selection a child may first be taught only the words that are phonetically reliable, but he cannot get very far! Before long he has to accept that, whereas *go, so*, and *no* are pronounced in the same way, this does not apply to *do* or *to* and *who* which have to rhyme with *shoe* which, however, does not rhyme with *goes* or with *does* (in a common pronunciation of the derivate from *do*)—and what can be made of the *wh* in *who* and *whole*; of *one* and *bun*; of *all* and *ought*; *has* and *was*; and many other common words? It is true that secondary clues in the context will be a help, but searching for these in the early stages is impracticable when three-quarters of the adjoining words are misleading. Moreover too much frustrated searching may well form bad habits of irregular eye-movements and, as we saw in Chapter 2, the reader must at quite an early stage gain some skill in analyzing the shapes of syllables and words and in relating them to the corresponding sounds and meanings. However carefully protected, the beginner soon has to grapple with a capricious diversity of mental associations or relationships. Up to a certain point he can rely on a logical relationship between the visual and spoken forms of words, and between different words that are made up of similar syllables, but he has no means of telling when the relationship is going to let him down. There is no alternative, with our present spelling, for the beginner but to memorize the numerous irregularities among the common words, to learn them by rote. Is it any wonder that there has always been a tendency (a necessity?) to lay too much stress on learning to spell compared with learning to read.

The unavoidable inconsistencies among the most common words give rise to the most obvious weakness in the phonic method of teaching reading. The child may rapidly learn to taekle unknown words or even an invented word such as *Poppollington*, to relate *band* with *sand* and cross-relatc to *bend* and *send*, but this does not help him cope with *many, can't, pane*, or *want*. The supply of systematic syllables socn runs out. The galaxy

[1] Ibid., p. 67.

49

of misleading spellings denies to the child the opportunity easily to build on his collection of syllabic relationships and cross-relationships. The auditory element which we saw (Chapter 2) resides in every child is continually perplexed if not frustrated. As some phonemes depend on two characters that are not even adjacent (e.g. the letters *o* and *e* in *bone*) the left-to-right sequence in reading has to be disturbed when deciphering the sound. These inescapable difficulties explain why in Book 1 of a well-known series of reading primers based on 49 easy words, the sound of *I* is represented by no less than 4 different spellings; it also explains why J. C. Daniels and H. Diack admit that halfway through Book 1 of the *Royal Road Readers*,[1] based on their Phonic Word method, "30 odd 'special' words (e.g. *I, you, to, do*) which do not conform to the simplest phonic rules are introduced in order to make it possible to write interesting stories."[2] In the same publication[3] they give examples of pupils who give a "phonetic rendering of irregular words" (e.g. *once* read as *onky, talk* as *talc*) and conclude that these errors "may be said to be errors on the right side since, even when they make errors of this sort, pupils are applying in a logical way the principles upon which alphabetic writing is based." Staggered or phased methods in which words of increasing difficulty are introduced according to a scale worked out on sound phonetic principles (e.g. the schemes devised by the linguistic expert, Leonard Bloomfield,[4] or James P. Soffietti[5]) have something to recommend them because they stress the importance of the alphabetic principle (in conjunction with whole words) from the start, but they too are soon impelled to involve the reador in hosts of exceptions, semi-irregularities, and "sight words."

INCONSISTENT APPEARANCE OF CHARACTERS

The actual shapes of the roman characters also cause difficulty for a child learning to read. To begin with, the lack of sufficient differentiation be-

[1] Chatto & Windus, London, 1954.
[2] *Progress in Reading*, p. 5. J. C. Daniels and H. Diack, University of Nottingham Institute of Education, 1956.   [3] Ibid., p. 45.
[4] "Linguistics and Reading." *Elementary English Review*, 1942, Vols. 19 and 20; pp. 125–30, 183–6. Bloomfield died in 1949 but his writings and ideas have been developed by C. L. Barnhardt in *Let's Read: A Linguistic Approach* (Appleton-Century-Crofts, New York, 1961). Another linguist, C. C. Fries, expanded them further and added conclusions of his own in a most stimulating and thoughtful book: *Linguistics and Reading* (Holt, Rinehart and Winston, New York, 1962–3).
[5] "Why Children Fail to Read: A Linguistic Analysis." *The Harvard Educational Review*, 1955, Vol. 25, pp. 78–83.

tween certain characters makes for poor discrimination and thus learning becomes more taxing. For instance it is only too easy for a child to confuse *d* and *b*; *p* and *q*; *n* and *u*; *n* and *h*. Similarly, *o*, *c*, and *e* are very apt to be mistaken one for the other—whereas *c* and *k*, which represent the same sound, can be readily and needlessly distinguished! This default in the roman alphabet may perhaps be better appreciated by re-reading the previous paragraph in whikh deliberate spelling mistaces were introduced by interkhanging *o*, *c*, and *e*. Unless the reader happened to detekt *all* eight mistaces more easily than he will have detekted the interkhanges of *c* and *k* in this paragraph, the degree of lakc of differentiation between *o*, *c*, and *e* will be made krystal klear.

Even more misleading are the variations of each character, particularly between upper-case (capitals) and lower-case. This is of especial relevance to the look-and-say method. In its pure form look-and-say avoids the phonetic difficulties altogether and in fact jettisons the alphabetic principle, but (leaving aside for the moment whether or not this can be justified) it also fails to recognize that the variations in the form of each character present the child with another series of inconsistencies. It is perhaps impossible for an adult to appreciate how baffling it can be to a child to discover that the indefinite article **a** can also appear as *A* or *a*; that *the* can be *The* or *THE* or*the*. They may seem all the same to us but to a child, striving to acquire the first elements of reading, these kinds of variations are inevitably perceived as being quite distinctive and inexplicably inconsistent. A simple word like *bag* can appear in at least ten forms—

BAG, Bag, Bag, bag, bag,*bag*, bag, bag, Bag, Bag

The present alphabet may have only 26 letters but, even if we leave out differences in the design of type-faces and in handwriting, we make use of no less than 66 variations amounting to distinct characters. An analysis of the ten commonest words in English[1] shows that they can be printed or written in 48 different ways (*Figure 2*). While it is true that a few upper-case (capital) characters resemble their lower-case equivalents (e.g. S, s: C, c) and that a teacher is able, if she is aware of the child's difficulty,

[1] These ten words occur more than once in every four words of continuous English— see Godfrey Dewey, *Relativ Frequency of English Speech Sounds*, p. 19. (See footnote, p. 42.)

to take care to use only one variant of each character, all the traditional reading books likely to be used in the class contain many variants: for example, in the earliest pages of the first book of a well-known reader, the word *and* appears in four different forms (*AND*, &, and, *and*); in another first reader the 27 specially selected look-and-say words are presented in a total of 41 variants.

THE	The	the	*the*	*the*	*The*		6
OF	of	*of*					3
AND	And	and	and	&			5
TO	to	*To*					3
A	a	a					3
IN	In	in	*In*	*In*			5
THAT	That	That	that	that	*that*	*That*	7
IT	It	it	*It*	*It*	*it*		6
IS	is	*is*	*Is*	*Is*	*Is*	*Is*	7
I	*I*	*I*					3
							48

Figure 2. The ten commonest words in the English language can be printed or written in forty-eight different ways.

With the orthodox alphabet a child has to accustom himself to relating several—at least three on average—different visual patterns to each spoken word, and has, in effect, to make the correct choice between three separate alphabets—e.g. bAg is a wrong choice and so is "brown" in the case of a proper name. It is more accurate therefore to speak of the orthodox alphabets in the plural.[1] Although the eye is capable of being conditioned to

[1] For this reason on all succeeding pages reference is usually made to "orthodox alphabet(s) and spelling." The expression "traditional orthography" ("T.O.") is also widely used and it means the same thing, but for the sake of consistency it has normally been avoided in this book.

different patterns which vary only to a small extent, e.g. B, *B*—as is the ear to different regional accents (a subject we shall return to later)—there can surely be no doubt that radical inconsistency of visual patterns must impede the instant linking between the visual pattern of the whole word and its meaning which is the heart and aim of the look-and-say method. The necessity of having to comprehend and continually remember that there is a relationship between *A*, a, *a*; *B*, b, *b*; etc. surely shows that, with the orthodox alphabet at any rate, the look-and-say method cannot be as effective as is believed or as free from reasoning processes as its extreme protagonists suggest.

FRUSTRATION OF CHILD'S LOGIC AND REASONING POWER

These particular strictures apply equally to the phonic method and to the various mixed methods which are nowadays employed in so many schools. On top of the variations in representing each phoneme, the average child therefore has to tackle at the same time two or three variations in the shape of each character: the 793 different ways of representing the 40 phonemes are thereby increased to make a total of over 2,000 possible variations. The combination of both these types of inconsistency and unreliability means that a valuable element in the learning process is lacking, viz. whenever possible the learner should be enabled to form meaningful relationships between different concepts and to confirm what he has already learned by applying it to other but similar situations. This kind of linking can be seen to operate when children mistakenly but logically talk of "mouses who runned" or say "I *were* a good girl"—only to be baffled when the parent corrects the mistake by explaining: "Yes, you *were* a good girl, but you must say I *was* a good girl." When learning to count, a child's logic is not impeded: the numbers up to twelve call for an effort of memory alone, but once the teens are reached the rational, relationship-building element in the child's brain comes to bear and carries him through the 20s, 30s, 40s, and so on to the 100s and 1000s in one triumphant rush. By comparison, teaching the same child to read presents difficulties as great as if, say, in the 30s he had to use 5 for 2; 7 for 5; and 2 for 6; so that whereas the printed and written forms 20, 21, etc. ran logically, the 30s were to run in a sequence of—

$$30 \; 31 \; 35 \; 33 \; 34 \; 37 \; 32 \; 37 \; 38 \; 39$$

and the child were compelled to remember that because the 30s were peculiar, 35 stood not for what it now appears to stand for but for 32, and so on. This kind of numbering would obviously be a denial of normal mental relationships and would make arithmetic an even harder subject to teach than it is already, but would it present more taxing difficulties than having to remember that *women* sounds different from *home*, *comet*, or *come* or that *THE* is the same as *The* or *the*? Children, provided they have normal hearing, seem inclined by themselves to seek out rules that link their experience of speech with the visual symbols, but their search is all too often frustrated. The twin processes of analysis and synthesis are repeatedly baulked. It would scarcely be surprising if the simultaneous presentation of so many problems, so many contradictory concepts, did not merely put an over-severe strain on the memory of many five- or six-year-olds but also damaged the ability to reason logically and to form good habits of problem solving. Is it to be wondered that in many children one detects a gulf between what should be the complementary skills of listening and reading?

The virtue of initial success in any new activity barely requires mention. Once a child has failed to surmount early instances of illogicality it is arguable that he may stick at this point and that this prevents him from progressing and gives rise to a swelling sense of frustration, confusion, and disappointment that hampers further efforts. My hypothesis is that this is when many backward readers are born. The great majority of these children never succeed in overcoming their bad start. The unpleasant feelings they associate with characters and their representations of syllables and words are welded into their minds and inhibit and sour their approach to reading through the years of adolescence until by adulthood the habit of *not* reading is securely formed. In quite a few cases it may also well be that the early strain of coping with the tangle of difficulties involved in learning to read English actually unleashes various physiological, psychological, temperamental, or social predisposing and causative factors that would otherwise have remained unimportant—

Individual differences that would otherwise have a negligible influence on his school life in general and reading in particular become significant variables. Slight abnormalities, that would otherwise be functionally unimportant and hardly play a role in the perception and differentiation of a small set of letters in consistent one-to-one relation to the phonemes they spell, become critical factors when the reading process requires the perception and differentiation of hundreds and even thousands of . . . word spellings. . . .[1]

Is it far-fetched to postulate that a child's first wrestling with the vagaries of the English alphabet(s) and spelling may prepare the ground for doubt about the adult world of teachers and parents, and nurture emotional and temperamental traits that will later be expressed in truancy and worse? As we have seen, delinquency and backwardness in reading are old companions.

BURDEN OF PROOF

Successful experiments in the past with teaching reading by means of various phonetic alphabets (see Chapter 6) have furnished evidence that the roman alphabet and English spelling do together create special difficulties for children in the earliest stages of learning. The teachers concerned frequently became enthusiastic converts to the new alphabets but unfortunately these earlier trials were conducted without the rigour necessary for scientific research and the findings were largely ignored and forgotten. An attempt to apply modern research techniques to the problem was made by W. R. Lee whose report was published in 1960.[2] Among other things, he investigated methods of teaching reading in over thirty other countries and set out to relate the greater phonetic regularity of spelling in certain languages with the teaching methods employed in the respective countries and with their reading standards. There is cause to believe, for example, that it takes a British or American child from one to two years longer to learn to read than it takes children whose mother tongue is, say, Italian, Castilian Spanish, Finnish or, particularly, Russian. In these languages the correspondence between the printed word and the spoken word, while not perfect, is, when compared with English, very simple and systematic. Spelling does not constitute a serious problem for the reader. By the end of the first year at school a child can usually read any word from its characters without effort whether or not he understands its meaning. In Italian, for example (which, incidentally, makes use of only 27 phonemes compared with the 40 spoken in English) the characters

---

[1] James P. Soffietti. "Why Children Fail to Read: a Linguistic Analysis." *The Harvard Educational Review*, 1955, Vol. 25, p. 73.
[2] *Spelling Irregularity and Reading Difficulty in English.* National Foundation for Educational Research in England and Wales, London, 1960.

provide an almost completely reliable clue to the sounds of the syllables.[1] For an Italian child, acquiring proficiency in reading is largely therefore a matter of practice to perfect mechanical skill allied with increasing the child's store of words and meanings; words may be learned as wholes, but the child readily becomes aware of the alphabetical nature of syllables and thus of reading and writing. Russian is an even easier medium for learning: it has 32 characters for its 32 phonemes and, in addition, it makes use, with only a few exceptions, of the same character forms for upper-case (capitals) and lower-case; it is thus phonemically both more reliable and consistent.

One might pardonably expect that phonic methods would be more favoured in countries whose languages are phonetically regular and that look-and-say methods would be prevalent where the spelling is more irregular. Lee, however, was unable to discover any clear relationship. Furthermore, because of the lack of common standards of assessment and of other variables such as the differences in the age at which children start school, he decided that international comparisons between reading attainments were of dubious validity.

Some light has, however, been thrown on this question in a report of a carefully controlled experiment with two methods of teaching reading in the Philippines. In Pilipino, the national language, the correspondence between spoken sounds and printed symbols is close and, as might be expected, the most widespread method is a purely phonic one (called the *cartilla* method). The experiment was designed to test the comparative merits of this phonic method with those of a mixed method that combined look-and-say (especially in the early stages) with phonic practices and sound-blending. The research data suggested that the mixed method yielded better, but only slightly better, results. Another interesting, and significant, finding was that when tested in English (which they all learned simultaneously as a second language), the children taught to read Pilipino by the mixed method turned in rather better results that did the phonic group.[2]

Lee also developed a method to investigate whether English words with irregular spellings are more difficult to read than words spelt regularly.

[1] A literate Englishman, even though knowing no Italian, could read, say, a Milanese newspaper to a blind Italian. Between them they would soon be able to clear up the handful of character-sound relationships that might cause difficulty. See also John Hart's deception that he could speak Welsh (page 77).

[2] "An Experiment with Two Methods of Teaching Reading," by Tensuan, Emperatriz S., and Davis, Frederick B. *The Reading Teacher*, Vol. 18, No. 1, pp. 8–15. International Reading Association, Newark, Delaware, U.S.A., 1964.

Errors made in reading selected prose passages aloud by two groups of children were classified in two categories: errors arising from words that were (1) "more" regular and (2) "less" regular. His conclusion was that "the lack of a regular correspondence between sounds and letters . . . was a minor cause of reading difficulty, particularly where isolated words were concerned . . ."; that ". . . 'irregularity' was a cause, but evidently by no means a major cause, of reading difficulty among the children who took part in the inquiry." But, as Lee himself made clear, most of the children had been taught initially by a "whole word" (i.e. look-and-say) method and that "this may of course have influenced the result" and that "complete beginners and the very worst readers were not and could not be included." Unfortunately the children in question were between six and twelve years old (*sic*) and had already learned to read. Lee's categories are also suspect in that his "less" regular category consisted of words that are more frequently used by young children than the words in his "more" regular category; this, clearly, must have increased the likelihood that, despite their "less" regular spellings, these words would be read correctly. (Lee, for instance, regarded the use of *v* in *have*, etc., as "less regular" than *f* (*hafe*), his preference being based on the prevalence of the word *of* in which *f* is "more regularly" used to convey the phoneme. In the attempt to be objective in assessing "more" or "less" regularity, the criteria became questionable.) Lee's investigation is open to other objections. To demonstrate conclusively whether or not our spelling and alphabet are the root cause, the HCF in the failure to read properly requires a far more elaborate design and form of test.

The analysis of our written and printed language outlined in this chapter will, I hope, nevertheless persuade the unprejudiced reader that English spelling and the roman alphabet have at least a strong prima facie case to answer. It is true that some 80 per cent of the English-speaking population *do* in the end learn to read more or less satisfactorily and for their own enjoyment—though no one knows at what price in childhood misery this is achieved and a high proportion of the successful adult readers admit to being indifferent at spelling. It is undoubtedly true also that the other factors we have discussed can prevent people from learning to read effectively. But the nature of our alphabet(s) and spelling cannot be ignored in any objective, real investigation of the reading problem: to do so is comparable to investigating plant growth and ignoring the qualities of the soil, the air, and of sunlight. As with most prosecutions, it is easier to assert than to prove. Proof leading to conviction can be provided only by the results of a large-scale enquiry, carried out with scientific rigour, in which comparisons are made between groups of children taught to read by means of a phonetic alphabet and carefully matched control groups taught by means of the orthodox alphabet. The final and definitive stage of an enquiry of this type has now been completed and is described in a later chapter.

5 How did the English Alphabet and Spelling Happen?

A LANGUAGE crystallizes a people's history, it is the repository of tradition, the product of social evolution, and therefore there is a tendency to consider its characters and spelling as well as its speech as being sacrosanct, "natural," and somehow "right." This, together with the understandable practical objections to spelling reform, the difficulty of observing the precise processes of learning in children and of recalling the stages of one's own early attempts to read, perhaps explains why so many teachers and educationists, though aware of the alphabet's deficiencies and the inconsistencies of English spelling, have underestimated them—indeed they have for the most part been so unaware of their importance in the learning processes that they have dismissed them as an irrelevancy. There has, however, usually been a small though fluctuating minority who have thought otherwise. Special teaching alphabets appeared as early as Elizabethan times, and by 1880 at least fifty systems of spelling reform had been invented and forgotten. My own teaching alphabet (and spelling), although its purpose is merely to help beginners to master reading with the *orthodox* alphabet and spelling, and therefore is the antithesis of spelling reform, comes at the end of a long chain and has not been concocted in a vacuum. A brief account of these early experiments, especially Fonotypy devised by my grandfather, Isaac Pitman, makes a logical and necessary introduction (see Chapter 6) but, first, it may be helpful to complete and

59

reinforce the analysis of orthodox spelling in the previous chapter with an outline of the key linguistic and historical forces and accidents that made such confusion possible.[1] This will, I hope, also convince the reader that our alphabet(s) and spelling are neither "right" nor "natural."

The alphabet used by the English-speaking peoples is derived from characters developed by the ancient Phoenicians. Their writing was based on consonantal sounds but when the Greeks adopted the characters they added seven vowels—*alpha, iota, upsilon,* the long and short *e* and the long and short *o*: *eta, epsilon; omega, omicron.* According to the most likely theory, the Etruscan alphabet provided a link between the alphabets of the Greeks and the Romans; the latter modified some of the characters (e.g. the upper case Greek Δ became *D*; Σ became *S*), dropped some (e.g. *theta, phi,* and *chi*), and added others (e.g. *G, Q, R*). This alphabet was carried by the legionaries and imperial officials to all parts of the Roman Empire and was eventually adapted to suit the needs of the local languages.

The alphabet of the Anglo-Saxons therefore consisted mainly of adapted Latin characters. By means of digraphs the five Latin vowel characters —*A, E, I, O, V*—were increased to eighteen; two Anglo-Saxon runic characters were incorporated—*wen* for the sound of *w* (wuh) (written like a *p*) and þ for the voiceless *th* sound; a new character ð was also invented to represent the voiced *th* sound but was sometimes used indiscriminately with þ; the character *h*, except when used initially, indicated the guttural sound; *f* and *s* had to serve double purposes—*f* equalled *v*; *s* equalled *z*.[2] With these and other devices it was possible to write words that approximated fairly well to phonemic representations of the spoken Anglo-Saxon language even though, because they reflected different local pronunciations, they were by no means uniform throughout the island. Enough examples have been given to suggest that "improvisation" or "makeshift" is a more accurate description than "adaptation." The roman alphabet may have been sufficient for the purposes of Latin,[3]

[1] For a more comprehensive study of this complex subject the reader is referred to, among other sources, *Spelling* by G. H. Vallins (with a chapter on American spelling by John W. Clark). André Deutsch, London, 1954; *Principles of English Etymology* by Walter W. Skeat. Clarendon Press, Oxford, 1892; *The Alphabet* by David Diringer. Hutchinson, London, 1968; and "Augmenting the Roman Alphabet: some orthographic experiments of the past four centuries," by David Abercrombie. *The Monotype Recorder*, Vol. 42, No. 3, London, Winter 1962–3.

[2] For a long time *s* was also written angularly—ꞩ; coins, for instance, up to the reign of William and Mary, carry the word ꞩAXONUM or its abbreviation—ꞩ.

[3] The Emperor Claudius evidently believed the roman alphabet to be deficient, for he introduced an inverted F (ⅎ) for the *w*/*v* sound to distinguish *v* from *u*; a reversed C (Ɔ) for the combination *ps*; and the half H (Ⱶ) for an intermediate sound between *u* and *i*.

but it was seriously inadequate in the case of a language such as Anglo-Saxon that employed different and a greater number of phonemes. It later proved to be deficient at every stage in the growth of the English language and, as we saw in the previous chapter, its adaptation to modern English could scarcely be clumsier, although for some other contemporary languages—e.g. Italian, Spanish, and Portuguese, partly because they are Latinic—it works well enough.

Figure 3. These minuscule characters were compiled by the late Stanley Morison[1] from the *Liber Machabaeorum* in a bible written in a script authorized by Maurdramnus, the Abbot of Corbie, Picardy, in A.D. 772–81. They demonstrate that by this date the shapes of most of the present-day lower-case alphabet had been established.

The shapes of our characters were similarly designed in relation to Latin and were in part determined by contemporary writing instruments and the texture of the writing surfaces. Most of our majuscule (capital) characters were originally perfected for carving Latin inscriptions in stone with a chisel (*Plate I*). The minuscule characters (Figure 3), printed as well as hand-written, are the result of a series of modifications spread over centuries: when not merely smaller versions of the majuscules, some of the essential shapes were formed by eliminating a part of the majuscule (*H* became *h*); the shapes of *d*, *f*, and *b* are thought to have been influenced by the strokes of the reed or quill pens which, sliding across the surface of parchment or vellum, substituted curves for the angular strokes of monumental carving. The advent of copperplate engraving and of the steel pen and paper—and the resulting spread of private correspondence and the habit of joining up the characters in a word—led to cursive writing and yet more curves.

[1] *Notes on the Development of Latin Script*. Cambridge University Press, 1949.

The roman alphabet is by no means the only culprit. The sources of many types of illogicality in our spelling are to be found also in—

(*a*) The etymological origins of words, the blending of the different tongues that give rise to the English language, and the continual assimilation of foreign words.

(*b*) Changes in pronunciation that made the original phonemic representations of words anachronistic.

(*c*) The individual, and often mistaken, preferences of printers and dictionary compilers.

English is one of the most hospitable of languages. Over the centuries it has absorbed with varying degrees of adaptation a profusion of words and phrases from invaders, neighbours, and, on occasion, from nearly every tongue. Among the conglomeration of inconsistencies two root systems of spelling are still discernible: one based on Old English (Anglo-Saxon) principles and seen also in words, usually of one or two syllables, adapted from other Germanic languages (e.g. *sun, earth, day, find, apple, butter, eye,* etc.) and the other based on principles derived either from Norman-French (e.g. *chamber, circle, guile, language, feudal, attach, discover,* etc.) or from adapted Latin, introduced via French forms or directly from the classical tongue (e.g. *capital, religion, feminine, general, calculate, emerge, persecute,* etc.). The language is also richly supplied with words taken over without much alteration from Greek, modern French, and a miscellany of other tongues (e.g. *khaki, llama, tobacco, mattress, pagoda, hookah, mufti, kraal, taboo, wigwam, bungalow,* etc.). The new words are still arriving: Ancient Greek, for example, is still being quarried to provide the extra words required by science and technology. The latest (1964) *Concise Oxford Dictionary* recognizes *communicado, espresso, crime passionel, psephology, dirndl, transistor,* among others. No other language possesses such a copious vocabulary and there is a very credible theory that it is the mixing and interplay between words with contrasting origins that has provided English poets with such a sensitive and flexible instrument. But the price has been levied in the parallel mixture of spelling principles—indeed " . . . happy is the spelling that has no history."[1]

The impairment of the essentially phonemic representation of the spoken language was a long-drawn-out process. By the twelfth and thirteenth centuries spelling was still more or less phonemic but less so than the earlier Anglo-Saxon spelling. This was in part because of changed

[1] A. Lloyd James. *The Spectator*, No. 5,381, pp. 207–8, 15 August 1931.

pronunciation but it was also brought about by developments in the language and changes introduced by French manuscript scribes under whose influence much of it was respelled. Latin was the lingua franca of the monastic system, then virtually the only source of education and learning. It was the chief mode of learned written communication. If not Latin, scholars and poets expressed themselves in French and when the spoken, popular language—a fusion between Anglo-Saxon and Norman dialects—demanded to be written, it was natural for the scribes to be guided by the Latin and French they were accustomed to. One result was that the roman alphabet shed several of its "adaptations." Some of the Anglo-Saxon representations were replaced by French ones, thus—

The digraph *th* replaced both þ and ð;

qu was introduced to replace the hard *cw* in words like *queen* and *quick*;

k began to be used to denote the hard sound of *c* before *e* and *i*, because to the French scribes *c* had the sound of *s*—hence *king* (cyning), *keen* (cene), *kelp* (culp), *kitchen, kin, kiss, kiln, kernel, kite,*[1] but *cellar, receive, forcible*—though in some words the hard *c* became *ch*—Saxon *cirice* turned into our word *church*;

v was used both as a vowel and a consonant in Roman days and the values for it became interchangeable—Dr. Johnson in his dictionary (1755) still treated *u* and *v* as the same symbol. It also replaced the *f* in many words (e.g. *life, live; calf, calves; roof, rooves; belief, believe*) but the *f* remained in an unstressed word such as *of*;

because the existing *u* represented at least three separate sounds, the French scribes added the *o* to make the digraph *ou*, so that the Old English *hus* became *house*;

when *u* was apt to be confused with *m, n,* or *v*, they changed it to *o*—which accounts for *some, son,* and *love*.

Among the most purposeful innovations of the period was the doubling of a consonant to indicate that the preceding vowel in a closed syllable was short. Credit for this unfortunate but well-intentioned device is awarded to a Northumbrian monk called Orm who (c. 1200) wrote a long poem called the *Ormulum* which consisted of homilies on the gospels and in which this doubling rule was sternly adhered to—

"... annd off goddspell icc wile zuw
zét summ del mare shœwenn ..."

[1] It also lingers on in a rare word like *ceorl* and in *Celtic*.

The same device can be seen in many of our words ending in *-ff*, *-ll*, *-ss*, *-ck*, etc., and in the medial double *-tt-* when endings are added to short-vowelled words like *fat* (*fatted*) or *bit* (*bitten*). This medial doubling was necessary because of another departure from phonemic representation: the final *-e* in many words had ceased to be pronounced as a distinct syllable and, instead, denoted that the preceding vowel was long (cf. *fate*, *fat*; *fated*, *fatted*).

The earlier medieval scribes did try, if sometimes clumsily, to represent the sounds of the spoken language, though later there was a tendency to reproduce older and existing conventions and to ignore changes in pronunciation. This process of "petrifying" spellings that were phonemically outdated was strengthened by the introduction of printing. Caxton (1422–91) on the whole followed the spellings in contemporary manuscripts without question, and ignored any lack of correspondence with the sounds of contemporary speech, yet he was forced to make certain choices among the varying spellings in the manuscripts he set up in type and added a new stage to the centuries' long process of consolidation—not that his own spelling was by any means consistent. He thus launched printing on a path that was to perpetuate the gap between sight and sound.

William Blades in *The Life and Typography of William Caxton*[1] shows that Caxton's alphabet consisted of 25 lower-case *letters*—as opposed to characters which displayed almost as many minor variants as in manuscript writing. There was no *j*; *u* and *v*, when used initially, were interchangeable as characters to convey the two different sounds (e.g. for the sounds both of *vee* and *uh* in *valliance* and *unto*), but the character *u* appeared for both in all its medial uses which we now distinguish (e.g. *resolution*, *Saturn* and *over*, *marvelled*). There were two distinct versions of *r* and two of *s* (*s* and *ſ*). It is clear that the choice of which *r* to use was dictated almost always by the convexity of a preceding *o* or *e*; the choice between *s* and *ſ* was determined by the character's position in the word, *s* being always printed at the end of a word and *ſ* elsewhere.

The influence of the first printed books was not widespread but Caxton handed on his spellings to other printers and gradually printing caused spelling to be regularized and codified. It was unfortunate that the spread of printing coincided with a period of major changes in pronunciation. Between the time of Chaucer and the time of Shakespeare occurred what has become known as the "great vowel shift" which put

[1] Joseph Lilly, London, 1861.

thirteen of the vowel sounds out of key with those of the fourteenth century, and yet in most cases their visual representation remained unaltered by the printers. While it is true that the uniformity and accuracy of the early printers fell a long way short of modern standards—an author did not always see proofs, and fresh mistakes were apt to be made in "correcting" his personal spelling, and variant spellings were employed to "justify" the length of lines—the printers' need for uniformity, combined with the authority lent by the printed word, not only got rid of certain archaic, inefficient spellings but it also did much to consolidate spellings that were phonemically already outdated and to "fix" English spelling in its medieval mould. It made it phonemic, if at all, only in the historical sense, with the result that today it is as likely to represent the sounds of the past as of the present.

The spelling of the hand-written (compared with the printed) language was slower in achieving uniformity and, not surprisingly, it was also phonemically more accurate. Queen Elizabeth I, a well-read woman and influenced by "literary" spelling, happily penned *clark* (clerk), *hart* (heart), *Godz* (God's), *desiar* (desire), and many other substantially phonemic spellings. The Elizabethans saw no necessity to standardize the spelling even of their own surnames, as evidenced by the 73 recorded variations in the spelling of Raleigh and by the following variations of *Shakespeare* used by members of the poet's family—

Chacsper	Shackspeare	Shakispere	Shaxkspere
Saxpere	Shackspere	Shakspeare	Shakyspere
Saxspere	Shackspire	Shakspere	Shakysper
Schackspere	Shagspere	Shaksper	Shaxper
Schakespeare	Shakesepere	Shakspeyr	Shaxpere
Schakespeire	Shakespeere	Shakuspeare	Shaxspere
Schakespere	Shakespere	Shaxeper	Shaxsper
Schakspere	Shakespeyre	Shaxkespere	Shaxpeare
Shakspare	Shakespear		

The spelling in the earlier editions of Shakespeare's plays is instructive. In the Folio edition, which copies at least some of his own spellings, we come across *tuch* (touch), *vane* (vain), *hare* (hair), *forst* (forced), *tung* (tongue), *tanted* (tainted), and many similar words. An analysis of the differences between the manuscript and printed (1591) text of Sir John Harrington's verse translation of Ariosto's *Orlando Furioso* shows that the printer introduced numerous changes: one single folio contains no less than seventy corrected spellings, e.g. *dead* for *ded* and *damage* for *damadge*.[1]

To what extent changes in Elizabethan printed texts may represent deliberate corrections or be printer's errors, printer's licence, or even house-style is debatable. Nevertheless an entirely new principle was introduced during the sixteenth century, that of "etymological spelling." Self-conscious attempts were made to conform as closely as possible with the spelling of the original Greek or Latin. A similar erudition was not applied to the portion of the language derived from Anglo-Saxon whose spelling remained unaltered—*queen*, for example, was not replaced by the more etymological *cwen*. This new principle arose from the rediscovery of the classical cultures and was in line with the Renaissance belief that there must always be one "right" mode—in spelling as well as in architecture. There was a craze for making the etymology evident to the eye, even if this meant the introduction of mute characters; the needs of the ear were forgotten and thus our spelling became even more ideographic and less truly alphabetic. Even worse, the imposed etymologies were frequently inaccurate; in particular, the innovators were too ignorant to realize that the majority of Latinate words had reached us via Old French and were not directly derived from classical Latin, and they were misled in thinking that Latin was entirely derived from Greek. In fact, the true etymology was not infrequently smothered. Some of the changes were justified, at any rate etymologically but, though—fortunately perhaps—the reform was never carried out completely, our written language has ever since been littered with additional misleading spellings. Here is a selection, including some choice pedantic blunders—

The *b* in *debt* and *doubt* was inserted to show the connection with the Latin *debitum* and *dubitum*, although the words reached us via the Old French *dette* and *doute*. Wycliffe's Bible (1360) tells us to "forgeue to vs our *dettis*" and Cranmer's (1539) to "forgeue vs oure *dettes* as we forgeue oure *detters*," but the Geneva Bible (1557) changes over to "*debtes*" and "*debters*" and the Authorized Version (1611) prints the modern "*debts*" and "*debtors*."

The *d* in *advance* was intended to represent the Latin *ad*, although the earlier form *avance* was derived from the French *av* which arose from

[1] *Proof-Reading in the Sixteenth, Seventeenth, and Eighteenth Centuries* by Percy Simpson, pp. 74–75. Oxford University Press, 1935.

the Latin *ab*; the *d* in *admiral* comes from a confusion of the Latin *admirabilis* with the proper source, the Arabic *amir*, meaning a "commander" or "prince"; the Latin *silva* was mistakenly traced to the Greek ὕλη, and the error is immortalized in *sylvan*.

The *g* in *reign*, *impugn*, and *feign* makes the spelling remote from the pronunciation, but at least it can be traced back to the Latin *regno*, *impugno*, and *fingo*; the *g* in *sovereign* is more absurd as its roots come from the Old French *soverain* which in turn came from the Latin *superanus*; similarly *foreign* stems from Old French *forain* and Latin *foris*. The reasons for adding characters were frequently arrived at by applying false analogies: the *c* in *scissors* may show that the word comes from the Latin *scindere*, but there is no possible justification for adding it to *scythe*, *scimitar*, or *scent*; nor for adding *-ue* to *tongue* as if it ought to end like the French *langue*; nor the *s* to *island* which comes from the earlier *iland* and the Anglo-Saxon *igland*, meaning "stream land," and yet has been confused with *isle*, derived from the Latin *insula*: similarly *delight* was confused with *light*, though it really comes from the Latin *delitum*. A side-effect of some of these absurd spellings has been to change a word's pronunciation: for example an *l* was inserted during the sixteenth century in *fault* (originally *faute* from Old French) to indicate that it was derived from the Latin *fallere*. For a long time the *l* remained mute (Pope rhymed it with *ought*, *thought*, and *taught*), but eventually the visual appearance of the word prevailed over the tongue. On the other hand *vitailles* was altered to *victuals*, because of the Latin *victualia*, and yet the old pronunciation *vittles* still persists; similarly the old pronunciation survives in the name of the Oxford college *Magdalen* as well as in the adjective *maudlin*.

A significant stage in the development of English spelling was reached with the publication of the Authorized Version of the Bible (1611). It is often stated that Dr. Johnson, a century-and-a-half later, was the first to fix our spelling, but the suggestion that the task had been already determined for him in its essentials by the Authorized Version is far more convincing. This view has been argued by, in particular, William Barkley[1] and, earlier, by the great Victorian philologist, Walter W. Skeat: "Broadly stated, the changes in our spelling since the time of Shakespeare are remarkably few and unimportant, especially if considered with reference to the numerous changes that had taken place previously."[2] Even the

---

[1] See especially *A Last Word*, pp. 8–9. Pitman, London, 1961.
[2] *Principles of English Etymology*, p. 328. Clarendon Press, Oxford, 1892.

WYCLIFFE—1380

1. IN the bigynnynge was the word and the word was at god/ and god was the word/ 2. this was in the bigynnynge at god/ 3. alle thingis weren made bi hym: and withouten hym was made no thing. that thing that was made 4. in him was liif, and the liif was the liȝt of men/ 5. and the liȝt schyneth in derknessis; and derknessis comprehendiden not it. 6. A man was sente fro god to whom the name was Ion/ 7. this man cam in to witnessynge, that he schulde bere witnessynge of the liȝt, that alle men schulden bileue bi hym/ 8. he was not the liȝt, but that he schulde bere witnessynge of the liȝt.

TYNDALE—1534

1. IN the beginnynge was the worde/ and the worde was with God: and the worde was God. 2. The same was in the beginnynge with God. 3. All thinges were made by it/ and with out it/ was made nothinge/ that was made. 4. In it was lyfe/ and the lyfe was the lyght of men/ 5. and the lyght shyneth in the darcknes/ but the darcknes comprehended it not. 6. There was a man sent from God/ whose name was Iohn. 7. The same cam as a witnes to beare witnes of the lyght/ that all men through him myght beleve. 8. He was not that lyght: but to beare witnes of the lyght.

CRANMER—1539

1. IN the begynnynge was the worde, and the worde was wyth God: and God was the worde. 2. The same was in the begynnyng with God. 3. All thynges were made by it, and without it, was made nothynge that was made. 4. In it was lyfe, and the lyfe was the lyght of men, 5. and the lyght shyneth in darcknes, and the darckens comprehended it not. 6. There was sent from God a man, whose name was Iohn. 7. The same cam as a wytnes to beare wytnes of the lyght, that all men through hym myght beleue. 8. He was not that lyght: but was sent to beare wytnes of the lyght.

GENEVA—1557

1. IN the beginnyng was the word, and the worde was with God, and that worde was God. 2. The same was in the begynnyng with God. 3. Althinges were made by it, and without it was made nothing that was made. 4. In it was lyfe, and the lyfe was the light of men. 5. And the light shineth in darkenes, and the darknes comprehended it not. 6. There was a man sent from God, whose name was Iohn. 7. The same came for a wytnes, to beare wytnes of the light, that all men through hym might beleue. 8. He was not that light, but *was sent* to beare wytnes of the light.

RHEIMS—1582

1. IN the beginning vvas the WORD, and the WORD vvas vvith God, and God vvas the WORD. 2. This vvas in the beginning vvith God. 3. Al things vvere made by him: and vvithout him vvas made nothing. That vvhich vvas made, 4. in him vvas life, and the life vvas the light of men: 5. and the light shineth in darkenesse, and the darkenesse did not comprehend it. 6. There vvas a man sent from God, vvhose name vvas Iohn. 7. This man came for testimonie: to giue testimonie of the light, that al might beleeue through him. 8. He vvas not the light, but to giue testimonie of the light.

AUTHORIZED—1611

1. IN the beginning was the Word, and the Word was with God, and the Word was God. 2. The same was in the beginning with God. 3. All things were made by him, and without him was not any thing made that was made. 4. In him was life, and the life was the light of men. 5. And the light shineth in darknes, and the darknes comprehended it not. 6. There was a man sent from God, whose name was Iohn. 7. The same came for a witnesse, to beare witnesse of the light, that all men through him might beleeue. 8. He was not that light, but *was sent* to beare witnesse of that light.

Figure 4. These extracts are taken from the first eight verses of the first chapter of St. John's Gospel in six early bibles: Wycliffe (1380), Tyndale (1534), Cranmer (1539), Geneva (1557), Rheims (1582), Authorized Version (1611). They demonstrate that by 1611 (and almost by 1582) the pattern of contemporary spelling had been virtually crystallized.

short extract on the opposite page (Figure 4) from the original printed Authorized Version (King James's Bible), compared with the same passage from the bibles of Wycliffe, Tyndale, Cranmer, and the later "Geneva" and "Rheims" Bibles, makes it clear that by 1611 the pattern was already set, that most of the worst spelling inconsistencies and illogicalities were already solidly built into the system—if one can still call it such (Tables VI and VII; Figures 4 and 5). The most obvious differences from the spelling of our own day are, as in Caxton's, the use of *u* where we have *v* and vice versa; of *i* instead of *j*;[1] and the interchangeability of *y*, *i* and *ie*—the Authorized Version includes both *charity* and *charitie*; it was still the custom also to employ alternative spellings to shorten or lengthen words so that lines of type could be neatly "justified."[2] But these differences are not of great moment compared with the earlier radical changes in the representation of phonemes, and they can be looked upon merely as alternative characters in the same way as (*vide* Caxton) *s* had an alternative in the now obsolete ſ and there were two forms of *r*. In more than one sense King James's Bible became Holy Writ! The roman characters in the column headings (see Figure 5) are so beautiful that it is understandable why they eventually superseded the more florid characters in the main body of the text which still shows the influence of the earlier manuscript bibles. The bishops assembled at Hampton Court no doubt felt unable to discard the conventional word-shapes based on medieval Gothic characters, but it is interesting that they preferred the more ancient—but now contemporary —classical characters for the headings and for the initial drop capitals at the start of chapters, together with the roman lower-case versions for the rubrics and marginal references (the latter in a pleasing italic). Their descendants are fortunate that divine invocation reinforced the royal command to authorize such beautiful characters, but would that those learned bishops had matched their typographical discernment with an attempt also to authorize and popularize a rational mode of spelling by relating what was to be printed with what was to be read twice each Sunday from every lectern in the kingdom!

Much of the false and incomplete erudition of the Tudor "reformers"

---

[1] This may appear surprising because "v" and "j" were both available in the printer's case as roman numerals—the "v" being used for 5 and the "j" being an alternative to "i" by itself, or as the last in a series: iij = 3.

[2] For instance, the words *young child* in the account of Our Lord's birth and early childhood in *St. Matthew*, Chapter II, were spelled variously—*yong child* (vv. 8 and 11); *yong childe* (vv. 14 and 20); *young childe* (vv. 9 and 13). By about 1640, however, standard spellings were considered more important.

The creation	of the world.
The creation of man.	The firſt Sabbath.
Mariage inſtituted.	The fall of man.
The promiſed ſeed.	Abel murthered.
The genealogie	of the Patriarchs, &c.
Methuſelah.	Noahs Arke.
Noah entreth	into the Arke.
The Arke reſteth.	Noah ſacrificeth.
The Rainbow.	Noahs generations.
The firſt Monarch.	Babel builded.

Figure 5. Here are fifty words taken at random from the Authorized Version (1611)—they happen to be the column headings in the first five pages of Genesis. It will be seen that forty-six were spelled exactly as they are today. Of the four others, two of them (*mariage*—the French spelling—and *murthered*) appear with their present-day spellings elsewhere in the 1611 Bible; *arke* and *genealogie* can also be found to conform to present practice in bibles of 1651 and 1653.

These fifty words incidentally provide telling examples of the misuse of characters: "t" is made to do duty for four quite different sounds—*the* (dhuh), *creation* (shuh), *Sabbath* (thuh), *first* (tuh); "a" appears in four guises—*man, creation, fall, arke*; and so does "u"—*instituted, murthered, Methuselah, builded.*

70

TABLE VI
Comparative Spellings from six early Bibles

	Wycliffe 1380	Tyndale 1534	Cranmer 1539	Geneva 1557	Rheims 1582	Authorized 1611
a	( )	creacion	creacyon	creacion	creation	creation
a-e	take	take toke	take	take	take	take
ai	feith	fayth faithe faith	fayth	faith fayeth fayth	fayth faith	faith
ai-e	reyned	rayned	rayned	rayned	rained	rained
aigh	( )	strayght streyght	strayght strayt	strayght	straight	straight
a-ue	plague	plage	plage	plague plage	plague	plague
ay	day dai	daye	daye	day	day	day
aye	preiede preyed preied	prayed	prayed	prayed	prayed praied	prayed
ea	grete greet	great greate	great greate	great	great	great
e-e	there	there	there	there	there	there
ei	veil	vayle	vayle	vayle	vele	vaile
eig-e	regned	rayned	raygned	raigned	reigned	reigned
eigh	( )	wayght	wayght	waight	vveight	weight
ey	thei	they	they	they	they	they
eye	obeischid obeied	obeyed	obeyed	obeyed	obeied	obeyed

These comparative spellings from six early bibles in English make clear how the lack of characters led to at least twelve improvisations in order to convey the sound of *a* in *day*. The character *a* by itself can with reason be said to be reserved for the vowel's (normal) sound in *man* (e.g. Latin *manus*).

TABLE VII
Fifty common words as spelled in six early English Bibles

	Wycliffe 1380	Tyndale 1534	Cranmer 1539	Geneva 1557	Rheims 1582	Authorized 1611
the	the	the	the	the	the	the
of	of	of	of	of	of	of
*and	and	and	and	and	and	and
to	to	to	to	to	to	to
*a	a	a	a	a	a	a
*in	in	in	in	in	in	in
*it	it	it	it	it	it	it
that	that	that	that	that	that	that
I	I	I	I	I	I	I
is	is	is	is	is	is	is
*for	for	for	for	for	for	for
be	be	be	be	be	be	be
was	was	was	was	was	was	was
you	you[1]	you	you	you	you	you
as	as	as	as	as	as	as
with	with	with	wyth	with	vvith	with
he	he	he	he	he	he	he
have	have	have	have	have	have	have
*on	on	on	on	on	on	on
by	bi	by	by	by	by	by
*not	not	not	not	not	not	not
*at	at	at	at	at	at	at
this	this	this	this	this	this	this
are	(ben)	are	are	are	are	are
we	we	we	we	we	vve	we
his	his	his	his	his	his	his
*but	but	but	but	but	but	but
they	thei	they	they	they	they	they
all	alle	all	all	all	al	all
*will	wole	will	will	wil	vvil	will
*or	or	or	or	or	or	or
which	whiche	which	which	which	vvhich	which
*from	fro	from	from	from	from	from
*had	hadde	had	had	had	had	had
(has	has	has	has	has	has	has)[2]
one	oon	one	one	one	one	one
our	our	oure	our	our	our	our
*an	an	an	an	an	an	an
been	ben	bene	bene	bene	been	been
my	my	my	my	my	my	my
there	there	there	there	there	there	there
no	no	no	no	no	no	no
their	hir	there	their	theyr	their	their
were	weren	were	were	were	were	were
so	so	so	so	so	so	so
*him	hym	him	him	him	him	him
your	[1]youre	youre	youre	your	your	your
*can	kan	can	can	can	can	can
would	wolde	wolde	wolde	would	would	would
*if	if	if	if	if	if	if

* Alphabetically spelt.
[1] Wycliffe used the old English form of y.   [2] The form used was "hath" not "has."

This is how the fifty commonest words (reported by Dr. Godfrey Dewey in 1923) were spelled in six early English bibles. Only sixteen, at most seventeen, spellings can be said to be truly alphabetic (marked with an asterisk); if we take these seventeen as representing the normal sound values, the remaining thirty-three spellings are misleading and irrational.

was fixed in the language by the printers who, together with the dictionary makers, stereotyped (!) the spellings, though meanwhile, between the seventeenth century and today, the never-ending shifts in pronunciation have continued to enlarge the breach between the spoken and visual languages. The need for authoritative spelling became irresistible. The poet Dryden, as member of a committee set up by The Royal Society (founded 1662) to improve scientific terminology, urged the need for a central authority (similar to the *Académie Française*); Swift, fifty years later, likewise advocated that the language be finally fixed "after such Alterations are made in it that shall be thought requisite" and described as "a foolish Opinion advanced of late Years, that we ought to Spell exactly as we speak."

The first effectively authoritative compilation of spellings, definitions and derivations did not however appear until the publication of Dr. Johnson's dictionary (1755). Johnson has thus been saddled with unjustified odium; Bernard Shaw, for instance, cavilled at "Dr. Johnson's monumental misspelling, which is now more sacred than the creed and the catechism."[1] But, as already mentioned, the Doctor's painful labour largely consolidated and systematized spellings that were for the most part fixed already. Although Johnson believed that the most elegant speakers were those who deviated the least from the written word, when coping with spellings then still doubtful he ignored the spoken sound and went back to the word's derivation. Nevertheless he had to explain that even in words of which the derivation was apparent he was often obliged to sacrifice principle to custom, and wrote—

> ... In this part of the work, where caprice has long wantoned without control, and vanity sought praise by petty reformation, I have endeavoured to proceed with a scholar's reverence for antiquity, and a grammarian's regard to the genius of our tongue. I have attempted few alterations, and among those few, perhaps, the greater part is from the modern to the ancient practice; and I hope I may be allowed to recommend to those, whose thoughts have been perhaps employed too anxiously on verbal singularities, not to disturb, upon narrow views, or for minute propriety, the orthography of their fathers. It has been asserted, that for the law to be *known*, is of more importance than to be *right*.[2]

Although he is often accused of making howlers, Johnson's scholarship was prodigious and he insisted that his recommended spelling "is still

[1] From a letter to *The Times*, 27 December 1945.
[2] From the Preface of *A Dictionary of the English Language*, sixth edition. London, 1785.

controvertible" and helpfully included two spellings of some words, e.g. *"choak, choke"*; *"soap, sope"*; *"fewel, fuel"*; "that those who search for them under either form may not search in vain,"[1] and went on to say: "I have left, in the examples, to every author his own practice unmolested, that the reader may balance suffrages, and judge between us. . . ."[2] Despite this modest reservation Johnson's dictionary soon became accepted as the universal authority, and with a few exceptions (e.g. his insistence that *c* could never end a word—hence his *musick*—and his preference for *authour, terrour*, etc.) the spellings he recorded and justified are still with us.

[1] Preface, ibid. [2] Preface, ibid.

6   Four Centuries of Spelling and Alphabet Reform

DURING THE PAST FOUR CENTURIES small numbers of teachers, educationists, philologists, linguists, and others have wrestled with the problem of the relationship between spelling and pronunciation. Some have limited themselves to methods of overcoming the special difficulties faced by children learning to read; some have been concerned with devising a phonetic alphabet, subsidiary to the roman one, in order to indicate the "correct" pronunciation in dictionaries and grammars or textbooks; and yet others have devised and sought to promote radical systems of spelling and alphabet reform for the ultimate benefit of the whole community. Their solutions range from minor modifications and palliatives to completely new alphabets with characters that bear little or no visual relationship to the roman ones. While most propose that the reform should be introduced in a single dose, others prefer a series of gradual instalments.

Obvious simplifications of existing spelling (e.g. the removal of mute and double characters) are common to most of the proposals but their principles can be classified under five rough groups, though many of the proposed systems contain elements of more than one group. In the first four groups the deficiencies of the roman alphabet are made up by—

(1) additional characters, resulting in an augmented roman alphabet;

or (2) diacritical marks or accents added to the roman characters;

or (3) combinations of roman characters, resulting in additional digraphs;

or (4) employing different colours to signal the sounds of printed words, the characters being unchanged—strictly speaking this is merely a method of teaching but as the purpose is the same as that of the reformed alphabets this group deserves a place in this chapter.

The fifth group is separate in that it consists of systems that—

(5) replace the roman alphabet with a new set of characters.

I. AUGMENTED ALPHABETS

Before English spelling was fixed and during the period when etymological spelling was very much the fashion, a few far-sighted men were conscious of the dangers inherent in these changes and so-called "reforms" and were already promoting more rational, alphabetic proposals. In 1568 Sir Thomas Smith, a Secretary of State to Queen Elizabeth I, published a dialogue[1] in Latin between himself and a young man called Quintus which lambasted the stupidities of English spelling. His solution was an alphabet of thirty-four characters which included the Saxon ð for the voiceless *th* and the þ or a Greek θ for the voiced *th*; among his other concoctions were new symbols for the soft *g*, for *y* when used as a consonant, for *v*, and for *sh*—though the hard *ch* was represented by *c* and the soft *c* by *s*. For the vowels, instead of introducing new symbols, he added accents or diacritical marks to the existing characters to indicate their length and quality, e.g. *â*, *ä*, *a-*.

This Alphabetum Anglicum, as Sir Thomas Smith called it, will be found in Appendix II. It was the forerunner of the many augmented alphabets that were to appear during the next four centuries. Though their inventors' understanding of phonetics was often imperfect and unscientific and there were, in particular, differences in the minimum number of characters thought to be required, all these alphabets were constructed on the principle of adding new characters, sometimes with and sometimes without diacritical marks on the old or new characters.

Another Elizabethan, John Hart, who held the position of Chester Herald, issued *An Orthographie, conteyning the due order and reason, howe to write or paint thimage of mannes voice, most like to the life or*

---

[1] *De recta et emendata Linguae Anglicae Scriptione*, Paris, 1568.

nature.[1] He also devised a system of teaching reading entitled *A Methode or comfortable beginning for all unlearned, whereby they may bee taught to read English, in a very short time, vvith pleasure.*[2] He made use of several additional characters, arguing "... nor is any man bounde to the shape of this or that letter, but that which is easiest to be written, and best giueth the Reader the vnderstanding of the writers meaning, and is most easiest to be taught, to the ignorant of all letters." To demonstrate the effectiveness of his method, he described how—

> As by the way of pastime, I haue done from a Welshmans mouth, though I vnderstood no worde thereof, and did reade it againe to him, and diuers others of that language, so as one amongst them (which knew me not) sayde vnto the rest in Welsh, that I coulde speake Welsh so well as he. But the rest knowing the contrary, laughing tolde me what he sayde, whom I forthwith certified, that I did it, by an order and certaine knowledge what I did write, and not by any acquaintance with the tongue. The like haue I done to the Irishe, and may as easily doe of the Barbarian, or Russian speaches ...[3]

The illustration from his works (*Plates IV* and *V*) shows the elegant design of his characters; he was particularly concerned to make them easy to write. He goes back to the Saxon ȝ; creates new characters for *ch*, *sh*, *le*, and the voiced and voiceless *th* (Appendix II). Like Sir Thomas Smith, he in addition uses diacritical marks, under the vowels. It is interesting to read his strictures on the then contemporary alphabetic method of teaching (see Chapter 2, page 20); the characters, he maintained, were—

> ... misnamed much from their offices and natures ... call it [h]ache, by ignorance of the inuention, leauing out the first h, whose office and qualitie shoulde be vvell expressed vnto vs, by the names of chalke or cheese, as by the name of ache ... bringeth to the lerner, rather confusion than help. Vvhich I finde as reasonable, as if a nurse should take in hand to teach a child, to go first vpon high pattens or stiltes, or vpon a coarde, or on the hands, before he should be taughte as the naturall and reasonable order is. ...[4]

Two augmented alphabets[5] were devised by Alexander Gill, High Master at St. Paul's (1608–35): the first contained a quantity of new characters, but the second reduced them to four only, together with diacritical marks and simplifications such as *biznes, mountainz, hart, lif*.

---

[1] Published in London, 1569. It was reprinted by my grandfather in 1850 with Hart's original phonetic spelling.

[2] "Imprinted by Henrie Denham," London, 1570.

[3] From the Preface (first page) to *A Methode* ...

[4] From "The Epistle Dedicatorie" (second page) to *A Methode* ...

[5] See Plate VI.

Gill is said to have influenced the spelling of Milton who was a pupil at St. Paul's. The poet was, for example, averse to mute characters and wrote *femal*, *facil*, *apostat*, and avoided etymological spellings that conflicted with pronunciation, writing: *iland*, *suttle*, *sovran*, etc.

One method of creating new symbols was to add to or adapt the structure of existing characters. The joining of double characters by means of a ligature was proposed by, among others, Charles Butler (1633)[1]:*ææ* for *ee*, ∞ for *oo*. He also replaced digraphic symbols with single characters to which a short bar or horizontal mark was added; the *u* normally linked with *q* was omitted; soft *g* was replaced by *j*; and an inverted *t* (ꓕ) for *th*. A few years later Cromwell's brother-in-law, John Wilkins, read a discourse[2] to the Royal Society in which he recommended the use of a *y* with a peculiar tail, the Greek α and γ, and diacritical marks.[3] His arguments are telling but the system was exceedingly complicated and also aesthetically displeasing, the Greek characters differing in size from the rest of the text.

A century later (1768) Dr. Benjamin Franklin[4] proposed an alphabet with six elegant, if insufficiently distinct, new characters but he dispensed with others (*c, j, q, w, x, y*) that he felt served no essential purpose. Thus *g* "has no longer *two different* Sounds, which occasioned Confusion; but is, as every Letter ought to be, confined to one;—The same is to be observed in *all* the Letters, Vowels, and Consonants, that wherever they are met with, or in whatever Company, their Sound is always the same." The six new characters represented (see Appendix II) the sounds *folly*; *ship*; *-ing*; *think*; *they*; and *umbrage* (the first syllable of which would ap-

---

[1] *The English Grammar or the Institution of Letters, Syllables, and Words in the English Tung.* Oxford, 1633.

[2] *An Essay towards a Real Character and a Philosophical Language*, 1668.

[3] Wilkins also devised another system which was intended to be a shorthand and was not at all alphabetic. His peculiar symbols represented certain ideas (as opposed to sounds) and were a form of "glyphs" or symbolic representations of concepts independent of language. Earlier, in 1588, Timothe Bright, Doctor of Physic at St. Bartholomew's Hospital, had designed the first English shorthand which was limited entirely to glyphs or, as he called it, a system of "characteries" and a parallel system of "characters." Comparable analyses of concepts have been P. M. Roget's 826 "categories" in the "tabular synopsis" employed in his famous *Thesaurus*; C. K. Ogden's 850 "Basic" words plus international words such as radio, tea, etc.; and the 880 concepts of Lancelot Hogben's *Interglossa* which may be written numerically and spoken or written in polysyllabic Latin words. Glyphic systems should not be confused with alphabetic writing or phonetic shorthand systems. They are something quite on their own. (See "Communication by Signs," by Sir James Pitman. *New Scientist*, Vol. 25, No. 433, pp. 580–1. London, March 1965.)

[4] *A Reformed Mode of Spelling. A Scheme for a new Alphabet and reformed mode of Spelling; with Remarks and Examples concerning the same; and an Enquiry into its Uses, in a Correspondence between Miss S——n and Dr. Franklin, written in the Characters of the Alphabet*, 1768.

SENATVS·POPVLVSQVE·ROMANVS
IMP · CAESARI · DIVI · NERVAE · F · NERVAE
TRAIANO · AVG · GERM · DACICO · PONTIF
MAXIMO·TRIB·POT·XVII·IMP·VI·COS·VI·PP
AD·DECLARANDVM·QVANTAE·ALTITVDINIS
MONS · ET · LOCVS · TAN   IBVS · SIT · EGESTVS
[TIS · OPER]

I Inscription on Trajan's Column (c. 176 A.D.) still to be seen in Rome. The characters are well suited to be carved on stone with a chisel and were no doubt sufficient for the purposes of Latin, but they have proved to be a very inadequate inheritance with which to convey the sounds of spoken English.

INCP EPLA· AD
HEBRAEOS·

MULTIFARIE MUL
TISQ:MODIS· OLIMDS
LOQUENS PATRIBUS IN
PROPHETIS· NOUISSIME
diebuf iftaf locutuf é nobif infilio
quem confatute heredem uniuerfor-u per qué
fecit et faecula· Quicum fit fplendor gloriae
et figura fubftantiae eiuf· portanfq: omnia
uerbo uirtutif fuae· purgationem peccator-u
facienf· fedet addexter-a maieftatif in excelfif·
tanto melior angelif effectuf quanto differen
tiuf prae illif nomen heredtauit· Cui enim dixit
aliquando angelorum filiuf meuf eftu· ego hodie
genuite· Et rurfum ego ero illi in patre· Et
ipfe erit mihi in filium· Et cum iter-u introducit
primogenitu in orbem terrae dicit· Et adorent
eum omnef angeli di· Et ad angelof quidé dicit·
Qui facit angelof fuof fpf· et miniftrof fuof flam
mam ignif· Ad filium aute· Thronuf tuuf df in
fctm fcti· Et uirga aequitatif uirga regni tui·
Dilexifti iuftitiam et odifti iniquitaté· propte

II Extract from a Bible inscribed at Tours about 850 A.D. It is the Latin
Vulgate version as revised by Alcuin of York. Note the mixture of roman
capitals, the capitals known as uncials, and the small characters or
Caroline minuscules. Compare this manuscript in Latin with a printed
page in English.

THE HOLY GOSPEL
OF IESVS CHRIST ACCOR-
DING TO IOHN.

CHAP. I.

The i parte:
THE ACTES
of Chrilt be-
fore his ma-
nifeftation,
whiles Iohn
Baptilt was
yet bapti-
zing.

The Gofpel at
the third Maff:
vpō Chriftmas
day. And euery
day at the end
of Maffe.

The preface of the Euangelift, commending Chrift (as being God the Sonne incarnate) to the Gentils, and fetting out the blindnes of the Iewes in not receiuing him. 15 Then the teftimonie of Iohn Baptift firft to the folemne legaur of the Iewes: as fecondly, vvhen he favv IESVS come to him: 35 thirdly, to his ovvne Difciples, alfo, putting them ouer from him felf to IESVS. 47 the made it plainer to them that he is Chrift, 40 and fo began he alfo to haue Difciples.

IN THE beginning "vvas the **WORD**, 1 and the **WORD** vvas "vvith God, and "God vvas the **WORD**. † This vvas in 2 the beginning vvith God. † Al things 3 vvere made "by him: and vvithout him vvas made ` nothing. That vvhich vvas 4 made`, † in him vvas life, and the life vvas the light of men: † and the light fhineth in darkeneffe, and 5 the darkeneffe did not comprehend it. † There vvas a man 6 fent from God, vvhofe name vvas Iohn. † This man came 7 for teftimonie: to giue teftimonie of the light, that al might beleeue through him. † He vvas not the light, but to giue 8 teftimonie of the light. † It vvas the true light, vvhich ligh- 9 teneth euery man that commeth into this vvorld. † He vvas 10 in the vvorld, and the vvorld vvas made by him, and the vvorld knevv him not. † He came into his ovvne, and his 11 ovvne receiued him not. † But as many as receiued him, "he 12 gaue them povver to be made the fonnes of God, to thofe that beleeue in his name. † Vvho, not of bloud, nor of the 13 vvil of flefh, nor of the vvil of man, but of God are borne.

ET VERBVM
CARO FAC-
TVM EST.
† AND "THE VVORD VVAS MADE FLESH, 14 and dvvelt in vs (and vve favv the glorie of him, glorie as it vvere of the only-begotten of the Father) ful of grace and veritie.

III The "Rheims" New Testament, 1582 A.D. Typographic conventions were already well established, but note the two separate lower-case 'v's for 'w'—the French *double*-v—and the u in place of the present-day v. See also Tables VI and VII.

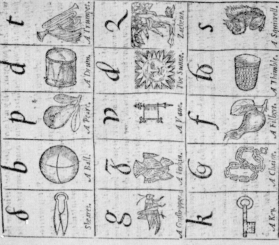

IV Elizabethan augmented characters devised by John Hart (published in *A Methode*, 1570). Note the new characters for *sh*, *j*, *ch*, and the voiced and voiceless *th*. (See also Appendix II.)

In de nam ov de fadr
and ov de sun, and ov
de holi gost, so biit.

de lords prei-ʃr-bi-lijs, and ten kom-m-aund-ments.

Our fadr huiʃ art
in hevn hal-lu-ed bi
dei nam. dei king-
dum kum. dei uil bi dun
in erʃ, aʒ it iʒ in hevn.
Giv-uʒ dis dei, our de-li
bred. And for-giv-uʒ
our tres-pas-ses, aʒ ui
for-

A Methode.

lord hav mer-si-up-on-
us, and, in-klein our herts tu kip dis lau.

dou ʃault not mak tu
dei self, ani gravn-i-maʒ
nor de leik-nes ov ant
ting dat iʒ in hevn a-
buv, or in derʃ be-neʃ,
nor in de uatr undr d-
erʃ, dou ʃault not bou
doun tu dem, nor uur ʃip
dem; for ei de ʃord dei

V Extracts from the Lord's Prayer and the Ten Commandments and inscribed in John Hart's augmented alphabet (1570). He also used diacritical marks under some of the vowels. (See also Appendix II.)

VI An extract from Edmund Spencer's *The Faerie Queen* in the alphabets designed by Alexander Gill. The first edition (1619) (*left*) contains new characters and modifications of existing ones, many of them added in red ink on the printed page. The second edition (1621) (*right*) is less complex but makes frequent use of diacritical marks.

16 If any half vowel, doo folow : r,
our speech serueth wel, too spel them toogether.

17 And this stryk (,) is excepcion general,
too spel woordz truly, when thær rulz fail al.

18 Not wel, thér is neuer tru sillabl',
without vowel, diphthong, oz half vowel.

19 And thoth half vowelz be speld best alón,
yet the next consonant it dependeth on.

20 By ez, oz z, the plural' doo ges,
whooz simpl'z genitiuz, end éz, oz z.

¶ The 12. Chapter,

sheweth the vse of this amendment, by matter in
prose with the same ortography, conteining
arguments for the premisses.

An exer-
cyz foz
exampl'.

Er-in iz shewed an exercyz of the amended oztogra-
phy befoz shewed, and the vc of the prikz, strykz, and
notz, foz deuyding of sillabl'z accozding too the rulz
befoz shewed. Whær-in iz too be noted, that no art, exercyz, mixtur, scienc, oz occupacion, what-soeuer, iz included in ón thing only : but hath in it seueral distinccionz, elementz,
principl'z, oz deuizionz, by the which the sám cometh too hiz perfet vc.
And bicauz the singl' deuizionz foz english sped), ár at this day so vn-
perfetly pictured, by the elementz (which we cal letterz) pzouyded foz

Of pzo-
fit the
grætest
iz too be
chózn.
Ignozance
cau-
zeth ma-
ny too fal
t offend.

the sám, (az may apper plainly in this fozmer trætic) I hau set fyrth
this wozk foz the amendment of the sám : which I hóp wil be tákn
in good part accozding too my mæning : foz that, that it hal saui char-
gez in the elder sozt, t saui græt tym in the zyth, too the græt comodi-
ty of al estátz, vntoo whom it iz necessary, that thér be a knowledg of
their duty, vntoo God chefly, and then their duty ón too an other : in
knowing of which duty, consisteth the hapi estát of manz lyf : foz ignozanc cauzeth many too go out-of the way, and that of al estátz, in
whom ignozanc dooth rest : thær-by God iz greatly dis-plæzed, the
comon qietnes of men hindered : græt comion welth'z deuyded, ma-
gistratz

VII A page from *Bullokar's Booke at Large, for the Amendment of
Orthographie for English Speech* (1580). Bullokar minimized the use of
augmented characters and represented the 44 *"divisions in one voice"* by
means of diacritical marks, ligatures, and the abbreviations and contractions supplied by the "black letters" earlier used for printing Latin. (See
also Appendix II.)

Môft plain and familiar exâmpleſ (täken out
of the Eṅgliſh Primrôſe) ſhewiṅg the grëat
unčertaintîe of the ſoundſ of the
vowelſ, and fôrčeſ of the conſo-
nantſ, wherẹbŷ the Eṅgliſh-
toṅguẹ iſ expreſt : & how
tô knôw them. with
čertaintîe.

A

a	man-tlẹ	dan-dlẹ	dan	
ä	män-ğer	dän-ğer	dänc	
â	com - män-ded	dân-čer	dâwn	Lâu-rel
a	Mạu-ričẹ(Mo-ričẹ)Ląu-renčẹ			lo-rel
a	me-tạl (me-tl)	Phạ̈-raôh	(Phä-rô)	

E

e	fea-ther	wea-ther	pe-riſh.
ë	fé-ver	wëa-ver	Pë-reſh.
ê	ê-ven (ee-vn)	Stê-phẹn	(Stee-vn)
e	e-vil (i-vl)	dẹ-vil	(di-vl)
e	her (Hur)	ma-ner	(Ma-nour)
ç	er-rand(ar-rant)Ser-ğeant		Sar-dinc
ẹ	ſho-vel (ſhu-vl)	ra-vẹl	(ra-vl)

A   win-

VIII Examples of the diacritical marks employed by Richard Hodges, from
his spelling book, *The English Primrose* (1644). (See also Appendix II.).

pear to have done duty for the phonemes not only in a word like *such* but also in *order*, *perform*, and *works*. Together with various other devices, the new characters provided that "there be no distinct Sounds in the Language *without Letters* to express them." Franklin decided that *c* could be omitted, *k* supplying its hard sound and *s* the soft; but he relied on digraphs (e.g. *piur* for *pure*) including combinations with his new characters to solve some of his problems. To differentiate long vowel sounds from short ones, he doubled the character, e.g., *mend* and *remeen'd* (remained); *did* and *diid* (deed); but he treated *folly* and *ball* (also *pull*, *pool*, and the semi-vowel in *we*) as possessing the same sounds. Like other reformers Franklin gamely dismisses opposition: "The objection you make to rectifying our alphabet, 'that it will be attended with inconveniences and difficulties,' is a natural one; for it always occurs when any reformation is proposed; whether in religion, government, laws, and even down as low as roads and wheel carriages.—The true question, then, is not whether there will be no difficulties or inconveniences; but whether the difficulties may not be surmounted; and whether the conveniences will not, on the whole, be greater than the inconveniences. In this case, the difficulties are only in the beginning of the practice ..."

Another eighteenth-century American, Dr. William Thornton, also borrowed from the Greek to construct a Universal Alphabet which "ought to contain a single distinct mark or character, as the representative of each simple sound which it is possible for the human voice and breath to utter. No mark should represent two or three distinct sounds; nor should any simple sound be represented by two or three different characters."[1] His alphabet also included an inverted capital ʃ for *sh*; a square *o* for the vowel sound in *law* and *fall;* and an *o* with a dot in the centre for *wh*.

Among the Victorian spelling reforms I shall concentrate attention on Fonotypy, the augmented alphabet invented by my grandfather, Sir Isaac Pitman. This has nothing to do with family pride, but it is because the principles of Fonotypy have provided the foundation for my own Initial Teaching Alphabet, the central subject and purpose of this book. My grandfather is well known as the inventor of the system of phonetic shorthand that bears his name, but Phonography, as he called his shorthand, was only the beginning. A logical and reliable relationship between characters and sounds was the essence of his shorthand, and he believed that the same principle could be employed with equal success to improve

[1] *Cadmus, or a Treatise on the Elements of Written Language*, pp. 11–12. Philadelphia, 1793.

longhand. His early life as a country schoolmaster had convinced him how difficult it was to teach children to read and he believed that his proposal would also provide an effective teaching medium. The result was Phonotypy (or Fonotypy), a system of printing with an augmented roman alphabet. His shorthand was published when he was only twenty-four and, although it was later refined and improved and much of his time was spent in publicizing it, issuing shorthand manuals and journals, and so on, an ever-greater energy and a large part of a long life—in fact until his death at the age of eighty-four—was devoted to Fonotypy and spelling reform (see pages 95 and 102). At an early stage he wrote: "As Phonography becomes the general medium of written communication, phonotypic printing must follow. We shall, therefore, advocate Phonography as a means for the attainment of the great need—Phonotypic Printing." It is no exaggeration to say that he looked upon his system of shorthand as a means of advocating spelling reform; indeed a large fraction of the profits from his shorthand manuals, together with contributions from A. J. Ellis and a band of other Victorian reformers, went to finance the campaign for spelling reform, the casting and rejection of numerous experimental metal types; the launching of several journals, a 750-page bible, Milton's *Paradise Lost*, reading primers, and other works printed throughout in Fonotypy.

These activities centred around the Phonographic Corresponding Society and the Phonetic Council and in time were backed by many eminent men. They received a big impetus from the Education Act of 1870 and the campaign against adult illiteracy; a parallel spelling reform sprang up in America. My grandfather's original conception was considerably amended and improved in conjunction with A. J. Ellis and others, but by 1846 "Messrs. Pitman and Ellis distinctly pledge themselves not to make any further alterations in the forms or uses of the letters of the practical Phonotypic Alphabet . . . or in the theory upon which it is founded."[1] This was a pious hope and many more costly experiments and changes were tried, from which Ellis soon dissociated himself, regarding with disfavour the later versions—they amounted to a total of at least seventy-two varieties of the alphabet—produced by Isaac Pitman on his own.

The earliest version of Fonotypy was an augmentation of the capital (upper-case) roman characters only, using what printers term "caps" and "small caps." The decision was soon taken to adapt it also for lower-case.

---

[1] *The Phonotypic Journal*, Vol. 5, No. 54, p. 171, Bath, June 1846.

No. 1, *January*, 1844.

ɪ ɛ ʌ ɵ ꭥ ʊ (heard) ʉ, ɪ ꞇ ʌ ɵ ʊ ꭒ,
ᴌ ɵ ꭥ ꭒ, ᴡ ʏ ʜ, ᴘ ʙ ᴛ ᴅ ᴄ ᴊ ᴄ-ɢ, ꜰ ᴠ
ɵ ᴀ ꙅ ᴢ ᴢ, ʟ ʀ, ᴍ ɴ ꭒ

Specimen:

NUꭨIꬻ HWOTEVER IZ MꭥR TꙀ BɪꞆ
DꞆᴢᴀRD, OR MꭥR DEʟᴀTꟻUʟ, ᴅᴀN ᴅꞆ
ʟᴀT OV TRꭥꭵ : FOR IT IZ ᴅꞆ SꭥRꞀʾOV
WIZDUM ʜWEN ᴅꞆ MᴀND IZ HᴀR-
ᴀST WIᴅ OBSKꭤRITI, DISTRᴀKTꞆD Bᴀ
DꭑTꞀ, RꞆNDERD TORPID OR SᴀDEND
Bᴀ IGNORᴀNꞀ OR FꭥʟꞀITIZ, ᴀND TRꭥꭵ
ꞆMꞆRJꞆᴢ ᴀᴢ FROM ᴀ DARK ᴀBIꞀ, IT
ꞀᴀNᴢ FꭥRꭵ INSTᴀNTꞆNIUSʟI, ʟᴀK ᴅꞆ
SUN DISPURSIꭵ MISTS ᴀND ᴠꞆPURᴢ,
OR ʟᴀK ᴅꞆ DꞆN DISPꞆʟIꭵ ᴅꞆ ꞀꞆDᴢ OV
DᴀRKNꞆꞀ.

No. 3, *June*, 1846.

ɪ ꞇ ɑ ɵ ꭥ ꭒ, i e a o u ꭒ, ꭘ ɵ ꭒ,
w y h, p b t d ᴄ j c g, f v ᵵ d s z
ʃ ʒ, l r, m n ŋ.

Specimen.

Nuᴛiŋ hwotever iz mɵr tꙀ bꞇ
dezjrd, or mɵr deljtful, ᴅan ᴅe
lꞁt ov trꭍt : for it iz ᴅe sɵrs ov
wizdum. Hwen ᴅe mꞁnd iz harast wiᴅ obscꭒriti, distracted bꞁ
dꭑts, renderd torpid or sadend
bꞁ ignorans or fɵlsitiz, and trꭍt
emerjez az from a darc abíꞀ, it
Ꞁꞁnz fꭥrt instantɛniusli, lꞁc ᴅe
sun dispersiŋ mists and vꞆpurz,
or lꞁc ᴅe dɵn dispeliŋ ᴅe ꞀꞆdz ov
darcnes.

No, 5, *Proposed Jan.*, 1852.

ɪ ꞇ ɑ ɵ ꭥ ꭒ, i e a o u ꭒ, ꭘ ꭥ ꭒ, w
y h, p b t d ᴄ j c g, f v ɵ d s z ʃ ʒ,
l r, m n ŋ.

Specimen.

Nuᴛiŋ hwotever iz mɵr tꙀ bꞁ
dezjrd, or mɵr deljtful, ᴅan ᴅe lꞁt
ov trꭍꭵ : for it iz ᴅe sɵrs ov wizdum. Hwen ᴅe mꞁnd iz harast
wiᴅ obscꭒriti, distracted bꞁ dꭑts,
renderd torpid or sadend bꞁ ignorans or fɵlsitiz, and trꭍꭵ Ꞇmerjez
az from a darc abíꞀ, it Ꞁꞁnz fꭥrꭵ
instantɛniusli, lꞁc ᴅe sun dispersiŋ
mists and vꞆpurz, or lꞁc ᴅe dɵn
dispeliŋ ᴅe ꞀꞆdz ov darcnes.

No. 2, *October*, 1844.

ɪ ꞇ ꝗ ɵ c (heard) ɵ ꭥ, i e a o u ꭒ,
ꞁ ꝗ ꭒ ꭒ, w y h, p b t d ᴄ j k g,
f v ᵵ d s z ʃ ʒ, l r, m n ŋ.

Specimen.

Nuᴛiŋ hwotever iz mɵr tꙀ bꞁ
dezjrd, or mɵr deljtful, ᴅan ᴅe
lꞁt ov trꭍt : for it iz ᴅe sɵrs ov
wizdum. Hwen ᴅe mꞁnd iz harast wiᴅ obscꭒriti, distracted bꞁ
dꭑts; renderd torpid or sadend
bꞁ ignorans or fɵlsitiz, and trꭍt
emerjez az from a dark abíꞀ, it
Ꞁꞁnz fꭥrt instantɛniusli, lꞁk ᴅe
sun dispersiŋ mists and vꞆpurs,
or lꞁk ᴅe dɵn dispeliŋ ᴅe ꞀꞆdz ov
darknes.

No. 4, *Jan.*, 1847.

Ꞇ ꝗ ꭗ ɵ ꭥ ꭒ, i e a o u ꭒ, ꞁ ꭘ ꭥ ꭒ,
w y h, p b t d ᴄ j c g, f v ᵵ d s z
ʃ ʒ, l r, m n ŋ.

Specimen.

Nuᴛiŋ hwotever iz mɵr tꙀ bꞆ
dezjrd, or mɵr deljtful, ᴅan ᴅe lꞁt
ov trꭍt : for it iz ᴅe sɵrs ov wizdum. Hwen ᴅe mꞁnd iz harast
wiᴅ obscꭒriti, distracted bꞁ dꭑts,
renderd torpid or sad'nd bꞁ ignorans or fɵlsitiz, and trꭍt emerjez
az from ɑ darc abíꞀ, it Ꞁꞁnz fꭥrt
instantaniusli, lꞁc ᴅe sun dispersiŋ
mists and vapurz, or lꞁc ᴅe dɵn
dispeliŋ ᴅe ꞀꞆdz ov darcnes.

No 6, *Romanic Alphabet.*

aa, bb, cc, dd, ee, ff, gg, hħ ii, jf,
kc, lƚ, mm, nn, oo, pp, qc, rr, ss, tt,
uu, vv, ww, xcs, yy, zz.

Specimen.

Nothing whatever is more to be
desired, or more delightful, than
the light of truth : for it is the
source of wisdom. When the mind
is harassed with obscurity, distracted by doubts, rendered torpid
or saddened by ignorance or fals-
ities, and truth emerges as from a
dark abyss, it shines forth instantaneously, like the sun dispersing
mists and vapours, or like the dawn
dispelling the shades of darkness.

Figure 6. Five versions of Fonotypy (from *Life and Labors of Sir Isaac Pitman*).

81

VOWELS.

Short hand.	Long hand.	Type	Example of its sound.	Name.
N.1 ⌐	𝒵ᵢ	Ɪ i	feet	i
⌐	𝒥i	I i	fit	it
2 ⌐	𝓔ε	Ɛ ɛ	mate	ε
⌐	𝓔e	E e	met	et
2½ ⌐	𝓐æ	Æ æ	mare	æ
3 ⌐	𝓐ɑ	A a	psalm	a
⌐	𝓐a	ɑ a	Sam	at
4 ⌐	𝒪σ	Θ ɵ	caught	ɵ
⌐	𝒪σ	O o	cot	ot
5 ⌐	𝓤u	U u	cur*	u
⌐	𝒲y	ᴜ u	curry	ut
6 ⌐	𝒪σ	Ọ ọ	bone	ọ
7 ⌐	𝓤uu	Ш m	fool	ш
⌐	𝓤u	Ш u	full	шt

COMPOUND VOWELS.

⌐	5 ᵢ	Ɪ̶i	high	i
⌐	𝒫σ̇	Φ ꝺ	hoy	ꝺ
⌐	𝒱x	8 8	how	8
⌐	𝓤y	Ψ y	hew	y

COALESCENTS.

◡	𝒴y	Y y	yea	yɛ
◠	𝒲w	W w	way	wɛ

BREATHING.

⊂(·)	𝓗h	H h	hay	hɛ

CONSONANTS.

Short hand.	Long hand.	Type	Example of its sound.	Name.
\	𝒫p	P p	pay	pi
\	𝓑b	B b	bay	bi
│	𝒯t	T t	toe	ti
│	𝒟d	D d	doe	di
/	𝒞ɡ	Ꞔ g	chew	ɡɛ
/	𝒥j	J j	jew	jɛ
—	𝒞c	C c	call	cɛ
—	𝒢y	G g	gall	gɛ
⌣	𝓕f	F f	few	ef
(	𝒱v	V v	view	vɛ
(	Ɏ ɫ	Γ t	thigh	it
(	℔ ꝺ	Ꝺ đ	thy	đi
)	𝒮s	S s	seal	es
)	Z z	Z z	zeal	zɛ
⌣	ʃʃ	Σ ʃ	mesh	iʃ
⌣	𝒵z	Ƹ ʒ	measure	ʒi
(	𝓛l	L l	lay	el
⌐	ℛr	R r	ray	rɛ
⌢	ℳm	M m	sum	am
⌣	𝒩n	N n	sun	en
⌣	𝒴ɳ	Ŋ ŋ	sung	iŋ

* Additional exemplificative words for this vowel, when *unaccented*, are *a*muse, m*a*nna, princip*a*l, principl*e*, mettl*e*, met*a*l, form*a*l, gosp*e*l, ev*i*l, pist*o*l, cons*u*l, pill*a*r, temp*e*r, elix*i*r, ten*o*r, murm*u*r, bos*o*m, schis-m, *o*pen, doz*e*n, Germ*a*n, lem*o*n, gall*a*nt, tal*e*nt, &c.

Figure 7. The First of Isaac Pitman's Phonographic (shorthand) and Phonotypic alphabets reproduced from *The Fonotypic Bible* of 1845.

The five versions, between 1844 and 1852, given in Figure 6 show how Fonotypy developed. The 1847 version was a joint effort with A. J. Ellis who maintained that, despite any defects, it should be considered as the accepted, stable version for teaching and other general purposes; the 1852 version was preferred by Isaac Pitman because it recognized the values of European vowel sounds, and would thus help promote English as an international language, whereas the 1847 version catered for English speakers only.

As my main example I have chosen the versions of 1845 and 1846 (Figures 7 and 8), not because they can be said to be better than later versions but they are reasonably representative and were used in the first Fonotypic Bible. The 1846 version, for example, made use of 16 vowels

ᴂI GOSPEL ACORDIꙄ TU JON.

ᴄAP. 1.

IꞤ ᴅi biginiꞧ woz ᴅi Wurd, and ᴅi Wurd woz wiᴅ God, and ᴅi Wurd woz God. 2 ᴅi sɛm woz in ᴅi biginiꞧ wiᴅ God. 3 Ɵl tiꞧz wɛr mɛd bꙓ him; and wiᴅꙅt him woz not enitiꞧ mɛd ᴅat woz mɛd. 4 In him woz lꙓf; and ᴅi lꙓf woz ᴅi lꙓt ov men. 5 And ᴅi lꙓt ʃꙓnet in darᴄnes; and ᴅi darᴄnes comprihended it not.

6 ᴅɛr woz a man sent from God, huuz nɛm woz Jon. 7 ᴅi sɛm ᴄɛm fɵr a witnes, tu bɛr witnes ov ᴅi Lꙓt, ᴅat ɵl men tru him mꙓt biliv. 8 Hi woz not ᴅat Lꙓt, but woz sent tu bɛr witnes ov ᴅat Lꙓt. 9 ᴅat woz ᴅi tru Lꙓt, hwiᴄ lꙓtet evuri man ᴅat cumɛt intu ᴅi wurld. 10 Hi woz in ᴅi wurld, and ᴅi wurld woz mɛd bꙓ him, and ᴅi wurld nu him not. 11 Hi ᴄɛm untu his on, and hiz on risivd him not. 12 But az meni az risivd him, tu ᴅem gɛv hi pꙒur tu biᴄum ᴅi sunz ov God, ivn tu ᴅem ᴅat biliv on hiz nɛm: 13 Hwiᴄ wɛr bɵrn, not ov blud, nɵr ov ᴅi wil ov ᴅi fleʃ, nɵr ov ᴅi wil ov man, but ov God. 14

And ᴅi Wurd woz mɛd fleʃ, and dwelt amuꞧ us, (and wi biheld hiz glori, ᴅi glori az ov ᴅi ᴏnli bigotn ov ᴅi Faᴅur,) ful ov grɛs and trut. 15 Jon bɛr witnes ov him, and ᴄrꙓd, sɛiꞧ, ᴅis woz hi ov huum ꙓ spɛc, Hi ᴅat cumɛt aftur mi iz prifurd bifor mi: fɵr hi woz bifor mi. And ov hiz fulnes hav ɵl wi risivd, and grɛs fɵr grɛs. 17 Fɵr ᴅi lɵ woz givn bꙓ Mozes, but grɛs and trut ᴄɛm bꙓ Jizus Crꙓst. 18 No man hat sin God at eni tꙓm; ᴅi ᴏnli bigotn Sun, hwiᴄ iz in ᴅi buzum ov ᴅi Faᴅur, hi hat diᴄlɛrd him.

19 And ᴅis iz ᴅi reᴄord ov Jon, hwen ᴅi Juz sent prists and Livꙓts from Jirusalem tu asc him, ᙿ Hu art ᴅꙒ. 20 And hi confest, and dinꙓd not; but confest, Ɨ am not ᴅi Crꙓst. 21 And ᴅɛ asct him, ᙿ Hwot ᴅen. ᙿ Art ᴅꙒ Ilꙓja. And hi set, Ɨ am not. ᙿ Art ᴅꙒ ᴅat profet. And hi ansurd, No. 22 ᴅen sed ᴅɛ untu him, ᙿ Hu art ᴅꙒ, ᴅat wi mɛ giv an ansur tu ᴅem ᴅat sent us, ᙿ Hwot sɛest ᴅꙒ ov ᴅꙓself. 23 Hi sed, Ɨ am ᴅi vɵs ov wun ᴄrꙓiꞧ in ᴅi wildurnes. Mɛc strɛt ᴅi wɛ ov ᴅi Lɵrd, az sed ᴅi

Figure 8. The opening of the Gospel According to John in *The Fonotypic New Testament* of 1846. Note the differences in the alphabet in Figure 7 which has two extra characters (Numbers 2½ and 5).

and 24 consonants of which 11 vowels and 6 consonants were new, *c*, *q*, and *x* being dropped. This enabled each of the essential sounds in the language to be represented unambiguously—that is digraphs were completely dispensed with. Most of the new characters were invented but, significantly, they resembled the style of the retained characters.

The problem of which variety of pronunciation of English speech the phonetic characters should represent has always, if needlessly, vexed spelling reformers and it was this that gave rise to much of the endless experimenting. The opinion of Professor Max Müller, the famous philologist, who became a supporter of Fonotypy, is worth quoting on this point because it shows how clearly Isaac Pitman realized that a practical alphabet for the reader, capable of being used as a teaching medium, might tolerate and needed to embody a limit to "phonetic truth" as my grandfather called it—

> What I like in Mr. Pitman's system of spelling is exactly what I know has been found fault with by others, namely, that he does not attempt to refine too much, and to express in writing those endless shades of pronunciation, which may be of the greatest interest to the student of acoustics, or of phonetics, as applied to the study of living dialects, but which, for practical as well as for scientific philological purposes, must be entirely ignored. Writing was never intended to photograph spoken languages: it was meant to indicate, not to paint, sounds. . . . Language deals in broad colours, and writing ought to follow the example of language, which, though it allows an endless variety of pronunciation, restricts itself for its own purpose, for the purpose of expressing thought in all its modifications, to a very limited number of typical vowels and consonants. Out of the large number of vowel sounds, for instance, which have been catalogued from the various English dialects, those only can be recognized as constituent elements of the language which in, and by, their difference from each other convey a difference of meaning.[1]

Though the intention and purpose was to reform the spelling of the whole community, it was soon discovered that Fonotypy was a dramatically effective aid in teaching children and illiterate adults to read (and to write) orthodox as well as Fonotypic spellings. The resemblance of the Fonotypic characters to roman characters—originally intended to reduce adult opposition to the reform—paradoxically made the new reader's transition to the orthodox effortless: in the words of Isaac's brother, Benn Pitman—

> An added interest was created in favor of the new system when it was found that the transition from the Phonetic to the Romanic letters was a

[1] *Fortnightly Review*, pp. 556–79, Vol. 25, April 1876.

comparatively easy task. The general resemblance between the old and new styles was so great that the pupil's ability to read the new method enabled it to readily decipher the greater number of words in the common print. It was thus demonstrated that the easiest and speediest way of learning to read Romanic spelling was to *begin* with the Phonetic system.[1]

Fonotypic reading classes were organized in many parts of the country, not only in schools but also for the inmates of workhouses, reformatories, and jails; for the members of a Phonetic Sunday School movement and a temperance society of working men in Broadway, Westminster, and elsewhere. At a meeting in Manchester in 1849 Benn Pitman, an able publicist and teacher of reading by the new medium on both sides of the Atlantic, reported that in a few months 1,300 illiterate adult Mancunians had been taught to read and write phonetically.

Fonotypy was used with success by missionaries in Africa, China, and India; in Nova Scotia it was applied to Micmac, a written version of an American Indian language that until then had been only spoken. By 1845 Fonotypic type had been brought to Boston, Massachusetts, from Bath by Stephen Pearl Andrews (see Appendix II). Among the best documented reports of its effectiveness was that of a large-scale experiment in ten schools at Waltham, Massachusetts, between 1852 and 1860. The children were able to read Fonotypic texts fluently after six to eight months when they made the transition to reading in the orthodox alphabet(s) and spelling. In their report for 1852–3 the town's school committee recorded that—

> We advocate Pitman's Phonetics simply as an aid in education, and as an introduction to ordinary orthography. It has been proved in repeated experiment that if a child upon his first learning his letters, is taught the Phonetic Alphabet, and is confined to Phonetic books for the first six or eight months of schooling, he will at the end of his first year's schooling read common print, and *spell in common spelling* better than children ordinarily do at the end of four or five years' instruction. It has also been proved by repeated experiments, that if an adult of ordinary intelligence is ignorant of his letters, he may learn to read the Bible, or the newspaper in two months' time by giving his attention to Phonetics two hours a day for six weeks, and to common print for the remaining fortnight.

The results of this experiment are given also in a report of the American Philosophical Society (1899)—

> We tested it thoroughly for six or seven years in the town of Waltham, Massachusetts, which then had about eight-hundred children in the public

[1] *Life and Labors of Sir Isaac Pitman*, p. 145. Cincinnati, 1902.

Ma-riz Lam.

Ma-ri had ɑ lit-l lam,
 its fles woz hwɪt az snɷ,
and ev-er-i-hwɑr đat Ma-ri went,
 đe lam woz ʃʏr tɷ gɷ.

He went wiđ her tɷ skɷl wun da;
 đat woz a-genst đe rɷl;
it mad đe ɕil-dren lɑf and pla,
  ˈ tɷ se ɑ lam at skɷl.

Sɷ đe teɕ-er turnd him ɤt,
 but stil he liŋ-gerd ner,
and wat-ed pa-ʃent-li a-bɤt,
 til Ma-ri did a-per.

And đen he ran tɷ her, and lad
 hiz hed up-on her ɑrm,
az if he sed: "Ɨ·m not a-frad,—
 yɷ·l kep me from el hɑrm."

"ɕHwot maks đe lam luv Ma-ri
  sɷ,"
 đe e-ger ɕil-dren krɪ;
"ɷ, Ma-ri luvz đe lam, yɷ nɷ,"
 đe teɕ-er did re-plɪ.

"And yɷ, eɕ jen-tl an-i-mal
 tɷ yɷ, fer lɪf, ma bɪnd,
and mak it fol-ɷ at yɷr kel,
 if yɷ ɑr el-waz kɪnd."

Figure 9. "Ma-riz Lam." From the *First Phonetic Reader*, by Benn Pitman.
American Phonetic Publishing Association, Cincinnati, 1885.

schools. The effect upon the school life of the town was very marked. The saving of time in teaching the children to read and to spell enabled us to introduce exercises for the eye and the hand, thus cultivating habits of observation, skill in drawing and writing, and geometrical ability. The fonetic print corrected the brogue of Irish children and the Yankee dialect of the American in a surprising manner. An improvement in the moral and intellectual tone of the schools was also noticeable, arising certainly in part from giving the children interesting reading instead of such absurd falsehoods as that of saying "sea," "you," "pea," spells "cup."

Fears were expressed that this method should injure the pupils' spelling. In order to test that question, I took pains to procure, several times, lists of words which had actually been used in Boston, Roxbury, and other places, with the percentage of failures on each list. Springing these lists, without warning, upon classes of the same grade in Waltham, we always found our percentage of errors very much smaller than in other towns, sometimes I think only one-third as large. We also questioned each pupil in our high-school as to the amount of time which he or she had devoted in his or her whole school life to fonotypy and fonography. Comparing these times with the percentage of errors in spelling, by the same scholars, we found that those who had read the most fonotypy made the fewest mistakes.

An even larger experiment with another augmented alphabet was started in the schools of St. Louis in 1866 and continued for some twenty years. This alphabet, invented by Dr. Edwin Leigh, contained over seventy characters (Appendix II). The first primer only was printed in Leigh's alphabet, the transition to the roman alphabet being made after six months. It was reported that time spent in learning to read was reduced by one-and-a-half to two years. By 1870 the school superintendent, William T. Harris (later to become Commissioner of Education at Washington), was saying—

> Each year increases our admiration of the work. Gain in time—quite one half—distinct articulation, and better spelling represent the undoubted advantages. I am satisfied that with the time we now have to devote to the higher readers, our teachers have it in their power to accomplish results in this department that we have hitherto considered impossible.[1]

From Illinois which also tried out Leigh's alphabet the Board of Education reported in 1871: "Pupils are found in their second year of schooling who have read many books. They learn to read so quickly and by comparatively so little effort, that reading is a pleasure, which could not be said under the old system."[2]

[1] From a *Report of a Public Meeting on Spelling Reform*, 29 May 1877, p. 9. Isaac Pitman, Phonetic Institute, Bath, 1878.
[2] Ibid.

One could give many more examples of augmented alphabets from those in my grandfather's library now at 39 Parker Street, London: for example, the Anti-Absurd alphabet (1844) invented by a Polish reformer of English spelling, Major Beniowski, which relied almost entirely on inverted characters; or the aesthetically pleasing 50-character alphabet designed by the poet Robert Bridges (1927–34: Appendix II). More recently (1962) the U.S. Simpler Spelling Association recommended a 41-character alphabet—the S.S.A. Fonetic Alfabet. Though intended particularly for use as a teaching medium, its promoters believed it also offered a "practical working basis for eventual fonetic spelling reform of English for general use." Among the 18 additional characters are 8 digraphic characters and a single character word-sign for *the* (see Appendix II). Capital (upper-case) characters are indicated by a heavy version of the lower-case character or, in handwriting or when typewritten, by an asterisk placed before the character.[1]

There is also John R. Malone's New Single Sound Alphabet[2] (see Appendix II) which, though put forward as a medium for teaching children to read, was originally devised for easy conversion into a binary code, to feed information into computers. All his 40 "single sound" characters are upper-case (without ascenders or descenders), the ratio of height to width being a constant 7:5; the same block-type characters are used to provide a lower-case alphabet, the vertical measure of the characters being reduced by about 29 per cent so that the 7:5 rectangle becomes a square. Malone claims that his system is very nearly fully consistent with the "Latin" conventions of most European spelling—e.g., Polish, Czech, Spanish, Italian, Turkish, German—thus facilitating language learning as well as electronic scanning combined with machine translation. All but one of the 21 orthodox characters retain their customary sound values. There are 19 new characters, few of which resemble orthodox characters.

This summary would also be incomplete without a mention of the International Phonetic Alphabet (IPA) which, while a tool for transcribing variations in the sounds of speech, is not a spelling reform even if it is a form of augmented alphabet. It was not without predecessors, the peculiarities of English spelling as well as the multiplicity of local accents giving rise to several earlier pronouncing alphabets and dictionaries: e.g.

[1] The *U.S. Simpler Spelling Association* also advocates a digraphic system (see page 96).
[2] Now called Unifon; previously called Shaw-Malone. Promoted by the Foundation for a Compatible and Consistent Alphabet. See also "The Larger Aspects of Spelling Reform", by John R. Malone; *Elementary English*, Vol. xxxix, No. 5, May 1962, Illinois U.S.A.

one by William Johnston (1764) which employed italic and black-letter characters and by Thomas Spence (1775) whose ten ligatured characters were cut by Thomas Bewick. Nowadays the IPA, which is issued by the International Phonetic Association (founded in 1886), is employed by most, but not all,[1] professional phoneticians and linguists as well as by lexicographers to indicate the conventionally correct pronunciation of words in standard dictionaries. Phoneticians of many nations, in designing this means of transcribing the speech of all languages, and of dialects within languages, drew largely upon the characters designed by Pitman and Ellis; it was derived in part also from Henry Sweet's scheme of Romic characters. Many of those used for English are to be found in the table in Appendix II. With the help of numerous modifiers, it is capable of distinguishing several hundred different sounds and so catering for all languages.

A reading system based on the International Phonetic Alphabet was tried out in 1914 by an infant teacher, Miss McCallum, at a school in Lumphinnans, Cowdenbeath, Fife. It was reported that the one-for-one relationship between character and phoneme made it unnecessary to select only "phonic" words or to reject the most difficult words in common use, and this meant that she was able to base her lessons on the children's own vocabulary. After a year, when they could "read any matter presented to them in phonetic symbols, and can write the same to dictation," they made the transition to the orthodox alphabet and it was recorded that their reading was then "much more fluent, natural and intelligent than is commonly found in an infant school."[2]

2. DIACRITICAL MARKS

A smaller group of reformers and/or teachers have avoided introducing additional characters, limiting themselves to certain simplifications and to diacritical marks. The pioneer of this group was William Bullokar who found that the orthodox spelling of his day led to "quarels in the teacher,

---

[1] While American linguists and phoneticians use the International Phonetic Alphabet and are thus in step with the great majority of their colleagues in the rest of the English-speaking world, others have introduced minor modifications of the standard version, in order to cater for special American pronunciations; yet others, such as George L. Trager and Henry Lee Smith, Jr., have added major changes that amount virtually to a special alphabet.

[2] Jackson, R. "Phonetics and Phonetic Texts in the Teaching of Reading." *Miscellanea Phonetica*, Vol. I, pp. 33-37, 1914.

and lothsomnesse in the learner, and great payne to both: and the conclusion was that both teacher & learner must go by rote, for no rule could be followed . . ." He argued his case in (1580) *Bullokar's Booke at Large, for the Amendment of Orthographie for English Speech:*[1] "wherein, a most perfect supplie is made for the wantes and double sounde of letters in the olde Orthographie . . . for the easie, speedie, and perfect reading and writing of English, (the speech not changed, as some vntruly and maliciously, or at the least ignorantlie blowe abroade) . . ."

He believed that there were 44 "divisions in one voice" and therefore a need for 26 consonants, 8 vowels, 7 diphthongs, and 3 "half vowels" (i.e. *l, m, n*). He maintained that a reformed alphabet should be as close as possible to the existing one and that "no new nor vnaccustomed letter (not used in the olde) shall be brought in: but the whole supply made by adding a little strike or turning, to, or neere one of the olde letters, (most agreeing for conference with the olde printing)."[2] His claim is perhaps a little overstated for he introduces ligatures and other devices—e.g. œ, oo (∞), ph (ꝓ), sh (ꜧ); a liquid *l* with "a turne neare the top of it"; *y* with a "crooked foot" when it is a consonant—and by using the old "black letters" (*Plate VII*) he is enabled to draw upon numerous abbreviations and contractions employed in the printing of Latin, making a total of 92 characters if we include what he called their "pairs" (e.g. *A, a*) but excluding his ampersand. As explained earlier, it is not possible to fit all the alphabets described in this chapter into precise categories, but Bullokar's cannot be truly termed augmented because most of his additional, unmarked characters are combinations of orthodox ones and are essentially digraphic (see *infra*). If this is thought to be too nice a distinction, it must be noted that he disputed the augmented methods adopted by his contemporaries Sir Thomas Smith (1568) and John Hart (1569) because they "brought in diuers of new figure and fashion, hauing no part in figure or fashion of the old, for whose soundes they were changed in figure, or newly deuised, strange to the eye, and thereby more studie to the memory." Without actually increasing the number of characters he endeavoured to provide the reader with a distinctive instruction for each essential sound and to warn him of various pitfalls. His vowels (as in Sir Thomas Smith's system)

---

[1] Published by Henrie Denham, London. He also issued a pamphlet entitled *A Short Introduction or guiding, to print, write, and reade Inglish speech*. Henrie Denham, London, 1580. A revised edition of this second pamphlet (1581), copiously annotated by Bullokar in his own hand, was bought by my grandfather and is the only copy known to exist. Among his other works were *Aesops Fablz in tru Ortography with Grammar-nóts* . . . and *William Bullokarz Pamphlet for Grammar* . . . Edmund Bollifant, London, 1586.   [2] Ibid., p. 19.

carry various "strykz, prikz, & notz" to show their length and quality; he dispensed with mute characters and, whenever possible, with the final *e* which was then used even more frequently than it is today; he was against etymological spellings such as the *b* in *debt* and *doubt*.[1]

In Tudor England, according to another reformer, Richard Mulcaster, "the right writing of our English tung" was "yet in question."[2] He adds: "is it not a verie necessarie labor to set the writing certain, that the reading may be sure?" Mulcaster, however, was far more cautious than Bullokar, let alone Smith or Hart; custom, he argued, should be as important a consideration as sound and reason in deciding upon the most appropriate spelling; "by the mean of Art" reason, custom, and sound provided a "triumvirate in their gouernment of the pen." He limited his reforms to clearing away certain obvious abuses and to "sharp" or "flat and quick" accents on vowels.

An ingenious and complex employment of diacritical marks appeared a century later with the publication of a spelling-book called *The English Primrose* (1644) by Richard Hodges, a Southwark schoolmaster (*Plate VIII*). He declared on the title page that it was: "Far surpassing al others of this kinde, that ever grew in any English garden . . . The Easiest and Speediest-way, both for the true spelling and reading of English, as also for the True-writing thereof: that ever was publickly known to this day." In the introduction he explained that the roman alphabet and English spelling made it impossible that learning to read—

. . . should bee pleasing to the Scholars. 'Tis most true, that they poor boys bee often chiden, rebuk't, knockt and whipt, when the fault is not in them, that they apprehend not what is taught, but in the uncertain, and perplext, and intricate expressing of our Tongue, by letters wrong named;[3] and by their various sounds and forces attributed to them.

Significantly, on his title page he places words from *I Corinthians*, chapter xiv, verse 8, to which might well have been added verse 7—

7. And even things without life giving sound, whether pipe or harp, except they give a distinction in the sounds, how shall it be known what is piped or harped?
8. For if the trumpet give an uncertain sound, who shall prepare himself to the battle?

[1] *Plate VII* and Appendix II.
[2] *The Elementarie*, 1582.
[3] This is the same criticism as raised by Sir Thomas Smith (see page 76).

He explains that by means of his marks he expresses "the true sounds of al the vowels and diphthongs, and make manifest, the forces and powers of al the consonants which are proper to the English Tongue, and yet use our ancient and usual characters, and adde onely to them some marks of distinction." Hodges also wrote about homophones;[1] among various reforms he believed that some, but not all, double consonants should be abolished and that *peeple* was better than *people*; he grumbled about the tautology of *c* and *k* in words like *lack* and *luck* but accepted that "for the present" one must put up with them (Appendix II).

A contemporary example of this method is the Diacritical Marks System (known as DMS) invented by Dr. Edward Fry, Professor of Education at Rutgers University, New Jersey. It is intended merely for teaching purposes and the marks are "vanished," possibly by being printed in successively lighter shades of grey, as the reading habit is established. Orthodox spelling and both upper- and lower-case characters are retained; the marks can all be made with a standard typewriter. Fry's basic rules are as follows—

(1) Characters for "regular" consonants and short vowels unchanged.

(2) Silent characters are "slashed" (*wrīte̸, ri̸ght*).

(3) Long vowels are indicated by a short bar over the character (*mā̄de̸, māi̸d*).

(4) Short unstressed neutral vowels carry an overhead dot (*ȧgo, lemȯn*).

(5) What he terms "other consistent" sounds are indicated by a bar underneath (*i̱s, a̱utō̱*).

(6) A bar beneath both characters signals a digraph (*s̱ẖut, c̱ẖat*). Exceptions to these six rules have an asterisk above the offending character (*ȏnce̸, ȯf*). The character *r* is singled out for special treatment in words like *fu̱r, fi̱r, he̱r, acre̸*, the *r* being raised to the status of a vowel; but in *a̱rm* and *vā̱ry* it is considered as part of a short or long sounding digraph. Similarly *y* appears unmarked in *funny*, as *ȳ* in *mȳ* and *cȳclȏne̸*, and as *y̱* in *y̱es* (Appendix II).

Another recent example of diacritical marks is Professor William Craigie's[2] system of indicating pronunciation to foreign students of

---

[1] *A Special Help to Orthographie or the True-writing of English*, 1643.

[2] *English Reading Made Easy* and *The Pronunciation of English*, Oxford University Press, 1922 and 1917.

English. Together with a number of fixed rules (e.g. in words of one syllable ending with a consonant the vowel is always pronounced short) and the printing of "wholly irregular" words in italics, various marks are placed above, below, or after certain characters to convey pronunciation without tampering with the spelling: thus ᴗ and - tell the student that a vowel is short or long (*răpid, sēcret*); $\bar{s} = z$; $\bar{x} = gz$; $\mathit{ş} = zh$; $n\bar{g} = ng + g$; $\mathit{ġ}, d\mathit{ġ} = j$; $\acute{c}, \acute{s}, \mathit{t}, ch = sh$; $\hat{e}, \hat{e}a = $ long a (*fête, grêat*); a dot beneath a character denotes that it is silent (*limḅ*); a dot after a vowel denotes that this syllable bears the main stress (*acro·ss*); and so on.

3. DIGRAPHIC SPELLING

A third group of spelling reformers have contented themselves with reducing inconsistency as much as possible and with devising relatively logical spellings within the restricted resources of the roman alphabet. Inevitably this gives rise to the use of digraphs not found in orthodox spelling and thus increases the employment of characters to represent more than one sound. On the other hand these systems have immediate, though spurious, attractions: they depart no more than is strictly necessary from orthodox spelling; they eliminate the inconvenience and practical difficulties of introducing new characters or marks—which if intended for a major programme of spelling reform for adults means revolutionizing the printing and typewriter industries; the resemblance between the new and old systems is said to reduce resistance from the public, though in fact it is debatable whether the digraphic approach necessarily preserves greater similarity to orthodox texts than do the augmented or diacritical systems or whether the public's resistance is reduced.

Numerous brands of digraphic spelling were promoted by mid-Victorians. Among the first and most influential was Glossic (1870), devised by A. J. Ellis after he had lost faith in converting people to Fonotypy. Glossic was simple to understand and the intention was to use it concurrently with orthodox spelling "in order to remedy some of its defects, without changing its form, or detracting from its value." Based on forty-three sounds, Glossic[1] could be used to teach children to read, though a more elaborate notation, "Euniversel Glosik," was designed to reproduce dialects for phonetic discussion (Appendix II).

---

[1] See *Transactions of the Philological Society*, pp. 89–118, London, 1870.

The system can be best explained by the following summary of "Objekts" and "Meenz"—

Objekts: Too fasil·itait Lerning too Reed,
Too maik Lerning too Spel unnes·eseri,
Too asim·ilait Reeding and Reiting too Heerring and Speeking,
Too maik dhi Risee·vd Proanunsiai·shen
ov Ingglish akses·ibl too *aul* Reederz,
Proavin·shel and Foren.

Meenz: Leev dhi Oald Speling untuch·t
Introadeu·s along·seid ov dhi Oald Speling
a Neu Aurthog·rafi, konsis·ting ov dhi
Oald Leterz euzd invai·rriabli in dhair
best noan sensez.
Emploi· dhi Neu Speling in Skoolz too
Teech Reeding in *boath* Aurthog·rafiz.
Alou· eni Reiter too reit in dhi Neu Speling *oanli* on aul okai·zhenz widhou·t loozing kaast, proavei·ded hee euzez a Risee·vd Proanunsiai·shen; dhat is— *aknol·ej dhi Neu Speling konkur·entli widh dhi Oald.*

A similar scheme was E. Jones's Analogical Spelling (1875) which was based on forty symbols, fifteen of them being digraphs of roman characters. He made concessions to the extent of preserving the *k* in *kill*, the *-ay* in *day*, and *-ow* in *cow*, etc. Meanwhile Ellis had decided that his Glossic was still too far removed from orthodox spelling and made further concessions with yet another system called Dimid'iun,[1] though it does not appear to differ greatly from Glossic. His purpose in both cases was to provide a system of spelling that could be immediately used by any printing works which possessed a fount of roman characters. The veteran spelling reformer makes a moving, if not despairing confession—

If nomic[2] reederz ar tou hav the sleitest dificulty in reeding the new speling, goud bey tou our haaf loaf! Ingglish reederz wohnt goh tou scool agén, eh pourr cohz ((et pour cause))—a burnt cheild dredz the feir! Hens, if posibl, every thing prizénted tou thair eyz shoud bi whot thay aulrédy understánd. In uther wurdz the new speling must bi bilt on the leinz ov thi oald.

Revolewshun *may* bi the best solewshun, but ey doo not inténd tou wurk in that direcshun eny longger. Mey paast expeeriens, whitch haz been boatth grait and painfoul, wornz me tou trey anuther road. It iz not without egzurting grait fors ohver misélf thut ey-uv rinounst a pewrly fonetic alfabet. But Glosic woz mey furst step in the new direcshun, and Dimidiun or "háafway speling" is mey secund.

[1] *Dimid'iun Spel'ing or Haaf ov whot is needed.* Lundun, 1880.
[2] Nomic: "dhe fonetic euzejez ov our prezent cústumery speling."

IX Isaac Pitman at the age of thirty-two.

From
Bernard Shaw

Phone & Wire: AYOT SAINT LAWRENCE,
CODICOTE 218. 7/8/1947   WELWYN, HERTS.

I said that the first thing to be provided is an alfabet. But this is not enough. The schools cannot experiment until we provide them with a primer with reading and writing exercises. I am half inclined to draft it myself.

Meanwhile write up in letters of gold round your office England Knows Nothing of Phonetics, Hates Education, But Will Do Anything For Money.

No digraphs.

Cockerell cannot suggest any artist-calligrapher with brains enough.

I greatly enjoyed your visit.

G.B.S.

X Postcard sent by George Bernard Shaw to Sir James Pitman (7th August 1947). Shaw insisted that the saving of printing and paper costs was a telling argument in favour of a new alphabet entirely divorced from the legacy of Rome.

It iz thi owtcum ov thurty sevn yeerz ov consienshus wurk, coménst and carid on for edewcaishunul and filolodjicul purpusez.

In his later years Isaac Pitman was also convinced that the most practical course was to promote a system of spelling reform limited to the resources of the roman alphabet. After various experiments[1] he announced the following Three Rules of the Spelling Reform, based still on his forty discrete sounds (Appendix II)—

RULE 1.—Reject *c*, *q*, *x* as redundant; use the other consonants for the sounds usually associated with them; and supply the deficiency of twelve other letters by these digraphs—

ch	'th	th	sh	zh	ng
*ch*eap	*th*in	*th*en	wi*sh*	vi*s*ion	si*ng*
aa	ai	ee	au	oa	oo
p*a*lm	p*a*le	p*ee*l	p*a*ll	p*o*le	p*oo*l

Write *ay* for the second vowel, and *aw*, for the fourth, *at the end of a word*; as *pay*, *law*.

RULE 2.—*A*, *e*, *o*, *u*, *ending a syllable* (except at the end of a word; as, *sofa*), represent a *long* vowel; as in *fa-vour*, *fe-ver*, *ho-li*, *tru-li*.

RULE 3.—*A*, *e*, *i*, *o*, *u*, in *close* syllables (and *a* at the end of a word), represent the short sounds in *pat*, *pet*, *pit*, *pot*, *put*. Use *ŭ* for *u* when it is pronounced as in *but*.

Write the Diphthongs thus: *ei*, b*y*; *ou*, n*ow*; *iu*, n*ew* (*yu* initial); *ái*, K*ai*ser; *oi*, c*oy*.

NOTE.—In the First Stage concede to custom *I* instead of *ei* for the first personal pronoun; *n* for *ng* when followed by *k* or *g*, as *bank* (bangk), *anger* (ang-ger); *father*, *piano-forté*, *pianist* (*for* faather, piaano-foarté, piaanist). When the letters of a digraph represent separate values insert a (·) between them as short·hand (not shor·thand), be·ing (not by·ing). Proper names and their adjectives, addresses, and the titles of books, should not be altered at present.

Isaac Pitman's monthly journal *The Speler*, first issued in January 1895, was for the most part printed according to these "First Stage" rules and to the end of his life he advocated this more limited reform with the same energy and persistence as he had devoted to Fonotypy.

During the first half of this century the interest in digraphic systems continued; one of the most widely supported grew from the researches of the Simplified Spelling Society and of the sister organization in the U.S., the Simplified Spelling Board. Both organizations believed the goal

---

[1] Based on a set of *Five Rules* for the improvement of English spelling, issued by the American Spelling Reform Association and the American Philological Society.

to be a system in which single or combinations of roman characters unambiguously represented the essential sounds of English, but they differed over tactics, the Americans believing in a series of graduated reforms whereas the British, while making a start with new readers in schools, wanted to extend a completely reformed spelling gradually throughout the adult community. The proposals underwent many revisions over a period of nearly fifty years, their final (British) form appearing in 1938 and 1948, the latter as the sixth edition with the title *New Spelling*[1] by Walter Ripman and Walter Archer; this was subjected to further amendment of detail in 1956 which enabled the proposals to be supported fully by the U.S. Simpler Spelling Association.[2] The system of consonant and vowel sounds represented by New Spelling was arrived at after a thorough statistical analysis of the linguistic structure of the language (Appendix II)—

TABLE IX

New Spelling in brief, arranged on a phonetic basis, but not including the amendments agreed to with the U.S. Simpler Spelling Association

		CONSONANT SOUNDS			
pin	bin	tin	din	kin	got
fat	vat	set	zest	chat	jet
hot	lot	rot	win	whim	yet
		(N.B. karry, sorry, hurry)			
met	net	sing (N.B. thank)		(lokh)	
shut	vizhon	thing	dhis		

		VOWEL SOUNDS			
bat	bet	pit	pot	but	good
		pity			
		pityus			
faadher	maed	feel	haul	goez	muun
far	faer	feer	short	loer	puur
stary	kaotik	being	story	heroik	bluish
	krie	kount	koin	hue	
	fier	sour	emploir	puer	
	dial				
		fur	sister		
		sturing			

[1] First issued in 1910 as *Simplified Spelling*. Revised in 1938 by Professor Lloyd James, Professor Daniel Jones, Harold Orton, Walter Ripman and I. J. Pitman. The influence of Professor R. E. Zachrisson and his Anglic (see pages 100–1) was acknowledged in the Foreword by Professor Gilbert Murray. Pitman, London, 1938 and 1940.

[2] This incorporates the Simplified Spelling Board. See also *supra* (page 88). The Simpler Spelling Association's augmented alphabet was adopted in 1958.

The principles of the system deserve to be summarized—

No new characters or diacritical marks.
Avoidance, as far as possible, of digraphs not already in use or familiar, but with the exception of *dh*, *zh*, *aa*, *uu*, and in effect also *ae*.
Each character or digraph to be self-sufficient, so that its significance should not depend on any other character.
Economy in the use of characters without causing ambiguity or inconsistency.
Minimum departure from orthodox spelling; the appropriation to each symbol of the sound with which it is most commonly associated.
Allowance to be made for existing divergencies of pronunciation—e.g. the distinction between *weather* and *whether* heard in different speech areas.
The convenience of the coming generation to be the objective, and not to be sacrificed to the habits of the adult generation of today.

New Spelling was on the whole systematic but it was never intended that it should be phonemically perfect "because reason suggests that the gap between the old spelling and the new should be made as small as possible *without sacrifice of simplicity and consistency*."[1] The truth of this assertion can be seen from the following example—

> Befor repliing, it mae be wel to konsider anudher objekshon which iz ofen urjd: dhe introdukshon ov anudher speling wood maek aul dhe egzisting books uesles. I am not kwiet kleer whie dhis objekshon shood be soe redily urjd; for shuurly it iz kwiet unreezonabl. Dhe introdukshon ov a nue speling iz not dhe wurk ov daez or weeks; it wood be imposibl (eeven if it wer dezierabl) at wuns to suplie in dhe nue speling aul dhe books dhat ar wonted, and to remuuv aul dhe oeld books in dhe oeld speling. Evribody wood be aebl to reed dhe oeld speling widhout difikulty; dhoez braut up on dhe neu speling wood be familyar widh dhe oeld, dhoe dhae wood hardly look upon it widh admiraeshon.[2]

Dr. Godfrey Dewey's World English Spelling, which grew out of the system agreed by the two societies, is similar to New Spelling: the digraph *th* is not replaced by *dh* in words like *that, rather, with*; and *thh* is employed in "voiceless" words such as *thought, nothing, both*: also the roles of *oo* and *uu* are reversed, e.g. in *pull* and *pool* the form has become *puul* and *pool*, but *good* and *book* become *guud* and *buuk*. World English Spelling is intended for use as a teaching medium that would lead to permanent spelling reform.

A system of spelling very similar to the most recent version of New

---

[1] *New Spelling*, p. 15.   [2] Ibid., p. 95.

Spelling was tried out in an experiment in which sixteen British schools participated between 1915 and 1924. The transition to orthodox spelling varied from school to school, some fixing an arbitrary date and others making it depend on the individual child's progress. The transition was found to cause no difficulties and estimates of the time saved in learning to read ranged from six months to two years. The conclusions reached from the experiment were summed up as follows—

(1) That children learn to read fluently matter in a simple phonetic spelling, and to write correctly according to the system, in the course of a few months.

(2) That, as a consistent spelling presents no bar to free expression, the original compositions of children who use a phonetic spelling are markedly superior in matter and manner to the compositions of children of the same age who use the traditional spelling.

(3) That, in reading aloud, the children who use a phonetic spelling acquire a clearer enunciation than children taught to read throughout in the current orthography.

(4) That, contrary to expectation, the transition from the phonetic to the ordinary spelling is attended by no difficulty, and indeed, that children who pass from the former to the latter, acquire something like proficiency in the ordinary spelling sooner than children do who are familiar with no other.

(5) That the better mental discipline introduced into the reading and writing lesson leads to improved work in other subjects of the School course.[1]

A more recent demonstration of the efficacy of a phonemically reliable digraphic alphabet as a teaching medium has been provided by Dr. Frank C. Laubach. His *Let's Reform Our Spelling Now*[2] is again very similar to New Spelling, except that he introduces a single diacritical sign and admits some 54 alternative forms in order to increase the similarity to orthodox spelling (Appendix II).

Another recent and, though small, encouraging experiment with a digraphic alphabet was carried out by Dr. Helen Bonnema, at the time a school principal at Denver, Colorado, in the Jefferson County District. Her Dictionary-Key system eliminates upper-case characters, discards *c*, *q*, and *x*, and bases its characters on the pronouncing keys provided in brackets after each entry in the *American College* and *Thorndike-Barnhart* dictionaries widely used in U.S. schools. The diacritical marks employed in these dictionaries are however discarded in favour of the digraphs supported by the U.S. Simpler Spelling Association (see p. 96), assisted

[1] *The Best Method of Teaching Children to Read and Write*, p. 2. Simplified Spelling Society and Sir Isaac Pitman & Sons Ltd., London, 1924.
[2] New Readers' Press, Syracuse, New York, 1966.

by a single non-roman character—the inverted ə—to represent the un-stressed vowel. With this system Dr. Bonnema believes that—

> The child always has the security of proceeding from the known—the dictionary notation of word sounds—to the unknown or new-to-him, standard spelling. He establishes self-confidence in learning to read before he has to face the intricacies, the contradictions, the illogic of our standard spelling, which he does not face all at once. [1]

Once the child can *write* anything he wishes in the Dictionary-Key system he makes the transition to orthodox spelling in easy stages, a process which involves learning what she terms the "48 general spelling rules."

Among the most persistent campaigners for a digraphic system of reform was Dr. Mont Follick, Labour M.P., who devised his own system, consisting of 23 single characters and 16 digraphic combinations[2] (Appendix II). Though Follick believed in the need for a permanent spelling reform, he approached the problem from the point of view of an expert on teaching English to foreigners—he was the founder and proprietor of the Regent School of Languages, London. He insisted that it was only the spelling with the roman alphabet that needed improvement, not the roman alphabet itself. Digraphs would best do what was required. A systematic romanic alphabeticism, he argued, would make it very much easier for the foreigner, literate in any language printed with roman characters, to learn to read and speak English; it would also help the English child learning to read, but this was not his first concern. Follick believed passionately that his reform could establish English as the world's major second language. It is not, however, for his own particular alphabet that he is likely to be best remembered, but rather for his two Private Member's bills in the House of Commons (1949 and 1952) advocating the need for reform, with which I am proud to have been closely associated. In fact he invited me to draft his second bill and to take charge of it as if it were I and not he who had been successful in the ballot. His first bill was defeated on a second reading by only 3 votes after a five-hour debate; his second bill achieved a majority of 12 votes and was also successful in Committee

[1] "Writing by Sound: a New Method of Teaching Reading." *Spelling Progress Bulletin*, March 1961, Hollywood, California.

[2] Follick's alphabet was completed by 1914 but not published until 1934. See *The Influence of English* by M. Follick. Williams and Norgate, London; *The Case for Spelling Reform* by Mont Follick. Pitman, London, 1965; also *The late Dr. Mont Follick—An Appraisal: the Assault on the Conventional Alphabets and Spelling*, paper delivered by Sir James Pitman, K.B.E., M.P., at Manchester University, 7 February 1964: Pitman and University of Manchester, London and Manchester, 1965.

despite ministerial opposition. After a good deal of "horse-trading" by me behind the scenes, he was induced to withdraw the second bill in return for an offer by Miss Horsbrugh, then Minister of Education, to pledge her interest and goodwill "towards proposals by a competent research organization to investigate possible improvements in the teaching of reading by means of a system of simplified spelling."[1] In both bills it was left to others to determine the form of the new medium. There is no doubt that his pioneering work smoothed the way to the official blessing given to the research into my own alphabet, for the second bill, as I drafted it, required the National Foundation for Educational Research to carry out the necessary research and this was what eventually occurred, the Foundation working in collaboration with the University of London Institute of Education and with support from charitable and Government funds (see Chapter 9).

Of the many other systems that come in this group I shall limit myself to mentioning only three more: first, the fonetik crthqgrafi invented by the American Frederick S. Wingfield,[2] because it goes to the opposite extreme of most of the systems limited to roman characters in that his words bear only a remote resemblance to orthodox spellings: by using the redundant *c*, *j*, *q*, and the colon (:) to represent certain vowel sounds, the character *r* for others, *x* for *ng* before *g*, and various other devices he makes the English language look like this—

> Dhis fonetik mo:d v rjkcrding Ixglish kaen bj jzili print'd, taipritn, jvn telagraeft. It iz dh qutkvm v prsistnt eksperimnt, investigeishn, n kmpaersn widh vdhr methadz, thruqut 14 yirz. Evri yusidzh haz bin thctf'li djsaid'd vpqn, haeving kqnstntli in maind dh "lcng vyu" v qrthograefik rjfcrm, dht dh most meritorias speling wwd bj a saiantifik homqgrafi widh an aedikwatli enlqrdzhd aelfabet. Dh sistm holdz widhin its beisik strvktshr dhaet rjm:t pqsibiliti. At dh preznt taim it haez potenshl yusflnes aez a pqpiular crthoepik ko:d fcr diksh'neriz, baiqgrafiz, ensaiklopjdiaz, teksts qn k'rekt pronvnsieishn, n fcr dh paerenthetik indikeishn v pr'nvnsieishn v streindzh wr:dz n prqpr neimz. Dh seiving in letrz iz aprqksim'tli 7 tu 15%. It iz wvn v dh most jzili lr:nt v cl sistmz v speling rjfcrm. Its frst n fainl rek'mendeishn iz dh pqsibility v vltim't traensishn tu niu letrz fcr dh preznt ae, th, dh, sh, tsh, zh, dzh, ng.

Two interesting systems have been devised by Swedish linguists: Professor R. E. Zachrisson and Dr. Axel Wijk. The former's Anglic[3] is very similar to New Spelling, but Zachrisson permits the retention of

[1] *Hansard*, 7 May 1953.
[2] *Fonetik Crthqgrafi*. Northwest Printery, Chicago, 1942.
[3] *Anglic, an International Language*. Almqvist and Wiksell, Uppsala and Stockholm, 1932.

forty-two "wordsigns" or ideographic representations of short, common words, thus bringing his system a stage closer to orthodox spelling. Dr. Wijk (see also p. 48) reduces the gap further still by maintaining that less than 10 per cent of the total vocabulary display "irregular" spellings, yet he estimates that these amount to 15–20 per cent of the running words on an average page. His Regularized English[1] is limited therefore to the replacement of (Wijk's) "irregular" spellings by (Wijk's) "regular ones inherent in the present orthography"; to the introduction of *aa* for the broad *a-* sound when not followed by *r*; *f* for *ph*; and a handful of other reforms (Appendix II).

4. COLOUR SYSTEMS

Colour has been employed to convey the correct sounds for teaching purposes in a manner that is very similar to diacritical marks. Among the earliest were the Dale series of reading primers, published in 1900;[2] the latest is the Words in Colour system,[3] developed by Dr. Caleb Gattegno, which makes use of no less than forty-seven colours. All the different versions of a sound are indicated by one particular colour; identical spellings which have different sounds are printed in different colours. A comparable colour system has been proposed by J. K. Jones.[4] In a system I devised myself in conjunction with Charles M. Smith[5] the orthodox spelling and characters were similarly preserved but each of the vowels was printed in a particular colour—red, orange, yellow, green, blue, violet; diphthongs were indicated by a blend of the two appropriate colours; the short vowels were printed only in outline; the longer vowels in solid. The way in which the colours were used is shown by the following three sentences that represent all the sixteen vowel sounds—

	RED	ORANGE	YELLOW	GREEN	BLUE	VIOLET
Solid characters	*Pa*	*may*[6]	*we*	*all*	*go*[6]	*too*
Outline characters	*That*	*pen*	*is*	*not*	*much*	*good*

[1] *Regularized English*. Almqvist and Wiksell, Stockholm, 1959.
[2] *The Dale Readers* (6 vols.) by Nellie Dale. George Philip and Son Ltd., London, 1900–2.
[3] See *Forward Trends*, Vol. 7, No. 4, pp. 141–4. The Guild of Teachers of Backward Children, London, 1964.
[4] *Colour Story Reading*. Nelson, London, 1967.
[5] *Phonetic Orthography*. Sir Isaac Pitman & Sons, London, 1937.
[6] In some language areas these are pronounced as pure vowels.

	RED–YELLOW	RED–VIOLET	GREEN–YELLOW	YELLOW–VIOLET
Parti-coloured characters	*I*	*now*	*enjoy*	*music*

These colours appeared in every character, however many, that represents a vowel sound, the long sounds entailing more weight of colour than the short ones. Similar phonetic clues were provided for the consonants: when the top or bottom half of a digraph was printed in outline, this denoted that the two characters combined to make one sound; mute consonants were signalled either by printing them in outline or in the same colour as the vowel characters they accompanied.[1]

5. NON-ROMANIC ALPHABETS

A few reformers have decided to have no truck with roman characters, spurning the slightest compromise with orthodox spelling and rejecting augmentations, diacritical marks, digraphs, or colour. Instead of "tinkering" with the roman alphabet they advocate its replacement by a completely new set of purpose-built characters. These alphabets should not be confused with cyphers or systems of more rapid writing. An early example was the curious "visible" speech invented by A. Melville Bell (the father of Alexander Graham Bell and a collaborator of my grandfather); Bell's symbols were designed (1867) to be pictorial representations of the arrangement of the vocal organs required to produce the sounds necessary to the language.[2] Among others who tried their hand at designing this type of alphabet were Isaac Pitman (1843)[2] and Daniel Jones and Paul Passy (1907)[2]—see also Figure 10.

The most trenchant publicist for a complete rejection of the roman alphabet was Bernard Shaw. The old Fabian in politics was a phonetic

---

[1] I decided to reject colours as a means of signalling different sounds, while retaining the shapes of the words as conventionally printed, for three main reasons: (1) the cost of supplying a sufficient quantity of reading material in many colours is very high, if not prohibitive; (2) whereas colours can be helpful in teaching reading, it makes writing most difficult: it is surely a mistake to deny a child, accustomed to seeing characters in different significant colours, the opportunity of writing words in colours himself, but this imposes yet another burden—as well as deciding which characters to write and remembering their shapes, he has in addition to remember which crayon to pick up; (3) even when he does choose the correct crayon, he is just as likely to be defeated by *once, all, the, sugar*, etc., because of the lack of any one character to represent each sound required.

[2] See Appendix II.

revolutionary and ridiculed the compromising Fabians among the spelling reformers—

> I am dead against any mixture of Johnsonese and Phonetic[1] . . . we all know the old alphabet as we know the Lord's Prayer. To stick 17 new letters into it would be as puzzling as to stick 17 words into the Prayer. "Give us this day our daily bread with a sufficiency of carbohydrates and a glass of beer" would be metabolically justifiable but not psychologically desirable.[2]

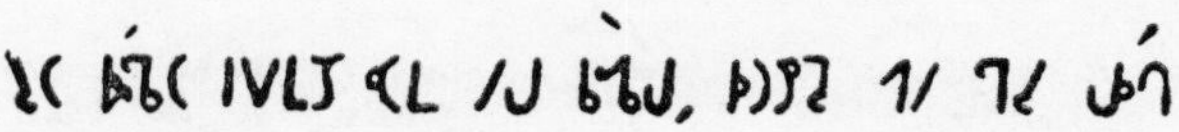

John Wilkins (1668).

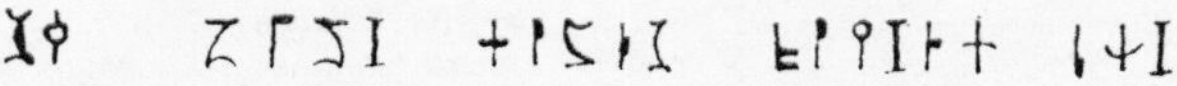

Isaac Pitman (1843).

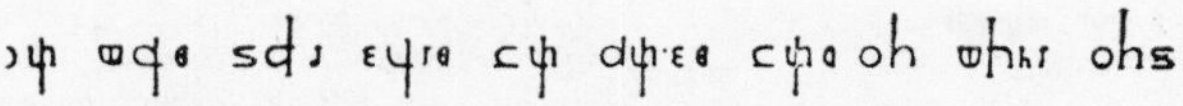

Daniel Jones and Paul Passy (1907).

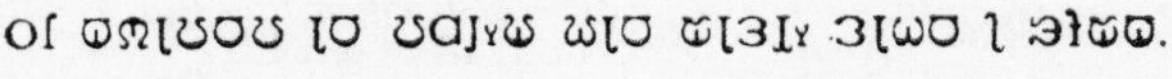

A. M. Bell (1867).

Figure 10. Examples of non-romanic alphabets, collected by Professor David Abercrombie.

In Shaw's view *woz* for *was* and *pees* for *peace* were "obscenities." In his will he bequeathed a large sum to further alphabetic reform, part of which was to be spent in creating a new alphabet containing at least 40 characters which would enable the English language to be written without indicating single sounds by groups of characters or by diacritical marks—the pronunciation to resemble that recorded by "His Majesty our late King George V and sometimes described as Northern English."[3] Of the 40 characters 16 had to represent vowel sounds. As is well known, the will was disputed in earnest by two of the three residuary legatees (the British Museum, the Royal Academy of Dramatic Art), against the wishes

[1] Note from G.B.S. to Daniel Jones, 18 August 1947.
[2] Letter from G.B.S. to Sir James Pitman, 16 December 1947.
[3] Clause 35 (2) in Bernard Shaw's will, 1950.

of the National Gallery of Ireland, but a "compromise" settlement was reached which permitted sufficient money to be set aside to carry out Shaw's intention: the Public Trustee as administrator was enabled to offer a prize of £500 for any design accepted and to provide for the transliteration, publication, and presentation to every public library in the British

ANDROCLES AND THE LION

alike, *fly for their lives, the gladiators bolting into the arena, the others in all directions. The place is emptied with magical suddenness*].

ANDROCLES [*naïvely*] Now I wonder why they all run away from us like that. [*The lion, combining a series of yawns, purrs, and roars, achieves something very like a laugh*].

THE EMPEROR [*standing on a chair inside his box and looking over the wall*] Sorcerer: I command you to put that lion to death instantly. It is guilty of high treason. Your conduct is most disgra – [*the lion charges at him up the stairs*] help! [*He disappears. The lion rears against the box; looks over the partition at him; and roars. The Emperor darts out through the door and down to Androcles, pursued by the lion*].

ANDROCLES. Dont run away, sir: he cant help springing if you run. [*He seizes the Emperor and gets between him and the lion, who stops at once*]. Dont be afraid of him.

THE EMPEROR. I am not afraid of him. [*The lion crouches, growling. The Emperor clutches Androcles*]. Keep between us.

ANDROCLES. Never be afraid of animals, your worship: thats the great secret. He'll be as gentle as a lamb when he knows that you are his friend. Stand quite still; and smile; and let him smell you all over just to reassure him; for, you see, he's afraid of you; and he must examine you thoroughly before he gives you his confidence. [*To the lion*] Come now, Tommy; and speak nicely to the Emperor, the great good Emperor

132   133

Figure 11. From the Shaw Alphabet edition of *Androcles and the Lion* (Penguin Books, Harmondsworth, 1962).

Isles, the Commonwealth, and the United States of copies of Shaw's *Androcles and the Lion* printed on facing pages in the orthodox and the new alphabet. No less than 467 new alphabets were submitted, of which four were considered to possess outstanding merit. In the end the design submitted by Kingsley Read was adopted after it had been modified in consultation with the other three winners—Pauline M. Barrett, J. F. Magrath, S. L. Pugmire—with whom the £500 was divided equally. The new characters, once learned, are easier and speedier to read and to write than roman characters. Their essential simplicity and legibility can be seen by comparing character with character in the two versions reproduced from *Androcles and the Lion* (Figure 11 and Appendix II); they also demonstrate unmistakably the great saving in space—and thus of ink, paper, type, machine time, labour, storage, transport, and writing time—made possible by this new alphabet. Shaw urged that the mind ought not to wait upon the pen but that the pen ought to wait upon the mind. He once sent me a postcard advising me to "write up in letters of gold round your office England Knows Nothing of Phonetics, Hates Education, But Will Do Anything For Money."[1] Shaw used to declare that the failure of Fonotypy compared with the success of my grandfather's shorthand was because Fonotypy, though instantaneously read, offered no practical benefits, while his shorthand, which to a novice was wholly illegible, yielded great and marketable value. But it was not Shaw's intention that the roman alphabet should ever be totally abandoned. He foresaw an alternative system that would parallel and, provided it was found to be functionally better, that would gradually but inevitably supplement the roman alphabet just as, over several centuries, arabic numerals had paralleled and largely replaced roman numerals.

*   *   *   *

In 1906 a list of reformed spellings for 300 words, recommended by the American Simplified Spelling Board, was endorsed by President Theodore Roosevelt who adopted them in his official correspondence. They were also approved by the majority of American educationists of the day and by the American National Education Association. This appeared at the time to be an important first step and it was followed up with a vigorous and influential campaign supported financially by Andrew Carnegie to the tune of some 300,000 dollars. By no means all the 300 recommendations were widely adopted and indeed the National Education Association withdrew its official support in 1921, but it is because of these events, together with the influence of the American lexicographer Noah Webster[2]

---

[1] Postcard from G.B.S. to Sir James Pitman, 7 August 1947. (*Plate X*).

[2] Webster also compiled a spelling-book used in teaching reading which became a best-seller with a reputed sale of 80 million copies.

(1758–1843) whose dictionary, particularly the earlier versions, specified certain innovations, that all Americans spell a small minority of words differently from the British and all the other users of the English language —e.g. *honor*, *center*, *labor*, *leveled*, *defense*, *program*—and that some Americans write *thru*, *thoro*, *catalog*, and so on.

The most that can be said for the American reform is that it was well-intended; none of the fundamental inconsistencies were tackled and, while the smallest improvement may appear to be better than none at all, it is arguable that the price for this handful of reforms is the necessity to Anglicize or Americanize and reset the type of many publications whose market embraces the whole English-speaking world. Limited though it was, the American reform amounted to a small-scale disaster for world-wide communication in the English language. By changing words like *centre* and *honour* to *center* and *honor*, it strained at the gnat only to swallow the camel. There would have been more point if changes had been made in the beginning of these words—i.e. the first, important stressed syllable instead of the unaccented ending. The condoning of the misleading *c* and *h* showed an astonishing misapprehension of the objective—whereas *senter* and *onor* would have been very helpful; in fact, *sentur*, *sentr*, *sentor*, even *sentyr*, or almost any final syllable, provided recognition was given to the fact that *c* furnishes a treacherous start to the word, would have been as well-conceived as *center* was ill-conceived. By appearing to be progressive, the American so-called "reform" merely prevented the chance of any worthwhile reform becoming acceptable. Worse still, the need for universal acceptance was overlooked; any change in convention that is not acceptable by the whole of the English-speaking world is a breach in the foundations upon which communication is founded. No attempt seems to have been made to induce non-American writers of English to agree to the changes and therefore American publications became to some extent unpalatable in all other countries including Canada—and vice versa. This has become a handicap to the interflow of knowledge, because a book, for example, has to be of major importance to justify the expense of reset-ting, even though few words are involved; for the rest publishers, whether in the United States or Britain or elsewhere, are naturally liable to hesitate before marketing a book with "foreign" spellings.

These differences between the two major branches of the English-speaking world represent the total achievement of much devoted effort, thought, and expense by a great many spelling reformers during the last century and a half—and, apart from a few minor improvements, such as reducing the incidence of final *-e* and the clearer differentiation between *u* and *v*, the previous two centuries achieved scarcely as much. The reasons why spelling reform has made so little headway are self-evident and so manifest that I shall touch upon only a few of them. First, it has to be recognized that the spelling reformer is asking a great deal of his own generation; many individuals will agree intellectually with the criticisms of orthodox spelling but few are prepared to accept the inconvenience and dislocation inevitable in adapting their reading habits—much less their writing habits—to even the most limited changes which, in any case, will bring benefits to posterity only and none whatsoever to those who are already literate. Another very convincing objection is that spelling reform cannot make spelling more simple unless full liberty is given to "spell as you please," that is to say: to spell as you speak. But unless all were to speak identically, or nearly so, which they do not, such licence would lead to the breakdown of the invariable, agreed, socially accepted forms that make printed, if not written, communication convenient. It is likely that a writer would be considered illiterate by a reader with a different pro-nunciation. Indeed, a licence to spell as you please is the reverse of spelling *reform*. The alternative is to insist that the new form of spelling must reflect what is the one-and-only, "acceptable" pronunciation and, quite apart from the difficulty of agreeing what this should be, this imposes a new kind of burden on the memory. Should we base the reformed spelling of the word *either* on the sound represented by *iether* or *eether* and, if we come from the South of England, we may prefer to leave out the *r* and opt for *iethe* or *eethe*; similarly is it to be *stuepid* or *stoopid* (U.S.); *birds* or *boidz* (Brooklyn); *hat* or *at* (Cockney); *sor thum* or *sau thum* or perhaps even *saur thum*? The sounds associated with *r* involve innumerable complications.

This whole question is discussed at length in the next chapter and I hope I have said enough to show that spelling reform would by no means abolish the problem of learning how to spell; at best it would merely replace the need to memorize the existing arbitrary spelling con-ventions by the need to memorize a new set of arbitrary conventions dictated by some kind of so-called authorized and inevitably in many cases unacceptable pronunciation.

These very tenable objections are supported by others that are more subjective. For the majority, the word-forms they read and write are understandably so closely linked with the language in which they think and feel and express themselves that they are sacrosanct and the refusal to countenance the smallest alteration is bolstered with ridicule and an almost aggressive loyalty to the established form. In particular, when deciding how our sons and daughters should be educated we are only too apt to look in the mirror and there find satisfying evidence that what is best for the new generations is what was good for ourselves. At all costs let us defend, albeit subconsciously, the goodly heritage and pass it on unaltered!

It is not difficult to see why the spelling reformer has always been good for an easy laugh, even among the Elizabethans. There were, as we know, learned men who recognized that it was not feasible to pronounce words as they were then spelled—but also that there was very little which could be done about it. At any rate it seems possible that Holofernes in *Love's Labour's Lost* was speaking with his tongue in his cheek in two senses—

> *Holofernes.* He draweth out the thread of his verbosity finer than the staple of his argument. I abhor such fanatical phantasimes, such insociable and point-devise companions; such rackers of orthography, as to speak dout, fine, when he should say doubt; det, when he should pronounce debt,—d,e,b,t, not d,e,t: he clepeth a calf, cauf; half, hauf; neighbour *vocatur* nebour; neigh abbreviated ne . . .
>
> *Love's Labour's Lost* Act V, Scene 1.

Three hundred years later my grandfather and A. J. Ellis had to be patient with the same brand of derision: *Punch* in the 1840s described their phonetic printing as "decidedly the most insane thing out of Bedlam,"[1] and made heavy-handed fun with what would happen to certain surnames if spelled in accordance with the "Phonetic, or Fanatic, principle of writing"—

> We can feel acutely for the long-established proprietors of these aristocratic names, if they are suddenly cut down from five or six syllables to only one or two, and thus put (literally speaking) upon half-pay. It is pitiful to consider how much they would lose in the eyes and ears of distinction! . . . Can you imagine the noble CHOLMONDELEY sinking in *Chumla*? . . . Again, how would anyone who had been christened MARJORIBANKS be able to recognize himself in the diminutive *Margbanx*? The great ST JOHN, also, would run with fright from *Cingin*, WEMYSS would abjure *Wims*, and PEPYS have a horror of *Pips*. . . . We advise the gentlemen whose complaints we have given a public voice to, to reform their names themselves, and to pronounce them in a manner more *consonant* with their real spelling; and by this remedy they will escape being put into the Procrustean bed by Mr

[1] "The Fonetic Solution for Hard Names." *Punch*, Vol. XVI, p. 84, 1849.

PITMAN'S alphabet, and coming out considerably less in print than they ever did before.

Thirty years later (1879) *Punch* printed a cartoon of my grandfather (Figure 12) and remarked that a letter of his to *The Times* was—

> . . . mainly a commendation of Vegetarianism and Teetotalism, which he, being now "siksti-feiv yeerz of aij", has practised for the last forty years. He testifies that—
>
> "Theez forti yearz have been spent in kontineus laibor in konekshon with the invenshon and propagashon ov mei sistem ov fonetik shorthand and fonetik spelling, korrespondenz, and the editoarial deutiz ov mei weekli jurnal."
>
> His "weekli jurnal" is of course the *Fonetik Nuz*, still alive and kicking, as the People say—kicking against etymology and common sense. Its longevity seems even more wonderful than its editor's survival of his "forti yeerz"

AN EVERGREEN VEGETARIAN

Figure 12. A cartoon of Sir Isaac Pitman which appeared in *Punch* of 15th February, 1879.

regimen to the "aij" of "siksti-feiv." His circulation has been maintained on that regimen, but what can have supported that of his paper?

Spelling Bees have for some time dropped out of vogue, or else a "Fonetik" Spelling Bee might answer Mr. PITMAN'S purpose of propagating his peculiar orthography. He would not, of course, be deterred from that expedient by any remark which might possibly be made that he had a Spelling Bee in his bonnet.[1]

The phonetic conservatism of the British was well characterized by Robert Bridges, the late Poet Laureate—

> . . . [the general reader) would admit the desirability of the letters having some fixed correspondence with sounds, yet he likes to think that ours in a manner share the pride of English liberty, and he would consider it almost an impertinence to enquire too narrowly into their behaviour. He has moreover a suspicion of all fine distinctions, and a prejudice against anything which threatens the comfort of an accustomed convention. He gets on, so he thinks, amazingly well as he is, and does not wish to be disturbed or have new paths opened to him.[2]

Divisions in the ranks of the spelling reformers have frequently weakened the campaign. Although during the first half of the century many on both sides of the Atlantic reached agreement under the twin banners of the U.K. Simplified Spelling Society and the U.S. Simpler Spelling Association, the large number of competing systems have led to a dispersal of energy only paralleled by the sects of dissenting Christians or the extreme left in politics. This tendency was satirized in the 1880s by an anonymous "Phreneticus" in lines entitled *Graphophonomachia: the Battle of the Signs and Sounds*, which depicted a horrid monster named Orthograph or Malefido who sits in a sunless vale protected by Custom against the assaults of the reformers—

> . . . Yet none the less
> The crippled monster bleeds at many a wound.
> First patriarchal Isaac[3] smote him hard
> With missiles forged in shapes unknown to men,
> Like the weird talismans in Egypt found,
> Graven uncouth, or those mysterious signs
> On Babel's arrow-headed cylinders.

---

[1] *Punch*, Vol. LXXVI, p. 61, 1879.
[2] *English Pronunciation*, p. 3. Clarendon Press, Oxford, 1913.
[3] Isaac Pitman.

XI Before the children learn to read systematically, pictures of well-known objects demonstrate the association of the concept with the appearance of the word printed in i.t.a.

XII *Upper :* Sir James Pitman demonstrates the practical value of being able to read.

Lower : The walls of the classroom and even the nature table provide reading practice.

But ere brave Isaac pierced the giant's cave
To thrust him to the heart, a digraph-shower
As thick as Vallombrosa's autumn leaves
Hurl'd him back breathless. Then his puissant peer,
Strong Alexander,[1] seized the two-fork'd forms,
Gather'd them, shaped them, polish'd them anew,
And with his own darts smote the giant down.
Again uprising, Malefido urged
Myriads of Mutes to beat the invader back
With soundless death. So Alexander failed.
Next a Welsh Knight[2] devised a magic charm
To lead the Mutes by many a devious path:

The multiplicity of solutions propounded over the centuries reflects not
only the failure to find one that is acceptable but, to my mind, it also
results from mistaken tactics. The understandable tendency to suggest
ever less provocative proposals (cf. the limited reforms promoted by
Regularized English with the far more thorough-going New Spelling,
though this itself was minimal in that it rejected additional characters) has
not merely jettisoned the radical measures essential to a spelling system
worthy of the name, but proved equally ineffective in overcoming hostility,
scepticism, and inertia. After half a lifetime as a spelling reformer and
after playing an active part in supporting Dr. Follick in his campaign for
New Spelling in Parliament and elsewhere, I decided therefore some years
ago that we were wasting our time and that it would be more sensible as
well as more desirable to concentrate on the more pressing part of the
problem: the teaching of reading. But meanwhile I had a promise to fulfil.
Shaw a few years before his death had written to tell me that he considered
I was ". . . the best equipped adventurer in the field"[3]—and later:
". . . remember: you are the man for the reform. You have no enemies and
a great phonetic name. My name is well known; but it raises clouds of
savage prejudice; and I am too old, too old."[4]

In the summer of 1947 I had motored down to Ayot St. Lawrence with
Professor Daniel Jones to try to persuade Shaw to leave funds to further
the aims of the Simplified Spelling Society and to dissuade him from

[1] Alexander J. Ellis, contriver of Glossic.
[2] E. Jones who advocated the use of *e* as a modifier to indicate long vowels.
[3] Letter from G.B.S. to Sir James Pitman, 19 July 1944.
[4] Letter from G.B.S., aged ninety-one, to Sir James Pitman, 16 December 1947.

backing a non-romanic alphabet. As it happened it was Shaw who converted me! I could therefore but agree to carry out the wishes in his will and to be responsible, at the request of the Public Trustee, for running the competition for the Shaw alphabet.

Quite apart from coming to believe that spelling reform, as normally understood, had no future and that the only hope of achievement lay in a root-and-branch transformation of the alphabet which would have to be extended and redesigned from first non-romanic principles, I could see that such an alphabet would have a further special virtue. It could offer a supplementary alternative to our present cumbersome system of handwriting. Designed as shorthand but with the simplicity of longhand, it could exist for personal use alongside the roman characters and thus reduce, in my grandfather's words[1]—

> . . . the greatest disparity, in point of facility and dispatch, between these two methods of communication: the former, speech, has always been comparatively rapid, easy and delightful; the latter, writing, tedious, cumbrous, and wearisome. It is most strange that we, who excel our progenitors so far, in science, literature, and commerce, should continue to use a mode of writing, which, by its complexity, obliges the readiest hand to spend at least *six* hours in writing what can be spoken in one. Why do we use a long series of arbitrary marks to represent what the voice utters at a single effort? Why, in short, are not our *written signs* as simple as our *spoken sounds*? It cannot be said that this is impracticable. . . .

There is certainly no reason why "hand-writing man", just because he has evolved and is now committed to particular visual forms for purposes of reading, should necessarily reproduce the same forms—often very badly!—in his personal correspondence. A new form of handwriting based on reliable phonemic principles could, provided it was speedy and convenient, soon catch on and not only replace the present assortment of illegible fists but also escape from the cumbrous legacy of ancient Rome with its incised stone lettering.

For this reason among others I welcomed the competition for Shaw's alphabet and very readily took on the job of organizing it, even though it was little more than a labour of love and one that would not conceivably yield serious benefits in my own lifetime. But the task is done. A Shaw alphabet has been created and published in the form he wished, and all may judge it for themselves. Perhaps there will be later and better systems?

[1] From introduction to *Phonography* (5th edition), pp. 5–16. Samuel Baxter, London, 1842.

Meanwhile, whatever the fate of Shaw's alphabet, generations of children and people from other countries have to struggle with the inconsistencies of roman characters and English spellings when learning to *read*. I asked myself: why should they have to wait until the adult community, for the most part literate, is converted to the need for Shaw's alphabet or any other non-romanic system, designed primarily to simplify *writing* and printing? There have always been a few teachers aware of the difficulties created for beginners by orthodox spelling, but I knew that they boggled at the idea of an overall spelling reform—and yet the evidence proving the success with children of the earlier experiments with Fonotypy, Dr. Leigh's alphabet, and New Spelling, though perhaps not sufficiently scientific or precise by modern standards, was impressive; there was a powerful prima facie case for believing that an alphabet and spellings inherited, virtually unchanged, from the Middle Ages is the root cause of difficulty and failure in reading, and that children do learn to read with a phonetic alphabet in a shorter time; for believing that the easiest way to learn to read orthodox spelling is to begin by learning with a rational and helpful alphabet—in other words that the transition need cause no difficulties. All this evidence seemed to have been forgotten and hidden by the controversy surrounding the attempts to convert the whole community.

An alternative approach was needed. By stages I reached the conclusion that the only way forward was to have a second but immediately practical type of reform, for new readers only. As an old advocate of New Spelling I had been sure that the schools were the best point of departure, yet now, unlike the New Spellers, I saw this not as a first stage in the changeover, not as a means of converting the whole community, but as an end in itself. Moreover, I had never been completely happy about a digraphic solution. Essentially this makes concessions to adults who can read at the expense of those, usually children, who are mentally confused by the employment of digraphs. The most urgent necessity was a radical and phonemically efficient reform which would be geared to reading rather than writing and be employed only during the early stages of learning, designed specifically to help make the job of learning to read and write *roman* characters and *orthodox* spelling speedier and less painful. This would be its *only* purpose. Restricted in this way to teaching, its necessity and the expense of casting and printing with new characters would be easier to justify.

None of the existing alphabets discussed in this chapter was completely suitable for the teaching of reading only, though Fonotypy came nearest to the kind of system I had in mind. I decided therefore to try to devise an alphabet based on my grandfather's principles but which took account of all that had been learned since his day. It would eliminate digraphs and provide an unambiguous "invariable" relationship between the characters and the phonemes required to speak English—*the*, the commonest word in the language, must not (cost what it might) appear to begin with *t*. Concentration on reading rather than writing, on facilitating the easiest possible transfer to roman characters and orthodox spelling, on the needs of beginners instead of the whole community, would certainly lead to the creation of a system that was imperfect when judged by the criteria of a complete spelling reform. But there would be no temptation to erode the root principles with compromises introduced to win over sceptical adults and it would be far more radical than most of the latter-day conciliating reforms with their lists of "regularities" and/or cumbersome additional digraphs which required characters to possess two, three, or even twelve sound values and which superficially, by eschewing new characters, seemed to prepare the beginner for orthodox spelling but in practice retained the very worst of the difficulties. I realized that I might be accused of selling traditional spelling reform, however mild and compromising, down the river because my kind of alphabet, if successful, would extinguish part—and the most convincing part—of the traditional reformer's case: if the problem of teaching beginners could be solved, the arguments against the dislocation and expense of a thorough-going spelling reform would be strongly reinforced. These considerations made me ponder, but not for long. The potential benefits to, maybe, generations of otherwise backward readers were too great.

The outcome of this conclusion is the Initial Teaching Alphabet—i.t.a. for short. The version described in the following pages was arrived at after years of study, experiment, and refinement.

Part II

Part 1

7   The Initial Teaching Alphabet

ſhe iniſhial teeɥiŋ alfabet has been desiend wiſh ſhe siŋgl puɼpos ov simplifieiŋ ſhe task ov leɼniŋ tœ reed iŋgliſh. as sœn as flœensy in reediŋ wiſh ſhe nue alfabet has been aɥeevd, a transiſhon is mæd tœ reediŋ wiſh ſhe orſhodoks rœman alfabet(s). i.t.a. dus not pretend tœ bee a nue **meſhod** ov teeɥiŋ; it is meerly a nue **meedium** ſhat can mæk aull ſhe egzistiŋ meſhods ov teeɥiŋ mor effectiv. . . .

Although some of the i.t.a. characters are unfamiliar, an adult does not find passages in the new alphabet difficult to read, even when he meets it for the first time. After very little practice they can be read by the average experienced reader speedily and without conscious effort. This is understandable because not only are the majority of the roman characters retained, but most of the additional characters bear a visual resemblance to and carry the familiar sound values of the roman characters or the pairs and groups of roman characters they replace. It was for this reason that the new alphabet was originally named "Augmented Roman," a title it was later thought advisable to discard because many people, particularly parents, were confused by it and supposed that their children were to be taught in some extinct alphabet similar to Greek or Hebrew rather than in an extended form of the alphabet with which they themselves were familiar. The correct typographical description is Ehrhardt Pitman Initial Teaching Alphabet (Monotype Ehrhardt Series 453); the new characters were designed by C. N. Fellowes and D. H. J. Schenck of the Monotype

Corporation who based their design upon an i.t.a. alphabet devised in 1953 by the famous calligrapher Alfred Fairbank. With this handsome foundation they skilfully fulfilled the requirements set them and produced characters that possess elegance as well as clarity and are also acceptable bedfellows with the existing roman typeface. The relationship of the characters to the respective sound values owes much to the skilful analysis of phonemes and most usual spellings set out in *New Spelling* by Walter Ripman and William Archer.[1]

Here is the printed form of the i.t.a. alphabet (Table X) and the names given to the characters. I have arranged the characters by rote because this has the advantage of being familiar and thus more convenient than any other order. It also is an international convention dating from early times— *aleph, beth . . . alpha, beta . . .* It will be seen that up to *z* two characters (*q* and *x*) are discarded and only the five traditional characters for vowels are replaced by new characters; the five traditional symbols come after *z* together with the fifteen other new characters (making a total of twenty augmentations) each of which effectively represents one phoneme only. Ten of the orthodox characters are renamed so as to indicate the sounds with which they should be associated and to avoid the misdirection suggested by the traditional names (e.g. *aitch* becomes *hay*; *double-u* becomes *way*). It is not suggested that a child need ever learn any character's name but, however much teachers may refrain from uttering them, the children themselves are apt to hear them. Some teachers may in any case feel the need to name the characters when correcting a child's handwriting. Indeed a character cannot for long remain nameless.[2] Printers need

---

[1] See footnote on p. 96.

[2] Characters need spoken names so that they may be talked about and phonemes need written names so that they may be written about. The names of characters ought to relate to the sounds they represent and be distinguishable from the names of all other characters, notwithstanding variations in pronunciation of the different speech-groups. The names of ten characters have accordingly been changed. Fortunately the initial elements of Nos. 1, 5, 9, 15, and 20 are such that the disturbance of traditional convention is minimal (and it is only temporary until the transition to the orthodox alphabet). To avoid confusion, the corresponding five short vowels have also been given new names. The addition of the *d* or *n* to all the names of the long vowels and of *t* or *g* to all the short ones not only maintains consistency but also of itself emphasizes the length of the long and the shortness of the short. It is important to respect the final consonant in the names of characters, and in particular the final *d* in *ahd* (No. 34) in order in this case to avoid confusion with the old name of the re-named *ray*.

The names of the phonemes (see Table XII, page 132) also ought to relate and be similarly distinguishable. The characters *k* or *p* have been used as endings for all the short vowel phonemes and *b* or *m* (or *me*) for all the long ones. Phonemes may be represented thus |*ak*|, |*aim*|, |*puh*|, |*buh*|.

TABLE X

Initial Teaching Alphabet by Rote

No.	Character	Name[2]	Example	No.	Character	Name[2]	Example
1.	æ	ain	æbl	23.	y	yay	yellœ
2.	b	bee	but	24.	z	zed or	zœ
3.	c	kee	cat			zee	
	d			25.	ʂ	zess	aʂ
4.	ḑ	did	ḑog	26.	wh	whee	whie
5.	єe	een	єeḉh	27.	ḉh	chay	ḉhurḉh
6.	f	ef	fun	28.	ţh	ith	ţhin
7.	g	gay	gæt	29.	ʄh	thee	ʄhen
8.	h	hay	hay	30.	ʃh	ish	ʃhip
9.	ie	ide	ies	31.	ʒ	zhee	meʒuer
10.	j	jay	jam	32.	ŋ	ing	siŋ
11.	k	kay	kiŋ	33.	ɾ	er	her
12.	l	el	lip	34.	ɑ	ahd	faʄher
13.	m	em	man		a	ask	
14.	n	en	not	35.	a	at	at
15.	œ	ode	œpen	36.	au	aud	autum
16.	p	pee	pæ	37.	e	et	egg
	q			38.	i	it	it
17.	r	ray	rat	39.	o	og	on
18.	s	ess	sit	40.	u	ug	up
19.	t	tee	top	41.	ω	oot	bωk
20.	ue	une	ueʂ	42.	ω	ood	mωn
21.	v	vee	vois	43.	ou	oun	out
22.	w	way	wet	44.	oi	oin	oil
	x						

instructions. A car number BHX 378 is inconceivable without the ability to speak it. It is as well therefore that the characters' names should not be misleading, at any rate during the early stages.

The function of the twenty additional characters is to make up for the deficiencies of the orthodox alphabet which, as we saw in Chapter 4, amount to a lack of at least seventeen characters. The reason for the four apparently gratuitous i.t.a. characters is that, as will be explained below, (1) both c (*kee*) and k (*kay*) have been retained; (2) the new character ᴡh (*whee*) is preferred to hw; (3) ƨ (*zess*) has been provided as an alternative to z (*zed*); and (4) ɼ (*er*) has been provided as an alternative to r (*ray*). It would have been possible to manage with fewer augmentations (see page 42); on the other hand it was tempting to introduce even more. A balance had to be struck between simplicity and effectiveness. The fewer the sounds catered for and the fewer the characters, the smaller the burden of learning in the first instance, but too crude a classification of sounds makes the identification of words more difficult; a more precise classification of sounds, in excess of the basic 40 phonemes in English, may make the identification of words somewhat easier, but at the expense of increasing the burden of learning and the difficulty of eventually making the transition to orthodox print. My final choice of 40 phonemes and 44 characters represents a balance that seems to be reasonable.

Fourteen of the augmentations are somewhat digraphic in that they are a combination of two or more roman characters. The combinations chosen are those shown by Ripman and Archer[1] to be the most usual in the representation of English speech syllables and therefore the most easily recognized by the eye when the time comes to transfer to orthodox print. Moreover a child finds it much simpler to learn the single, distinct characters ſh (*thee*) or ʈh (*ith*) instead of having to remember that the two separate characters which he has learned as having their own two particular values are also to be "thought of" as combining together in certain words, but not in others, to supply a single and quite different value. The same is true of ɕh (*chay*) for *c* plus *h* (but the traditional spelling has been retained in loch). The creation of these characters makes it possible for *h* to stand only for the phoneme that occurs at the beginning of a word like *hat* instead of having, as in New Spelling, to help represent five other different phonemes as well: *that* (ſhat), *thin* (ʈhin), *when* (ᴡhen), *church* (ɕhurɕh), *ship* (ʃhip). Similar reasoning applies to the other digraphic i.t.a. characters, although in one instance (ɔin) both the phonemes can actually be heard by a sophisticated ear yet not by the child.

Op. cit. Once the decision had been taken to create new characters, I possessed greater freedom and flexibility than was permitted by *New Spelling*, and there was no need to resort to confusing and ambiguous characterizations such as *dh* to distinguish between the two sounds of *th* in *the* (*dhe*) and *thin*, which in i.t.a. become ſhe and ʈhin. Similarly, *zh*, *uu*, and *aa* could be dispensed with and system introduced into the use of *ng*.

To the child these digraphic i.t.a. characters appear as and stand on their own as single, distinctive characters in the same way as we accept *w* as a single character although in fact it is digraphic, a double medieval *u* (*double vee* in French). The intention is for the constituent parts of the digraphic augmentations to coalesce sufficiently to be clearly distinct and memorable in the child's mind and yet also, with the ultimate transition to orthodox print in mind, to bear a strong visual relationship to the two or more separate roman characters by which the sound is normally represented. It is but a small step for the child, later on, to accept the unligatured *ch* as but a variant of ꨄ (*chay*), *sh* as but a variant of ʃh (*ish*); for ꨄurꨄ to turn into *church*, ʃhip into *ship*, bєєn into *been*, and so on.

With the i.t.a. alphabet each of the 44 characters can be directly and unambiguously presented to the reader as carrying a particular one of the 40 phonemes in the English language. He *always* knows where he is. Each character can be relied upon to convey invariably the same sound in speech, a sound appropriate to the part of a word it is helping to represent. There are no falsely implied relationships.

Instead of one character for six different sounds—
　　fat, fated, father, what, water, any
we have six different characters—
　　fat, fæted, faⱦher, whot, wauter, eny
and similarly with the other examples of inconsistency given on page 43—
　　me, met, pretty, Derby (the English town)
　　mєє, met, pritty, ꝺarby
　　fin, final, concertina, meringue
　　fin, fienal, consєrtєєna, meraŋ
　　hover, lover, rover, mover, choir, wolf, women
　　hover, luver, rœver, mꝏver, cwier, wꝏlf, wimen
　　pun, puny, full, rule, busy, bury
　　pun, pueny, fꝏll, rꝏl, biᴣy, bery
　　Confusion is likewise eliminated in those contrasting pairs and groups that so frequently muddle a child, such as
　　not her: mother; shorthand: northern; mishap: bishop; school: such
　　not heɼ: muⱦheɼ; ʃhorthanꝺ: norⱦheɼn; mishap: biʃhop; scꝏl: suꨄ

i.t.a. also abolishes the misleading differences in spelling that conceal a common factor of pronunciation; there are no falsely implied dis-relationships—for instance the variety of representation of the sound common to—

>*Caesar, quay, these, me, seen, tea, chief, seize, fatigue,*
>*machine, people, suite*

is represented consistently—

>ſee�249ar, kee, ſheeɤ, mee, ſeen, tee, ɕheef, ſeez, fateeg,
>maſheen, peepl, ſweet

similarly

>*chauffeur, most, yeoman, sew, boat, show, foe, go, brooch,*
>*folk, whole, soul, bureau, mauve*

become

>ſhœffur, mœst, yœman, sœ, bœt, ſhœ, fœ, gœ, brœɕh,
>fœk, hœl, sœl, buerœ, mœv

and *straight, halfpenny, make, fail, hay, great, eight,*
>*eh!, cabaret, fete, veil, deign, gaol, gauge*
>stræt, hæpenny, mæk, fæl, hæ, græt, æt,
>æ!, cabaræ, fæt, væl, dæn, jæl, gæj

and *aisle, assegai, McKay, ayes; seismic, height,*
>*eying, eye; I, phial, ice, indict, lie, sign, maligned,*
>*high, sighed, island, isle; choir; beguiling,*
>*guide, buy, guyed; sty, dye, style; rhino, rhinestone;*
>*rheinberry rhyme, rhyming*
>iel, assegie, mackie, ieɤ; sieɤmic, hiet,
>ieiꞑ, ie; ie, fieal, ies, indiet, lie, sien, maliend,
>hie, sied, ieland, iel; cwier; begieliꞑ,
>gied, bie, gied; stie, die, stiel; rienœ, rienstœn;
>rienberry, riem, riemiꞑ.

Admittedly, some of these words are not likely to be met with by a child of, say, five who is just beginning to learn to read because their meaning would be beyond his comprehension. To show how a child's early acquaintance with i.t.a. appears to him, some extracts from i.t.a. Readers are shown in *Plates XV* and *XVI.*

It will be noted that i.t.a. employs lower-case characters only, capitalization being achieved merely by making these larger. Lower case has been chosen because the child meets it far more frequently in books and because the presence of ascenders and descenders (i.e. characters that go above or below the line) endows each printed or written word with a more distinctive and thus immediately recognizable and memorable shape and outline. (Lower-case characters can truly be said to be more *characteristic* and differentiated from one another).

The replacement of the multiple variants of the roman alphabet such as *THE*, *The*, *the*, *the*, *the*, *The*, by the invariable and unequivocal *the* entirely removes the variations in the visual patterns of every single word. This in itself reduces the total of visual variations by a factor of probably more than five. If we also take into account the 658 different spellings that represent the phonemes as suggested on page 43, it will be seen that on balance there is an enormous gain in simplicity: in return for accepting 20 additional characters this load is lifted from the i.t.a. reader and he can concentrate unimpeded on perfecting his familiarity with only 44 associations linking character to sound. What is more, these associations are phonemically reliable and indicate each word by means of a rational and **unambiguous** visual image.

By breaking down the task of learning how to read into two main stages, the child is able at the very beginning of the first stage immediately to make adequate links between the printed or written words and his experience of the spoken language. The stability and reliable quality of i.t.a. fosters "constructive remembering" and furnishes him with a reliable alphabetic system with which to synthesize sounds from the characters. Repetition is free to reinforce associations between visual images and speech, and all confusion is eliminated. More complex words and sentences can be tackled with confidence because the child seeks out familiar groups of characters, knowing even from his short experience that he can build on them and that their values are always dependable. Many, not all, children find it difficult to learn several new things at a time and prefer to make sure about one thing before they move on to the next. By being temporarily protected from the illogical conundrums of orthodox spelling every child, and the one-thing-at-a-time child in particular, feels secure and can also therefore seek out meaning and comprehension from the secondary clues offered by the context. They are not bogged down by excessive memorizing and, as the syllabic relationships develop, they quickly solve the unfamiliar word by a syllable attack which replaces the per-*character* analysis and phonic synthesizing which, incidentally, can very easily become a bad habit, leading later on to slow reading speeds that are difficult to eradicate. Above all, the child is more likely to enjoy his reading from the start, to delight in the discovery that he can read to himself and so tell himself stories. As soon as he has gained fluency and skill at reading passages in i.t.a., and has sufficient linguistic competence, he is ready for the second stage, to make the transition to the roman alphabet. This he does with no significant loss in effectiveness. Confident in his own new-found ability to extract meanings from words, the inconsistencies and illogicalities of orthodox spelling seem far less puzzling and most of them turn out to be, as the Chinese put it, "paper dragons."

That is the essence of the case for the i.t.a. alphabet. The ease and speed with which the transition to reading the orthodox alphabet can be made of course constitutes its most decisive test. The mental processes involved and the extent to which the need for an effortless transition has influenced the design of i.t.a. are examined at length later in this chapter. Meanwhile we must deal with a closely allied question, that of the relationship of i.t.a. to the variations of pronunciation which are found within the English language which many fear must complicate the functioning of a phonemic alphabet, particularly if it is to be printed or written in a standard form.

VARIATIONS IN PRONUNCIATION

It is in the sounds of the vowels that variations are particularly noticeable and numerous. Bernard Shaw, when instructing his trustee in his will about the requirements of a new British alphabet, expressed the problem very succinctly: ". . . by infinitesimal movements of the tongue countless different vowels can be produced, all of them in use among speakers of

TABLE XI

Varieties of Pronunciation

	Kenyon & Knott[1]		Daniel Jones[2]	
	Entries	Variants	Entries	Variants
p. 100	34	67	35	71
p. 200	45	79	49	71
p. 300	37	90	41	77
p. 400	39	83	36	89
	155	319	161	308

[1] J. S. Kenyon and T. A. Knott. *A Pronouncing Dictionary of American English.* G. and C. Merriam, Springfield, Massachusetts, 1943 (date of preface).

[2] Daniel Jones. *English Pronouncing Dictionary*, Eleventh Edition. Dent, London, 1957.

English who utter the same vowels no oftener than they make the same fingerprints." Five minutes' study of any standard pronouncing dictionary will confirm what our ears tell us when we listen to someone with an "accent" different from our own. Table XI shows the quantity of the variants calculated in a random sampling of even the "cultured" pronunciations given in a well-known English and an equally well-known American publication. This works out at an average of just over two recognized, widely different pronunciations for each word in American speech and 1·9 for each word in English speech, even though Daniel Jones records only the limited "educated" southern variety of speech known as "Received Pronunciation (R.P.)." If we add the multiplicity of other variants of English pronunciation in America, England, Wales, Scotland, Ireland, Australia, New Zealand, West Indies, West Africa, and other Commonwealth and ex-Commonwealth countries with all their sub-variants, there is no doubt that, so far as listening is concerned, the total is virtually infinite. How, then, is it possible to construct a printed or written form of speech based on accurate representations of phonemes? How can it be done even within the confines of the United Kingdom in which the southerner says *food* (fꞷd) and *pub* (pub), and the northerner says *fŏŏd* (fꞷd) and *pŏŏb* (pꞷb), in which the Cockney says *woif* and *'ouse* and most of the rest of us in the country utter some variant of *wife* and *house*?

It is remarkable, and also significant, that we nevertheless do manage to understand each other. As Shaw also wrote:[1] ". . . the vowels used by the English people are as various as their faces, yet they understand one another's speech well enough for all practical purposes." The ear has been conditioned (in the Pavlovian sense) to tolerate very wide variations and to extract meaning from them all. In the speech of a single individual it is possible to detect three variants in the pronunciation of the definite article, the commonest word in the English language: (1) the apple; (2) the pen; (3) *the* best way; and no less than nine variants in the pronunciation of *and*: (1) bacon *n* eggs; (2) buttons *en* bows; (3) china *r[en]* glass; (4) apples *end* apricots; (5) India *[r]en* Japan; (6) charity *ern* good learning; (7) obvious *ernd* evident; (8) coming *eng* going; (9) *and* it came to pass. Practice in the unconscious art, in adjusting to these and other variants, begins virtually in the cradle and nowadays children, before they start to learn to read, are likely to acquire a considerable facility in understanding the great variety of pronunciations heard on television and radio,

[1] Preface to *The Miraculous Birth of Language*, by R. A. Wilson, p. xxvi. Dent, London, 1942.

even when the words they listen to have only a rudimentary relationship to the words they speak themselves. All that is necessary is that there is in any spoken sentence a linguistic resemblance to one or more versions of words they have heard and understood, sufficient to make comprehension possible; there is no need for a precise identification with or even similarity to the speech of any one listener.

A similar, but even more adaptable, process takes place when anyone reads. To the extent that the child "hears" the printed words in his head and works them out, he hears them in his own individual way of speaking. A northern child will read *food* as *fŏŏd* and a southern child as *fōōd*, and the same with *pŏŏb* and *pub*. This applies to reading with the orthodox alphabet(s) and spelling as much as to reading with i.t.a.—though with the latter the child soon discovers, almost certainly without realizing it, that the relationship of the printed i.t.a. language to his own spoken one is consistent and can always be relied upon. The pronunciation on which i.t.a. happens to be based will occasionally differ, as does the speech on the radio or television, from the one he has learned to speak. This in turn will differ in some respects from the speech of his own parents, because speech is personal—compared with printed words which are standard and universal. Speech is evanescent in time, but printed words are timeless. The printed form of any language tends to be the same in one book as in another, in one year and another, because it has to be widely shared, regardless of its readers' accents; and this inevitably has to apply even to a new printed language that seeks to represent the phonemes with greater accuracy. It has to be based on a single, notional pronunciation. Speech may well be personal and diverse but this is no argument for idiosyncrasy and diversification in print.

In the case of i.t.a. what is essential is that any pronunciation to which it is linked should not only be completely consistent and instantly understandable but that it should provide a printed form that bears as close a relationship as possible to the existing orthodox printed language—to help the learner eventually to read the orthodox being, after all, i.t.a.'s only purpose. The initial teaching alphabet was not invented to transcribe speech differences, but to establish a working relationship between the printed words and meaning; to be phonemically reliable so that the link between the printed and the spoken word is sufficiently effective to enable the printed word to be easily identified. The primary purpose of i.t.a. is not to teach pronunciation, though it can help remove bad speech habits (see pages 159–60), and the child will not be confused in that i.t.a. is not phonemically perfect. All that matters in order that i.t.a. may make *reading* easier is that the "acoustic impression"[1] should be adequate; that the spellings should convey the speech of mythical speakers who would be easily understood by any child in Birmingham, London, Glasgow, New York, Sydney, Auckland, Calcutta; in Kingston-on-Thames; Kingston, Ontario; or Kingston, Jamaica. The chosen form must be acceptable throughout the English-speaking world. It will be accepted —and to a large extent mingled in each child's head with the local pronunciation—just as easily as is the voice of the Queen broadcasting a Christmas message or of the U.S. President addressing Congress or the English of film actors whose voices are reproduced in all parts of the globe.[2] The child will learn and evaluate the i.t.a. characters in his own pronunciation, and will learn to read passages printed in i.t.a. without being aware that others ever could pronounce them differently, or that there might be a pronunciation problem at all. Indeed considerable liberties may be taken unbeknown to the majority of children or of grown-ups. For instance, the word sœlɟieɹ can be understood and recognized instantly by each reader even though, personally, he may pronounce it sœlja, sœljer, sœljia, or sœljier. This is likewise true of iether or been, even if the child has grown up to say eether or bin.

The effect produced in the reader by i.t.a. spellings can best be described as being that of a carefully articulated and not colloquial pronunciation, normally one which could be supported by at least one of the two pronouncing dictionaries[3] or by the *Oxford English Dictionary* and *Webster's*. This amalgam of pronunciations would be widely understood and accepted if delivered from public platforms, on television or radio, or on the stage, even though it would be difficult to discover any adult or child who speaks it in everyday life. It differs from Received Pronunciation but is similar to that adopted by Ripman and Archer in their *New Spelling*.[4] It also has, as intended, the advantage of achieving spellings in i.t.a. that are, relatively, closer to the orthodox spellings than would be possible with other pronunciations. I.t.a. opts for fœod and not fœd, for pub and wief

---

[1] See *Regularized English*, by Dr. Axel Wijk, p. 157.

[2] A further analogy is provided by (1) the Englishman who speaks some French and whose pronunciation, particularly of the vowels, is a good deal worse than his vocabulary or grammar—provided his mispronunciations are not too gross, he is understood; (2) dialect speech on the stage or in broadcasts, though the producer needs to exercise care in judging precisely when dialect starts to impede comprehension.

[3] Daniel Jones and Kenyon & Knott, op. cit.   [4] Op. cit.

and not pωb and wɔif. Each reader contentedly associates the i.t.a. form with his own particular pronunciation. Nor is anyone liable to have difficulty with stuepiḍ or wuɹk if, as some Americans, they say stωpiḍ and wɔik; or with mie tie if as Cockneys they say mɔi tɔi or mæ tæ as in very affected suburban London speech. These dialect variations are so consistent that the pronunciation is self-accommodating and the meaningful relationship between print and speech is readily maintained (see also [j] on page 138 on the *a* in words like *castle* and *bath*). Each group of readers will extract from the print their own personal version of the sound that happens to be for them the vowel sounds that possess significance. Attention has been paid not only to the pronunciations common in Scotland, Wales, and Ireland, but also those in the South of England and the North Midlands which also have their own distinct differences. In all these areas—and also in the United States, Canada, and Australia—I have listened to children reading the same i.t.a. words with their own national, regional, and sub-regional, accents. Indeed any mother, if blindfolded, could pick out her own child's voice in an i.t.a. class by means of the unmistakable individual tone and accent the child gives to words it sees in the silent, standardized, i.t.a. print.

In its search for an acceptable pronunciation which is also closest to the appearance of orthodox spelling, i.t.a. finds itself favouring pronunciations that are almost pedantic. Thus ḍelicæt is used rather than ḍelicit, ſundæ and not ſundi as in the lines from the songs: "The lass with the delic*ate* air," "Sun*day*, sweet Sun*day*, my one *day* with you" (see also note [f] on page 134). Abbreviations are normally written in full—misteɹ, missiꙅ—though certain other abbreviations are left unchanged. Pronunciations should, if anything, be "bent" to suit the orthodox spelling, rather than the other way round: often is therefore preferred to ɑufen or even ofen; and progress (verb) to prœgress. This also explains the noticeably Scottish and Irish flavour in the case of the augmentation ᴡh (*whee*) and the use of the vowels before *r*. In both these instances the Scottish pronunciation is preferred not only because it is unambiguous, very precise, and clear, but because it looks requisite for those who speak it, and because, since it conserves the orthodox appearance of the words, it prepares the way for the transition to orthodox print: ᴡheꙗheɹ is distinguished from weꙗheɹ, the bird teɹn from tuɹn, and fiɹ from fuɹ for those who make these distinctions in their speech, while for those who do not make them there is no more cause for hesitation than there is in the case of cat and kitten whose alternative characters for the same sound are accepted by *all* without difficulty. When they are ready for the transition stage, all children are helped by the linguistic clarity and the conservative effect this choice has on i.t.a. spelling because wheℐer will become *whether* and weℐer will become *weather*. The same applies to corn and faun, born and laun, etc.: the Scot automatically differentiates the words in each pair and by following his example i.t.a. spelling remains closer to the orthodox.

A similar choice has had to be made between rival pronunciations in pairs of words such as—

massed : mast	masst: mast
stupor : stooper	stuepor: stⲟⲟper
balm : bomb	bam: bom
cot : caught	cot: caut
aural : oral	aural: oral
saw : sore	sau: sor
higher : hire	hieer: hier
merry : marry : Mary	merry: marry: mӕry
flower : flour	flouer: flour
layer : lair	lӕer: lӕr
ewer : your	ueer: yⲟⲟr

In some regional pronunciations the words in each of these pairs sound identical but in every case the i.t.a. characterization and spelling echo those alternative pronunciations that discriminate between them. Not only does this enable i.t.a. to keep closer to the orthodox spelling, but it also allows for a proper respect for the interests of readers whose speech makes these discriminations; those whose speech does not recognize the discriminations will disregard them happily when they see them in print. No child is ever presented with a form that is not immediately understandable. The principle of retaining the *r* is advisable for a further reason. Most people who rhyme *sore* and *saw* do so only when the word is followed by a pause or by a consonant. When each is immediately followed by a vowel, the *r* returns to furnish the distinction: all those who say ℐe ca woꭍ for ℐe car woꭍ produce the *r* in ℐe car iꭍ. Another advantage of preserving these discriminating pronunciations in print is that it avoids the unnecessary creation of words which look and sound alike. For a southern Englishman both *father* and *farther* should phonemically be faℐer, but this would merely heap confusion on confusion. All such words cannot be eliminated by i.t.a., but it may be worth noting that i.t.a. *could* (but does not) distinguish many of them without lessening ease in reading—e.g. bɑrk (tree), bɑrrk (dog). On the other hand words which look alike but sound different are of course spelt differently—e.g. bœ (archery), bou (obeisance); rou (quarrel), rœ (a boat); woond (injure), wound (coiled); sueer (drain), sœer (sempstress).

To fail to adopt a completely phonemic system may at first appear as a betrayal of the central principle of the new alphabet, but these departures from phonemic perfection are not only justified but advantageous, provided the learner is furnished with an adequate "acoustic impression" and an effective clue by which the word can be identified—e.g. sœldier is quite adequate as a clue; and provided also that—

(1) orthodox spellings are conserved—e.g. letter—or a closer similarity ensues—e.g. about rather than ubout—and thus the extent of the eventual transition is reduced; or

(2) a meaningful relationship is indicated between one word and another —e.g. sun-dæ, hand-cuff, pœst-card, as opposed to sun-dy, haŋ-cuff, pœs-card.

There is no point in preserving phonemic purity for its own sake. After all, we are not concerned with a root-and-branch system of spelling reform. Whereas any close continuity or resemblance cannot be achieved in the cases of *once* and *ought*, there would be more loss than gain by interfering with letter and dustbin or by making sœldier any less like *soldier*. To allow, in certain instances, more than one characterization for a single phoneme (e.g. c and k; t and tt) does no great harm and certainly is not to be likened to the opposite process of allowing a single character to represent other than its own particular phoneme. Purists may be disappointed that the short unstressed "*i*" is represented not only by i and y but also by e in printed and ekwætor and by æ in sundæ, dœtæj, etc.—see (*f*) on page 134; similarly, that the short unstressed *schwa* is represented by a, e, i, o, u,y, au, ou, in about, happen, æpril, kiŋdom, upon, mɑrtyr, restaurant, portsmouþ, and by ue and ie in pictuer and ʃropʃhier; they may grieve that an even more serious departure from this central rule (albeit a "consistent" departure) has been made in the case of the neutral vowel in the speech of certain regions—see (*h*) on page 135. But all these departures from phonemic perfection are minor and have been most carefully weighed and can be justified because they serve our essential purpose—to make the eventual reading of orthodox print easier.

The situation is also made clearer when the i.t.a. characters and their combinations are arranged opposite the 40 phonemes (Table XII, page 132).

The table is a simple, possibly over-simplified, explanation of the character-to-sound relationships of i.t.a. It should suffice for most readers who are advised to turn to page 139. The following sections (*a*) to (*j*) have, however, been added for anyone who wishes to go more deeply into the analysis of characters, of sounds, and of the alphabetic patterns in our traditional print which underlie the design of i.t.a. and the choice of its spellings—

(*a*) *Double consonants.* If the word is normally spelt with a double character, this is preserved in i.t.a. spelling, even though there may be no strict phonetic justification for it. One might expect the word *middle* to become midl, but midl has been preferred because the clue to the intended sound is one hundred per cent effective[1] and there is the advantage that it remains closer to orthodox spelling—in fact tautology by character is not actively misleading and in this instance can even be helpful. This rule applies to all words with double consonants (e.g. ill, beginnig, jabbd, foggy, etc.) whether or not the double consonant has phonetic significance in orthodox spelling (cf. *midday* and *midden*; *innate* and *innocent*).

(*b*) c (*kee*) and k (*kay*). Alternative characterizations have been preserved for the phoneme *kuh*; phonetically one or other is redundant, but their incidence in orthodox spelling is nicely balanced[2] and to eliminate one or the other would cause a considerable upheaval and cause difficulties when the transition stage is reached. Moreover, to keep both is not likely to confuse the reader. This same reasoning and the lack of serious objections to tautology has preserved cc, ck. The *c* is therefore kept in cat, the *k* in kig, the *ck* in back, the *cc* in tobaccœ. The roman character *x*, which contains more than one phoneme, is achieved by combining k and s (e.g. foks), or g and s (e.g. egsact), or k and ſh or ʒ (e.g. lukſhuerius). Similarly *qu* is achieved by combining k and w (e.g. kwɛɛn, kwick) or by k alone—e.g. kɛɛ (*quay*), tork (*torque*). In an earlier version of i.t.a. the character k was

---

[1] The difference lies only in the division into syllables. In typewriting the division at the end of a line would fall at mid-dle rather than at mi-ddle, which seems to be logical. The need to divide words such as mid-day, in-navigable, etc., in this manner is even more justified, because there is a slight pause in speech. Admittedly mid-dle is not in the same category but even if it were no child could understand the logic of printing a double character in the one case, but only a single character in the other. In any event no teacher has reported any sign of difficulty in practice by reason of this tautology.

[2] See also Ripman and Archer's analysis in *New Spelling* (sixth edition), pp. 20–23.

131

TABLE XII

Initial Teaching Alphabet by Phonemes[1]
40 (+1) Analysis[2]

	Consonants				Vowels	
No.	Example	Name*		No.	Example	Name*
1.	pæ	puh		25.	appl	ak
2.	but	buh		26.	faðer	ahm
3.	top	tuh		27.	egg	ek
4.	ḍog	duh		28.	æbl	aim
5.	cat / kitten	cuh		29.	it	ip[5]
				30.	eeḍh	eem
6.	gæt	guh		31.	on	ok
7.	fun	fuh		32.	aull	aub
8.	vois	vuh		33.	up	uk
9.	þhin	thuh		34.	œpen	ome
10.	wiþh	then		35.	tꝏk	oop
11.	sit	suh		36.	mꝏn	oob
12.	zꝏ / az	zuh		37.	ies	ibe
				38.	out	oum
13.	ʃhip	shuh		39.	boi	oim
14.	meʒuer	zhuh		40.	uez	ume
15.	ḍhurḍh	chuh				
16.	jam	juh				
17.	man	muh				
18.	not	nuh				
19.	siŋ	ung				
20.	lip	luh				
21.	riŋ	ruh				
22.	hat	huh				
23.	wet	wuh				
24.	yellœ	yuh				

(+1) The central, neutral or relaxed vowel.[2]

urd	uhr	uh
her	faðer	happen
sir	eliksir	pensil
fur	arþhur	upon
myrtl	martyr	meþhyl
	pœlar	about
	auþhor	atom
	ʃhropʃhier	fuetiel
	figuer	ferruel

* See footnote 2 on names on page 118.
[1] Strictly speaking, this should be "diaphones," but see explanatory footnote on page 41.
[2] See (h), pages 135–7.

adopted as a compromise for *c* and *k*, but Ripman and Archer's analysis of the incidence of *c* and *k* in orthodox spelling, together with the consideration that children find little if any difficulty in accepting this limited use of alternative characters, justifies the retention of both characters instead of ʞ. This use of c and k (unless ꞅ and z, r and ɼ, be counted as being effectively different) is the only departure from the principle that there should be only one visual representation for any one of the forty sound classifications.

(*c*) z (*zed/zee*) and ꞅ (*zess*). To the child these characters are virtually indistinguishable and they both represent the phoneme *zuh*, but ꞅ (*zess*) is used wherever in orthodox spelling the sound is represented by *s*. In fact the orthodox character *z* appears seldom for this sound, whereas *s* is misleadingly used very frequently: cf. zꝏ, ꝺuzen, zeebra; aꞅ, woꞅ, hiꞅ, ꭍœꞅ, flieꞅ, etc., etc. These two i.t.a. characters help to overcome this difficulty and to make the transition smoother, ꞅ being visually a link with *s*; at the same time ꞅ and s are far more dissimilar and certainly sufficiently so to enable a discrimination to be made between hiꞅ (*his*) and hiss. A comparable similarity in appearance has been attained in w (*way*), ꝏ (*oot*), and ꝏ (*ood*), though here we are dealing not with three identical phonemes but with three related yet detectably different ones. So closely related are they that they may be interchanged without diminishing significantly the clue to the reader. It is thus fortunate that a similarity exists between the characters which is matched by a similarity in the phonemes.

(*d*) ꜭh (*chay*) and tꜭh, stion, tuer. When *t* precedes *ch* in normal spelling, it is retained in i.t.a., though phonetically it is tautologous; e.g. matꜭh, hutꜭh, witꜭh because the sound *chuh* can be split into the two constituent sounds *tuh* and *shuh* (tʃh) and, in effect, we are merely duplicating the *tuh* to create *tuh-tuh-shuh*. This does not apply to whiꜭh. In words like kwestion and nætuer, the sound in colloquial speech is that of *chuh*, but there is no need to depart thus far from the orthodox spelling. The pronunciation of *tuh* and *yuh* when spoken rapidly in sequence becomes *tshuh*, i.e. *chuh*. (The identity in pronunciation between the three different forms: briet yuꞃ thiꞃꞅ, briet ꜭhuꞃ ꭍhiꞃꞅ, and brie ꜭhuꞃ ꭍhiꞃꞅ makes clear both the vestigial y (*yay*) sound between the sound of ʃh (*ish*) and any succeeding vowel and also the fact that ꜭh (*chay*) contains a tʃh and that ttʃh is the same as tꜭh and ꜭh.) Similarly the vestigial *yuh* "glide" which is inescapable after *shuh* and *zhuh* in words like speʃhial and œʃhean justifies the retention of the *i* and *e* which have the same short semi-vowel value as *y*. In words like *sure* and *azure* the glide is in effect conveyed by the *yuh* sound which is represented initially by the character ue in the diphthong as in ʃhuer and aʒuer.

(*e*) j (*jay*), dʒ (*didzhee*), and dj (*didjay*). When the orthodox spelling is *dg*, dʒ is used instead of j: e.g. wedʒ, judʒ. Besides being closer to the orthodox spelling this does not impede recognition of the sound because *juh* is made up of the two phonemes *duh* and *zhuh*. Similarly dj is used in such words as adjust.

(*f*) i (*ip*), y (*yay*), e (*et*), and æ (*aim*). The sound of y is what is known as a semi-vowel, and thus the sounds of y and i are closely related; where precisely the vowel begins and the consonant ends is difficult to determine. In *yet* the sound of the consonant-element is dominant and so it is in *million*; in *lanyard* the *y* could be described as a consonant or a vowel; in *very* it is unmistakably a vowel. Three practices emerge—

(1) These two phonemes are usually represented by either y or i, as the orthodox spelling has made conventional. In the rare Welsh name iœlœ it is right to keep the *i* of the orthodox spelling as it is in spaniel; in the name yvonn as in very it is right to keep the *y*; in yellœ and million the choice is even clearer.

(2) In ærea, galleon, etc. the *e* is kept as in the case of ekwætor, printed, where the sound is that of *i* rather than *y*.

(3) æ is retained in words such as sundæ, birʃhdæ, dœtæj, etc.

(*g*) ue, yue, yco. When the phoneme which *y* represents is linked with the other phoneme *oob*, they merge to produce the phoneme *ume*; y[*yuh*] and co [*oob*] = ue [*ume*]: e.g. due, fue, uenicorn. This is the first of the choices open; it will be seen that ue is preferred whenever a word in orthodox spelling begins with a *u*. When it begins with a *y* (e.g. *yule, yew, you*), the *y* is preferred and there is a further choice between yue and yco and the preference is obvious: yuel, yco, yco. Where it begins with *ew* (e.g. *ewe, ewer, Ewell*), ue is preferred. We thus have—

ue		yue		yco	
ues	(*use*)	yuel	(*yule*)	ycoʃh	(*youth*)
uenicorn	(*unicorn*)	yuegoslav	(*Yugoslav*)	yco	(*you*)
uenit	(*unit*)			ycorʒ	(*yours*)
ue	(*ewe*)				

There are of course many other ways in which y, i, ee, co, co, ue, could be combined to yield what could easily be read as representing the sound of ue, but these possibilities only emphasize what has been stressed earlier: that the purpose of i.t.a. is to assist reading and not to provide a medium for precise transcription. Only two criteria are relevant: Will it be easy to read? Does it resemble as nearly as possible the orthodox form of the same word?

(*h*) *Neutral vowels* (*urd, uhr, uh*). This *apparent* departure from restricting the use of a character to only one sound value is due to the prevalence in the speech of many of what is termed the central or neutral vowel—or, as I prefer to call it, the relaxed vowel—which is in two main groups, either long (stressed) as in *sermon, work, surf,* or short (unstressed or weak) as in *about, upon, sofa* and *pillar, energy, Arthur.* Strictly speaking, there is an intermediate group as in the middle of the word *fostering* which differs from *stirring.* In orthodox spelling it has never been directly represented and the question arises whether there is as great a need for a special i.t.a. character as in the case of the other 40 sounds. One difficulty is that on the one hand in speech areas where the *r* tends to be dropped children find difficulty in reading *fern, first, turn* because the presence of the *r* puzzles them and therefore a specific new character, with no trace of an *r*, would help them; on the other hand children in speech areas where the *r* is strongly pronounced would be equally misled by the absence of any *r*. Another difficulty is that a new character for the neutral vowel would have to appear in a great many words and even give rise to an alternative spelling wherever lack of stress transforms a vowel's sound (e.g. *and, have, to,* etc., would need to have one spelling for their unstressed (weak) form and another for their stressed form).

My grandfather exhaustively discussed whether or not it was desirable to exclude the neutral vowels from a phonemically adequate alphabet. In the end he decided that it was possible to exclude them, as has been the case with Pitman's shorthand which has managed well enough without them and has satisfied millions of users for more than a century. Although it means retaining four alternative representations for the long (stressed) neutral vowel—er(her), ir(sir), ur(fur), yr(myrr); and having no less than eighteen—a(about), e(happen), i(pensil), o(kiŋdom), u(upon), ie(fertiel[1]), ou(portsmouth), ue(ferruel), ω(tω), ar(pœlar), er (muther), ir(eliksir), or(author), ur(sulfur), yr(martyr), au(restaurant), ier(ʃhropʃhier), uer(pictuer)—for the short (unstressed) neutral vowel, it has been found to be justified; no doubt this is because, being a

---

[1] American pronunciation only.

relaxed vowel, it is easier for the reader to relax it. For instance, it is easier
to pass in reading from the emphatic *and* (and it wos ſhe sabbaſh) to the
relaxed form (bæcon 'n eggs) rather than in the reverse direction. A single
character could easily have been introduced for each and in fact the symbols
have been brought into existence by me—ʋ (long) and ɑ (short)[1]—but
their introduction would have necessitated considerable and unnecessary
departures from normal spelling which would have been particularly
harmful and indeed confusing in some parts of the English-speaking
world.

Carried to its logical conclusion, it would have involved many variant
forms. Even the commonest word *the* would have needed to appear in
three forms ſhi appl, ſhɑ pen, and ſhee wun ɑnd œnly wæ. In its
stressed form the neutral vowel may be conveniently implied by the use of
the alternative character ɼ (*er*). Moreover, with its similarity to r (*ray*), this
character achieves the desired compromise for those who utter, as in Scotland, what I call the "controlled" vowels (e.g. who pronounce *tern* and *turn*
with a difference which relates the former to *ten* and the lattter to *tun*). It
thus "optionally modifies" the vowel which precedes it. In Scotland there
is no need for the teacher to call the attention of the child to the small
difference between ɼ and r because the Scottish child pronounces the *e*
and *u* in *tern* and *turn* differently and very strongly pronounces the *r*.
Elsewhere however the teacher should call the attention of the child to the
difference between ɼ and r because teɼ in *tern* and tuɼ in *turn* have to
him the same sound value (though spelled differently) and with, in many
cases, not even a trace of the sound of *ruh*, and without the differing
values as in *terrify* and *turret*.

With the single exception of *colonel*, the long (stressed) neutral vowel
always appears in orthodox spelling with the corresponding character *r*,
and i.t.a. retains this in its modified form (ɼ), following *e, i, u,* and *y*.
Similarly, although there is in the speech of many no invariable connection
between the short (unstressed) neutral vowel and the character *r*, this is
employed in the modified form whenever the *r* appears after *e, i, u,* and
y. Many people, not only in Scotland, use at least two, if not even three
different vowel sounds in saying *her, sir, fur, myrtle*, but their pronunciation does not then contain the long (stressed) neutral vowel but a vowel
noticeably close to the usual value of *e, i,* and *u,* or *y* followed by an *r*.

---

[1] The two characters are available in printers' founts and on some typewriters: they are
intended only for phoneticians who may wish to make use of i.t.a. for their special purposes.

Because they are generally understood without difficulty there is every-thing to be said for keeping thus close to the orthodox spellings for such words as heʀ, siʀ, fuʀ, and myʀtl. The value of Scottish pronunciation and of careful, enunciated, almost pedantic speech is here again very relevant, because this in itself makes it practicable to eliminate the neutral vowel from the i.t.a. alphabet. The final syllable in perʈhʃhier which is pronounced by the Scots to rhyme with *shire*, and not with the neutral vowel, demonstrates this; moreover, the elimination of the neutral vowel from the alphabet prevents *Countess of Ayr* appearing like *County Sur-veyor*, or *She was a tanker* like *She was at anchor*. Another advantage of avoiding new characters for the neutral vowel is that helpful or instructive cross-relationships are retained as in: perʈhʃhier, ʃhier-haull; pœlar, pœlarity; metal, metallic; auʈhor, auʈhority; rector, rectorial. Simi-larly the use of the character ie in the final syllable of words such as fuetiel is justified because the spellings are in closer agreement with the orthodox spellings—i.e. if the English pronunciation be preferred to the American, the latter child being more easily accommodated in that for him the adjust-ment is no more than the kind of relaxation he applies to so many words.

What might be termed a side-effect of providing the ʀ (*er*) character is that whenever the character r (*ray*) is preceded by i.t.a. short vowels e, i, u, or y, the i.t.a. character would have needed to be doubled in order to preserve the sound of the vowel (i.e. if not doubled, it would become one of the characters used to represent the sound of the neutral vowel—er, ir, ur, yr). It is thus convenient to continue to print very, spirit, curæj, and syrup instead of needing to change them to verry, spirrit, etc. To be consistent it is likewise necessary to convert only one of the rs (*ray*) into an ʀ (*er*) to represent the neutral vowel in words which in ortho-dox spelling contain the double r before the neutral vowel: e.g. eʀriŋ, stiʀriŋ, puʀriŋ and to revert to r (*ray*) as in muʃheriŋ, i.e. whenever a vowel follows.

When the short (unstressed) vowel appears without a succeeding r the full vowel sounds provided by i.t.a. are again considered to be sufficient, whether the neutral vowel is positioned at the start of a word (abœut, enuf, obæ, upon), in the body (metal, œpen, pensil, kiŋdom, minimum, fuetiel, ferruel), or at the end (sœfɑ, to, ʈhe before a con-sonant). These representations not only convey meaning unambiguously if a little pedantically to readers in all speech areas, but they also conserve the orthodox spellings.

137

(*i*) ḍ (*did*). In the early stages of learning to read i.t.a. the extension downwards of the upright stroke in d, so that it appears ḍ, has been found helpful by children because it increases the characteristic value and lessens the risk of confusion between d and b—the "mirror" reversal referred to in Chapter 3. (Other similar characters—n and u; a and d; n and h; v and y; o and ɑ; c, e and o—were also considered and special types were designed for n and u, but it was decided to make no further changes in the retained roman characters because to do so would have entailed reducing the similarity between i.t.a. and orthodox characters.) The child is also helped to discriminate between these two characters by the method by which he is taught to write them. As can be seen from the printed b, the crayon or pencil is employed in a continuous line, as if it were the numeral 6, with a very straight back. On the other hand the child writes ḍ with a discontinuous action—a straight downstroke, a lift, and then a semicircle.

(*j*) Ambivalent a. In certain speech areas the sound given to a and ɑ is not consistent (or, in linguistic terminology, does not lend itself to diaphonic treatment). Whereas anyone who says pꝏb (rather than pub) is certain also to say mꝏᴅh, lꝏv, ʃꝏv, hꝏg, etc., those who say cɑsl (rather than casl) never say cɑt (rather than cat); equally those who say casl (rather than cɑsl) do not say pam for *palm* (rather than pɑm). To overcome this difficulty, an "in-between" a (a, a, ɑ) has been adopted. When reading in i.t.a. those who say baᴛh associate the a with a, while those who say baᴛh associate it with ɑ. This character, being a compromise between two already closely related shapes, involves too sophisticated penmanship for practical use in the classroom. It is intended for use only in print or in typewriting; moreover, it is desirable that teachers should encourage the child to interpret it as a or ɑ according to his or the particular regional pronunciation. At any rate it has been found to be workable and it enables i.t.a. to adhere to the principle of not subordinating the speech of the more discriminating speaker (e.g. in the case of mast and masst) and of ensuring that no reader will ever discover an i.t.a. character that for him has one value in one word and a different value in a different word (e.g. cat and cast will, as expected, have the same value to one kind of reader while cast and cɑrt will have the same value for another).

These rules will at first appear to be very complex and it is scarcely necessary to stress that they do not have to be mastered by the child. As a reader the child is happily unaware of them. Even the teacher of a class of new readers does not need to understand them in detail, although they are essential to a complete and comprehensive description of how the new alphabet has been constructed and is printed. They have also to be understood by anyone who prepares duplicated, or blackboard, material in the alphabet for teaching purposes. But the child, as a writer, should be left happily free to write as he pleases, provided only that he uses what is after all merely an *inter*medium in such a manner that his writings are understood. I have been pleased to see displayed on classroom walls compositions in which even єєꞷ has been written for *you*!

Despite these departures from phonemic perfection i.t.a. does succeed in reducing the task of learning over 2,000 representations of 40 phonemes to one of learning the values of only 44 characters. For the very young reader—and it is for the *reader* that i.t.a. has been designed—the values of the 44 characters in relation to the sounds they represent remain uncompromised. Overriding every other consideration is the desire to establish an easy working relationship between print and meaning—with sound playing a beneficial part in assisting it. Comprehension is all-important even at the earliest stages of reading and must be enlisted to buttress word recognition. While the representation of the sounds by i.t.a. characters need not be phonemically perfect, they are a reliable guide through sound. The characters must represent sounds which, if spoken out loud by anyone or if imaginatively heard in the reader's mind, would be unfailingly understood in context as syllables and words and sentences. Reading is a practical art and we are not concerned with teaching children to rattle off a collection of meaningless but correct sounds. The importance attached to meaning is well illustrated by the treatment of a word like *the* which is invariably ꞇhe even though it is often pronounced ꞇhєє, ꞇhi or ꞇhɑ—ꞇhe is preferred because it happens to be the orthodox spelling. The same applies to the word *to*; in the sentence "He said *to* me that he could see clearly close *to*, but needed glasses *to* see at a distance," the word *to* has three distinct sounds in the speech of most people, but i.t.a. adheres to the single form tꞷ. There is no justification here in creating different forms for the orthodox, invariable spelling; to do so would mean confronting the child with an unnecessary complication and only impede the ability to recognize and extract the intended meaning from the print.

The reader will by now, I hope, understand some of the niceties involved in perfecting this alphabet, how it may appear that, while i.t.a. enables a logical system of representing speech to be established, it then at once proceeds to weaken it with exceptions and reservations. Although the central principle of phonetic simplicity and reliability is never departed from for the purpose of *reading*, although the sound represented by each of the 44 characters is invariable and unambiguous, there are indeed in its *writing* many compromises with "pure theoretical phonetic truth," between this and the need to adhere as nearly as possible to orthodox spelling and the conventional appearance of words. The reason for this has already been explained, but it deserves reiteration. Being a medium for teaching reading—or as some may prefer: a learning device—and not a spelling reform, the choice of i.t.a.'s spellings has been very flexible. Its purpose is limited as well as temporary. Phonetic considerations are relevant only in so far as they impede or foster the process of learning to read, the extraction of meaning from the silent page. Each decision has to be weighed and assessed in relation to the eventual objective: to provide an easier, surer way of teaching meaningful reading of texts printed in the roman alphabet and with orthodox spelling, and to infuse the process of learning with enjoyment from the very start. In designing the characters and in deciding how they can be best employed in the representation of each word, this objective has been paramount.

TRANSITION TO THE ROMAN ALPHABET(S) AND
ORTHODOX SPELLING

The divergencies from orthodox spelling caused by the systematic use of the Initial Teaching Alphabet can be estimated as follows: for the purpose of the calculation, the frequencies with which various words recur in continuous English are based on the sample provided by Dewey's *Relativ Frequency of English Speech Sounds*[1]—

(*a*) Words unchanged,
    e.g. *and, in, it, for, not, but, had, did, got*   26·5%
(*b*) Words changed, but only by a minor modification,
    e.g. ſhe, ſhat, iʒ, our, been, suɥ, ſhell, gꙩd.   23·75%
(*c*) Words changed, but with the retention of much that is
    familiar, e.g. hav, mꙩv, nou, gon, hors, tiem   10·5%
(*d*) Words radically changed, e.g.
    aut (*ought*),   hꙩ (*who*),   wun (*one*),   duʒ (*does*),   39·25%
    jæl (*gaol*),   hœl (*whole*),   cof (*cough*).   100·00%

[1] Op. cit.

These last three categories are necessarily matters of individual opinion, but different analyses are unlikely to differ much in total. The last group includes some of the most frequently recurring words in English and they are the easiest words to guess from the context and the more readily remembered. Roughly speaking, 50–60 per cent of words are virtually unchanged or subject to only minor modifications and, notwithstanding the variety of compromises permitted by the i.t.a. system, the inconsistencies and contradictions of orthodox spelling lead to at least 40 per cent of the changes being classed as "radical."

Despite this high figure, the transition from reading i.t.a. texts to reading orthodox texts is smooth and effortless. The case for the new alphabet stands or falls on the validity of this assertion because i.t.a. would possess little merit if early progress were bought at too high a price in later progress, if the time gained in bypassing the difficulties of orthodox spelling was equalled or exceeded by the time taken by the average reader in making the transition to orthodox texts. It would likewise be rightly dismissed as a curiosity if it transpired that readers taught with its help had an inferior comprehension of orthodox texts, were poorer at orthodox spelling, or—and this is the most vital test—produced an equally depressing percentage of backward readers among adolescents and adults.

The research described, together with the selection of teachers' opinions in a later part of this book, is the most satisfactory and, indeed, remarkable proof that what is claimed for the new alphabet is justified and now set beyond any but prejudiced doubt. The rest of this chapter is limited to examining the mental processes involved in the transition and to re-emphasizing that the requirements of the transition stage have throughout governed and influenced both the design of the i.t.a. characters and the manner in which they are used.

Most children who begin to learn reading at five or six are ready for the transition stage by the age of six or seven, though such educational generalizations are always dangerous and many by this age will have graduated much earlier to orthodox texts. Once the pupil has acquired complete fluency in reading and comprehending i.t.a. texts suitable to his experience and vocabulary, age and intelligence, so that he can read effortlessly in great "gulps," he is ready to face the difficulties and inconsistencies of orthodox spelling. To write in these terms is, however, misleading as there is in reality no sudden or abrupt change. The transition process has to be thought of as an adjustment rather than as the learning of something new or the unlearning of what is already established. The child ready for the transition stage can read already. He utilizes considerable linguistic skill in dealing with printed words and the fluency acquired in reading i.t.a. is transferred smoothly over to the orthodox medium. There may be a temporary slowing down in the speed of reading or hesitation over the irregular words, almost amounting to a setback. But it will be minor and short-lived, for he is not being asked to tackle a printed language that is strange and wholly unknown but one with which he is already on familiar terms, and for which i.t.a. has groomed him. The similarity between the appearance of i.t.a. words and of words with orthodox spelling and characters means, in effect, that an extra-curricular transition stage begins "unofficially" as soon as the child becomes aware of the orthodox word-shapes on advertisement hoardings, in newspaper headlines or comics, and elsewhere outside the classroom wherever he happens to meet them; for instance, *Bus Stop* differs so little from bus stop (which he can read) that the situational clue is well able to help him bridge the minor dissimilarity. Each success in reading a word in orthodox print yields a double advantage: not only does it pave the way for the transition, but it also demonstrates to the child that he is on the right road to "reading grown up."

Earlier in this chapter I drew attention to the adaptability of the human ear and the ease with which it is conditioned to varieties of pronunciation. The *adult's* eye would appear to be more resistant to new conditioning, or at any rate to be prejudiced and thus impeded, if only emotionally, by unfamiliar spellings or typography. A different set of perceptive faculties in the brain is concerned and yet this greater resistance is curious because compared with the ear, which operates in time and has but a moment to register each fleeting spoken word, the eye (which operates in space) can examine the words at relative leisure and has the advantage of the permanent record of print. So far as printed words are concerned, it might perhaps be suggested that the eye has less practice in being conditioned to different forms. On the other hand most of us have managed eventually to be conditioned to the ten variants of roman characters (BAG, Bag, *bag*, etc.) and were expected to make these relatively far more drastic transitions at an even less mature age and with far less confidence and experience than possessed by the five-, six- or seven-year-old child making the transition from i.t.a. to orthodox spelling. It can be argued that the transition from BAG to bag and *bag* is one of substitution only and does not amount to

XIII *Upper :* Dr. John Downing supervises his experiment.

Lower : A well-stocked book corner.

XIV "I see the dog." Words hand–written on the blackboard in i.t.a. are linked directly with their appearance in print as well as with their spoken sound and with the concept as drawn by the child.

a radical change in form, but the brain is in fact so conditioned to these variant forms as to be unaware that they exist, as has been demonstrated by Sir Alan Herbert[1]—

> "To-day I am MAKing aN inno6£vation. as
> you mayalready have gessed, I am typlng this
> article myself Zz½lnstead of writing it, The
> idea is to save time and exvBKpense, also to
> demonstyap demonBTrike = =damn, to
> demonstratO that I can type /ust as well as
> any blessedgirl if I give my mInd to iT""""
> Typlng while you compose is realy
> extraoraordinarrily easy, though composing
> whilr you typE is more difficult. I rather
> think my typing style is going to be
> different froM my u6sual style, but Idaresay
> noone will mind that much. looking back i
> see that we made rather a hash of that
> awfuul wurd extraorordinnaryk? in the middle
> of a woRd like thaton N-e gets quite lost?
> 2hy do I keep putting questionmarks instead
> of fulstopSI wonder. Now you see i have
> put a fulllstop instead Of a question mark
> it nevvvver reins but it pours."

. . . but a mor spesific comparison can bee mæd bie obʃervɪŋ ʃhe ɛɛʃ wiʃh whiɕh ʃhe aɖult ie can bee condiʃhonɖ tꙍ reeɖɪŋ teksts printeɖ in i.t.a., ɛɛven ʃhœ ʃhe caracterʃ ar outsieɖ ʃhe reeɖer'ʃ preevius ekspeeriens anɖ ar approɕht wiʃh nun ov ʃhe preparatory teeɕhɪŋ enjoiɖ bie ʃhe ɕhielɖ puepil.

It does not necessarily follow that children will be able to adapt them-selves in what is, after all, the opposite direction. The transition from ʃhe to *the* and from hors to *horse* is not likely to present much of a problem, but it is at least arguable that the transitions from wuns, hꙍ, aut, and ɖꙍ to *once*, *who*, *ought*, and *do* will raise difficulties of quite a different order. Because wuns, etc., are more rational it has to be conceded that, compared

[1] "A Criminal Type." *Punch*, Vol. 159, p. 62, London, 28 July 1920.

with adults, i.t.a. children are required to make the difficult jump from the rational to the irrational, from the systematic to the unsystematic.

Time and plenty of practice are needed for the seven-year-old to be able to recognize and instantly recall the irregular words, especially when presented out of context, but this difficulty should not be exaggerated. The transition is aided by several factors, one of which may be discerned in the design of the i.t.a. characters, particularly their upper halves which in all but the misleadingly spelled words incorporate what amounts to a "built-in" link with orthodox characters. The sophisticated adult reader pays most attention to the "top coast-line" of words and sentences—

When masked at the bottom the result
is easy to read: when masked at the
top it is seen to be harder to read.

When masked at the bottom the result is easy to read: when masked at the top it is seen to be harder to read. In designing the i.t.a. characters the orthodox top coast-line has been left largely undisturbed and the features by which the new characters can be discriminated are wherever possible located in the lower half of the lines of print, as shown in these two specimens—

this is printed in an augmented rœman alfabet, the purpos
ov which is not, as miet bee suppœsd, tœ reform our spellin
but tœ improov the lernin ov reedin

The beginner tends to examine the whole characters—both bottom and top—and therefore makes full use of the special i.t.a. features. As he gains in fluency and becomes familiar with the shapes of whole words, at any rate those which recur very frequently, he increasingly ignores the bottom half and, like the sophisticated adult reader, merely skims along the top coast-line with sufficient concentration to devour the meaning. Because the top coast-line of i.t.a. sentences is so very similar to the top coast-line of orthodox sentences, it is correct to say that the transition starts as soon as the i.t.a. reader begins to acquire fluency.

The effectiveness of the top coast-line in easing the transition should not be exaggerated. It can operate only in the case of words where the changes, if any, are not radical. No typographical device, however ingenious, can be expected to bridge the chasm between aut and *ought*, between wun and *one*, between hœ and *who*—or in the case of many of the 39·25 per cent of radically irregular spellings. Contextual clues and meaning also play a most important part in tiding the reader over at the moment of transition and in the weeks immediately following it, during which he gradually becomes familiar with and learns to recognize the irregular words instantly. This does require practice and repetition but the adaptation is relatively effortless because by the time the child is ripe for the transition he must—and this needs continual reiteration—he must already be able to read in i.t.a. with fluency and comprehension. Though the transition occurs smoothly it is true that the radically irregular words may sometimes cause a slight slowing down in the speed of reading or even in a few cases a "plateau," but it is only temporary and the ability to read the difficult words even without the prop of context increases alongside the continuous growth of linguistic skill and general intellectual development.

It must be emphasized that the transition is to a new visual form only. Context and meaning provide the vital, additional bridge between the two alphabets. Just as they buttress the initial process of reading i.t.a. texts, they also help the pupil to take the transition stage in his stride. In effective reading with either alphabet context and meaning always in fact dominate the process. Read these two notices—

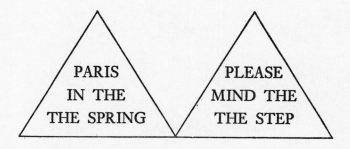

PARIS
IN THE
THE SPRING

PLEASE
MIND THE
THE STEP

Most people read them incorrectly and fail to spot that the word *THE* is repeated twice, because the brain has the habit of adjusting what can be seen so that it is in accord with what is understood. Linguistically we anticipate what is coming, we tend always to seek complete meanings, to sift and select probabilities. When at the start of a sentence a child meets upper-case (capital) roman characters for the first time, they do not worry him even if they are unfamiliar—because he has by now mastered the art of reading; because of his ability to read lower-case characters his sense of probability tells him what they represent, particularly if he has come successfully to substitute and he has been told that roman characters have alternative forms that are used on certain occasions. When read as a whole even an extreme example—*Once upon a time*—is readily sifted to produce its probable and true meaning by those to whom Wuns upon a tiem is already familiar and understood without conscious effort; on the other hand *emit a nopu ecnO* will cause most readers to stumble because, unless it is read from right to left, it makes no sense. An Englishman landing in New York does not have to switch over to a new spoken language as would a Frenchman or German; he does not laboriously substitute in his head his own vowel-sounds for those heard all around him, but simply absorbs the meaning from what he hears with the aid of a rapid, unconscious process of sifting and adjustment, ignoring, even if he notices them, most of the phonemic variations. In the same way a child of five, six, or seven making the transition to orthodox texts knows enough and is confident enough to search out the meaning and thus master the inconsistencies and ambiguities of the spelling without so much as realizing he is doing it.

8   i.t.a. and the Teacher

THE MOST SUPERFICIAL SKIMMING of the last few pages should be enough to convince the sceptical that i.t.a. is no threat to the roman alphabet and that it does not introduce even the thinnest part of a wedge of spelling reform. But I have found that among those who accept intellectually the arguments in favour of i.t.a. there are quite a few who resist it emotionally. Though the eye and the parts of the brain concerned with vision are capable of being rapidly conditioned to new symbols, the printed roman character is apparently sacrosanct and surrounded by taboo. The most bizarre or most slovenly distortions of handwriting will be tolerated and not seriously impede recognition of meaning, but the American spelling of words like *color* or *program*—or likewise the British *colour* or *programme* —can arouse a degree of irritation and ridicule comparable to that provoked by Picasso's two-nosed women or the pictorial assaults of Pop-art. To the adult i.t.a. does of course involve a challenge to habitual thinking and this kind of emotional antagonism is to be expected among some teachers and educationists, particularly among those whose destructive attitudes have been steeled in the conflicts between the different methods of teaching children how to read. It is best therefore to start this chapter by restating unequivocally that i.t.a. is neither a spelling reform nor a new method of teaching. It is a teaching medium only: one that can be used with advantage in conjunction with *any* of the existing methods or with an eclectic combination of two or more of them. Every teacher who adopts i.t.a. as a medium is free to stick to the method he or she prefers and the favoured method can continue to be used without any modification, or with only such minor ones as the teacher will find helpful.

The advantages that i.t.a. brings specifically to the teacher who favours phonic methods can be summarized as follows—

The provision of sufficient characters to represent accurately each of the 40 phonemes required for the English language.

The replacement of digraphs, whether contiguous (e.g. *th*) or separated (e.g. *bone*) by single characters (ſh, œ). The characters *t* and *o* (and *h* and *e*) are thus confined to their own unique sound values; the left-to-right sequence is maintained consistently and is not reversed when deciphering digraphic sounds, whether separated or adjacent.

The vocabulary need not be specially restricted—indeed it may be as natural as that spoken to the child. The practice of writing can also proceed with an equally unrestricted vocabulary. Ideal opportunities are given for writing practice to reinforce the phonic element in reading.

Each i.t.a. character represents a single phoneme only: the ambiguities and inconsistencies of orthodox print and spelling are removed, enabling full advantage to be taken of constructive syllable and word building and the recognition of reliable syllabic cross-relationships. The frequency and effectiveness of repetition are greatly increased as a result of the large decrease in the quantity of spellings.

To the teacher who favours look-and-say, global, or whole word and sentence methods i.t.a. means—

The elimination of separate characters for capitals and of the numerous variants of the roman alphabet, and their replacement by a single set of characters which in words or sentences form a consistently stable basis for repetition and reinforcement.

This simplification makes it easier for the pupil to acquire distinct, unambiguous, stable, visual images of the patterns of words and sentences. They are repeated more frequently, thus reinforcing the impact of the word image.

Pattern can be more easily and certainly associated with meaning and, in due course, with sound. Learning is not confused by competing patterns.

The greater similarity in the appearance of syllables helps in acquiring a larger stock of familiar units which in turn allows words not hitherto in the look-and-say vocabulary to be identified.

It has been calculated that with i.t.a. 220 syllables are sufficient to express 70 per cent of the language and that the remaining 1,150 syllables are closely related.

For the extreme 100 per cent look-and-say teacher—if any such exists —who assumes that analysis of characters and synthesis of sounds play no part whatsoever in learning to read and that the pupil, so far as reading goes, might just as well be deaf or learning Chinese ideographs, I confess that most of these purposes could be well achieved by limiting a child's first reading primers to lower-case roman characters. Secondly, it might be argued that in learning to read by this hypothetical 100 per cent look-and-say method the elimination in some cases of the inconsistencies of orthodox spelling might indeed be considered disadvantageous because it would also entail in some cases a change amounting to the elimination of the distinctive shapes of words. But I just do not believe that such extreme look-and-say learning ever persists even in the early, much less the later stages—I suspect that the children themselves (unless born as deaf-mutes) discover the basic phonemic, alphabetic nature of orthodox spelling for themselves.

It would be hypocrisy for me to pretend that I have no views on this tedious conflict between teaching methods,[1] and yet I count myself as

---

[1] My experience over many years of the teaching of shorthand (which involves a comparable acquisition of skill coupled with linguistic meaning) makes me favour a look-and-say approach, in which recognition and perception of the whole word, its *general* aspect or (shorthand) "outline," precedes the recognition and perception of the *particular* elements of which the whole is built up—if only because the automatic reflex reactions of a skill tend to be inhibited if intellectual rational processes are too greatly encouraged.

When reading or writing an unknown word such as *Poppolington*, the child, while learning, and the student of shorthand both need to "think it out," but in the case of the frequently recurring majority of words it is better if they can read and write them automatically without conscious thought processes. If the learner, from the very beginning, starts to acquire this automatic skill with a few words, there is nothing to prevent him from employing an intellectual attack on an unfamiliar word whenever it is necessary; on the other hand the learner who employs a predominantly intellectual attack at the outset on every word finds it hard to give it up and rely effortlessly on the automatic, speedier process. This is not to suggest that auditory discrimination (without the association of the appropriate characters) should not be taught from the start—indeed it may well be taught before the first steps in reading; but I believe that the further ability to discriminate characters visually and to associate them with sounds can be more successfully learned after rather than before the acquisition of a foundation of familiar, well-learned whole words—eventually these will be seen *also* to have an alphabetic structure.

The basis of reading, even when it comes to rare proper names, involves an effortless, look-and-say mastery of the syllables of the language. By and large the reading process has a close link with look-and-say, the writing process with the phonic method: the skill of habituation is normally more established earlier in the receptive activity—reading—an automatic skill in writing taking longer to acquire.

a neutral in that I agree with i.t.a. teachers who rely on any combination of the two. For these teachers *both* sets of advantages will accrue. The stability and invariable quality of the i.t.a. reading system, its genuine and completely efficient alphabeticism will, I believe, show conclusively that the conflict is unreal. Two methods have evolved because they reflect different parts—visual and auditory—of the reading process. Before he gets very far the child has to be able both to recognize the shapes of syllables, words and sentences and to analyze the constituent character-sound relationships of familiar words. The new medium, by removing the disadvantages suffered by both methods when used in conjunction with the orthodox alphabet(s) and spelling, can finally turn this unreal conflict into a natural alliance. The visual and auditory capacities in every child will then be free to supplement each other with benefit not only for those who now fail to read properly but also for those who now succeed. Meaningful relationships between the growing store of the two sets of symbols will form in the child's mind and he will be free to test and confirm his new understanding with the help of reliable comparisons and associations which, as we have seen, is a natural and important element in all processes of learning.

As no change in method need be involved, the scene in an infants' class where i.t.a. is used differs very little from that in a class using the roman alphabet. Words written on the blackboard and on the labels under pictures and on furniture, so as to familiarize children with the association of the concept and appearance of printed words before they are ready to be taught reading systematically, are, however, written in i.t.a. characters. Wherever words appear on apparatus or toys designed for pre-reading activities, i.t.a. characters are again used—if necessary pasted over the roman characters. Some have found it advisable to make an exception of the children's names, for example on exercise books or on lockers and coat-pegs; from a very early age many children are familiar with the conventional appearance of their own names (either in upper- or lower-case) and, because of their symbolic importance, they are apt to resent their being altered. An individual John who may have been taught the form "JOHN" is quite happy for another John to have his name written as "John" and for another in an i.t.a. book to be written as "jon." It is advisable to foresee and provide for the day when the class will become "mixed," a proportion of the children having made the transition, by writing i.t.a. words on yellow paper or with yellow chalk; later, words in orthodox characters and spelling can be written on white paper or with white chalk. This helps both groups of children to sort themselves out and directs their attention to the presentation most helpful to them, dependent on the stage they have reached. Becoming used in this way to both media helps to make the transition effortless and largely unnoticed.

Authority determines when the child shall attend school; the teacher decides when he is ready to start reading. It is not my concern to say at what age this should be. Let me no more than insist that the tests for "reading readiness" are no different in an i.t.a. class. Although the simplicity of the new medium enables words to be read at an earlier stage of intellectual development, it is safer if the teacher continues to rely on the normal indications that the child is ready to start systematic learning. A premature start can still set up resistance to reading and do damage to the child's confidence. In particular, it is necessary that the child is sufficiently advanced linguistically because, as we have seen, reading is essentially an extension of speech and, unless he has gained certain minimum verbal skills and experience, he is not ready for the printed or written word. A child's linguistic ability depends, of course, on his home background and the teacher is recommended in the pre-reading stage to concentrate on remedying any marked verbal deficiencies noted in individual members of the class and on helping children who are "linguistically deprived." More research and experience may eventually change our ideas of what is the right age to start reading—Sir Compton Mackenzie claims he could read before he was two[1] and a book has recently been published with the title *Teach Your Baby to Read*[2]—but as yet it is not anticipated that the typical age for starting to learn to read will be significantly advanced. Our concern is not to produce reading prodigies but to remove the barriers to successful reading, and this, in practice but incidentally, means that progress is rapid and exhilarating; fluent reading and a high communicative ability are normally achieved many months earlier than with the orthodox alphabet.

[1] "My mother was not particularly impressed by my being able to read before I was two. She and her sister Isabel had read Rollins' long Roman history before they were two and a half. Their mother had taught herself to read at two and by the time she was four she was reading Sterne's *Sentimental Journey* as a favourite book." *My Life and Times; Octave One 1883–1891*, p. 40. Chatto & Windus, London, 1963. The provocative question obtrudes itself: have many outstanding people learned to read very early because they were exceptional children or did they become exceptional adults because they could react positively to a highly communicative environment?

[2] By Glenn J. Doman. Random House, New York, 1964.

Which reading primers and supplementary books are adopted will again depend on the preference of the teacher. Several well-known series in the U.K., America, and Canada have been transliterated in i.t.a. characters, and the list of other books printed in i.t.a. has grown fast. Even so, schools find that the children learn so fast and read so voraciously that the supply of i.t.a. books is soon exhausted unless new and more generous ideas on the content of school libraries are adopted. The earliest i.t.a. classes were faced with a difficult but heartening problem in that children of four and five years old who had come to school unable to read had each got through about a hundred (*sic*) books and were clamouring for more. The most commonly reported shortage was of books with fairly sophisticated and advanced vocabulary and spelling but with large-scale type and ideas and stories suitable for six-year-olds. Teachers spoke of the i.t.a. children's "greed" for books: the book corners in their classrooms were continuously patronized and it was remarked how many five- and six-year-olds were eager to read not only during free periods but also during the mid-morning break or the dinner-hour.

When precisely a child is ready for the transition to orthodox print can be decided only by the teacher, but once the step has been taken there is no reason for hesitation. The transition should, nevertheless, not be forced. Time spent in gaining yet further competence in i.t.a., further linguistic ability, and wider experience through i.t.a. books is well spent. A late transition has much to recommend it, seeing that it will be, if anything, easier the later it occurs. In some classes the last book to be read in i.t.a. is re-read in an orthodox version and from then on i.t.a. is forgotten. Some teachers believe in dividing the transition into three intermediate stages: (1) the introduction of capitals and digraphs (e.g. *i* and *e* separated: *ie* instead of ie); (2) the introduction of "regular" irregularities (e.g. *mate, here, dine, bone, cube*); (3) the introduction of "shock" words like *once, all, enough*. Transitional reading primers that provide for these three stages are available, the shock words being printed in a distinctive colour; some books are printed partly in i.t.a. and partly in orthodox characters and spelling.

WRITING IN i.t.a.

As we saw in Chapter 2, learning how to write at an early age not only instils mastery of the motor responses and provides a means of self-expression, but it is also bound up with the acquisition of skill in look-and-say word recognition, as well as in phonic analysis and synthesis. The child's act of forming characters and words, thus becoming more familiar with their "feel" and shape and linking his own created symbols with the symbols of words written or printed by others, helps to associate the word-symbols with their sounds and meanings. The i.t.a. alphabet is more suited than the orthodox alphabet to these twin requirements because the shapes of the written and printed characters are identical instead of different. Writing emphasizes the reliability of i.t.a. When, as at present, a child learns to write words such as—

again, fall, private

he has to learn that in roman print they look considerably different—

again, fall, private

whereas when written in i.t.a. there is no difference—

agæn, faull, prievæt

agæn, faull, prievæt

Because of the omission of differing capitals, and even allowing for the correspondence between upper and lower case of some of the roman characters (e.g. *C, c*; *O, o*), the child taught handwriting by means of the 44 i.t.a. characters has actually fewer distinct symbols to learn. The first time one watches a class of five-year-olds writing i.t.a. words in their exercise books produces a sensation of marvel and disbelief. It is difficult for the adult, habituated during many years to form orthodox characters, to keep an open mind on this question, but there is no reason why i.t.a. characters should be more difficult for a child to form than orthodox characters. The augmentations—e.g. æ, ſh, єє, etc.—are in fact probably easier than *o, c,* and *e* whose accuracy depends so much on where to start and end the circular line. The characters a and au perhaps give cause for special attention, particularly for the adult. It must be remembered that to the open-minded five-year-old child ꜯh (*chay*) is not a rather peculiar combination of *c* and *h* but as much a single character as is *w* to the adult. The ease with which children acquire facility in writing i.t.a. characters is reflected in the greater ease with which teachers find they can

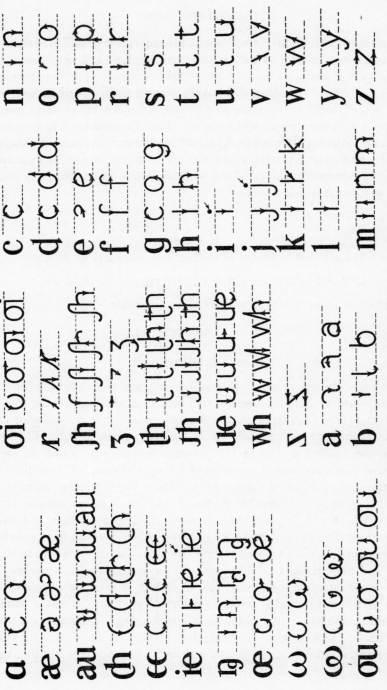

Figure 13. Pencil movements when forming i.t.a. characters.

decipher the children's early writing compared with corresponding efforts with orthodox characters (see illustrations, *Plates XIX—XXVI*).

In typical teaching practice the child is ready to start writing his first words in i.t.a. only a few weeks after he has taken his first steps in learning to read. Owing to the incorporation in i.t.a. of the roman lower-case alphabet with the exception of *q* and *x*, the child has plenty of practice at forming orthodox characters. In addition, the methods of forming the i.t.a. augmented characters should correspond as nearly as possible to the movements required for the orthodox characters. As with certain spellings, a few compromises are called for between the most efficient methods of forming the i.t.a. augmentations and the need to embed habits that will be useful when the transition is made to writing orthodox characters only. If i.t.a. were intended as a permanent reform, one might expect children to make the character ŋ (*ing*) by means of continuous movement of the crayon or pencil in order to add the semicircle at the top of the tail—

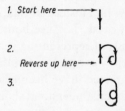

But so as to reinforce the correct habits required later to form a separate *n* and *g*, the following movements are recommended—

The illustration opposite shows the methods recommended for forming all the i.t.a. characters. The arrow-heads on the strokes indicate the direction of movement.

Perfection in i.t.a. calligraphy (or spelling) cannot and should not be expected of any child. It is not intended as a Procrustean discipline because months before the typical child is likely to produce reasonably accurate spelling and confident handwriting he will have learned to read and made the transition to reading orthodox characters and spelling—and also begun the transition to writing them. Most teachers nowadays accept the need for writing to be an activity that is enjoyed and, while insisting on neatness and care in the formation of the characters, refrain from correcting too many errors of spelling in their children's exercise books and compromise by correcting only the worst ones. This attitude is certainly desirable with children who learn to write in i.t.a., especially as they tend to write, as well as read, earlier and more copiously.

Because many of the i.t.a. spellings are only temporary and shortlived for the child, any insistence on accurate spelling—even to use the term "spelling"—can achieve little except to undermine the child's delight and confidence at discovering his power to communicate and express himself on paper. If he writes, say, haz instead of haʒ, or bocs instead of boks, it is not worth taking him to task, because both are phonemically accurate and are alternative methods of representing the same sounds—and in any case he will eventually write *has* and *box*. On the other hand, errors which suggest that the i.t.a. characters have been selected wrongly because the sound of the word has been misunderstood should always be corrected and explained. If *the* is spelt þe instead of ʃhe or *eat* is spelt it instead of eet, and the errors are allowed to pass unchallenged, they could delay the child's progress as a reader as well as a writer.

Occasional departures from the generally accepted i.t.a. spelling of a word may with advantage be tolerated to cater for marked local or even individual variations in pronunciation: the word *fertile*, for example, might be spelt fertiel in Scotland and the North of England, as furtiel in the South-West of England, as furtoil in Cockney London, and as foitl in Brooklyn.[1] Because i.t.a. is the opposite of a rigorous orthodoxy,

[1] In the interests of world-wide acceptability, American and British publishers of children's i.t.a. reading books may be expected to avoid the very few words that are pronounced with a radical difference in the two parts of the English-speaking world—e.g. leftenant (lꝏtenant) can be promoted to captæn and ʃheduel (sceduel) changed to prœgram. Instances of such words, at any rate in reading primers for children, are fortunately very rare. Speaking as a British and an American publisher who is continually plagued by the necessity and expense of Anglicizing American books and vice versa, I hope this plea will find a response among my colleagues across the Atlantic who must be equally plagued by the necessity and expense of Americanizing British, Canadian, Australian, etc. books (see also page 106).

considerable discretion and flexibility may be left to each individual teacher especially in the case of words that occur infrequently; on the other hand, to justify departures from accepted i.t.a. spelling, the expected gains should be more than marginal. The need to preserve the greatest possible resemblance to orthodox spellings must never be overlooked, particularly in common words that need to be repeated and reinforced.

It is useful, but not essential, for the teacher to be able to write any word in i.t.a. It is necessary to learn how to write simple words under the children's own pictures or on wall charts, and a good blackboard and flannel-pen technique is equally important. It is not as easy for an adult to learn to write words in i.t.a. as it is to read them, but the facility comes with very little practice. It is largely a question of understanding and remembering when the orthodox spelling needs to be altered in order to make it represent the word's sound. If in doubt reference can be made to the published i.t.a. spelliŋ gied and nœts[1] which relates each orthodox character or combination of characters to the corresponding i.t.a. character and gives comparative examples of representative words in the two media. The *Teachers' Instruction Pack*,[2] a programmed text designed to give teachers a working knowledge of i.t.a. characters and spelling, can also be recommended. The i.t.a. Foundation offers a correspondence course and has organized hundreds of "orientation workshops" for local education authorities and assisted at them. Experience with the pioneer i.t.a. classes has shown, however, that teachers have no difficulty in learning the twenty augmentations and knowing when to apply them or sufficiently simplify the orthodox spelling.

What about the parents? There is no need for them to learn to write and spell in i.t.a. but their general goodwill is very desirable and, if necessary, special steps should be taken to win it. Resistance to the new medium may be found among a small minority of parents, but only at the very beginning. Even in the pioneer classes a pithy explanation of the principles of i.t.a. and of the reasons why it is beneficial to the child has been sufficient to remove anxiety which has been finally dispelled by the unmistakable and rapid progress shown by their own children. As is normal in most homes, parents should be asked to interest themselves in and encourage their children's reading, though, until the transition stage is reached, the

---

[1] Published by Initial Teaching Publishing Co., London, 1964.

[2] Compiled by Elsie Crouch and John Leedhan, also published by Initial Teaching Publishing Co., London, 1964.

books provided at home should be printed in i.t.a. characters. To use books with roman characters is not as helpful as providing more i.t.a. books. It is excellent if children take some of their supplementary i.t.a. books home with them, but not the basic i.t.a. primers as this can lead over-ambitious parents to usurp the teacher's role and so set up conflicts between home and classroom. It is wise to tell parents that there is no need to discourage their children from puzzling out for themselves ortho-dox words they happen to notice in newspapers, hoardings or elsewhere. So far from setting up a muddling and harmful conflict with the i.t.a. words read at school, it shows that the child will soon be ready for the transition and is, in fact, in a natural and unselfconscious manner already starting to embark on it.

COMMON DOUBTS ABOUT i.t.a.

Any major innovation in the teaching of reading, notwithstanding that the actual methods are left intact, is naturally at first met with caution if not suspicion; even among teachers who accept the central premise of my arguments and are convinced by the effectiveness of i.t.a. doubts may still remain. This chapter therefore concludes with some of these doubts, together with explanations that will, I hope, remove them.

(1) *Will not a child who learns to read with the help of i.t.a. later find that writing in orthodox spelling is more than usually difficult?*

The information available so far from the research both in England (see pages 180–1) and America indicates that after the transition and a short period of learning orthodox spelling i.t.a. children spell with greater accuracy than do other children who have been taught all along with the orthodox medium. This is not unexpected, because i.t.a. children begin by spelling as they speak and this helps them after they have made the transition to appreciate that there is, basically, a systematic relationship between spell-ing and the sounds of words and syllables—despite the plethora of inconsistencies. Once a child has learned to read and has done so without concluding at the age of six or seven that he is "rotten at spelling," he begins, after the transition, to become aware of which words are spelled irregularly and which therefore he must learn. Correct spelling, inevitably, is the product of much reading and writing—and i.t.a. children are soon

sue pots on her red cœt.
ſhis is sue in her red cœt.
    sue runs off too plæ
in ſhe feeld.
ſhee plæs in ſhe feeld wiſh ken.

5

XV *Upper*: From *Ken and Sue*, the first of seven books in the *Oldham Readers* series. (Written by Maurice Harrison, illustrated by Susan Bailey: Initial Teaching Publishing Co., London, 1966.)

"yes, ie will help yoo.
ie liv in a hœl in ſhe ground
and ie am cœld at niet too.
ie wood liek too liv wiſh yoo."
    "ſhat wood bee fun,"
ſhe græ mous sed.
"ie wood liek too liv wiſh yoo.
let us fiend a nies plæs
too bild a hous."

Lower: From *A Day at Home*, the fourth of eight books in the *Clearway Readers* series, designed for remedial reading schemes. (Written by Stuart Bell, illustrated by Tony Goffe and Susan Bailey: Initial Teaching Publishing Co., London, 1965.)

22

the summer woʃ aulmœst œver.
"sœn it will bee winter tiem,"
sed faʃher ʃkwirrel. "ʃhen ʃhe dæʃ
will bee cœld and fœd will bee
hard tœ fiend. sœ lœk nou
for nuts and pœt ʃhem
in a sæf plæʃ
for yœr winter fœd."

bandy and ʃhe uʃher ʃkwirrelʃ
went aull œver ʃhe wœd
lœkiŋ for nuts.

bandy found a lot ov nuts.
hee hid sum in ʃhe ground
and sum in eny littl hœl
hee sau in ʃhe treeʃ.

XVI *Upper:* From *Bandy's First Jump*, the second of four books designed to extend vocabulary that form part of the *Downing Reading Scheme.* (Written by John Downing, stories by Faith Graham and Dilys Beeston, illustrated by Grace Lodge: Initial Teaching Publishing Co., London, 1965.)

when ʃhee cæm out,
ʃhee lœkt liek ʃhis.
billy did not nœ whot tœ dœ.
ʃhen hee sed,
"cum intœ ʃhe kitʃhen
and ie will drie yœ."

Lower: From *Billy Pig and Sally Lamb*, one of the growing library of 'Book Corner Books'. (Written by Doris Dickens, illustrated by Sylvia Treadgold: Initial Teaching Publishing Co., London, 1965.)

reading and writing more copiously in the orthodox medium than many children brought up on it. Moreover the i.t.a. child, having the advantage of being well grounded in the essentially phonemic nature of spelling, is better able on this structure to memorize the exceptions. Teaching the etymological roots of words scarcely arises until long after the age when a child has made the transition, though they certainly can then be helpful in memorizing some of the irregular orthodox spellings.

(2) *Is not the transition from i.t.a. to the orthodox medium more difficult in respect of writing than reading?*

Having gained some mastery of writing with one medium, to add variants of it is relatively easy. The initial achievement presents the largest challenge. The child taught to write in the orthodox medium has very soon to be able to discriminate between *the*, *The*, and *THE*. To substitute *the* for ʃhe or *The* for ʃhe makes virtually no demand of the child. After all it is well known with what little effort a bilingual child switches even from English to, say, French, or a schoolchild who learns Greek is able after a very short while to write ρυθεps and σιστεps vice *brothers* and *sisters*. The transition in writing is also helped by the similarity of i.t.a. characters to orthodox characters and by the manner and order in which the strokes in each character are made with crayon or pencil (see above). It is possible that i.t.a. versions of the common, shock words like cum, wuns, aull, sed, etc. will be persisted in after the transition—and after these can be effortlessly *read* in the orthodox versions—but this phase is not likely to last for very long: at the most six months and for the average child the period is shorter. For nearly all children fluency in reading precedes and indeed is a precondition of fluent and accurate spelling, and therefore the child who has had the benefit of i.t.a. is likely to make as favourable progress in his writing and spelling as in his reading.

(3) *Does i.t.a. have any effect on a child's speech?*

Oddly enough, the effect of reading i.t.a. texts does not influence the normal child's speech any more than reading texts in the orthodox medium prevents him from saying in his own pronunciation whatever words he is able to read with understanding. On the other hand the advantage of allowing young children to write as they speak is that it assists teachers in detecting bad speech habits. If a child writes ie ʃhωd ov been, it very clearly indicates that he hears and has learned to say the words wrongly. When it is explained that the sentence should be written ie ſhœd hav bεεn, an improvement is being fostered in the child's diction as well as in his writing. Children with bad speech behaviour are often the victims of poor auditory discrimination; when corrected orally they still fail to hear their mistakes. Their visual discrimination is however usually perfect and when they are able to see their own mispronunciations put on paper in i.t.a. and then corrected in i.t.a. they soon become aware of the differences they need to listen for. All this has nothing to do with regional pronunciations, which are a separate issue, the teacher being properly concerned only with instilling comprehensible, accurate, and consistent speech within the criteria of vowel and other sounds customary in the speech of each child including that of the particular locality—which more likely than not will be the way the teacher speaks herself. (The pronunciation of foreigners who learn English with the help of i.t.a., particularly in its specially adapted form [see Chapter 15], may well, on the other hand, be influenced greatly by the medium and therefore be modelled on a pronunciation that is widely accepted and understood.) Until recently teachers have acted on the supposition that their chief purpose is to teach reading and that improvement of "language" is a by-product; it can now, however, be argued that, with the removal of all the clutter that impedes children when learning to read, we shall come to recognize that their chief purpose is to teach "language" (including speech) and that reading and writing are but the visual half.

(4) *Is i.t.a. helpful to the bright and average child no less than to the dull child?*

The postponement of the worst difficulties in learning to read and the early and relatively effortless acquirement of the skill are at first sight more likely to be of most benefit to children with low intellectual ability or who for some other reason are apt to find reading difficult—i.e. the seventeen per cent and more who until now have grown up as backward readers. Reading is such a basic skill that they thus stand a better chance to avoid being dubbed—as unfortunately does occur at too many junior schools—as "bottom stream material" and thus, like an athlete who stumbles at the first hurdle, begin to fail scarcely before they have got properly started. But children of average and even outstanding ability also have much to gain from i.t.a. To begin with, it must be remembered that intelligence is not necessarily a passport to the easy acquisition of reading. Among the seventeen per cent of backward readers will be found a few with considerable intellectual potentiality and even a high level of linguistic ability and experience. It is difficult and often impossible to detect which among a group of young beginners may find reading difficult, and therefore to start them off with the simpler, more logical medium is, if nothing more, a sensible precaution. Quite apart from this, the use of i.t.a. is likely to enable each child in the infants' class—whatever its intellectual standard—to make optimum progress and therefore the brighter children do not have to mark time because of the hours that have to be spent by the teacher in helping the stragglers. Freed from the overriding problems and fears of spelling accurately, all children can start expressing themselves in written words at an earlier age and, as is clear from the pioneer classes, nearly all of them become copious writers as well as readers to the extent that it has been found difficult to supply them with enough writing paper let alone enough books suitable for their age and understanding. Fortunately the range of i.t.a. books has grown so fast that a child can be given reading matter to match his particular interests and to foster and enrich his individual development. I cannot believe that this is anything but beneficial though it is not unknown for educationists to argue that being able to read as early as five or six years old is harmful and distorts the healthy growth of character and personality. To force the pace beyond that at which children wish to learn to read is undoubtedly damaging, but once the decision to teach it has been taken the removal and postponement by i.t.a. of the most frustrating difficulties surely suggests that, even though the pace of learning will be quickened, there will be less rather than more strain on the child. We have much still to discover about the nature of intelligence and its relation to temperament, to creative ability, and so on, but it seems probable that its development is not unrelated to early experiences of problem solving. Learning to read constitutes one of the most challenging manifestations of problem solving met by a child and therefore if the difficulties are postponed and the solutions are seen by the child to be logical and systematic, it may perhaps enhance the ability to solve similar problems when the intellect is older and more mature. Besides, immediately successful reading increases experience and develops linguistic capacity. Time and follow-up research with children who have learned to read with i.t.a. may add to our knowledge of these processes.

9 How effective is i.t.a.?— 1. The First British Experiment

THE EFFECTIVENESS of the Initial Teaching Alphabet could be proved satisfactorily only by means of an elaborate and large-scale programme of meticulous research. Only this would finally substantiate (or disprove) the validity of the particular difficulties for the learner of reading inherent in the orthodox alphabet(s) and spelling, and would enable the advantages of i.t.a. to be measured with enough precision for schools to decide whether or not its adoption could be justified. Mere assertion and argument leading to intellectual conviction among teachers were obviously not adequate, nor would the enthusiastic opinions and uncorrelated empiricism of individual teachers who had adopted i.t.a. be likely to carry sufficient weight with the teaching profession as a whole. Rightly, educationists and teachers are cautious of accepting the claims of innovators, and i.t.a. would suffer the fate of earlier teaching alphabets unless its advantages could stand up to the most rigorous and scientific techniques of educational research. The findings could then speak for themselves.

In the spring of 1960 I succeeded, after years spent in creating a favourable climate, in persuading Lionel Elvin, the director of the University of London's Institute of Education and Dr. W. D. Wall of the National Foundation for Educational Research in England and Wales to recommend to their respective governing bodies that the research be undertaken. The project was moreover given the blessing of the Minister of Education and of the secretaries of the Association of Education Committees and the National Union of Teachers. An expert committee, appointed to initiate the enquiry and give it general guidance, consisted of: H. L. Elvin, M.A., Director, University of London Institute of Education; W. R. Niblett, B.A., B.Litt., Professor of Education and Dean of the University of London Institute of Education; W. D. Wall, B.A., Ph.D., Director, National Foundation for Educational Research in England and Wales; P. E. Vernon, M.A., Ph.D., D.Sc., Professor of Educational Psychology, University of London Institute of Education; Joyce M. Morris, B.A., Ph.D., Officer Responsible for Reading Research, National Foundation for Educational Research in England and Wales; Sir Cyril Burt, M.A., D.Sc., Hon.LL.D., Hon.D.Litt., F.B.A., Emeritus Professor of Psychology, University College, London; E. B. Fry, Ph.D., Professor of Experimental Phonetics and Head of the Department of Phonetics, University College, London; and myself. A Reading Research Unit was set up at the Institute and Dr. John Downing was engaged.

The core of the first British experiment[1] has been a comparison of the achievements of 873 children using i.t.a. with a control group of identical size that used the orthodox alphabet(s) and spelling. The age, sex, socio-economic class, and indices of intelligence in the experimental and control groups were matched as nearly as possible. The children in both groups attended schools in a selection of areas which together were considered to provide a typical cross-section of the school community. Every attempt was made to match such variables as pupil-teacher ratios, urban/rural locations, types of school organization, size of school, school amenities, and even such minutiae as number of cloakroom pegs and size of playground.[2]

To begin with, it was not easy to convince schools that they had nothing to lose by participating in the experiment. Early in 1961 certain education authorities were asked for their co-operation and they agreed to call meetings of head-teachers to discuss the invitation to join the experiment, a

[1] See *The i.t.a. Symposium. Research Report on the British Experiment with i.t.a.*, by John Downing. With contributions by H. L. Elvin, A. Sterl Artley, Sir Cyril Burt, Hunter Diack, R. Gulliford, James Hemming, Jack A. Holmes, A. R. MacKinnon, A. H. Morgan and M. Procter, Marie D. Neale, Jessie F. Reid, M. D. Vernon, W. D. Wall. The National Foundation for Educational Research in England and Wales, Slough, 1967. Dr. Downing's earlier interim reports will be found in *The i.t.a. Reading Experiment*. Evans Bros. (for the University of London Institute of Education), London, 1964.

[2] For fuller particulars of the research design and the procedures adopted see *The i.t.a. Symposium*, pp. 4–30.

pamphlet[1] to explain the nature and purpose of i.t.a. being sent out before-hand. No school took part in the experiment unless the head-teacher was willing and the class-teacher was at least agreeable. Many teachers, including some who took part, were sceptical of the whole idea of i.t.a.; others believed they were getting perfectly adequate results with the orthodox medium or did not feel able to risk submitting their children to an unproven novelty. At that time i.t.a. was considered such a bizarre notion that for the initial phase of the experiment which began in September 1961 it was possible to enlist no more than 20 schools to try out i.t.a., though there was no difficulty in finding 33 schools to provide control groups.

Recruitment of schools and volunteer teachers continued however and meanwhile two-day "workshops" were arranged for the teachers in charge of the experimental i.t.a. classes. Explanations were given of the function of the additional characters and the teachers were introduced to the first reading primers printed in i.t.a.; the principles of i.t.a. spelling were explained and discussed; and the teachers practised writing in the new medium and satisfied themselves that it need cause them no difficulties. Dr. Downing confirms,[2] as was expected, that the transition stage was of special concern to the teachers—

> They were often anxious about this aspect, and it seemed very important not to make a child switch from i.t.a. to T.O. too early. It was pointed out that Pitman's design for transfer was based on the development, prior to the transition stage, of two skills: reading from minimal clues (the "top coast-line" of the print)[3] and the use of contextual clues to meaning. These were unlikely to be developed before a child could read at *Janet and John* Book IV stage or even the book following. Judgment of readiness for transfer should not be based solely on the book reached, but should be based more on the quality of the reading. In particular, it would be very important , it was suggested, to ensure that the child was reading from such a book in a meaningful way.
>
> It was indicated that transfer from i.t.a. to T.O. should not be dramatic but that the child should be allowed to move over smoothly when he was ready.

Advice was also offered on the transition in writing and what importance to attach to spelling,[4] but it was emphasized that it was essential for the

---

[1] *The Augmented Roman Alphabet: a New Two-Stage Method to Help Children Learning to Read* by John Downing. University of London Institute of Education, 1961.

[2] *The i.t.a. Symposium*, p. 18.

[3] This is in fact a distortion of what I proposed in my original paper (*Learning to Read*) in which I emphasized the dominance of meaning. I have seldom, if ever, employed the phrase "minimal clues" and Dr. Downing, like others, has misunderstood what I have always stated (see pages 144–5).   [4] Ibid., p. 19.

purpose of the experiment that in both groups every teacher's methods should be held constant and, apart from changing the medium in the experimental group, that classes should be conducted along normal lines (e.g. in respect of the assessment of reading readiness, the proportion of time devoted to reading, etc.), methods being adapted and stages of instruction speeded up only to the extent that the children's progress demanded. From observation it appeared that most teachers involved in the experiment, whether in charge of i.t.a. or control classes, used an eclectic, mixed method (see Chapter 2), but it was possible for teaching methods to be matched only in the general sense that the traditional freedom to use the method a teacher found most appropriate for her class was preserved. Similarly, it was found impossible in this first experiment to match such intangibles as the quality of teaching or the extent of the teacher's training and experience. A pamphlet[1] was sent also to parents explaining i.t.a. and the nature and purpose of the experiment.

To ensure the maximum similarity between the experimental and the control classes, both used the same series of reading primers, the only difference being that for the experimental classes the text was printed in i.t.a. It was decided to employ the *Janet and John* series[2] (both in its look-and-say and in its phonic versions), because this was known to be more widely adopted by British schools than any other. The i.t.a. groups were, in fact, at a disadvantage compared with the control groups because the *Janet and John* primers, being merely transliterated into i.t.a., remained necessarily oriented to suit the needs of instruction with the orthodox alphabet(s) and spelling; the text was thus not designed to make full, deliberate use of i.t.a.'s consistency and reliability, nor did it include the wider vocabulary corresponding to the children's expanded linguistic prowess that i.t.a. makes possible. The classroom libraries of orthodox books were paralleled as far as possible by a library of books printed in i.t.a. Teaching apparatus with words spelt in i.t.a. characters was also provided and the teachers themselves adapted much of their existing equipment. To offset what is known as the "Hawthorne Effect"—the effect on teachers and classes produced by the knowledge that their work is the subject of special scrutiny and research—necessitated certain precautions: for example, the explanatory meetings and training workshops were duplicated by regular

[1] *How Your Children are being Taught to Read by the Augmented Roman Alphabet Method* by John Downing. University of London Institute of Education, 1961 (revised edition 1964).
[2] James Nisbet, Welwyn, 1949, and Harper and Row, Evanston, Illinois, 1949. This reading series is based upon the latter's *Alice and Jerry*.

meetings held for the teachers of the orthodox control classes to discuss the research and by refresher courses in established teaching methods; the research workers also made a point of paying visits to the control schools; parallel progress records were kept and both groups of children underwent identical periodic tests. In every way possible, care was taken to present comparable situations in the experimental and control groups, though in practice this was frequently impossible. Hordes of visitors poured into the few more accessible i.t.a. experimental schools, not only educationists and enquiring teachers but journalists, broadcasters, and television cameramen attracted by the newsworthy reports of dramatic successes in the i.t.a. classes. Fortunately the less accessible schools were left alone by visitors and the attainments of these children are available for comparison.

It is probable that the i.t.a. children were more distracted than stimulated by these attentions, and there are grounds for supposing that very young children accept the presence—or absence—of visitors much as they accept a sunny day. Teachers, on the other hand, are more susceptible, but in assessing the Hawthorne Effect one must differentiate between the stimulus that comes from knowing the results are being watched and the quite separate and growing stimulus provided by the success of the work under investigation. It is also fair to say that in the control classes the Hawthorne Effect on the teachers was heightened because, as we have seen, they were confident of their ability to hold their own and were even anxious to prove that the i.t.a. medium was ill conceived. Although the evidence available may not be sufficient to draw firm conclusions on the extent of this factor, Downing himself suggests[1] that the "importance of a Hawthorne Effect in the i.t.a. research has been exaggerated." In a second experiment begun in 1963, but not reported fully at the time of writing this chapter, an attempt was made to obtain an even more rigorous control. On this occasion the problem of variable standards and methods among the teachers was offset by arranging for a pair of teachers in the same school to share responsibility for both sets of classes (experimental and control) and by eliminating publicity. The results so far of this second experiment are stated to appear to be similar to those of the first experiment which is the subject of this chapter.[2]

[1] Ibid., p. 48.
[2] The comments on the Hawthorne Effect made by some of the experts who contributed to the Symposium which accompanied Dr. Downing's report tend to confirm this opinion: "It is impossible to decide whether these factors were, on balance, favourable or unfavourable to the teaching of the i.t.a., or had no effect." (M. D. Vernon, ibid., p. 156.) "It is further worth

It was not until the academic year 1963–64 that enough schools had volunteered to provide sufficient numbers for the two groups to be matched satisfactorily. By then over 2,500 children from 137 schools had been procured to try out i.t.a. and 97 schools had agreed to provide control groups, but the matching procedures reduced the actual sample to 41 classes and 873 in each group (supplied by 33 schools attached to 24 local education authorities). These numbers were further reduced by absences, removals, and so on and by adjustments to remove various other dissimilarities between the two groups. In most of the schools the classes initially consisted of 5-year-olds, but in some (e.g. Oldham) they were only 4 years old.

Introducing his report, Dr. Downing states[1] that ". . . matching of experimental and control groups is now as complete as it can be" and that: "Wherever a significant difference at the five per cent. level exists between the experimental and control groups on one of the background variables in respect of a particular set of data, this is reported along with the particular attainment test results which follow."[2] It will be seen that this kind of bias almost invariably tended to favour the control group and, indeed, Downing writes: "Where it has been difficult to equate the treatment or composition of the experimental and control groups in the two experiments the difference has tended to favour the control group (e.g. in the supply of books in both experiments), and as the superior attainments have generally been found in the experimental group, this suggests that this superiority of i.t.a. has tended to be underestimated in this research."[3]

remarking that we know very little about the alleged Hawthorne Effect (which arises as a concept from a study of *adult workers*) in terms of five to seven year old children and their teachers. *A priori* reasoning would suggest that it is probably very different and, since the first years of school are, for most children, a period of heightened emotionality anyway, it *may* be negligible." (W. D. Wall, ibid., p. 163.) "Nor am I much impressed by those critics who put this down to Hawthorne Effect. If Hawthorne Effect is indeed as great as some critics suggest, then we should have to write off here and now all research into method based on matched groups hitherto attempted, including much of the research on which the methods supported by the critics are based." (James Hemming, ibid., p. 121.) "Careful consideration of this point suggests that, even if the investigator's attempts were unsuccessful in producing similar stimulating effects upon the control group, then perhaps other conditions may have had a compensatory effect. Not the least of these would be the professional pride of the control teachers to 'prove' their teaching ability in the use of traditional orthography. Again, the reinforcing quality of everyday stimulation by the printed word in advertisements, television, comics, children's picture books, etc. seems likely to favour the control group. Still further, the availability and range of supplementary reading materials during the teething stage of the experiment seems to have favoured the control group. If we consider also the effect of parent teaching of reading by i.t.a. it seems, to the writer, that the ambivalent feelings of a number of parents to the new medium may have also put the experimental group in a less advantageous position." (Marie D. Neale, ibid., p. 143.

[1] Ibid., p. 25. [2] Ibid., p. 29. [3] Ibid., p. 48.

THE RESEARCH FINDINGS

The overall findings of the first British Experiment have been widely accepted as conclusive proof of the case argued in this book. They provide support for the basic premise that the orthodox alphabet(s) and spelling are a serious cause of difficulty in the early stages of learning to read and write and for believing that i.t.a. can achieve a sizeable improvement in children's reading standards and can reduce the quantity of backward readers. These conclusions are confirmed by parallel research undertaken in the United States which is reported on briefly in Appendix III by Dr. H. J. Tanyzer and Dr. J. R. Block.

My original intention was to reproduce in this chapter extensive verbatim extracts from the key sections of the official report of the research. By not attempting to paraphrase or simplify its findings, I would thereby avoid any suggestion of partisan distortion or omission. Regrettably Dr. Downing has refused to permit the quotation of the extracts and tables as I desired. Although great pains have been taken by myself and my co-author to present the research findings with complete accuracy and objectivity this has not been easy and Dr. Downing has only himself to blame for any undue condensation or unintentionally false emphasis. The reader is, of course, recommended to study the original document.[1]

I have kept my own personal comments and criticisms of the report scrupulously separate from the descriptions of the research. I have also limited my comments to the few instances where I feel the procedures were misconceived or the findings consequently misleading.

Reading in i.t.a. compared with T.O.

The detailed results were presented in relation to five major questions with a selection of seven related hypotheses. The first question asked: Can children learn to read more easily with i.t.a. than they can with T.O.?[2] If this proved to be the case, the research should show that the i.t.a. children made significantly more rapid progress in being permitted by their teachers to move on to each next more advanced book in the series of reading primers. To test this, the teachers were asked to keep individual

[1] *The i.t.a. Symposium.* See footnote on p. 163.
[2] Throughout this chapter, as in the research report, the abbreviation "T.O." (Traditional Orthography) is used in place of "the orthodox alphabet(s) and spelling."

record cards for both the experimental (i.t.a.) and the control (T.O.) groups and to note the date when each child successfully completed each book in the *Janet and John* series. Analysis of progress made after the first year at school; after $1\frac{1}{3}$ years; after 2 years; and $2\frac{1}{3}$ years demonstrates that the progress of the i.t.a. children was significantly more rapid, as will be seen from the table in the report[2]—

TABLE E1

PROGRESS IN READING BASIC READER SERIES

Percentage frequency distribution of reading primer reached

READING PRIMER REACHED	AFTER 1 YR.		AFTER $1\frac{1}{3}$ YRS.		AFTER 2 YRS.		AFTER $2\frac{1}{3}$ YRS.	
	Exp. (i.t.a.) %	*Cont.* (t.o.) %	*Exp.* (i.t.a.) %	*Cont.* (t.o.) %	*Exp.* (i.t.a.) %	*Cont.* (t.o.) %	*Exp.* (i.t.a.) %	*Cont.* (t.o.) %
Non-starters ..	6·6	5·2	2·2	0·3	2·1	0·3	0·7	0
At Books Intro., I or II ..	55·0	75·9	28·8	54·5	15·6	35·4	9·4	25·9
At Book III ..	17·8	15·7	12·8	17·2	7·8	17·1	5·0	19·1
At Book IV ..	10·9	2·8	14·5	13·3	5·1	12·0	4·3	11·2
At Book V ..	4·0	0·5	8·1	7·2	3·0	4·5	2·5	6·1
Beyond Book V	5·7	0	33·6	7·4	66·4	30·6	78·1	37·8
N	651	651	580	580	333	333	278	278
Median Primer Position ..	Intro., I, II	Intro., I, II	IV	Intro., I, II	Beyond V	III	Beyond V	IV
Kolmogorov-Smirnov[1] (one-tailed) test χ^2 (2 d. of f.) ..	49·51		92·71		85·02		90·21	
Per cent. level of significance ..	0·1		0·1		0·1		0·1	
Superior Group	Exp. (i.t.a.)		Exp. (i.t.a.)		Exp. (i.t.a.)		Exp. (i.t.a.)	

[1] Kolmogorov-Smirnov two-sample test. In SIEGEL, S. (1956). *Nonparametric Statistics for the Behavioral Sciences.* New York and London: McGraw-Hill, pp. 127-136.

[2] Ibid., pp. 30, 56.

These figures speak for themselves. After 1 year 20·6 per cent of the i.t.a. children had passed beyond Book III compared with only 3·3 per cent of the T.O. children (in other words i.t.a. is some six times easier to learn by those "apparently" ready for reading); after $1\frac{1}{3}$ years more than half of i.t.a. children (56·2 per cent) had passed that important milestone of progress, compared with only 27·9 per cent of the T.O. children. This lead was maintained as time elapsed and standards of reading rose until by the end of $2\frac{1}{3}$ years 78·1 per cent compared with 37·8 per cent had passed beyond Book V. It is perhaps even more important to note that after $2\frac{1}{3}$ years 45·0 per cent of the T.O. group had still not progressed beyond Book III compared with 15·1 per cent of the i.t.a. group. A comparison of the background data of the two groups (average age, size of class, etc.) indicated that these favoured the control (T.O.) group. The superior performance of the experimental (i.t.a.) group was achieved despite this bias.

The researchers also postulated that, if i.t.a. was an easier medium, children learning to read with i.t.a. should achieve significantly higher scores on reading tests in which what were termed "lower order decoding skills" have an especially important role to play. For this purpose use was made of the Schonell Graded Word Reading Test which consists of 100 separate words (without contextual clues), the pupil being credited with a point for each word read and pronounced correctly. For the experimental group the words were transliterated into i.t.a. and the test was given to both groups at the end of the first school year and after $1\frac{1}{3}$ years. Despite a bias in matching that favoured the control group, the experimental (i.t.a.) group achieved superior mean scores: 17·99 compared with 6·61 after 1 year and 33·93 compared with 14·74 after $1\frac{1}{3}$ years.[1] The distribution of scores is also highly favourable to i.t.a.: at the middle point of the range of scores, some 35 per cent of the i.t.a. children scoring 40 or above (a reading age of 9 and over) as against only some 8 per cent of the others.[2]

A further test, the Neale Analysis of Reading Ability, completed the first stage of the research. This consists of six passages of narrative prose and is designed to provide measures of accuracy, speed, and comprehension. As before, the passages were transliterated into i.t.a. for the experimental group but in all other respects the tests were identical. They were applied only once, just before the middle of the fifth term, and only to a sub-sample (459 children in each group). By all three criteria the i.t.a. children returned superior mean scores[3]—

[1] Ibid., pp. 31–2, 57.   [2] Ibid., graph 6, p. 75.   [3] Ibid., pp. 33, 57–8.

	i.t.a. children (N.459)	*T.O. children* (N.459)
Accuracy	24·79	13·68
Speed	26·41	24·77
Comprehension	6·99	4·86

Here again the distribution of the scores is particularly significant in the comprehension test, some 45 per cent of the i.t.a. children scoring $7\frac{1}{2}$ or more as against only some 25 per cent of the T.O. children.[1]

The report so far presents unambiguous evidence in favour of i.t.a. Though the relevance of reading speed during the very early stages, especially when divorced from the quantity and difficulty of what is read, may be doubted, the statistics demonstrate that the i.t.a. children found learning to read far less onerous and performed with markedly greater degrees of accuracy and comprehension than did the children confined to the orthodox alphabet(s) and spelling. To quote from Downing's final conclusions—

3. The traditional orthography of English is a serious cause of difficulty in the early stages of learning to read and write.
(*a*) T.O. slowed down children's progress in their series of readers.
(*b*) T.O. caused significantly lower scores on all tests of reading, but especially word recognition and accuracy. The reduction in the learning efficiency of the most able pupils in the t.o. classes was especially remarkable.[2]

Testing the transition

The acid test for the new alphabet was however the transition. Superior decoding, accuracy, and comprehension in i.t.a. were all very well, but could these skills be transferred to orthodox texts and be further developed? This question was linked to the third of Dr. Downing's hypotheses: "In i.t.a. classes, reading achievements in T.O. should not be inferior to previous achievements in i.t.a. once fluency in i.t.a. has been established." To assess the impact of the transition, parallel versions of the same Schonell and Neale tests were employed, comparisons being made of the i.t.a. group's scores when the tests were given in i.t.a. and (after an interval) in T.O. The first sub-sample (433) of the experimental group was put through its first T.O. Neale test during their fifth term, a month after undergoing the parallel test in i.t.a. The mean scores were as follows[3]—

[1] Ibid., graph 9, p. 77.   [2] Ibid., p. 51.   [3] Ibid., pp. 34, 59–60.

i.t.a. children (N.433)

	Tested in i.t.a.	Tested in T.O.
Accuracy	25·36	18·88
Speed	27·04	32·00
Comprehension	6·92	6·15

Though the scores in T.O. for speed were significantly superior, there was a significant falling-off in respect of accuracy and comprehension compared with the scores returned by the same children when tested a month earlier in i.t.a. The report, however, notes that approximately two-thirds of these children had not yet been thought by their teachers to be ready for the transition and had not yet been transferred to books printed in T.O.

In other words the proviso that "fluency in i.t.a. has been established" had not been met, and therefore a re-analysis of the test was carried out utilizing the results of only those 152 children who had been transferred from i.t.a. to T.O. materials by their teachers at least six weeks before being tested in T.O Their comparative mean scores were as follows[1]—

i.t.a. children (N.152)

	Tested in i.t.a.	Tested in T.O.
Accuracy	42·2	33·4
Speed	40·6	53·5
Comprehension	10·8	9·9

This second, more advanced group therefore appears to have lost ground in respect of accuracy and to a very small extent in respect of comprehension, though it actually improved its mean reading speeds.

Although Dr. Downing reports a "setback" immediately after the transition, he goes on to report that when tested again later at the end of the third school year and after they had time to become accustomed to reading T.O., the i.t.a. children (171 pupils) were shown to have made a complete recovery. In respect of all three criteria their mean scores in T.O. were very superior to what they had been in i.t.a. one-and-a-half school years earlier.[2]

i.t.a. children (N.171)

	Tested in i.t.a. in fifth term	Tested in T.O. in fifth term	Tested in T.O. at end of third year
Accuracy	28·79	21·31	39·98
Speed	29·47	36·80	60·73
Comprehension	8·18	7·16	15·36

[1] Ibid., pp. 34–5, 60–1.   [2] Ibid., pp. 38, 66.

This part of the research was summed up in the second of Dr. Downing's generalized conclusions—

> 2. The success of i.t.a. in improving T.O. literacy skills occurs in spite of an important setback in the growth of these basic skills at the stage of transition from i.t.a. to T.O.[1]

It is at this point that I feel justified in making some comments. Naturally, I hesitate to do so because it may suggest that, like an over-protective mother, I am unable to concede the mildest adverse criticism of i.t.a., but to say nothing would amount to condoning what I believe to be faults in the structure of the research as well as a number of wrong assumptions about the processes at the transition. I shall, however, limit myself to the following—

(1) Although numerous teachers have reported (e.g. Chapter 10) that the transition is normally smooth and effortless and in fact is scarcely noticed by the child, it is unreasonable to expect that there will be no setback at all. To state as in *Hypothesis 3* that "reading achievements in T.O. should not be inferior to previous achievements in i.t.a." is unreasonable if applied to children tested at the very moment of the transition or just after it. It is more than likely, though not inevitable, that their performance will be marginally inferior. What matters is that, even if they need to exert greater concentration and effort and even if their speed of reading slackens[2] somewhat, they should still be effective readers and able forthwith to regain and indeed improve upon the standards reached in i.t.a. This, in fact, was the case, for the research demonstrates that the purported setback is overcome and that "by the end of the third school year the t.o. scores are very superior to what they were in i.t.a. one-and-a-half school years earlier."[3] The significance of the ultimate findings are therefore in no way diminished. In other words any setback has to be considered in the context of the eventual superiority of the i.t.a. children once they have had a chance to become accustomed to the orthodox medium.

(2) The report itself assumes (*Hypothesis 3*) that the experimental group's reading achievements should be tested "once fluency in i.t.a. has been established." The need to establish complete fluency in i.t.a. before

---

[1] Ibid., p. 49.

[2] Another reason for suspecting the design of the research into the transition was the peculiar finding that the i.t.a. children read faster in T.O., though they were meeting it for the first time in their lives. This is more than anyone has claimed for i.t.a., and must cast doubt on the aptness and validity of the test (but see also pp. 177–8).

[3] Ibid., p. 38.

the transition is attempted has always been, among other conditions, emphasized in i.t.a. publications and seminars for teachers and, while the dangers of a premature transition can be exaggerated, I myself have always argued that fluency in the easier medium is a *sine qua non* for a successful transition to the more difficult one. It is astonishing therefore to find that this principle was disregarded by the researchers—especially when one considers the advice given by Dr. Downing himself to the teachers of the experimental group (*supra*, page 164). In the first test of the transition we are told "that approximately two-thirds of the children had not been transferred to reading T.O. books by their teachers when Neale A in T.O. was administered."[1] One feels entitled to ask: Why on earth not? Why not wait until they were ready? Quite a few teachers protested that their children were being forced to deal with orthodox texts long before they were ready for them and that they were concerned lest this might cause damage to the children's intellectual development.

Somewhat revealingly the report goes on to explain that the same test was applied to 152 children who had been transferred by their teachers from i.t.a. to T.O. at least six weeks beforehand. For three reasons this procedure strikes me as being inadequate: (*a*) For such a vital section of the research was it sufficient to rely merely on the judgement of individual teachers as to whether the children were ready for the transition? The report itself throws doubt on the teacher's judgement when it states that "Generally, in the first experiment, the transition stage tended to begin too early. In the second experiment it appears to have come later, but it seems that the use of i.t.a. requires a longer course than is often contemplated."[2] In the normal, everyday classroom situation the teacher's judgement can be relied upon, but in an experimental test of the transition, even in "field conditions," it is essential to adopt a more rigorous procedure and to make quite sure that *each* and every child taking part is fluent in reading i.t.a. This could have been ascertained by the achievement of agreed minimum standards on the three Neale tests. The information was available but it was never taken into account. These early tests of the transition were therefore meaningless.

(*b*) Why was it not considered necessary to test the children on the

[1] Ibid., p. 34.
[2] Ibid., p. 50. Elsewhere Downing has written, "As some guide as to when this stage would be reached, it was proposed that transfer should take place not before Book 4 had been completed (approximately a mid-grade 2 textbook) in i.t.a. and that even then these skills should be checked." "How i.t.a. began," *Elementary English*, Vol. 44, 1967, p. 45.

actual day they were thought to be ripe for the transition—or at any rate not more than a week afterwards? This would have meant testing each child individually, but surely it should have been an essential, not to say elementary step in the research?

(*c*) Why was this key test limited to a sub-sample of only 152 children? Why were not all the i.t.a. children tested in this way? No control group was involved in this part of the research which was concerned only with the performance of the same i.t.a. child before and after transition. There was no need for matching and thus for the severe reduction in the number of children tested. One would have hoped for the transition to be tested in the case of every child who had reached fluency (and comprehension—see next paragraph) in i.t.a. The residue who after an agreed period never reached this minimum standard might with some justification be considered as failures, related perhaps to some cause other than the use of i.t.a. No effort was made to probe this possibility.

(3) *Hypothesis 3* is at fault in omitting the criterion of comprehension. Fluency is not enough. This omission is surprising because, as we have seen, elsewhere in the report[1] Downing writes that "Pitman's design for transfer was based on the development, prior to the transition stage, of two skills: reading from minimal clues[2] . . . and the use of contextual clues to meaning." Although comprehension was tested by the Neale test and the information was available, it was not considered necessary to take fool-proof steps to eliminate children who were not yet able to read with comprehension in i.t.a. The extent of a child's comprehension of what he reads is much harder for a teacher to assess than his fluency but here once again each and every child should surely have been rejected if he was not yet ripe for the further test of transition.

The transition by the i.t.a. children was further investigated by means of the Schonell Graded Word Reading Test which was analysed in two ways: first, the i.t.a. results of 257 children were compared after $1\frac{1}{3}$ years with their results in T.O. after two years and a bit (the seventh term). This comparison was however not considered valid in relation to *Hypothesis 3* because only 52·2 per cent of the pupils had been transferred to T.O. books by their teachers. Therefore the results of 135 pupils who had been transferred to T.O. books by their teachers four months earlier were separated from the rest: this showed a decline in mean scores from 51·63 (i.t.a.) to 44·82 (T.O.).[3]

[1] Ibid., p. 18.   [2] See footnote on p. 164.   [3] Ibid., pp. 35, 62.

TABLE XIII

The distribution of alphabetic simplicity and difficulty in the Schonell test applied in the Research

	Regular	Irregular to the extent of a minor modification	Irregular but containing much that is familiar	Misleading
5	milk, egg	tree	littl	–
10	sit, frog, bun	book	–	scool, plæiŋ
15	clock	–	flouer	roed, træn, liet
20	summer	thiŋk	pictuer	peepl
25	–	dreem, thirsty	sheperd	dounstærs, biscit
30	–	sandwich, beginniŋ	croud	pœstæj, ieland
35	–	–	–	sauser, ænjel, seeliŋ, appeerd, nœm
40	–	–	attractiv, gradueally	canæry, imajin, nevue
45	–	applaud	–	smœlder, dispœsal, nurriʃht, diʃeexd
50	–	–	plauxibl	ueniversity, orcestra, noledʒ, audjens, situeæted
Total:	7	8	8	27
Percentage in Schonell test	14	16	16	54
Normal percentage in continuous English	26·5	23·75	10·5	39·25

Dr. Downing concludes this section of the report with an attempt to examine those words in both the Schonell and Neale tests which he believes are most likely to cause the pupil difficulty at the transition.[1] This part of the research also, I feel, calls for comment.

(4) The Schonell and Neale tests may have been very suitable for the original purpose for which they were designed and they are, I am sure, adequate if not ideal for comparing the standards of the experimental and control children at a time other than the moment of transition. On the other hand they leave much to be desired when testing the experimental group with itself before, at, and immediately after the transition. In four respects the tests employed seem particularly inappropriate—

(*a*) The testing of the single words in the Schonell test meant that the child was denied the benefit of contextual clues on which he had until the moment of the test been encouraged, rightly, to depend. He suddenly found himself placed in an unfamiliar, artificial situation. To measure simple decoding may be valid when comparing the mechanics of reading in one medium with those in another yet it has but little relevance, particularly in the case of the misleadingly spelled words, when testing the transition. In the other (Neale) accuracy test the four-second time limit made it similarly inappropriate.

(*b*) Furthermore, among the single words in the particular Schonell test appear an abnormally high percentage of misleading spellings. My calculation (*Table XIII*) is that only 14 per cent of the words in the test can be considered as "regular" (or unchanged from i.t.a.), compared with the normal 26·5 per cent (see analysis on page 140); 16 per cent of the test words can be counted as being "irregular" to the extent of a minor modification from i.t.a. compared with 23·75 per cent; and a further 16 per cent are "irregular" though containing much that is familiar, compared with an average of 10·5 per cent; but 54 per cent fall into the classification of being "misleading" and being radically different from their i.t.a. versions, compared with an average of only 39·25 per cent.

(*c*) Although in the Neale comprehension test the tester supplies the unread words, this denies the child the opportunity to puzzle out the meaning for himself, a process which lies at the heart of independent learning leading to understanding.

(*d*) In the Neale test the child is allowed only four seconds in which to read each word. This is no doubt correct for the purpose for which

[1] Ibid., pp. 35–8.

177

this test was designed, but it is surely not long enough for the i.t.a. reader not yet accustomed to orthodox spelling. To introduce a speed element at all strikes me as being inappropriate. The maintenance of a speed sufficient for effective reading (fluency with comprehension) is all that can or should be expected at and just after the transition; a small drop in speed is unimportant, particularly if the pre-transition speed was more than sufficient for this purpose. Variations in reading speeds among young children who, as here, registered mean speeds of only 30 words per minute are not of much practical importance; a difference of even ten per cent represents less than 3 words per minute!

Teachers reported that when tested in T.O. most of the children knew they were being tested for speed and not unnaturally were stimulated to higher speeds by the sight of the researcher holding a stop-watch. This kind of atmosphere must have been disturbing for very young children and diverted their efforts to beating the clock and thus detracted from their recently acquired ability to read. I state this bluntly in the knowledge that in tests of the transition the i.t.a. group speeded up, but this favourable finding in itself casts doubt on this aspect of the research because it is unbelievable that children will immediately read faster in the more difficult medium unless it is at the expense of accuracy and comprehension.

After the transition

The transition had been tested by comparing the standards of the i.t.a. experimental group before, at, and after the transition. Dr. Downing's third question asked: "After the whole process of beginning with i.t.a. and transferring to T.O., are reading attainments in T.O. superior to what they would have been without the intervention of i.t.a.?" In order to answer it, comparisons were made between the post-transition standards of the i.t.a. group and those of the control group who had started to learn to read at the same time. There were three main comparisons, *all carried out in T.O.*, the bias in the matching tending as before to favour the control group. It will be more convenient to mention the Schonell test first, though it actually was the second test to be used; it was applied to 291 pupils in each group at the start of their third year: the i.t.a. group returned a mean score of 29·70 compared with 24·39 for the control group.[1] This

[1] Ibid., pp. 39, 68.

result was significantly in favour of the i.t.a. children at the five per cent level. The Neale test was applied to 457 in each group in the middle of their second year and 194 in each group at the end of the third school year.[1] The mean scores were as follows—

	Mid-second year (N.457)		End of third year (N.194)	
	i.t.a. children	*T.O. children*	*i.t.a. children*	*T.O. children*
Accuracy	18·61	16·90	38·97	31·66
Speed	31·33	29·99	59·07	51·59
Comprehension	6·24	5·87	14·77	12·60

The superiority of the i.t.a. children in the first of these two tests may not be statistically significant at the five per cent level, but the report remarks that about two-thirds of these i.t.a. children had not then been transferred by their teachers to T.O. books. The second Neale test, like the Schonell test, showed that the i.t.a. group returned significantly superior results on all three counts.

These results provide an impressive vindication of all that has been claimed for i.t.a. They confirm that the setback, *if it exists*, is short-lived and that the experimental group soon regained and exceeded the standards they had achieved with i.t.a. Once they had been given a chance to practise with and become accustomed to the misleading words in orthodox texts, they became also in that respect superior to the control group. It may appear churlish not to be content with these findings, yet the criticisms made in relation to Question II are still applicable and in particular—

(5) Nothing was done to assess the readiness of the children (all of whom were tested solely in T.O.) for the transition (e.g. their standards of fluency and comprehension in i.t.a.). The test halfway through the second year took place when "about two-thirds of the pupils in the i.t.a. experimental group were still using i.t.a. materials and had not been transferred to T.O. books by their teachers." This seems to be an extraordinary admission in relation to a test in T.O. of children who, in the words of Question III (i.e. the question being investigated), have passed through "the whole process of beginning with i.t.a. *and transferring to T.O.*"[2] It says a lot for the new alphabet that despite their grotesque handicap the i.t.a. children's scores

---

[1] Ibid., pp. 39–40, 67–9.
[2] My italics.

were marginally superior to those of the T.O. group. Dr. Downing's Question III seems to be too imprecise. Insufficient distinction is made between the moment of transition (supposedly asked in Question II though in practice, as we have seen, ignored) and the continuing post-transitional period. For some unexplained reason the tests of the i.t.a. children appear to have been related neither to the date of the transition nor to the interval since its occurrence, but only to the date at which they first started to learn to read with i.t.a.! In other words no account was taken of the opportunities to practise reading in T.O. It is reasonable to ask why it was not considered obligatory, despite the possible difficulties of administration, to test each child individually on the day of its transition and also at regular intervals after it (e.g. 3 months, 6 months, 9 months, etc.).

Written composition and spelling

The next two questions in the report assessed the children's written compositions and their later attainments in orthodox spelling. In both cases the i.t.a. experimental group was superior to the control group.

To assess whether the i.t.a. or the T.O. group were able to write the more fluently, at greater length, and with a more extensive vocabulary, the compositions of 54 children in each group were compared during the seventh term, by which time the majority of the i.t.a. children had made the transition in their reading. The compositions were not specially prepared, but were collected without warning by the teacher or picked at random by the experimenter. It was found impossible to make a direct statistical comparison, because of large differences in the schools involved, but the overall impression is that the i.t.a. children were genuinely superior in their written composition work, both in the quantity of matter written and the richness of the vocabulary. The report also states that even if *all* the T.O. schools were up to the standard of the best T.O. school, the i.t.a. schools would still show a larger overall word-count and a greater total incidence of "more advanced" words.[1]

To assess the ability of both groups to spell T.O. words, the Schonell Graded Word Spelling Test was applied twice: individually in the middle of the third school year (374 pupils in each group) and as a group test in the middle of the fourth year (102 pupils in each group). Correct T.O.

[1] Ibid., pp. 40–2, 70.

spellings only were credited, a correct i.t.a. spelling being disallowed. The mean test scores were as follows[1]—

	i.t.a. children	*T.O. children*
Mid-third year (N.374)	28·44	25·34
Mid-fourth year (N.102)	39·11	32·25

Although the superiority of the i.t.a. group in the first test was not statistically significant at the five per cent level, it was so in the second test and both sets of results demonstrate that if one starts learning to read and write in i.t.a., it is easier later on to spell in T.O. Throughout, the i.t.a. children showed a consistent superiority and in the second test at the middle point some 43 per cent of the i.t.a. children scored 40 and over against only some 28 per cent of the T.O. children.[2]

"Low" and "high" achievers

The next section of the report compares what are termed "low achievers," "middle achievers," and "high achievers." In my view it is in part very misleading, having been based on premises that are surprisingly naïve. This statement cannot be dismissed as sour grapes because these findings in any case point very markedly to the superior effectiveness of i.t.a. By means of graphs, that for reasons already explained, may not be reproduced here, Dr. Downing attempts to suggest:[3] (*a*) that on most tests the high achievers among the i.t.a. children were superior to the high achievers among the T.O. children. The i.t.a. high achievers demonstrated a greater degree of superiority over the corresponding T.O. children than was found among the middle and low achievers; (*b*) that middle achievers taught by i.t.a., though less obviously superior to the corresponding T.O. pupils, nevertheless showed an important degree of superiority; (*c*) that among the low achievers on the earliest tests little or no measurable differences existed between the scores of the two groups. Later tests, however, suggested that the i.t.a. low achievers became superior to their T.O. counterparts, but that this was not true of the lowest ten per cent in both groups. When these i.t.a. children were being tested in i.t.a. (i.e. the first $1\frac{1}{2}$ years) no difference was found between their scores and those of the T.O. children. When in the middle of the second school year testing in T.O. took the place of testing in i.t.a., the low achievers of the i.t.a. group at first fell behind the T.O. group, but later,

---

[1] Ibid., pp. 43, 71.   [2] Ibid., graph 34, p. 89.   [3] Ibid., pp. 43–6, 73–90.

at the end of the third year, even the i.t.a. low achievers became generally superior to the T.O. low achievers.

Many of the strictures levied against the earlier results apply with at least equal force to these comparisons: they are once again invalidated, at any rate for the low achievers, by the unsuitability of testing single words out of context (Schonell) and of the time limitation in the (Neale) accuracy test, and by the failure to test for adequate levels of fluency and comprehension in i.t.a. before introducing tests in T.O. In addition, the following criticisms would appear to be justified—

(6) To test in T.O. children defined as low achievers even in i.t.a. is absurd, yet the conclusions Dr. Downing reaches about them are based on precisely such tests! The series of graphs which illustrate them include no data from tests carried out in i.t.a. later than the fifth term, apart from the teacher's records of reading primers reached after 2 and 2⅓ years (see table on page 169). This table demonstrates a considerable superiority among the i.t.a. children, and one suspects that a comparable superiority would have appeared if the experimental group had been similarly tested in i.t.a. for the Neale tests of reading rates, comprehension, and accuracy after 2 and 2⅓ years. The eventual superior showing of the i.t.a. low achievers in the Neale tests after 3 years, even in T.O. for which many of them could not have been ready, suggests that if tested in i.t.a. the margin between the two groups would have been even much wider. By definition the low achievers need a longer period before they become fluent and comprehend enough in i.t.a. to be ready for the transition. This delay does not matter greatly because the reduction in the *eventual* percentage of those who leave school as backward readers is far more important than whether the bulk learn to read a few months earlier.

(7) The tendency to remain a backward reader can be demonstrated more clearly if the Neale comprehension scores are related to reading ages (see Chapter 1) as, for example, in the test given to both groups in T.O. after 3 years (see *Table XIV*). Despite the gross handicap imposed on the backward i.t.a. children by testing them in T.O. for which they were not ready, 16 (49 − 33) per cent fewer than the control group had a reading age below a chronological age which may reasonably be supposed to have been approximately eight. The degree of incomprehension among the lowest achievers is indicated by the performance of the most backward who, despite three years of schooling, failed to score more than 5 points in the simplest of tests.

TABLE XIV

Reading comprehension measured by Neale Analysis of Reading Ability: Form B. Experimental and Control groups both tested in T.O. at end of 3 school years.

Score	Reading Age	i.t.a. %	T.O. %
Worst			
Below 6	Below 7	14	25
6–10	7·1–7·10	19	24
		33	49
Best			
11–15	8·2–8·10	26	21
16–20	8·11–9·6	16	10
21–25	9·10–10·10	15	8
Above 25	10·11–13	10	12
		67	51
		100%	100%

Though the vital comprehension and accuracy tests in i.t.a. are lacking, the table (*supra*, p. 169) recording the reading primers reached does tell us a great deal. The degrees of success in both groups can be divided into three categories[1]—

Book IV, Book V and beyond. These children can already be said to have reached the stage when they read for pleasure. They will never be below average, much less backward readers. Practice will steadily perfect their early skills.

Book II and Book III. Some of these children are likely sooner or later to master the essentials of reading, but most of them may never do so to

[1] Dr. Joyce Morris, in her investigation of reading standards in primary schools in Kent, adopted a similar division of reading primers: "Experienced teachers . . . had stated that, although the first four books of the better-known reading series varied in difficulty to some extent, it was possible to distinguish three standards of reading ability according to them. In practice it was customary for infant teachers to consider a first primer as dividing the poor and non-readers from the rest at the age of seven. Children at this stage would need systematic instruction in the junior school and a great deal of individual attention. Those who were well on in Book 2 or even reading Book 3 were at the second stage where reading ability was mainly mechanical. These children required a great deal of assistance and encouragement from the junior teacher if their progress was to be maintained, and their reading ability was to become a real tool for the acquisition of knowledge and pleasure. The ability to tackle a Book 4 was considered to mark the beginning of true reading, and children who had reached this stage or beyond . . . were able to make progress on their own, provided that they were given plenty of reading material." *Reading in the Primary School*, pp. 103–4. Newnes (for the National Foundation for Educational Research in England and Wales), London, 1959.

any high degree and therefore will end up as below average or backward readers; very few will remain semi-literate or illiterate.

Introductory Book and Book I. These children, after 2⅓ years, are not yet able to read primers that contain only 27 and 59 (27+32) words respectively. They are already "stuck" and have got off to such a poor start that they will almost certainly end up as backward readers or worse and many of them will make no significant progress even if they have the benefit of remedial teaching.

On this analysis 45 per cent of the T.O. group, having still not progressed beyond Book III, are prone to end up as backward readers or worse (unless saved by remedial teaching) compared with 15·1 per cent of the i.t.a. group. The percentages in both groups may perhaps be inflated but the comparison is apt. Whether this superiority of the low achievers among the i.t.a. children can be carried forward at and beyond the transition can be demonstrated only by testing them in T.O. when—and only when—they are ready for it. This was never done.

It may be asked, why then should there be even 15·1 per cent of potential backward readers among the i.t.a. children after 2⅓ years at school. This is a fair question and suggests that this 15·1 per cent at any rate must have been held back by some factor or combination of factors other than the difficulties of the orthodox alphabet(s) and spelling. As this no doubt applies equally to the control group, an additional 29·9 per cent (45·0–15·1) of them can be said to have been defeated by the orthodox alphabet(s) and spelling. The factors that explain the 15·1 per cent in both groups will include those discussed in Chapter 3—e.g. severely low intelligence; brain injuries and specific dyslexias; emotional, behavioural, or personality disorders; hearing or ocular defects—yet presumably children with these extreme disabilities were excluded from the research and all these factors together are, in my view, likely to account for only a very small percentage, far less than our 15·1 per cent, and there must be some other factor. By far the most feasible is that these children suffered from various degrees of what we defined earlier as "linguistic incompetence."

As we saw in Chapter 2, for most children listening and speaking precedes reading and writing. The simple words selected for a reading primer are assumed to be those already familiar to young children and meaningful to them in everyday use. Unless they know these words and unless, in addition, they possess a certain minimum linguistic ability which entails not merely being able to understand a short vocabulary of simple words but a facility to use them in meaningful sentences, children have little chance of beginning to learn to read. They are linguistically inadequate. They suffer, so far as reading is concerned, from a misfortune as disabling as partial sight or deafness. This is not to suggest that a child like this cannot catch up later on, but it will help explain why some children, after 2⅓ years at school and after the particular difficulties of orthodox spelling have been removed, are still defeated by *little* and *book*. They are unable to envisage the word they are struggling to read as being one in a meaningful sequence that prepares the way for and provides clues to the more difficult word even before it is reached. In reading, the linguistic context is a more powerful aid even than it is in listening, because the reader can hark back as well as cast forward; but none of this is possible, whether listening or reading, without a minimum foundation of linguistic competence.

Linguistic competence is a major "pupil variable." It is remarkable that the research took no account of it whatsoever (*a*) in determining which children were ready to start being taught reading; or (*b*) in order to ensure that children lacking a minimum linguistic competence were, like the blind, either excluded from the research or at least reported on as a separate section.

Moreover the failure to take conceptual and linguistic competence into account casts further doubt also on the statistics recording the transition. The children's performance must to some extent have been affected by richness or poverty of vocabulary and varying skill in the deployment of words. Because reading in i.t.a. is so much easier, linguistic difficulties are more apt to be concealed, whereas at the transition they tend to be exposed. This perhaps explains part of the purported setback—or, to put it more correctly, it explains the great range of differences in the time taken to reach the transition.

*   *   *

Suggested improvements to the research design

In this type of field research the difficulties facing the investigator are obvious and well known. It is even harder to be sure that one is drawing valid conclusions. Personally I am doubtful if any more formal statistical research into the basic tenets of i.t.a. is required, though in Chapter 13

185

the reader will find certain specific subjects which I feel may deserve investigation. The extent to which i.t.a. is adopted is more likely to be decided by the personal experience and recommendation of practising teachers. Should however the research described in this chapter be continued or should investigations into other teaching media be launched, I hope that those in charge will base their procedures on a deeper knowledge of the growth of the reading process in young children and on a more exact understanding of the nature and purpose of the new medium. Any future research into the transition should, I believe, be guided by the following principles, though they do not amount to a comprehensive programme—

(i) It is essential to devise adequate tests to ensure that each child assessed at the transition is ready for it. If found more practicable, there is no reason why the teachers themselves should not administer these proving tests, provided they are able to be objective. Agreed minimum standards should be set for fluency and linguistic competence in i.t.a. Scrutiny of each child's written compositions and an analysis of his vocabulary could provide an additional check of linguistic competence.

(ii) Each child who reaches the agreed minimum standards should be given the same test in T.O. at an equivalent level to that given earlier in i.t.a. on or not more than a week after the day on which he is first launched on the transition. (Enquiries should be made to eliminate any children prematurely and deliberately launched on the transition by their parents.)

(iii) At frequent, regular intervals the pre-transition children should be retested in i.t.a. (i.e. until they reach the agreed minimum standards when they will be ready for the test outlined in (ii) above). The post-transition children should also be tested at regular intervals.

(iv) Whether comparing the experimental group with the control group or with itself, tests for accuracy and comprehension should be isolated from any test for speed. Each child should be allowed to decide for himself when he gives up trying to read a particular word. If he fails to read any words, he should read the whole passage again and, if still necessary, he can be prompted, so that he has the benefit of contextual clues for the rest of the passage.

(v) In the earlier stages, certainly until the transition is long past, single word tests should be avoided and reliance placed only on tests consisting of continuous English. Comprehension tests, scrutiny of written compositions, and analyses of written vocabulary could continue to be employed to supply a measure of growth in linguistic competence.

(vi) In the post-transition period, until effective reading in T.O. has been firmly established, a clearer distinction should be made between reading skills and linguistic competence. The former could now be tested by means of rapid exposure of single words including some misleading spellings; the latter by presenting a gradation of even more difficult and infrequent words in sentences with plenty of contextual clues.

If the first British experiment with i.t.a. had incorporated these and similar principles, its findings would have been more meaningful. Nevertheless they merit careful study. As it happened, the shortcomings of the research all favoured the orthodox alphabet(s) and spelling and this makes its overall confirmation of the claims of i.t.a. the more remarkable.

10   How effective is i.t.a.?—
2. Verdict of the Teachers

THE STATISTICAL FINDINGS arrived at by the research team provide the essential, incontrovertible bare bones of the case in favour of i.t.a., but it is justifiable also to take account of the opinions of the teachers, some of whom now have many years' experience of the new medium. Enthusiasm for a fresh approach in teaching tends to be infectious and has to be discounted, yet in the case of i.t.a. it is too great to be ignored—and it must be remembered that all the teachers entered the experiment full of anxieties and virtually all as sceptics. Inevitably a teacher's opinion lacks the objectivity of the trained research worker but not infrequently teachers come closer to the growth processes of children's minds than the subtlest techniques of educational research. The more imponderable, immeasurable responses shown by the children equally merit study. Here, at any rate, is a small sample of teachers' opinions on the general effectiveness of i.t.a. They have been selected from comments invited firstly from teachers at the end of the third year of the British research programme, though not all the teachers quoted had the full nine terms' experience of the new medium; secondly from teachers in the United States where experience with the new medium began in 1963, when the first large-scale project began in Bethlehem, Pennsylvania. Their comments, taken over a substantial period of time, strikingly echo and confirm those of the British teachers. Inevitably the extracts may be said to have been hand-picked but they are typical of the opinions held by a great many, almost certainly the majority, of the teachers involved in the experiment. They can be assessed only individually and at their face value.

The extracts are arranged under the following headings: (1) general; (2) the transition; (3) keenness to read; (4) creative writing; (5) problem solving and concept forming; (6) handwriting; (7) morale and behaviour.

(1) GENERAL

I am firmly convinced after twenty-one years' teaching experience that the medium in which the child's first steps are taken in learning to read is a factor of great importance, particularly to early success. Since I began i.t.a. in September 1961, the standard of reading in the admission class is far superior to what it was when I was using orthodox spelling. This progress is maintained when the children move to a higher class. The consistency of rules simplifies the child's task, and he shows greater confidence in tackling new words. I have proved that many children discover for themselves the consistent relationship between i.t.a. letters and the sounds they represent.

> St. Wulstan's Roman Catholic Voluntary Primary School,
> Newcastle, Staffs.

Previous to introducing the i.t.a. method we found it difficult to arouse any interest in or enthusiasm for reading except among the very bright children who would learn from any medium. Now we find that every child soon obtains a mastery over sounds and words, and having gone through one book is most eager to go on and on. In fact I think that one of the biggest problems for the teacher is in keeping up with the constant demand of "Will you hear me read?"

> St. Patrick's Roman Catholic Infants School,
> Oldham.

This is the end of the first year of using i.t.a. in my school and I am very pleased with the result. The children in my school are from working-class homes and have very few books of their own. None of them can read when they first start school and most of them have real difficulty in learning to read. The able children learnt to read in approximately a third of the time, and all except a few children who have limited ability have made a much better start than they would have done with the traditional alphabet. They read with more understanding and can answer questions about the stories they are reading—even on the early books.

> Cadishead County Infants School,
> Cadishead, near Manchester.

A girl, aged 6½, having passed the transition to orthodox spelling, gained the Reading Prize in her Form at the 1964 Prize-Giving. Her elder brother, now 10½, of similar I.Q.—and, of course, identical home background—began to read at 8½, and at 9½ had reached the stage now attained by his sister, who thus has a 3-year advantage over her brother.

County Primary School,
Ridgmont, Bedford.

Teachers have argued that a normal child will learn to read anyway, no matter which reading scheme is used. This may well be true, but the claim of i.t.a. that this process is speeded up has undoubtedly proved true in my school. By means of i.t.a. children are now learning to read much quicker, and are through the reading scheme much quicker than in previous years. In some cases, this process time has been halved.

Top o' th' Brow County Primary School,
Bolton.

The Initial Teaching Alphabet has been used in this school with children who made little or no progress with the usual method, due to lack of intelligence, emotional upsets, poor health or background and other causes. The children have learned to read, some fairly quickly, some slowly and surely, with confidence and pride in their own ability. The most important point about this to me is that they do not feel, at this early age, 6–7 years, that they are failures.

St. Anne's Infants School,
Oldham.

. . . We come now, last of all, to the teacher herself, and all I can do is to speak of its [i.t.a.'s] effects on me, just an ordinary experienced teacher. I liked teaching children to read by orthodox spelling. There was concentrated effort on my part for a return varying from excellent in the brighter children down to an almost negative amount in a few of the less able children. Since using i.t.a. my effort is less strenuous and carries less strain, and the results are more rewarding, and far more advanced. I.t.a. has tremendous advantages over orthodox spelling. I am convinced it is the greatest contribution of this century in the educational field of infants.

Haworth County Primary School,
Haworth.

My experience has been that in this school every year, in spite of all efforts, some children have been transferred from the Infant to the Junior Department as non-readers. Since i.t.a. has been introduced, of the children taught by this method there will be *no* non-readers entering the Junior Department. . . . The children I refer to as non-readers are slow developers who have apparently found the difficulties of orthodox spelling too great to combat. Such children have all overcome the initial difficulty. Some are reading

190

he liek the story
caulld amanda best.
amanda is a littl
red cap. he am
the littl girl caulld
Jenny ho yo sent the
letter to. he am
5 years oeld. he walk
haem bie mie self. he
am sum tiems a
server at dinner-tiem

XVII Jennifer, 5 years.

ie liek storys. ie liek goldiloks and ie liek the three pigs wen the woolf chaeses them.

XVIII Angela, 5 years, 5 months.

deer mister Sir
Jaems pitman
thank yw fau
the buks
and ie liek
the buks
and ie liek
aull the buks
yw hav giv
us
wwd liek ie
tw cum yw
and heer her us
reeding. + ++ ++

XIX Lindsay—Letter sent to Sir James Pitman.

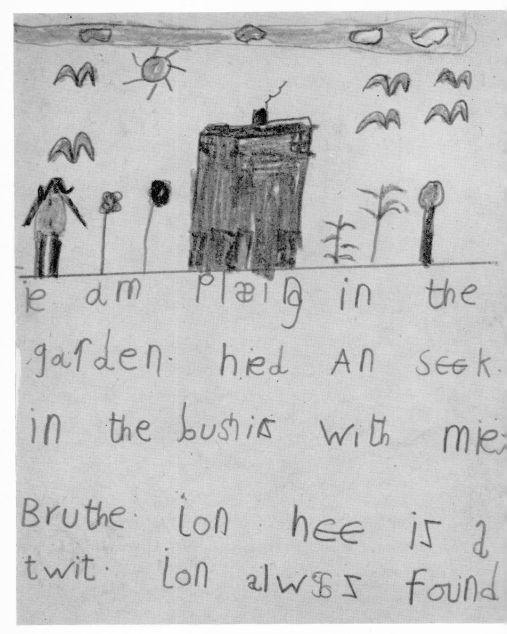

e am plæig in the garden. hied an seek. in the bushis with mie. Bruthe lon hee is a twit. lon alwes found

XX Josephine, 5 years, 8 months.

Wuns upon a tiem thaer livd
a man cauld aebrae ham and
a laedy cauld saera
wun dae sum trevelers caem
aebrae ham sau them and
sed doent goe past yw
lwk teerd sit doun and
aebrae ham went tw his
servants and the servaents
cwkd sumfwd and aebrae
ham twk it tw the
trevelers, the trevelers
sed tw aebraehem god is
sendin a baeby and
aebraehem nue that thae

XXI Richard, 9 years, 3 months.

Michelle.   Gardner.

mie muther and father

mie muther is a polees laedee
and shee cwks caeks
goes tw wurk at a polees staedoun
mie father
and hee has got blak haer. mie
muther has got blak haer tw. mie
muther has got broun ies. and mie
father has got blw ies. mie muther goes
tw the shops tw. befor muther goes
tw the shops shee maeks the beds.

XXII Michelle, 6 years, 4 months.

Roy Clarke

e. went tw the picturs and saw a
film cwlld scaramwsh it wos

gud won man hw fitts aull
the tiem and in evree fiet hee

never dies in the end tw men
had a saurd fiet and hee got

wwndid and the pwt a bandij
on his tumee amd the prins

tawkt tw him and then hee
fell ded gna thae bereed him

XXIII Roy, 6 years, 8 months.

missis ellecot is græt. Shee has
black hær and hie heel shoos.
Shee teeches in the mæn bildiŋ. thær
ar a lot in her class – ie wunder
hou meny. shee dusent wær ear-riŋ
but ie liek her patternd stockiŋs.
shee noes hou tu run her class
becos shee has got a bæby of her
very oen and thats hou shee noes
hou tu run it. shee luks after the
pee-ee apparætus. for us and washes
it if it gets mucky. eean.

XXIV Ian, 6 years, 1 month.

fluently and have completed transition. All will have reached Book 3. Of our children who have failed with orthodox spelling and have reached the age of 9+, all have now learned to read easily and well by using i.t.a., with the exception of two children whose I.Q. is well below 70.

Albert Road County Primary School,
Hinckley.

There was no doubt the language program was a success. We appreciate very much the growth the children enjoyed. But more exciting were the personality changes. Why does a child grow more in this area using i.t.a? We did not initiate i.t.a. to develop social growth but the by-products of the program that are mentioned as incidental will greatly influence the children's lives in the future. These children identify themselves as successful people and this early achievement builds tremendous self-confidence.

Locust Valley Elementary,
Locust Valley, New York, U.S.A.

On the whole, this group of children seemed to get more joy and satisfaction out of reading and writing on their own than any group of first graders I have worked with in my twelve years of teaching the first grade.

Oak Park, Michigan, U.S.A.

The children who, in our judgment, would read competently regardless of the medium have become independent readers at a much earlier stage. Enthusiasm is very evident and the children request library books daily. Almost all of the children, regardless of reading level, find enjoyment in extended reading activities. Since initial foundations have been laid, the parents have become increasingly enthusiastic at the success of their children and have expressed approval and satisfaction at progress made by their children when compared with their peers in classes using orthodox spelling.

Union Free School District No. 13,
Valley Stream, N.Y., U.S.A.

Our school is in a rural area and is definitely mediocre in linguistic background. Nearly every day Sister carries home stories written by her pupils and happily exclaims, "Look at the words my first graders are using. I never saw anything like it in my life." (Sister has taught first grade twenty years.) . . . Having taught primary grades many years, I can truly say i.t.a. is the most wonderful thing that has happened to reading in our century. All the *drudgery* is *removed*. Only the *joy remains*.

New Riegel School, New Riegel,
Ohio, U.S.A.

This group we are working with are a heterogeneous group whose Gates Reading Readiness Scores ranged from 100 to 48. Those at the upper end would have little difficulty with reading but are progressing more rapidly. Those at the lower end, while plodding, are building up a good foundation for word attack. These lower end youngsters would in all probability be ending up the year by finishing pre-primer or beginning primer material. Their exposure to i.t.a. will enable them to read at a higher level.

> Warren Township Public Schools,
> Warren Township, New Jersey,
> U.S.A.

We are quite elated with results, for not only are children learning to recognize any new word they meet, but they also are reading with a great degree of comprehension. . . . Motivation and interest level is extremely high because of the content of the reading materials. Enthusiasm shown by the boys is particularly significant.

> Summit County Public Schools,
> Akron, Ohio, U.S.A.

For us, i.t.a. works. Our children are reading substantially earlier and better than they had with orthodox texts. All our kindergarten children are well into reading. And while progress has been slower for most of the four-year-olds, all of them are reading successfully and many of them have advanced rapidly far into the Downing Readers. Our results tell us that we should continue to start reading in the four-year-olds and not wait even until kindergarten to start—for we cannot in good conscience deny the four-year-olds learning that is clearly within their capability and interest.

> Miss Mason's School, Princeton,
> New Jersey, U.S.A.

(2) TRANSITION

The teachers' comments on the transition to orthodox reading are of obvious importance—

When a child can read fluently in i.t.a. he can just pick up a book in orthodox spelling and read it. The transition takes place immediately, and no child in our school has needed any help at all. No special teaching need take place and certainly no special books or aids are necessary. We first were convinced of this in the very early days when we had a child who was leaving us to go to a school where i.t.a. was not being taught and where i.t.a. books were not available. We felt we must help this girl by putting her on orthodox reading before she left us, although she had not nearly completed the Infant Scheme. We were amazed to find that she could read the equivalent book in orthodox spelling without effort. This was a girl of six years old who we had considered below average in ability.

> Waterloo County Primary Infants School,
> Oldham.

The ease of transition to orthodox spelling surprised us very much. We gave no special help at all to any of our children, who transferred easily and naturally to orthodox spelling with hardly any pause in their fluency. We took the precaution of seeing that in the classroom there were a number of books in orthodox spelling which were also in i.t.a. and the children did make preliminary comparisons. I think this did play some part in the ease of transition.

Whitehouse County Primary School,
Bristol.

When the child reaches the required stage of fluency in i.t.a., transition to orthodox spelling seems almost automatic. Any reduction in reading ability is usually very insignificant and is very short-lived. In many cases it is not apparent at all.

Christ Church Junior Mixed and Infants School,
Burton-upon-Trent.

My teacher informs me that at the time of transition it is "almost a miracle," the way the i.t.a. readers transfer in the course of a few days to orthodox spelling.

All Saints' School,
Coalville.

The transition seems fairly effortless with the more capable children and it is surprising how little difference it makes to their powers of fluency and comprehension. The slower child is halted slightly but the progress is soon resumed.

Birstall County Infants School,
Leicester.

Once a child has become *really* fluent in reading i.t.a. he experiences no difficulty in reading books printed in orthodox spelling. I find that when read easily and at reasonable speed the child reads only the top half of the line of print. This appears to be so much like the top half of the line of print of the same matter in orthodox spelling that the child finds that he can read books printed in orthodox spelling with very little difficulty. He is able to read any unfamiliar words because the context helps him over the difficulties.

Alt Infants School,
Oldham.

The transition from i.t.a. to orthodox spelling creates a slight reduction in fluency and understanding, but this is very temporary and fairly insignificant.

Clarksfield County Infant School,
Oldham.

We find growing evidence that the change is happening all the time, even before the real fluency stage is reached, with reports of children reading orthodox books at home for enjoyment whilst they are using i.t.a. books at school. We have not yet made a specific attempt to change children, but find that (i) they change themselves, apparently in the twinkling of an eye; and (ii) with our visitors they will cheerfully read from an orthodox edition for them, and do not seem to think it strange.

> Malmesbury Park County Primary School,
> Bournemouth.

As the children have never been entirely cut off from orthodox spelling, they are aware of it from the beginning of reading. Therefore this step of transition is taken with ease and a sense of achievement. They are, so to speak, "throwing the props away." They know this is a step in their own development and, as such, it is with an enormous amount of self-satisfaction that they pass from i.t.a. to orthodox spelling. They take pride in it and are anxious to show their fellow pupils how easy it is and help them along the same pathway. Because they have been reading for meaning for so long, words they do not know are guessed from the context, which is surely true reading.

> Hem Heath County Junior and Infants School,
> Blurton, Stoke-upon-Trent.

The stage of transition seems to cause no difficulty at all. The children anticipate the transfer by their observations of "grown up" writing in everyday life, and by their use of book corner books in orthodox spelling as well as in i.t.a. When the actual transfer takes place their sense of achievement, and excitement at reaching this stage, carries them easily over any minor difficulties they may encounter.

> Leamore Infants School,
> Walsall.

The ease of transition is probably the most remarkable aspect of the teaching of reading through i.t.a. The first objections always posed by teachers and parents not conversant with the medium concern "unlearning" and the reading transition, and it would appear that the last causes the greatest concern. We who have used i.t.a. now know that as far as reading is concerned no problem appears to exist, no matter what the ability of the child may be. The difference between children is only evident by the stage at which each transfers, and once it is undertaken there appears very little hesitancy.

> St. Helen's Roman Catholic Primary School,
> Westcliff-on-Sea.

The child is able to make the transition to orthodox spelling quite effortlessly. The transition is *so easy* that we could hardly believe the evidence of our ears! The children do not seem to notice the difference between i.t.a. and orthodox spelling once they are reading fluently in i.t.a.

St. Mary's School,
Beaminster.

Ninety per cent of the Old Tappan first graders are now [by the end of the seventh month] in transition from i.t.a. to Roman Alphabet—traditional orthography. There is no difficulty.

Old Tappan, New Jersey, U.S.A.

Our school has a two year i.t.a. program for the pre-school child. In the first year—pre-kindergarten—the children learn to read and write with Pitman's Initial Teaching Alphabet. By the end of the year, they read fluently in i.t.a. The second year—kindergarten—these children are transferred to orthodox spelling. When school reopened in September, we found the following results: none of the children had lost his interest and fluency in reading i.t.a. books; three children had completed the transition to orthodox spelling on their own over the summer holidays—three months—but continued to read books in i.t.a. with the same amount of interest. Each child is encouraged to transfer when he reads i.t.a. so fluently that his interest motivates his eagerness to read "grown up" print. Teachers were amazed to find that capital letters presented very little if any difficulty at transition. They quickly associated the capitals with lower case letters.

The Anita Metzger School,
Ventnor City, New Jersey, U.S.A.

. . . I have now trained over a thousand teachers in our country and the immediate surrounding areas. . . . The progress of the children in i.t.a. has pleased the most doubtful administrator. In some classes all the children have made the transition and in the most limited classes 40 per cent already have made the transition. Although I caution all teachers *never to rush this change-over* I feel that the results that we have had are due to wide reading in the i.t.a. medium. It is then that the child has developed the skills of comprehension, confidence, competence and fluency.

Oakland Schools (administration),
Pontiac, Michigan, U.S.A.

(3) KEENNESS TO READ

Perhaps the most convincing evidence in favour of i.t.a. is the eagerness with which the i.t.a. children take to reading. Books are, from the start, things to be enjoyed. They are no longer drudgery—

The i.t.a. children have read a tremendous amount more than the orthodox spelling children. I have had to buy more sets of class readers in orthodox

195

Alphabets and Reading

spelling to cater for the children in their final year at school before going to the Junior Department. Some of the 6-year-olds who will be at the top of the school in September have already started on these new sets. By the Summer of 1965 I shall have difficulty in supplying the needs of the most able children.

Earls Hall Infants School,
Westcliff-on-Sea.

Before and after the transition the quantity of reading matter and the enjoyment and concentration with which it is read is noticeably greater than had the child been taught with the orthodox medium. Facility in reading is achieved so early that the child very soon gets the urge to read and is not content with going through the basic books but makes full use of the books in the school library. In fact most of the children have joined the Public Library and have no hesitation in taking back a book if, as they say, they "don't like it!" This applies to before and after the transition but especially in the latter case. In fact it is going to be difficult to maintain a supply of books for next year when our present Class II, who have been doing i.t.a. for two years, move into the top class. That the children are reading with enjoyment and concentration is very obvious to anyone entering the classroom during a Reading Period.

St. Patrick's Roman Catholic Infants School,
Oldham.

It is thrilling to see the four-year-olds gathered round the class library discussing the merits of the library books before choosing one for home reading.

St. Gabriel's Roman Catholic School,
Rochdale.

"In the six years I've taught here," enthuses Mrs. Marsha Brady, "this was the first time the children have always *wanted* to get back into the classroom to read. And to take books home when they didn't have to."

Long Beach Public School,
Long Beach, California, U.S.A.

(4) CREATIVE WRITING

It is possible that one day a researcher will evaluate some of the more general, less readily measurable educational effects of i.t.a., but meanwhile it is noteworthy that teachers in charge of i.t.a. classes have reported that the easier acquisition of reading brings in its train other benefits likely to influence and enhance the growth both of character and intellect. This is to the advantage of children who might not be expected to have found

196

orthodox reading particularly difficult as well as of potentially backward readers. The i.t.a. children, for example, show an unusual aptitude for writing creatively and spontaneously without help from the teacher, in some cases even before they reach their fifth birthdays. The language is their own and is laced with slang and baby-talk, but it is remarkably "free" and expressive. Because i.t.a. removes the burden of orthodox spelling, it enables children to write anything they are able to speak—

> In all the classes using i.t.a. there has been a greater surge of creative writing. There is no doubt at all that these children find no difficulty in conveying their thoughts to paper. They are so anxious to write their thoughts that their fingers cannot control their pencils to write at the necessary speed and so neatness is sacrificed. The value of the wonderful flow of language more than compensates for this. Our classes are vertically grouped, so it happens that all ages are in each class. Children learning to read and write in orthodox spelling often ask for help from the children using i.t.a., and so it happens that in the midst of a piece of work in orthodox spelling the teacher finds a word written in i.t.a. *Never* do the i.t.a. children ask for help from the orthodox spelling children—they usually have sufficient confidence to try alone. As the children are so confident in writing down their thoughts, their creative writing is not only increased but improved.
>
> Willowbrook Infants School,
> Leicester.

> I am firmly convinced that the creative writing has very greatly benefited during this experiment. We have one class of thirty-six children and they all write well and can express themselves very adequately. Even those whom we consider less advanced are writing two or three little sentences. Thirty of this class can really write quite a long story and use difficult words. The class teacher has remarked that she has never had a class before in which every child attempted to write. This is an age group just coming up to $5\frac{3}{4}$–6 years old. Some of the children who have now turned over to the ordinary reading books are writing well and beginning to spell words in traditional spelling.
>
> Cae Top Infants School,
> Caernarvon.

> Our children are still only $5\frac{1}{2}$ years of age, and to have gained the ability to read and write as well as they do is, in my opinion, a remarkable achievement. I should say that the children are pleasantly surprised when they discover that what they want to write they can spell, and I am sure that it will not be long before they regard writing to be as easy as speaking.
>
> Queen Mary Avenue School,
> Cleethorpes.

One of the greatest advantages of teaching reading by means of i.t.a. is in the improvement in the written work of the child. One of the drawbacks of teaching by orthodox spelling is that the child does not always have the confidence to reproduce in writing what he would like to put down. He is faced with a choice of two or three ways of spelling a word. The clever ones have not much difficulty, but the clever, lazy child will "settle for" writing a small amount correctly. The average child's work is often stilted, and the "poor child" is discouraged because he is faced with too many difficulties. Children taught by i.t.a. are able to write creatively and at length because they have it within their power to reproduce their thoughts without having to refer to the teacher for help. Although the child has to encounter and reproduce orthodox spelling later, I find that by that time he has a real interest in reading and his earlier training in looking carefully at words puts him in a better position to absorb traditional spelling and to reproduce the words without any adverse effect on the quality of his written work.

Alt Infants School,
Oldham.

Using i.t.a., the children soon realise that they can write whatever they can say, and so begin to write down their thoughts. As they read more widely they have more interesting things to write about and so the expanding process goes on. Imaginative writing improves as the children get ideas from the stories they read, and they are not prevented from writing more difficult words as they can spell anything they can say.

Abbey Hulton County Infants School,
Stoke-upon-Trent.

Creative writing has begun at least twelve months earlier than previously with most children. Those taught by traditional methods must find creative writing a most frustrating experience, and what they write can only be governed by what they can spell. These children, taught by i.t.a., have written with tremendous enjoyment and interest of their own experiences, and this alone would seem sufficient reason for continuing this method next year.

Holy Trinity Infants School,
Blackburn.

Creative writing begins at a much earlier age when using the medium of i.t.a. We find that little 5-year-olds just let themselves go when describing their experiences in relation to their family and friends. They get a great deal of pleasure from making little books with pictures and writing, and because they enjoy this activity they just write and write and write without the handicap of intricate spelling. The 6- and 7-year-old children also benefit and seem to feel capable of tackling any piece of written work in connection with their activities, since spelling is not the burden that it was.

Devonshire Road County Primary School,
Bolton.

Queues at the teacher's desk, asking how to spell every other word they wish to write, have completely disappeared. This relieves the teacher for general supervision. Three times the amount previously written is resulting from the freedom with which the child can express himself. It can use its speaking vocabulary—which, in the very early stages previously, used not to be its reading vocabulary, as so many words had to be avoided because of their irregular pronunciation.

> Malmesbury Park County Primary School,
> Bournemouth.

The effect of i.t.a. on underprivileged children in the Infants School has been quite remarkable. They have not only made more rapid progress in reading, but they are also expressing themselves in writing much more easily. We found before we started using i.t.a. that children were tied to their word books to find words which they could use in their writing. This led to stilted writing and the same phrases coming up again and again. The ease of writing in i.t.a. has weaned such children away from their word book and liberated them to express whatever idea they have in their mind.

> Whitehouse County Primary School,
> Bristol.

All educationalists visiting the school express wonder at the volume of creative writing produced by i.t.a. children; even those who have been learning just a term or two are able to write freely and imaginatively without asking the teacher frequently for spellings. This fluency is carried over after the transfer is made. Intelligent children, I find, continue to write more and more and produce their own booklets with great enthusiasm. They have no time for much picture-drawing, and obviously place great importance upon the full expression of their own ideas in writing.

> Pixies Hill Junior Mixed Infants School,
> Hemel Hempstead.

The Initial Teaching Alphabet never lets the child down in the disastrous way that orthodox spelling does. Thus he gets no setting back by reason of repeated incorrect efforts at words which in orthodox spelling are pronounced one way and written in an entirely different one. He becomes confident very quickly and can now communicate in a new way, which can at once be recognised, and at a *much* earlier stage in his school life.

> Newstead County Infants School,
> Blurton, Stoke-upon-Trent

After using i.t.a. for one year, we have been delighted with the improvement shown in creative writing by the reception class children. Never before have we had children of this age writing so freely and with such enjoyment.

> Derker County Infants School,
> Oldham.

Our i.t.a. children write exactly as they speak, i.e. in the vernacular. (This may well lead us into difficulties when, at a later stage, we are demanding a higher standard of grammatical expression and style, but I doubt it.) Some children will even write with impediments (and many have slight impediments since they have not completely discarded all "baby-talk"). One boy wrote "ʃhεε frɷ ʃhum frɷ ʃhe windɶ" when telling about Jack's mother's reaction to the beans exchanged for the cow in the story of *Jack and the Beanstalk*. This lack of inhibition enables the i.t.a. child to write with complete confidence.

> Castleton County Primary School,
> Rochdale.

From the very start of our change-over to i.t.a. it was obvious that the improved confidence in tackling reading would have its effect also on written expression. The volume of material that the child can now acquire through his reading can be so much more easily transferred into writing, his choice of expression is improved, and his actual written work is better at an earlier age than his non–i.t.a. colleague.

> St. Mary's Roman Catholic School,
> Wolverhampton.

We have found that the use of i.t.a. has helped the children considerably with creative writing. They are able to write without any help from the teacher much earlier and this consequently means that they are able to write much more. They are no longer frustrated because they cannot spell words and, therefore, they become very keen and thoroughly enjoy expressing their ideas in writing.

> Blakenall Heath Infants School,
> Walsall.

The children are able to be precise and are uninhibited as far as writing their own thoughts. They take more pride in creating different stories. Writing a title, caption, description or story is considered as easy as drawing a picture. Instead of saying "I don't know what to write," it is—"I know what I'll say."

> Evamere School, Hudson, Ohio,
> U.S.A.

In the beginning, the i.t.a. child, as compared to the orthodox spelling child, was at a disadvantage, this being a result of his older brother or sister and possible exposure to the regular alphabet with help from mother or dad. However, it wasn't long before the i.t.a. child was able to identify and write an equal amount of characters. As time went by the i.t.a. child soon took the lead in writing more words of one and two syllables. Amazingly, in a short additional time, our i.t.a. child was writing words comparable to his oral language and thus giving to us the well constructed, meaningful sentence which far exceeded the orthodox spelling child's vocabulary and sentence structure.

> Consolidated School,
> Jefferson Township,
> New Jersey, U.S.A.

Another aspect of i.t.a. deserving consideration is its effect on children's attitudes and on their written expression. We have found that i.t.a. children enjoy their work more and that their writing deals with topics beyond those usually expected from first grade children. Generally, we have found that by using i.t.a., children can read and write on any subject within their oral vocabulary. Displays of i.t.a. writing commonly deal with dinosaurs, space ships, holidays and any of a variety of topics of interest to children at this age.

> Marion County Public Schools,
> West Virginia, U.S.A.

Creative writing was the phase of which, in i.t.a. I was the most skeptical. It has been the most rewarding experience. There is no obstacle for anything about which the children wish to write, and I never realized that small children could think of such a variety of subjects to express themselves, although we have finished only half of our first term of i.t.a.

> Winburne Elementary School,
> Clearfield, Pennsylvania, U.S.A.

(5) PROBLEM SOLVING AND CONCEPT FORMING

Teachers report an earlier and more positive ability to form concepts and to solve problems. The effortless and surer achievement of reading also has an effect on the children's speech and enunciation, and on their performance in other school subjects—

I feel sure that the children who have learned to read through i.t.a. are greatly helped to understand much sooner the various activities in the classroom environment. The value of the non-variant of the symbols used must not be underestimated. It must have the greatest value in fostering the child's ability—because he knows that what he sees and writes is correct, i.e. there is only one way to write each sound. This is sound logic to the child and because he is unhampered by the variants of symbols, as in orthodox spelling, he can solve his own problems by his own rational processes. He is confident that he can succeed in learning activities other than reading and writing.

Willowbrook Infants School,
Leicester.

A much wider range of vocabulary can be used by the teacher on work cards and on notices. The children take these words into their vocabulary more rapidly because they have been able to concentrate on the meaning of the words, and not just on the reading of them. With the more rapid growth of vocabulary follows the more rapid growth of concepts, as demonstrated in the children's written work.

Countess Weir Infants School,
Exeter.

The medium determines the children's approach to reading for the rest of their lives. If it includes a "fool-proof" basis (i.t.a.), thus giving them a great deal of self-confidence plus an enjoyment from reading at the outset, then reading is meaningful and opens up a new world to the child. Early success, thus achieved, gives children confidence in all their school activities.

Hem Heath County Junior and Infants School,
Blurton, Stoke-upon-Trent.

The children's experience and knowledge has been expanded, not only by reason of their increased vocabulary, but more important because of their satisfaction and consciousness of their ability to read. Success produces success and the children become more literate in every sense of the word.

Whipton Barton Junior Mixed School,
Exeter.

As the i.t.a. children were promoted through the Infant School, there came a time in Infant II Class when the class consisted of half orthodox spelling children and half i.t.a. children. As the teaching progressed throughout the year, the gap between these children widened to such an extent that it was finally decided to put the orthodox spelling group on to i.t.a. Before this was done, however, it became more and more noticeable that in creative writing the i.t.a. children just got on with the job, whilst in comparison the orthodox spelling children bombarded the teacher with questions and requests for help. In reading, the i.t.a. children tackled their work with complete self-confidence, building when they did not recognise words, and eager to carry on without teacher assistance, and this was a complete contrast to the stumbling efforts of the orthodox spelling children. It is a unanimous decision of our Infant Staff that the use of i.t.a. has given self-confidence to all of our children, but has been most useful in helping to get our slower children over that first difficult hurdle.

Devonshire Road County Primary School,
Bolton.

The child's vocabulary is definitely extended more rapidly. This can be a particularly great boon to a child whose home environment is almost devoid of good speech. The child rapidly learns new words, and uses them to communicate with the teacher and other, more fortunate, children, from homes where natural, easy speech is commonplace.

> Christ Church Junior Mixed and Infants School,
> Burton-upon-Trent.

Free expression is genuinely "free"—very little recourse to Teacher for assistance. This "free expression" is also most noticeable in the children's speech as well as written work. Tongue-tied children are talking happily and their vocabulary has improved.

> St. Alban's Primary Infants School,
> Blackburn.

All learning situations are improved by a combination of consistency, logic, interest and involvement. The right climate for situational activity teaching is fostered by the inherent qualities of i.t.a., in particular the quality of reality . . . writing and reading are now no longer "subjects" but a part of language as real as the spoken word. *The phonic sound-barrier has been broken!* Exciting new demands are made upon the pilot. His plane requires different handling. It may be better now to encourage the *en*coding processes of writing *before* the *de*coding processes of reading. The child can now string a series of symbols consecutively to form a complete and satisfactory representation in print of his thought or speech utterance. The writing of numbers in *words*, and of the colours of the Cuisenaire Rods is leading children (and us!) to gain further enjoyment from mathematical language and truths. The development of language through activity seems now to have limitless possibilities.

> Moorlands Preparatory School,
> Clitheroe.

The teaching of reading with the slower children has always been a soul-destroying job, as no great progress was ever apparent in the early stages. Teachers became despondent and thought their efforts were largely wasted. Now even with the worst of readers some progress is evident and the better ones bring joy to the teacher's heart with their almost unbelievable rate of progress. The child's confidence in its ability to read appears to permeate its attitude to other work. No longer do they need teacher's constant attention, but are able to work on their own, so building up the child's belief in its own ability. No teacher that I know has yet failed to be impressed by the results obtained, and none have wanted to revert to orthodox spelling after once experiencing the thrill of teaching reading by the i.t.a.

> Moorlands County Primary School,
> West Bromwich.

It has been very noticeable that the children brought up on i.t.a. are able to concentrate on reading, writing and other activities for a much longer period—in short, their powers of sustained concentration have been greatly increased. As a result of their increased reading ability the teacher in the second-year class is able to present to the children various types of problems written in orthodox spelling for them to solve, e.g. instructions regarding shopping, buying and selling, making bills, weighing and measuring, etc., on individual cards. (This should lead to a better understanding of Number, Arithmetic and Mathematics.)

County Primary School,
Haworth.

In previous years, it was felt that a maximum expectation would be for children to learn five or six new words each day toward the end of the school year. This can be compared with the i.t.a. child's reading vocabulary that by the end of this school year will be almost limitless as far as their needs are concerned. Their teacher feels that the children because they have more to comprehend, are reading more, and have a larger vocabulary with which to articulate, are comprehending to a greater degree than any previous orthodox spelling class. She feels that instead of a vocabulary of possibly 400 words, they will have one of 4,000 words. It is felt that there is a definite relationship between the working vocabulary of a child and the degree with which he comprehends. New words introduced require understanding, or to say it differently, if new words cannot be introduced, the associated understandings and concepts are not present. To the degree that the child uses new concepts and understands them, so also to that degree will his comprehension develop. Since they are able to read more and wider, there is more to comprehend, and so their comprehension develops along with their reading ability. Since spelling is not a problem, the students can use their own choice of words to answer questions, and relate ideas. . . . It is the general feeling of the Principal and teacher involved in the program that although it seems that the immediate greatest benefit is the increased reading ability, that this is really only a preliminary advantage; that the greatest advantage gained in the program will come through the higher degree of expression and greater degree of creativity made possible by a broader, freer, and earlier ability to read.

The Ida Weller School,
Dayton, Ohio, U.S.A.

Kindergarten Teachers

For the lower socio-economic level child, learning proceeds at a much slower rate but the child is more sure of what he has learned and therefore establishes a stronger foundation for beginning reading.

First-Grade Teachers

Generally, the program resulted in children being able to read much faster, having more confidence in themselves because they can successfully attack new words, and showing an increased vocabulary, an enthusiastic desire to read independently, and good speech habits. Teachers like the Early-to-Read i.t.a. Program; stories are more sophisticated and much more interesting than T.O. basal series.

Second-Grade Teachers

Children seem to have a greater independence in reading and a much more varied reading interest. They are better equipped to follow directions and to engage in creative work. i.t.a. graduates seem to be more mature as a result of i.t.a. training. Slower children, however, still need extra work and help.

Third-Grade Teachers

The i.t.a. graduates work independently and can use reference books with ease. Creative writing is very good. They are able to attack new words with confidence, although not always with understanding.

Newburgh Public School,
Newburgh, New York, U.S.A.

Students realize early in i.t.a. that speech is the printed text. Students are able to see their own speech in print, make comparisons and detect their errors, thereby correcting their errors in writing and at the same time improving their speech.

Holmes Marshall School,
Piscataway Township, New Brunswick, N.J., U.S.A.

(6) HANDWRITING

Some teachers have noticed that very young children find certain of the i.t.a. characters more difficult to form than orthodox characters, but this is not the opinion of the majority. Despite this reservation, nearly all the teachers report that children learn far more quickly to write with i.t.a. characters than with orthodox characters—

Previously the child expressed himself in pictures at this stage because he had no command of words. So by the time he was reading sufficiently well to express himself fluently he had a control and co-ordination. Now he still uses pictorial expression but he knows and wants to use words. Being younger and without the previous practice he may initially have more difficulty in forming clearly and easily the i.t.a. alphabet—or any alphabet for that matter—and the result can easily be misleading, pointing to an undue difficulty in writing i.t.a. as opposed to orthodox spelling.

St. Helen's Roman Catholic Primary School,
Westcliff-on-Sea.

Children whose motor control had not seemed particularly good found no difficulty in forming the characters. Probably a was the most difficult.

Albert Road County Primary School,
Hinckley.

When we began to teach the children to form the i.t.a. characters we assumed that they would find them difficult to form, but we were soon proved wrong. Not one child has found difficulty in forming the characters. In fact, those which we found difficult, e.g. æ, a, ſh, œ, ie, were the ones which fascinated the children and were the ones they learned first. These characters were often to be found in their art work when they designed patterns for book covers, etc. They seem to enjoy the flow of line. Of course as there are only 44 i.t.a. characters there are fewer combinations for the children to learn, and so free writing is no burden as writing flows on with thought and there is no variant of symbol.

Willowbrook Infants School,
Leicester.

The i.t.a. child has no greater difficulty in learning to write the 44 i.t.a. characters. He does not have to learn a different set of capital letters and can concentrate on the 44 letters and know that the capital is just a larger version of the same symbol. We find that similar mistakes (like putting various symbols back to front) still have to be corrected, as they had to be when the children were being taught the orthodox spelling.

Dyffryn Infants School,
Llandudno.

The i.t.a. child has no greater difficulty than the child taught the orthodox characters. However, the 5-year-old does have considerable difficulty in making æ and au. We found that pattern making with all characters was a great help; also "writing" the characters with a finger in the air. This seems to help the rhythm required. Six- and 7-year-olds find no difficulty in writing i.t.a. characters.

St. Mary's School,
Beaminster

One of their favorite activities is creating the i.t.a. symbols in molding clay. From the isolated letters, they finally build words. This is challenging and interesting and I find most helpful in developing muscular control, which carries over to the printed page. At the close of the year, one of the most interesting experiences has been noting their development in color concept and originality of ideas expressed in art work! This remarkable attainment in the very young child, we attribute to the awareness and observation stimulated by the i.t.a. program. . . .

The Anita Metzger School,[1]
Ventnor City, New Jersey.

[1] Mrs. Metzger was the first teacher in the American continent to see the potentialities of i.t.a. and to try them out in a classroom.

Writing the sound-symbols, or characters, of the Initial Teaching Alphabet is similar in many respects to writing the traditional alphabet. The lines, circles and hooks of manuscript characters are changed only in that they often flow continuously from one to the other rather than being discrete elements. The additional characters of i.t.a. necessitate only the addition of the arch and loop. The procedure used results in characters which are described as a form of print which is halfway between the manuscript and cursive forms. Children have no more difficulty in beginning to write with this print than they ordinarily do with manuscript and they make the transition to cursive writing much more readily than do children who start on regular manuscript. Penmanship quality was excellent. The pupils seem to have produced a higher quality than ever before in traditional classes.

> St. Cloud Public Schools,
> St. Cloud, Minnesota, U.S.A.

(7) MORALE AND BEHAVIOUR

Children in i.t.a. classes are reported to possess not merely greater independence and self-confidence, but there is an observable improvement in their general behaviour. Their attitude towards school and lessons is said to be healthier and more positive—

Having taught with i.t.a. for twelve months and then transferred to a school using orthodox spelling, I would say without reservation that i.t.a. is far more satisfying both for teacher and children. Several of my class have completed the infant reading scheme in twelve months at school using orthodox spelling, but this does not compare with the i.t.a. class, where the exceptions after twelve months were the children who could *not* read fluently. Naturally this has an important effect on classroom morale and the enthusiasm of the teacher. Personally my greatest joy in teaching with i.t.a. was to see the children writing at great speed and prolifically—attempting words which I would find difficult to spell myself in orthodox spelling! They were confident and assured and this was reflected in many of the other activities in the classroom. I shall be starting with i.t.a. again in September, at my own request, which is surely the best recommendation for the medium that I can make.

> Haulgh County Primary School,
> Bolton.

The attitude of the child is far more positive to teacher and others. In some it has become slightly overbearing towards the unfortunates who have not read via i.t.a. and are therefore not as advanced. After two years of i.t.a. the children are very independent and will fend for themselves far better than before.

Tudno Infants School,
Llandudno.

The children are far more mature and responsible than the class which has been in school a term longer, on orthodox spelling. Both my teacher and myself were good teachers of orthodox spelling and our children here reach a high standard. But now—although the school is full of books—I doubt if we shall be able to keep up with this little lot! We were both very sceptical but are now sold!

Beacon Heath Junior Mixed and Infants School,
Whipton.

There is an easy, unselfconscious, assured attitude which colours all that the i.t.a. children do. They seem to come sooner to *shared* responsibilities, and an easy "give and take" with other children. Facility in language clarifies situations, instructions, intentions, and widens the sympathies.

Earls Hall Infants School,
Westcliff-on-Sea.

A class being taught by i.t.a. does not have behaviour problems, as there is no frustration in the initial stages of learning to read. Frustration in small children is the largest factor in behaviour in an Infant School. Their confidence is gained from the start, they are able at a very early stage to pick up books and be able to read. (This happens even in the Reception Class.)

Knolls Lane Church of England Infants School,
Oldham.

The improvement in self-confidence, initiative and general attitude to the school situation is very marked.

Firs Estate Infants School,
Derby.

A child of 7+ who had made no progress with orthodox spelling, and was almost a social misfit, was introduced to i.t.a. After a time his success in reading gave him a sense of achievement. His outlook noticeably changed, his general appearance improved, and his attitude towards his teacher, and later to his class-mates, became considerably more friendly and co-operative.

Shobnall Road Junior Mixed and Infants School,
Burton-upon-Trent.

It is very true to say that the class teacher of i.t.a. children finds an increased satisfaction in teaching—because the children are so obviously interested in reading. They want to read, and the child who through his inability to understand the mechanics of reading becomes bored and disinterested and therefore a problem child, now does not exist, which makes for a busy, enthusiastic, atmosphere in the classroom with teacher and children working in harmony.

Dyffryn Infants School,
Llandudno.

From our experience in teaching i.t.a. it would appear that being able to read at an early stage in school life is probably the most important factor in a child's attitude to school, and therefore his attitude to teachers and other children. The child appears to mature more quickly. By the end of the first school year, he seems to be more part of the school than in the past. How much this is due to the feeling of power which he gains from being able to read is difficult to say, because in these days of T.V., easier travel and a more affluent society, younger children have much wider experience than previously. By the end of the second school year the difference is even more noticeable. Generally speaking, a child is completely socially integrated. He plays more amicably with his fellows. He treats his teacher as an equal, asking for help where he requires it and discussing facts which he has gleaned from books and outside experiences. He is far less selfish and self-centred and does not seek to attract attention by small misdemeanours, because he appears to have a greater feeling of equality. Generally speaking, the children of average and above average intelligence are behaving more like younger juniors, they meet strangers without shyness, and have well developed senses of humour and a competitive spirit. All this leads to an ideal situation for true "activity teaching," but about 50 per cent of these children seem to prefer mental activity to physical and manual activity.

St. Hilda's Church of England Primary School,
Oldham.

I'm much happier. The independence it (i.t.a. program) gives the pupil virtually eliminates all discipline problems. But the best part is that because they work at their own rate, they all achieve success.

University City Public Schools,
University City, Missouri, U.S.A.

I notice that the children are quite independent in reading activities and they aggressively approach any problems they meet. It also proves that some 5, and all 6, year olds are capable of much more responsibility in reading than we give them in a traditional method. I.t.a. is proving to be an interesting adventure. The children are excited and the teacher is sometimes amazed.

O.H. Somers Elementary,
Mogadore, Ohio, U.S.A.

Strong point of the program is that the ego strength of the child is greatly increased. With the corresponding symbol and sound he soon feels confident that this is a reliable means for deciphering printed symbols. We have many happy children at the Foundation School. It became a child-motivated situation. Our findings in the i.t.a. program suggest that most children have profited considerably from this approach. The program is structured to meet the challenge of the child in the world of today. The story content (Early-to-Read i.t.a. Program) is on a level which stimulates their abilities. The one observed but unmeasured characteristic of first grade classes made by the author is the much improved classroom climate for learning that seems to have come about with the introduction of i.t.a.

Foundation School
Fredonia, New York, U.S.A.

To end with, here is a telling case-history—

The first case which comes readily to mind of a child becoming better adjusted to school and social environments through success in reading is that of Terence F. He is the last of a large family of rather poorish background, educationally as well as economically, who have all passed through the school. None of his elder brothers or sisters were really effective readers; some were quite definitely reading failures. Terence in particular was noticeably unkempt, wore "hand-down" clothes always too big for him, and on entering school had a definite speech defect. He was, however, a very pleasant child, as were the other children in the family, yet because they all had needed special treatment "reading-wise," often different work set for them, there seemed to be an air of failure about them, which prevented them from really facing their classmates on equal terms. Terence is the only one of his family to complete the Infant Reading Scheme while still in the Infant School. For the Staff it was a "red-letter" day, but not very special for Terence; for he had for long known that this was something he would just do. Our attitude to i.t.a. reading had always been that of course everyone would finish a certain number of books, some quicker, some slower, that it was really a matter of time. Once he gained phonic fluency in i.t.a., he began to "blossom out." He talked more to the other children, noticed his own defect less, volunteered more easily for "jobs," paired off with other little boys at playtimes, and what is more, occupied himself happily with his own book, Reading Corner book, or reading game, just as the other "reading-successful" children did. This, to me, seems a true sign of a child being adjusted to his school environment, for young children like above all to be doing something which everyone else is doing, yet doing it on their own.

St. Mary's Roman Catholic School,
Oldham.

11   Remedial Teaching with i.t.a.

T HE PRIMARY PURPOSE of i.t.a. is prophylactic, to prevent reading failure, but it can also be used most successfully with older pupils to remedy a previous defeat. It might be suspected that the introduction of new characters and unfamiliar spellings to a child already baffled by orthodox spelling would make confusion even worse; for those who have become "stuck" after achieving a minimal ability with orthodox texts, i.t.a. indeed entails a temporary transition in reverse, but none the less there is now evidence that i.t.a. can be a valuable aid to the remedial teacher.

Backward readers in need of remedial help can be classified under three broad categories[1]—

(1) The largest group have been defeated merely by the orthodox alphabet's spellings, although they are linguistically competent. The potential benefits of i.t.a. to this group are obvious.

(2) Children who are linguistically impoverished because of their early environment. With this group the first task is to improve their grasp of concepts and language, though at the same time i.t.a. may well help them to become verbal in speech as well as in print.

(3) A much smaller group whose brains are damaged or who are otherwise innately subnormal (e.g. Mongol or autistic children) or who are emotionally disturbed. The removal of the difficulties arising from the

[1] The deaf are a class apart and so are the blind; they are dealt with separately in the next chapter.

orthodox medium may (provided there is any hope at all) enable the teacher to promote conceptual and verbal competence in the pupil; in some cases i.t.a. has specific advantages (e.g. the constant left-to-right sequence of i.t.a. spelling is of direct value to specific dyslexics who "mirror-reverse" printed words).

It is already safe to assert that for many even in the last of the three categories i.t.a. is capable of providing "security" in the "learning situation," of reaching the child's consciousness with communicative relevance, and of showing that words do "make sense," that reading language is after all meaningful. I.t.a. does not merely overcome the backward reader's mechanical difficulties; it fosters comprehension—and comprehension extends experiences in the imagination—and this renourishes the will to read and renews self-confidence. This is of course the goal of every remedial teacher, whatever the medium. Unless he can conjure up the pupil's sustained co-operation failure will yet again reinforce failure. Frequently the non-reader is secretly so despairing and his ego is so bruised that little is left of even the desire to read. He dreads having to demonstrate once more that the teacher's optimism is misplaced. False pride in being no good provides a heady, tranquillizing self-protection. His attitude is at any rate likely to be ambivalent: one part of him is positive and wants desperately to read; another, negative part dreads what appears to be the certainty of continuing failure. In this typical situation i.t.a. can be a determining ally of the positive and starts with one immediate advantage: it looks different! An i.t.a. reading-book has only to be opened for this to be obvious. Although i.t.a. is essentially and intentionally close to the orthodox lower-case alphabet, typographically it is palpably a new proposition and sufficiently divorced from the orthodox medium—which is permeated with reminders of failure and misery—for it to be likely that the pupil's motivation will be rapidly rekindled. Once i.t.a. has begun to show that reading is not inevitably perplexing, the orthodox alphabet assumes the role of scapegoat—on occasion, a splendid therapeutic device in the convalescence of a child's or an adult's self-esteem!

Within the typical retarded reader exist the rudiments of acquired understanding. He may have formed some very bad reading habits and be inclined to mistaken, though possibly rational, interpretations of the values of characters (e.g. *go*, *to*, *not* read as *go*, *toe*, *note*) and in fact of the 70 per cent of all printed matter in which the characters are at variance with speech and thus misleading, but there are nevertheless some advantages in not starting from scratch. His years of failure have probably taught him enough to constitute a ready-made foundation for dramatically fast progress once i.t.a. has banished the difficulties that are confusing him. Very probably he is able to recognize a few orthodox words, most of which will be either identical or sufficiently similar to the words he now meets in i.t.a.; in addition, he is almost certain to possess an extensive experience of auditory discrimination and be familiar with quite a few character-to-sound associations. Like an aeroplane grounded on a snow-clogged runway, the retarded reader is only too often well primed and capable of a successful take-off, once the impediment is removed.

I am not suggesting that i.t.a. is a branch of magic. It would be quite wrong to claim that it is a panacea for all types of remedial case. Just as it does not set out to be a rival teaching method, it is not intended that i.t.a. should replace the special skills of the remedial teacher or any of the remedial techniques and aids such as jigsaw puzzles to promote visual perception, pictorial strips to develop sequential thinking, tape recorders to help relate the sounds of characters to their appearance, exercises to improve auditory blending, kinaesthetic methods, and so on. I.t.a. does, however, enable all these special techniques to be employed with greater effect, though there is a need to try it out further and systematically in connection with each and to compare the results of each technique when isolated from all others. The remedial teacher who decides to use i.t.a. can adhere to his preferred methods and techniques; basically, the only difference is that the reading books are printed in i.t.a., though, as is the case with the better kind of orthodox remedial reading books, i.t.a. remedial readers are now becoming available to match the varying ages and levels of interest and understanding which can range from backward infants, juniors, and secondary school children to adolescents and adults.[1]

When I originally began to think in terms of a serious research project, I was tempted to ask first for an opportunity to try i.t.a. out on badly retarded readers only, because I knew this suggestion would meet with less strenuous opposition—in the same way as new drugs are often

---

[1] Even so, caution is needed before crediting the adult non-reader with levels of understanding, of intellectual interests, and even of subject-matter higher than those of a child. His experiences are of course infinitely more extensive but his concepts, his vocabulary, and quite possibly his interests are nevertheless likely to be much narrower than might be expected. When instructors at the British Army School of Preliminary Education (see report below) left well-known fairy tales lying about the library, some of the soldiers described them as "smashing." When conceptual experience is low and linguistic competence is very limited, a start can be made only at the very bottom—and that bottom is outside the credibility of most fluent readers.

first administered to patients whose disease is otherwise incurable. In the end I decided against this course because I feared (as it happens, quite unnecessarily) that, being designed to prevent failure rather than cure it, i.t.a. might well be ineffective for remedial purposes. On the other hand there was also the risk that i.t.a.'s very success in the remedial classroom might lead to its being dubbed "remedial only," thus weakening its chances of universal acceptance as a prophylactic at the early stages—when the child first begins to read and must not be frustrated or doomed not even to make a start. This was why, when planning the research programme, it was decided to restrict it to its prime function, to concentrate on the initial teaching of very young children. Remedial teachers, however, soon began their own experiments with the new medium. The information on i.t.a.'s effectiveness as a remedial medium is limited to scattered reports on a small scale which cannot be correlated and, while they must be assessed with some reserve, they amount to a further prima facie case for i.t.a. that no remedial teacher can afford to ignore. It is also necessary to emphasize that most of these reports fail to do proper justice to i.t.a. because frequently it has been employed for only a very few hours a week and in an artificial teaching situation. Regular, *daily* practice is always desirable for any child attempting to master the complex skill of reading; for the backward reader it is essential. As a minimum he should practise for two hours a day on five, if not seven, days a week. Failing this, it is difficult to acquire the necessary reflexes and the memory span is too long for the effortless recall of what has been learned. With many remedial courses unfortunately, including some using i.t.a., it is not easy to arrange this degree of regular practice because the remedial teacher is a visiting specialist covering a group of schools and who can afford each child, say, a mere two half-hours weekly. In my view it is far more satisfactory if the class teacher can herself become sufficiently expert to conduct an i.t.a. remedial group—in other words, for the teacher merely to move from group to group instead of from school to school. Except in the most severe cases I am also convinced that it is preferable for the backward readers to be taught in a group rather than to be extracted one at a time from the classroom for an intensive, possibly self-centred session with a specialist.

The first attempt to measure the remedial value of i.t.a. was started in September 1961 by Keith Gardner, head of the Walsall Remedial Education Service. The size of the experiment was too small for conclusions to be surely drawn, but the results demonstrated that "children receiving remedial teaching in i.t.a. made significantly more progress than control groups who received their teaching in the traditional medium." It must be noted that these children received as little as one-and-a-half hours of teaching in i.t.a. per week and returned to orthodox texts in class during the rest of the week. Gardner also reported[1]—

> Firstly, i.t.a. has proved very effective in teaching reading to 7-year-old pupils in Junior School classes. In this kind of situation 83 out of 115 pupils in three schools made reading gains of two years or more in between October and June. All these pupils had a reading age of less than 6 years when work in i.t.a. began. This was attained in a normal classroom environment and in an area where there has been a high level of illiteracy for a number of years. Teachers have reported improvements, not only in reading, but in written expression, school attendance and behaviour. With these pupils transfer is effected very quickly. The quickest transfer in a matter of 6–10 weeks, the majority in 12–16 weeks, and the slowest may require a full school year.
>
> In the more orthodox Remedial Teaching situation, a wide variety of work has been carried out by specialized Remedial Teachers. In one experiment, 52 7–8-year-old pupils were selected, after an initial diagnostic period of one month. In each case the prognosis was considered to be very poor. After 50 hours' remedial teaching spread over 25 weeks the children were assessed on a Reading Scale in the traditional alphabet. The poorest gain was 18 months of reading age. Over half the pupils made gains of 3 years or more.

At Walsall i.t.a. was also tried out with children who had managed to achieve a minimal reading ability but who still lacked fluency and confidence, though here again only one-and-a-half hours per week were devoted to i.t.a., the children returning to a class using orthodox texts during the rest of the week. Gardner wrote—

> In this instance transfer takes place in reverse. Children who can read traditional material at about the 7-year level can read i.t.a. at an equivalent level without any prior instruction. The consistency of i.t.a., however, enables a wider vocabulary to be introduced very quickly, and the pupils have the means for gaining the required independence and confidence. The first results of this application of i.t.a. have shown that the introduction of the new medium has been very effective with the majority of children. There has been a new stimulation of interest in reading, and greater fluency and proficiency have followed.

Successful remedial teaching depends so much on the skill and sympathy of the teacher and the ratio between pupil and teacher, if not actually

[1] "Pitmans Initial Teaching Alphabet Applied to Remedial Teaching," *Forward Trends*, Vol. 8, No. 1, pp. 7–11. The Guild of Teachers of Backward Children, London, 1964.

one-for-one, is usually so much smaller that comparative evaluations with orthodox control groups present particular difficulties; on the other hand, the high degree of specialization and dedication of these men and women makes their opinions and recommendations of i.t.a. especially reliable. The remainder of this chapter is devoted to extracts from reports sent in at the end of the 1964 U.K. summer term and a little later in the U.S.—though, compared with the teachers quoted in the previous chapter, their experience of i.t.a. has been for the most part somewhat shorter. The extracts are arranged in three categories: (1) normal schools; (2) adults; (3) special schools for the E.S.N., partially sighted, etc.

(1) REMEDIAL TEACHING WITH THE INITIAL TEACHING ALPHABET IN NORMAL SCHOOLS

I.t.a. is more than a factor of great importance; it is the biggest breakthrough in helping the child who finds reading to be difficult in overcoming his troubles that I have seen in over 41 years of service in teaching, and my great regret is that I shall not be in school when it is generally adopted. I have not seen class teaching based upon the method and so am not in a position to judge, but I do know of its value for the backward child. When one remembers the playtimes and extra time devoted to helping those who just could not read, and has a boy of 9 with I.Q. of 70 who was going the same way and suddenly comes to one's room with the light of success in his eye and says, "Please, sir, will you listen to me read?" one is left in no doubt as to its value. . . . Before the introduction of i.t.a. one never saw the poor reader take out a book and work on his own, whereas now they do so regularly. They develop self-confidence and by success are made happier, more self-reliant and anxious to progress. The class teacher has now to guide and not to drive.

St. Peter-at-Gowt's Junior Boys School,
Lincoln.

Most of the children, First and Second year Juniors, made rapid progress with their reading after their introduction to the i.t.a. method, having previously failed in orthodox spelling. Much pleasure was derived from the success they experienced in mastering their books, thus giving them confidence and an appetite for more. A greater use of the School Library by these children has resulted. I have been impressed by the standard of creative writing produced by this remedial class and by the amount written. With less spelling difficulties to hinder them, the children take obvious pleasure in expressing themselves in writing. Another important aspect is that the teacher has little or no difficulty in reading through the written work thus produced!

Eastfield County Junior School,
Wolverhampton.

Remedial Teaching with i.t.a.

I.t.a. children do show more self-confidence and this is closely allied to the fact that i.t.a. restores their self-respect. Years of frustration in school are hardly conducive to progress in learning. I.t.a. has been the penicillin for illiteracy. . . . To see children in my Remedial Class, aged 10 and 11, reading and enjoying *David Copperfield*, *Kidnapped*, *Treasure Island*, *Robinson Crusoe*, etc., is a joy to behold.

Beever County Primary School,[1]
Junior and Infant Department,
Oldham.

In this school we work very much on individual lines. We try to present the child with an interesting situation or problem and set him to solve it. This involves use of apparatus—assignment cards, etc. Until i.t.a. made our remedial class a class of readers the learning activities of this group were greatly restricted. Reading has been a tremendous boon to the teacher, as to arrange individual work for non-readers presented colossal problems. The teacher of the remedial class has actually been experimenting with intensive writing on the lines suggested by Margaret Landon (for secondary school children) and of course it gave her tremendous satisfaction to come and show me work that bore comparison with work hitherto only attempted by our brightest children. With the exception of the ESN children the whole of the remedial class will be able to spend its fourth year with the other children in normal classes and the effect on morale both on teacher and children is incalculable. I am convinced that the sudden ability to read is at the root of this general improvement.

Albert Road County Primary School,
Hinckley.

Children (and parents) expect something more of the Secondary School. The brighter children obtain this from a wider variety of subjects studied— Science, Mathematics, possibly a foreign language, etc. The backward non-reader, on the other hand, very often can expect nothing more than the same old grind which has produced nothing but failure in the past. To introduce him to i.t.a. at this stage has a valuable stimulating effect. He must break with the past and all its associations of failure. He must meet the challenge of this new approach and move forward to literacy. . . . A new approach is good for the teacher as well as the child. It gives a fresh impetus to his teaching. Again, the i.t.a. system is so satisfying to teach because it makes sense. Teaching reading by the old method was full of frustration. A phonic method could not sensibly be employed because the constant exceptions to any given rule could only cause confusion in the mind of the child. Using i.t.a. we can

A description of the use of i.t.a. in this and other remedial classes in the Oldham area will be found in *Instant Reading* by Maurice Harrison, pp. 162–84. Sir Isaac Pitman and Sons Ltd., London, 1964.

tell the child a particular symbol stands for a particular sound, and it is always so. There are no exceptions. He can always believe what is in front of his eyes in black and white.

Oak Park County Secondary Boys' School,
Havant.

I have had recourse to i.t.a. for three six-and-a-half-year-old boys who, after two and a half years in school, were not reading at all—were virtually classed as non-readers. Result: Boy A—after nine months is reading orthodox spelling fluently; Boy B—after nine months is just changing over to orthodox spelling; Boy C—is reading Book 6 of the Downing Readers.

St. Alban's Primary Infants School,
Blackburn.

The i.t.a. has been very successful with our remedial reading classes of second and third graders. These boys and girls have progressed further in twenty weeks with i.t.a. than they had in two years using traditional techniques. The interest of the children is intense and they now attack a new word with a confidence heretofore unrealized. We no longer confuse the children by trying to apply rules that apply less than 50 per cent of the time. I feel that these children will be able to go on to the higher levels of education with the anticipation of success rather than of failure which would have been predicted before exposure to i.t.a. For these children i.t.a. has unlocked a door and opened it into the world of books. The results with our remedial reading classes have been so encouraging that we are going to introduce the i.t.a. into the first grade reading program.

Central School District #1,
Town of Moriah,
Mineville, New York.

Our experience during the past year has indicated that students who were having tremendous difficulty in learning to read appeared to find success with i.t.a. Students whose interest had lagged approached the remedial program with i.t.a. with great renewed effort. Their feeling of early success contributed greatly to a continuing interest and resulted in greater effort on the part of each student. . . . The enthusiasm in the i.t.a. class has been contagious. Even the slowest student is reading with better understanding and seems to be getting more enjoyment from the reading he does. We feel that i.t.a. does not insure that all students will learn to read at the same speed. There are varying needs and these must be met in individual ways exactly as would be done in a class using traditional orthography.

Union Free School District No. 2,
Uniondale, New York.

Remedial Teaching with i.t.a.

I have worked with twenty children that were taken from a sixth and a fifth grade. Their reading ability varied from low second-grade level to fourth grade. Some had no comprehension; some, no sound discrimination; and some, no pronunciation ability. They have all finished all the i.t.a. material made available to us. (Eleven readers and two workbooks.) The twenty are now in three groups. One group of eleven are in a fifth-grade reader (Houghton Mifflin), doing good work. The middle group of four is reading the last part of the fourth reader, and the last group of five is well started in the fourth-grade reader. The rapid and accurate rise in comprehension in all the pupils was most gratifying. The speed, smoothness, and interpretation attained in their oral reading is of good quality. They are able to attack new words with confidence and accuracy. The transition back into regular reading material seemed not to bother them at all.

Fruita Elementary School,
Fruita, Colorado, U.S.A.

The i.t.a. experiment at Schroon Lake and Moriah Central Schools involves thirty-two students at grade levels 2 through 6. These children were selected from the larger group known to be in need of remedial assistance. Our purpose is to attempt to discover the effectiveness of i.t.a. as a remedial tool; to establish the most effective levels where i.t.a. can be utilized in remedial instruction; to compare the effectiveness of i.t.a. with the orthodox alphabet and spelling used in the past. The children in this study are typical reading disability cases; the causes are multiple, complicated by reading failure from the beginning of their school experience. The majority suffer from poor auditory and visual perception and discrimination. Most have inferior visual memories; many others have poor auditory memories. There are numerous cases with speech problems, as well. The emotional states of these children range from reasonably normal to extremely upset. Many suffer from inadequate experience backgrounds, live in low socio-economic environments, and can be described as culturally deprived. . . .

. . . Since i.t.a. was begun, the change in the children's attitude toward school has been amazing! The i.t.a. program has been structured to insure this continued success. With the great improvement breaking the chain of unsuccessful progression in their education, the children show a marked difference in their ability to produce. Every child in the experiment exhibits improved spelling ability. (Those children who have not shown marked improvements on their test scores definitely exhibit a marked improvement in their ability to organize their thinking.) It does appear that the earlier i.t.a. is started, the more immediate is the evidence of progress; our testing shows the children in the lower grade levels exhibit more superlative successes more quickly than the older children. We feel this is only because the complexity of the problems of the older children, due to more exposure to failure in their past educational experience, prevents them from making progress as rapidly.

The following changes have definitely been observed in the entire group—

improved auditory perception and discrimination
improved auditory and visual memory
improved visual perception and discrimination
improved word attack skills
improved oral and silent reading ability
increased emotional involvement with reading material
increased development of independence in each child.

The last development is considered crucial for it is this very lack of ability to work alone that inhibits progress with traditional procedures. It is felt that there is encouraging evidence to support optimism with the i.t.a. experiment here in Schroon Lake. We look forward to the continued progress of remedial students with i.t.a. that will permit them to become functioning members of their classes and experience all the pleasure that goes with this accomplishment.

Schroon Lake and Moriah Central Schools,
Schroon Lake, New York, U.S.A.

The Initial Teaching Alphabet was introduced to a first year Junior class of twenty children in September 1964. During their first two years in school, this group had failed to learn to read, and the average reading age, according to the Schonell Reading Test, was 5 years 3 months. Many of these children had little interest in school work, they were noisy, talkative and very easily distracted. . . . On the 14th October the i.t.a. reading books arrived and were immediately put to use. These proved to be delightfully presented books and the bright illustrations attracted the children. Book I of the series was not used as this was too simple for Junior children. The class discovered that they could read Book II without difficulty which was a great incentive, and gave them a reading confidence which they had never before experienced. Progress was made rapidly on the first four books and, though it slowed as the books became progressively more difficult the interest never lapsed. Every child felt that they were achieving something and by the end of the Christmas term the average reading age had risen to 6 years 5 months. The most outstanding advance was made by a boy who in September had a reading age of 5 years 6 months, and in December had risen to 7 years 5 months. The latest test given to this same boy this week showed a reading age of 8 years 9 months. He has now transferred to orthodox print and is reading Book I of the *Wide Range Readers*. Two girls showed an advance of twenty-one months between September and December, and fourteen children altogether had made an advance of twelve months or more. Not one child had failed to make progress, the least advance being six months.

Apart from this there have been other benefits that the children appear to have derived from i.t.a. They discovered that they could now write freely, and, using the forty (plus 1) sounds, could spell most words needed in their stories. Encouraged to make books of illustrated stories, they produced a wide variety of ideas and began to use a much more descriptive vocabulary. From children who could hardly compose a simple sentence in September came descriptions such as the following: ſhe fier enjin cæm tꞶ scꞶl tꞶdæ, wee aull went out tꞶ see ſhe men skwirtiŋ wauter. Much amusement was caused by a most realistic piece of writing about the Beatles and a translation of one of their songs into i.t.a. Great enjoyment was gleaned from story writing and the children were always occupied and spent most of their spare time in writing. For these children i.t.a. has provided a new interest in school, stimulated a desire to write, awakened a liking for books and perhaps most important of all it has given them renewed self-confidence.

Pasir Panjang Junior School,
Singapore.

When previous failures steadily become aware that they too can read, their general behaviour is also likely to improve. This certainly seems to be the case with children in i.t.a. remedial classes—

Our little group—five 8-year-old children, with I.Q.s ranging from below 70 to 80, three of whom had been disturbing elements from the time of their admission to the school—having made no headway in orthodox spelling, began with i.t.a. last September. After a few weeks we noticed an improvement in behaviour—they were not constantly distracting the rest of the class or looking for notice. They were keen to learn. We planned the change-over to orthodox spelling for after Easter as these children leave our school at midsummer. This was forestalled by a child of very low intelligence and poor linguistic background, very soon after Christmas. Her example was soon followed by the others. Their reading ages in orthodox spelling now range from 7 years 6 months to 7 years 10 months. There has been a marked improvement in the behaviour of these children both in and out of class: they have become helpful and reliable, ready to take on little responsibilities and carry them through successfully.

St. Cuthbert's Junior and Infants School,
Withington, Manchester.

The interest aroused through this new approach excites children to make the initial effort to master the symbols and they are not plagued by a sense of previous failure. . . . This [better behaviour], to me, is one of the great achievements of this new way of tackling reading difficulties.

Wolsey Primary School
Croydon.

We are now receiving reports, from parental consultation, of anti-social behaviour disappearing, of much happier children at home as well as in school, of bed-wetting being cured—the phrase seems to be general, "You wouldn't think he was the same boy" (girl).

Malmesbury Park County Primary School,
Bournemouth.

Child No. 7. This child had serious behaviour problems apparently even more accentuated at home than in class where he was restive, inattentive, aggressive and sullen to the extent of remaining rigid for an hour at a time if displeased by any correction of his work or behaviour. When faced with formal reading, the child would say, "I can't read; I get the burps." In oral work the boy showed evidence of clearer thinking than that of the average child in the class, wider knowledge and a more extensive vocabulary; and he is one of those who immediately responded to the more logical and consistent application of i.t.a. After only two weeks of i.t.a., it was interesting to note the comment of his father to the effect that it was the first time that he had displayed any interest in his work or that homework had not been the cause of convulsive rage and head-banging on the part of the child. The aggressive behaviour towards his younger sister ceased and was replaced by entertaining her with i.t.a. stories which he read aloud. This boy, who could only produce three or four words prior to lapsing into a state of immobility in a "free-writing" or "news" period was immediately responsive to the linguistic key afforded by i.t.a. and was thereafter able to express himself in writing with ease, fluency and enjoyment.

Child No. 9: Above the average age of children in the class, this boy was a complete misfit academically in his own age-group as he was unable to read or write. A very mild, acquiescent and submissive child, he had been unable, despite persistent efforts on the part of his previous teacher, to acquire any reliable knowledge of phonics or any reading skills by a diversity of methods. At nine years of age, he was struggling with the reader designed for a 5–6-year-old. Introduced to this class only in mid-December 1964, unable to read one word in the Schonell word recognition test at that time, within one month of transfer to i.t.a. he registered a reading-age of 6·2 and this had increased to 6·9 by 1 March 1965. (Both these results are based on the version of the Schonell test in traditional orthography.) From writing complete gibberish this boy is now presenting well-expressed original work.

Child No. 11: Admitted in December, 1964, from a rural school in England this girl was excessively retarded in every respect to the extent of being unable to say her own name to the teacher. She was unable to recognize the written form of her name, match the appropriate flash-card or to copy it intelligibly, but her interest was aroused in the preparatory activities for the introduction to i.t.a. and her success in the first simple i.t.a. reader gave an unexpected boost to her confidence so that with the diligent help and co-operation of her parents she amassed an i.t.a. reading vocabulary of 150 words in two months and could, under supervision, build up and write simple phrases from her quite reliable knowledge of the phonemes of i.t.a. The scars and small scabs which dotted her arms as a result of persistent nervous scratchings had also cleared completely by this time. This seems directly attributable to the increased confidence she had acquired.

Alexandria Junior School,
Singapore.

This class is composed of boys and girls who would have been retained at the end of their first grade experience. They were experiencing much difficulty in many areas—particularly reading. The California Reading Test was given in September. Grade Placement scores ranged from 1·1–1·8. The California Test of Mental Maturity was also given these children in September. The range in I.Q. scores was 69–120. The same test, but a different form, was given in April. A significant change was noted. The I.Q. scores now ranged from 73–121. The average I.Q. gain on a pupil-by-pupil basis came to 9·5 and the range of improvement in the school year was from 0 to 22 points. The average gain in mental age was 16 months with the range being 5 to 29 months. The teacher has kept a record of the library books read. This has been very encouraging.

> Hickory Elementary School,
> Bel Air, Maryland, U.S.A.

Positive results of the program (with second graders in corrective reading) fall into three main areas. In the first place, sound discrimination improvement resulted in improved confidence and accuracy in recognizing and reproducing sounds, both orally and on paper. . . . In the second place, although I know that everyone who tries this approach reports the same phenomenon, I must mention again the amazing freedom of written expression. . . . The third result . . . was the joy and enthusiasm of the children. Every day was exciting and rewarding. Every session spelled "success" for each and every one of them. And this result, I believe, was the most important of all!

> Mrs. Marie Thomas
> Clallam Bay, Washington, U.S.A.

The linguistic poverty, so frequently met with in remedial classes, is also reduced by i.t.a. As explained above, the children's increasing familiarity with a printed word precedes and leads to its adoption in speech—

One of our major aims is to encourage slow readers to talk "with a purpose." This helps them to increase their "oral" vocabulary though they are reluctant to write such words for a while. By expanding their "reading" vocabulary they talk with more confidence and seek gradations of meaning, e.g. the universal adjective "nice" is now replaced by more appropriate ones— "pleasant afternoon," "enjoyable time," etc. This kind of phrasing, stimulated by i.t.a., becomes part of their normal speech and encourages them to respond to new situations without fear.

> West Howe Junior School,
> Bournemouth.

Having had considerable success by teaching reading with a phonetic approach for fifteen years, I approached teaching i.t.a. with enthusiasm and few doubts about its possibilities of success. However, I was most surprised at the ease with which the transition to orthodox spelling is being made by the children. In a class of ten children I have three reading groups—8-1-1. The superior group is reading fluently in orthodox print at a 1^2 reader level in the *4th month of school*, while the two other children are reading in books 4 and 5 i.t.a. respectively at this time. These two children came to school with poor linguistic backgrounds and speech difficulties. From past experience, I feel certain that they would need to be retained in the First Grade—had they not been taught the i.t.a. approach to reading. The ease with which children write creatively is an added asset of i.t.a.

> Valley School of Ligonier,
> Ligonier, Pennsylvania, U.S.A.

Yes, i.t.a. reading is a priceless tool for the detection and correction of speech difficulties. We feel most strongly on this point! The speech therapist who works with children in this building is overjoyed with the results i.t.a. has produced in making children aware of and alert to the various sounds of the English language. In September, he was skeptical of the entire program, but is now as enthusiastic as the teachers and I about i.t.a. reading. . . . Children who come from homes where a limited vocabulary is utilized by the parents (culturally disadvantaged homes) seem to make giant steps in vocabulary development. We feel that this is due to these reasons: (1) the independence of the child toward reading, which allows him to read more and thus increase his background of conceptions and perceptions; and (2) the type of reading material in the readers themselves. We appreciate the fact that children can now read material which is similar to their spoken language, and not be limited to a "nursery-school age" child type of language.

> Bald Eagle-Nittany Schools,
> Mill Hall, Pennsylvania, U.S.A.

(2) THE INITIAL TEACHING ALPHABET AND ADULT BACKWARD READERS

As far as is known, the earliest attempt to employ i.t.a. as a remedial medium with a group of adult backward readers took place at the School of Preliminary Education at Corsham, Wiltshire (a unit of the Royal Army Educational Corps); the following account has been provided by the Commandant—

The aim of this army school is to improve the standard of literacy of recruits who would otherwise be unacceptable, so as to enable them to benefit fully from their military training and to realize their fullest potential as trained soldiers and possibly as leaders. Every fortnight some thirty of these young men assemble at the school for a three month course. The great majority are by no means illiterate—the average reading age on entry is about 10 years and their average I.Q. is 85; a small number, however, about 8 per cent of the total, come with reading ages of less than 8 years. These men have always been grouped in small remedial classes where they can enjoy the maximum amount of individual help. I.t.a. was introduced as the standard learning medium in spring 1964 and, at the time of writing, some fifty students have completed the i.t.a. course.

Obviously with adults the use of i.t.a. presents special problems, in that it is not "initial." The great majority, even of the most backward, are familiar with at least the consonants of the traditional alphabet, and in only two cases has it been necessary to start with pre-reading exercises. The remainder, after a short introduction to the unfamiliar letters, using large letter cards and flash cards (home made), have started reading almost at once. We have used both the *Downing Readers* and the American *Early-to-Read* series. Both seem to be equally effective. From these, students go on to the large *Fairy Tale* series, *The Captain Roy* stories, and our own home-produced material. Most students become reasonably fluent readers in i.t.a. in about six weeks.

Provision of suitable reading matter is a major problem. Inevitably almost all published i.t.a. material is aimed at young children. The soldier student will accept the Infant Reader because he wants to learn. He will accept the classical fairy story because of its intrinsic merit. As fluency and comprehension improve, so he becomes more critical of "kid's stuff." We attempt to provide simplified adult reading matter by transliterating our home-produced readers in ordinary type with an i.t.a. typewriter. The result obviously cannot compare in clarity, attractiveness of layout and illustration with the commercially produced juvenile book.

No attempt is made to teach i.t.a. writing for two reasons. First, the shortness of the course does not give much time for written exercises. (We attempt to cover in six weeks ground that takes the child two or three years.) Secondly, since the student has already some knowledge of orthodox print, however misguided, it would only confuse him further if i.t.a. writing and spelling were to be imposed on him. If i.t.a. appears in the free writing that is done (usually in letters to their homes), this is acceptable.

The transition from i.t.a. to orthodox print probably presents even fewer problems with the adult than with the child. The adult is much more familiar with advertisements, posters, notices, newspaper headlines, and so on which he has seen all around him for years. It has been found as a general rule that the student changes from i.t.a. in his own time, as he finds that with increased confidence he can decipher and understand print that was previously either half comprehended by guesswork or else was sheer gibberish to him. In many cases improvement in reading i.t.a. and orthodox print is a simultaneous process, beginning as soon as the first impact of i.t.a. brings the miraculous realization that reading is a skill within the student's capability.

The supreme importance of psychological impact cannot be over-stressed. The child beginning to read comes with an open mind. The adult has a long background of failure and defeatism. We are able to say to him: "Here is something quite new and strange which you have never seen before. Give it a chance and it *will* help you." This approach has never failed. Then as soon as the student experiences some early success, the burden of failure is shifted from his shoulders to the orthodox alphabet and spellings—"There's nothing wrong with me. . . ." The psychological benefits of i.t.a. in modification of personality are most apparent in the increase of confidence and relaxation shown by all students in the periodical tape-recordings which they make, to assess their own progress. Even more significant is the marked improvement in *mechanical* arithmetic scores, although hardly any number work is done by the i.t.a. groups. This can only be accounted for by the increase in *general* confidence engendered by i.t.a.

We do not claim 100 per cent success for i.t.a. There have been one or two students whose innate dullness or lack of powers of retention make it as difficult for them to learn by i.t.a. as by any other method. But with the great majority of the most backward men, i.t.a. has been an outstanding success and is now the standard method adopted with all men with a reading age of 8 years 6 months or less.

School of Preliminary Education,
Royal Army Educational Corps,
Corsham, Wiltshire.

A start has been made with using i.t.a. with adult backward readers in several penal institutions. These extracts from two reports received from prisons in the U.S.A. are of unusual interest because of the marked association between reading failure and delinquency—

All new commitments who score less than fifth grade, approximately 5 per month, are assigned to the school as compulsory students unless excused because of infirmity or a lack of ability demonstrated during a prior incarceration. In an effort to improve our remedial program, we initiated the i.t.a. program in the summer quarter of 1964. A total of 37 inmates have participated over the ensuing 3 quarters with a great deal of success. The average grade level of these men at the time of commitment was 1·6. . . . Their average I.Q. was 77 with a range of 50 to 90. . . . After using the i.t.a. program for 9 months, we have attained the following results: The average advancement was 2·8 grades . . ., the average time spent in the program was 3·4 months, and 21 of the 37 inmates passed the fifth grade level. For the same period of time in our control group of 19 pupils using traditional orthography the average I.Q. was 77, but we found the average grade advancement to be only 1·2 grades. . . . The success we have enjoyed with i.t.a. should not be entirely attributed to the methods or materials. We do not believe we could achieve such satisfactory results with reluctant adults if the instructors had not received adequate training or were not genuinely interested.

We have been fortunate in finding enthusiastic and competent inmate instructors and in employing three professionally qualified part-time teachers from local school districts. It is the consensus of the certified instructors who have worked with such groups since September, 1961, that it is the most successful remedial program we have attempted, and the results presently indicate this. We have concluded from our studies of the program that the inmates find i.t.a. easier to learn because it is more consistent than traditional orthography. The men, once indoctrinated to the program, receive it more enthusiastically than the traditional orthography because it has a wider interest range and is less juvenile than the other remedial programs we have used.

We were concerned when we launched the i.t.a. program as to how these men would adjust in the transition to orthodox print. Our doubts were allayed . . ., and we found the men respond very readily to our regular grade school curriculum after completing the i.t.a. course. We are very pleased with i.t.a. and highly recommend it to others who are interested in teaching reading to adult illiterates.

Oregon State Penitentiary,
Salem, Oregon, U.S.A.

The i.t.a. program at San Quentin concerned ten men at first-grade literacy training level. Five of the ten men in the first-grade program were completely illiterate and five had very limited reading and writing ability at the time of their initial enrollment in the i.t.a. program. All had received previous training in reading with traditional orthography. Eight of the ten men made definite, positive progress with i.t.a. and yet, five of these eight had made no real progress with traditional orthography. Two men simply were not able to forget their earlier training sufficiently to fully utilize i.t.a.; i.e., they continued to name letters and to approach their reading problems by using the orthodox spelling. In spite of this we are enthusiastic because five of the men simply had not made worthwhile reading and writing progress with traditional orthography, and all five men are now reading and writing. Only one man made the transition from i.t.a. and he did it in a matter of four weeks; his ability to learn to read so quickly is really unusual with respect to the average illiterate student that we enroll.

We intend to continue with i.t.a. and the same teacher is going to teach this group during the summer session in order to insure continuity and to provide the opportunity for inmate students to make the transition. It should be noted that, in addition, instruction is being given in the evening school program with the i.t.a. approach being utilized as a remedial reading technique at the third-grade level. The third-grade level teacher also reports very satisfactory progress with this approach. The results of all work to date with i.t.a., although very inconclusive because of serious limitations in research design imposed by the pressure of other duties, nevertheless are very encouraging to the instructional and administrative staff at San Quentin Prison.

Department of Corrections,
California State Prison,
San Quentin, California, U.S.A.

(3) THE INITIAL TEACHING ALPHABET IN SPECIAL SCHOOLS FOR THE E.S.N., PARTIALLY SIGHTED, ETC.

If children with normal intelligence and faculties can find the illogical and unsystematic nature of orthodox spelling baffling, the task facing the physically, emotionally, and in consequence educationally handicapped child is daunting indeed. It is not difficult to understand why i.t.a. can help him—

The main "ingredient" which seems to help the children to read more quickly is the logicality of the system—the fact that once they know the sounds made by the symbols, they *know* they can word-build. Much of the lack of confidence with ESN children, we find, comes from the uncertainty of the English language. They are encouraged to try to write down their ideas as well as to read, only to find that any feeling of success is constantly undermined by illogical spellings in both spheres. In fact, free writing is delayed so long in traditional orthography that in many cases we never reach a stage beyond the composition of two or three simple sentences in sequence. In i.t.a., however, we find that written composition begins as reading begins and each reinforces the other, to improve vocabulary . . . with the children composing, based on their own experience and vocabulary, reading is no longer such a "classroom-based" activity. Previously we found that words met *outside* school hours were not connected in the child's mind with the same word met in a reading session *in* school. "Reading" tended to be divorced from reality however hard a teacher strove to give it practical realism. Now, quite a different attitude prevails, and in its way this is rather unexpected. Children on i.t.a. do not feel so involved with advertisements, bus destination boards, TV captions, etc., but the words they use in sentences of *their own* composition are at once related to the same words in their graded reading books and library books. Reading in school thus comes closer to their home and play environment because this is what they write about. Just before the end of term a child rushed up to me and said: "Look, there's *tractor* in my reading book. I wrote that in my words this morning." He was referring to the fact that he had written in his own free composition the very word he had just found in his reading book, and the excitement in his voice was enough to show his enjoyment of this situation. *He* was leading his reading book, for a change.

Audenshaw Hawthorns School,
Audenshaw.

In this E.S.N. Special School we have so far found that the alphabet is of value with only a proportion of the children. I am not yet in a position to make firm statements with regard to its overall value. That it has a value is beyond doubt but, as you know, in our type of school we are catering for children who have very limited intellectual ability (particularly at the lower end of the I.Q. range), limited memory spans, and additional handicaps having aural and visual bases. It will take time to assess accurately the value of i.t.a. with reference to such children. It is my intention over the next two years to observe closely such cases and conduct appropriate tests which should ultimately give us the accurate information that we seek. . . . It is evident . . . that many children have made accelerated progress in reading and that the written expression of these children has become more prolific and interesting.

The Park School,
Baguley, Manchester.

Before the transition the quantity of reading matter and enjoyment is greater because the child, having mastered the symbols and letters, can then build up any word written in i.t.a. and therefore read books which would have been beyond him if written in orthodox spelling. After transition quantity and enjoyment is much the same as had the child been taught to read by the orthodox spelling. But without i.t.a. some E.S.N. children would never get to this stage. With E.S.N. children the very fact of being able to read after many years of frustration and failure gives a measure of self-confidence in practical, social and imaginative activities.

Woodside Senior E.S.N. School,
Bolton.

I have used i.t.a. with my slower immature readers in my educable class. After one school year, there are five that are making the transition to T.O. . . . I was concerned about the loss of learning over the summer months and carefully prepared a review which did me a vast amount of good. They neither wanted nor needed it. I was amazed to see how little had been forgotten.

Grant School,
Dumont, New Jersey, U.S.A.

i.t.a. made it possible for them to see their own progress almost immediately. As one successful lesson led to another, they craved more and more knowledge. After all the years of failure, they can now read.

i.t.a. gives them a definite pattern to follow in order to learn to read. The teacher provides a pattern of behavior to follow. Combine the two and they create a stronger foundation on which the emotionally disturbed child can build a better future.

Highland Training School,
Highland, New York, U.S.A.

To summarize briefly, our experience here has been as follows: We have a population of 550 to 700 children among our 7,000 mental patients in this hospital. These children have been diagnosed generally as either cases of primary behavior problems or cases of childhood schizophrenia. Nearly all of them have reading disabilities in some significant degree. Many of them are non-readers. We have felt for a considerable time that there is a close relationship between their reading disability and their psychiatric problems. Although we have a competent staff of teachers, and small individualized classes, the teaching of reading in traditional orthography had been largely ineffective or extremely slow. We were quite willing to experiment with any new approach to the teaching of reading. . . . We began with six teachers, each teacher having both a class in i.t.a. and a matched class in traditional orthography composed of boys aged 6–10 years. The experimental and control classes were matched on the basis of I.Q., chronological age, and achievement tests. As a separate project, one of the teachers who was trained in the workshop began using i.t.a. with a group of 10–12-year-old boys, all non-readers, who had had about four years' instruction in orthodox spelling but who still could not read and were resistant to further training. The younger children are showing more rapid progress in learning to read through the use of i.t.a. than through the use of the orthodox alphabet and spelling. The 10–12-year-old boys have shown remarkably fast progress in learning to read and write with i.t.a. In addition, the newly acquired ability to read and write has shown a marked effect upon their psychological reaction toward each other and the classroom situation. They appear to be more co-operative, less anti-social, and motivated now toward academic progress.

Rockland State Hospital,
Orangeburg, N.Y.

I teach retarded children; however about three-quarters of my students are academically retarded or brain damaged—18 in all. One child was listed as a non-reader and now he is on page 51 in Book 2 of the i.t.a. *Early-to-Read Series*. Another child in Book 4 has a severe speech defect due to psychological reasons and with i.t.a. she has become more conscious of sounds. The majority have completed the programs and have come up two reading levels—over three, in some cases. Since their reading has improved, so has everything else, and one student has even gone back into the regular classroom; it's difficult to put into words what a morale builder i.t.a. is for my students as well as for their teachers!

R.D. 2, Fairfield,
Pennsylvania, U.S.A.

. . . Their I.Q.'s range from the low 50's to 75; their ages from 8 to 11 years. They had already spent from three to six years in school, divided variously between regular and special classes, before the introduction of the i.t.a. program. . . . No child, however, was put into the program who was coping with traditional orthography at a grade 1 or higher level, if he did so with an adequate degree of comprehension and with some word attack skills. . . . Some of the children have language problems because of their foreign background; many are culturally deprived; a goodly number have some emotional or organic problem, any or all of these factors contributing to or coupled with their mental retardation.

What have these children achieved? Of the 19 who had completed a year and a half of instruction in the Initial Teaching Alphabet as of February 1, 1965, one has made transition at the 2^2 level; eight were reading orthodox print at the 2^1 level after sweeping through the grade 1 basal reader in three weeks; three had learned the 44 i.t.a. symbols and were reading in Book 4 in the Pitman i.t.a. series (readability level, 2^2); four had learned 30 to 40 sound symbols and were reading in Book 2 in the i.t.a. (readability level, pre-primer to primer); and three had mastered only 20 sounds and were reading in Book 5 of the Downing series. To summarize: nine had made transition in reading successfully; three were close to making transition; seven were making slow progress.

When I asked the teachers for success stories from our original group of 19, they responded readily. Let me give you an example: twin boys, 11 years old; I.Q.'s 70 and 76, socially and physically mature for their age, from a typical middle-class family. The boys entered special class in the fall of 1963 after five years in regular classes, one year in kindergarten, two in first grade, and two in second grade. At that time their frustration level in reading on the Jastak Test was 1·1. They were placed immediately in the i.t.a. program and now, a year and a half later, have made transition and are reading at the 2^1 level in the traditional alphabet and spellings. The psychologist who has tested the boys several times is convinced that they never would have learned to read through instruction in the traditional medium in other than a clinical setting, if at all. When I asked the teachers for "failure" stories, I could get none. In their opinion, every child was making progress, however slow that progress might be. . . .

. . . The most exciting aspect of the i.t.a. program in classes for the educable retarded has been the great interest in reading and writing displayed by the children. They came to the i.t.a. with none of the frustration we used to find with orthodox print and this has been true even in our few cases of children who, after a year with the i.t.a. in first grade, were continued on the i.t.a. in special class. The children have, for the first time, shown a preference for books over puzzles, for pencil and paper over games. Given free time, they ask for permission to borrow the i.t.a. library books in their classrooms, to read to each other, or to write on the chalkboard. They also persevere in their reading and writing tasks more independently and for longer periods of time than formerly. Another by-product has been an improvement in the appearance of their written work. Symbols are more carefully formed; papers are neater. . . .

. . . At this point we are fully aware that the Initial Teaching Alphabet is not a panacea for all of the reading problems we encounter with the educable retarded and that there are many yet-unanswered questions about its use with these children. On the other hand, observation of our educable retarded pupils in the classroom setting, especially their interest in and motivatior for reading and writing, has encouraged us to believe that for many, if not for all, the Initial Teaching Alphabet is a medium with which they can approach the task of learning to read and write with enjoyment and success rather than frustration and failure.

Special Services, Bethlehem Area Schools,
Bethlehem, Pennsylvania, U.S.A.

We have used the i.t.a. *Early-to-Read* program with junior high level educable mental retardates who, at the ages 14–16, still had not learned to read. In some few cases the reading impairment was so severe that simple phonics—even the sounds of letters—were unknown. At the end of five months the majority of the group of 10 are in Book Five and progressing nicely. Even the most severely handicapped (I.Q.s of 46 and 52) have progressed to knowing the vowels plus some consonant sounds and are reading in the beginning of Book Two. We consider this to be most satisfying progress especially since some of these pupils have been exposed to traditional methods of reading for periods of 6 to 8 years without *any* success. We are most happy to have started this system over the objections of critics since we find the i.t.a. system to have one advantage over their systems of reading instruction—*it works!*

Fort Crailo School,
Rensselaer, New York, U.S.A.

The value of an unmistakable connection between speech and reading is even clearer and its need is even greater for the E.S.N. child. To be impeded by the alphabetic obstacles to forming the relationships is bad enough: to be also "verbally defective" would seem to present a barrier that is impregnable, but here again i.t.a. is capable of assisting the learning of language as well as reading—

Some children have to be taught in an almost complete vacuum. Where conversation is restricted to staccato phrases and ejaculations in the home, the child does not feel the urge to read which motivates most children, some to an almost passionate degree. These children show up as verbal defectives on the Raven and Crichton Tests, and as things are they must almost inevitably be non-starters on the path of language. However dull they may be, and I fear that there must be a residue for whom nothing lasting can be done, I feel that the verdict must be that all can be helped to be less underprivileged than they might otherwise have been by use of i.t.a.; I know of no other means by which this might be accomplished. . . . I feel very strongly that one cannot say too often, "better than would otherwise have been possible," and that this will be true at a variety of levels. I think that the logic and purpose of it all is even more important than the simplicity, because there will still be those children to whom it will not be simple, and with whom it will still be a long term job. It does not matter a great deal whether to a group of

232

backward children, who are shipwrecked in a stormy sea, i.t.a. appears as a high speed rescue launch or a lifebelt—the ultimate result is the same. Indeed the relief of the latter might well be more than that of the former. This is a great educational advance, and despite what some critics have said, a tool of proved merit. One doesn't need a set of statistics to detect the all-round improvement in children who have sampled its benefits.

> Northmoor County Primary School,
> Oldham.

Is the i.t.a. of value with E.S.N. children? We would answer in the affirmative. If a child is capable of learning how to read he will learn more quickly and more easily using the i.t.a. than with the orthodox alphabet and spelling. Furthermore his writing will go along with his reading and not be inhibited by an inability to spell. . . . Never before had we seen original written work by E.S.N. children at this end of the school, and it was a pleasure to see the great satisfaction the children obtained from it. It gave them freedom from an emotional blockage in allowing them to use a means of communication that had always been beyond their capabilities. Not only were the children able to do original written work but they were also able to do written comprehension exercises . . . the child's lack of language becomes apparent as a limiting factor in reading progress sooner with i.t.a. than with orthodox spelling. So many of the E.S.N. children come from subcultural homes that it has always been necessary to broaden their experiences and with i.t.a. this need has become more pressing much sooner. Although these children can now read more material sooner than before it is too early to say that they can learn from a book. This may come with a progressive broadening of experience, although it is doubtful if we can do more in this direction than we are already doing. The time at our disposal is limited, but it may be that the child's success in reading could produce a greater interest from the parents. I look forward to the day when an illiterate parent will come to us for the same satisfaction that the child has obtained from learning to read. Meanwhile the reading ability of the i.t.a. child is outstripping his experience, knowledge and vocabulary.

> Torfield School,
> Hastings.

The next comment was sent by a teacher in a school for partially sighted children; in the majority of cases in this particular class they suffered from additional disabilities such as emotional instability, E.S.N., or missing phalanges of the hand—

When i.t.a. was introduced last September (with an absolute minimum of books and apparatus being available) we were faced with a batch of newly admitted children completely lacking in self-confidence and with a marked

233

aversion to begin any form of academic training. I.t.a. proved to be an ideal way to launch these children into learning. Their enthusiasm was immediately apparent and their appetite for reading was such that it was difficult to obtain sufficient i.t.a. reading material to satisfy this. Our school year ends in two days' time and on reflection I cannot think of any previous occasion, during my eight years as headmaster here, when my colleague and I have felt so thoroughly satisfied with the improvement in the children's increased vocabulary, expansion of their experience and knowledge and their unflagging interest in reading.

Corporation Park School for
Partially Sighted Children,
Blackburn.

The next two extracts come from reports sent in by approved schools[1] for boys, both of which run regular remedial classes—

This school has a particularly high proportion of boys whose school life has been one of failure and rejection. It is not surprising that our first experience of them shows them to be truculent and difficult. Those who are unable to read, or whose reading skills are only partly developed (about 30–40 per cent of the school intake) are usually the ones who tend to be the most troublesome, though of course this is not always the case. Once the first barriers have been broken down, and they understand that they are not to be treated half so badly as they expected, they settle half-heartedly to the classroom, not visualizing any more success than formerly. The preliminary stages of reading by the i.t.a. method have proved so easy to negotiate that for the first time most boys realize that they are going to see some reward for their efforts. This has had the effect of settling their classroom behaviour, getting much more work out of them than they are used to giving, while at the same time allowing them the satisfaction that comes with success, and allowing much more immediate scope for creative and constructive expression. "Civilizing" is perhaps too strong a word, but in a lesser degree it describes the effect the i.t.a. method has had on some very backward and recalcitrant boys. In only one case out of eighteen did one boy continue to be despondent and difficult after ten weeks or so of the course, declaring that "he would never learn to read." He was shown a pile of a dozen or so books in i.t.a. which he had already read, and his frustration evaporated.

The results of the second year with i.t.a. showed that every boy in the remedial group was well able to read, and the *average* progress for the group in Comprehension, Spelling and Word Reading was 13·5 months, 10 months and 15·5 months respectively. In June 1964, we were able to say that every boy in the school could read, and the worst reader had a reading age of 6·9 years, although his Comprehension Age was 8·1 years, and he had made

[1] A school to which delinquent children are sent by a juvenile court.

16 months' progress in 12. From then on i.t.a. became the reading method for the remedial group and will continue so until something better can take its place. The same marked improvements as previously have been noted in the last school year. The 9 boys in the group have made remarkable progress, only 2 have failed to make over 12 months' progress, while improvements of 24 and 30 months in reading were achieved by two others. Such has been the change in character of the remedial group over the last three years that we have come to expect the boys, no matter how retarded on entry, to improve. It has been argued that the teacher responsible has far more influence than a particular medium but in this case the teacher had spent most of his career with this type of child, and only met success on this scale after the i.t.a. experiment. . . .

The difficulty of learning several new symbols was expected to be too much for this type of child, but it turned out that there was no difficulty at all, and the boys enjoy the fresh approach to reading. We found that the letters were quickly learned and the quick build-up of confidence in the early stages left its character on the child's learning process from then on. Most children rapidly develop a surprising ability to attack intelligently new and complex words, and since the sounding and blending of the words follow logical and single patterns, their efforts are immediately rewarded.

It is also noteworthy that the boys seem to understand more than they can actually read. Tests applied in orthodox print to boys learning in i.t.a. have shown that while the Word Reading score may be fairly low, the score for the Comprehension test is comparatively much higher. We have noted a difference in one case of as much as 32 months, while a general improvement was being maintained. The difference diminished after transition, showing that the reading skills are settling down. It has been observed that some pupils who are still at the pointing stage have their fingers under a word half a line away from the one they are saying. Sometimes, even in the early stages of the i.t.a. course, we see a boy assimilate a whole sentence as a continuous unit, instead of picking out each word separately. This is quite a new feature in remedial teaching and can only be put down to the confidence bred by i.t.a.

One last and most important effect of i.t.a. as far as a Junior Approved School is concerned is the way in which the method has been known to settle a boy who is anti-school. Many boys come to us with terrible school records. Many teachers have tried many methods and every kind of approach, all without success. The result has been to spoil the child completely for subsequent schoolwork. Schools cease to be places where he may express himself adequately. They are the scenes of his failures, his disappointments, his disgrace. In the classroom at St. Vincent's the non-reader can achieve immediate success, followed by more of the same. Instead of being blamed for failure, or sensing that he is wasting yet another teacher's time and energy, he begins, for the first time in his life perhaps, to respond favourably to the attentions of a teacher. In place of disillusion is success, combined with praise for well-directed effort. We have in the school at present a number of boys whose classroom behaviour is exemplary, yet whose previous school reports are damning. In some cases the improvement extends even beyond the class-room.

St. Vincent's School,
Tankerton.

Red House Farm School is a Home Office Approved School that caters for the retarded, ascertained E.S.N., and maladjusted delinquent boy in the chronological age range of 13 to 15+. The numbers catered for are approximately ninety of which a small percentage—5 per cent—are seriously maladjusted whilst the remainder usually have some small behaviour problems, which would be expected in a school of this nature. . . . The ability of the boys varies considerably but for the purpose of an informal experiment in the use of i.t.a. the twenty-four boys of lowest ability were chosen. . . .

The use of the Initial Teaching Alphabet for remedial purposes with the older retarded pupil presents some extra problems but sometimes gives a bonus. Many pupils have the hard sounds of the traditional alphabet so ingrained in them that it is difficult for them to recognise the soft sounds of the letters. When this occurs it means that the i.t.a. has to be taught completely; however, if some previous attempt at teaching by the phonic method has been tried with the pupil it usually means that basic soft sounds plus a limited but useful vocabulary has been built. As most teachers of retarded readers will agree, the barrier to progress using traditional orthography comes when vowel and vowel consonantal blends have to be introduced; a great deal of retardation and frustration of learning can be traced back to this cause. The Initial Teaching Alphabet helped to overcome this problem and the pupils found themselves reading with a greater fluency than they had done previously once the new i.t.a. symbols were mastered. . . . Each pupil was dealt with individually and some made progress faster than others according to their degree of retardation. At the start of the experiment the mental reading ages ranged from 4+ to 7+ Burt reading scale and individual I.Q.'s ranged from 58 to 80. Before the experiment was three weeks old a pattern had begun to take shape, namely that the more severely retarded boys with the higher I.Q.'s were making rapid progress. Some of the more severely retarded low I.Q. boys were taking longer to master the new symbols but this was not surprising as they were also having difficulty in mastering the basic sounds. . . .

We allowed the experiment to continue in this form for two terms from January 1965 to Summer 1965 during which time we have had in addition to the original twenty-four boys, a turnover of fourteen new boys to the group making a total of thirty-eight pupils since January 1965. During this period each boy has either learned to read or improved his reading age, the smallest advance in the six month period being 2·5 years M.R.A. to the greatest advance 4·1 years, M.R.A. These measurements were taken after transference using the Burt reading scale. As a completely academic exercise and purely for our own curiosity we transcribed the Burt reading scale into i.t.a. and here the average mental reading age of each pupil was in excess of two years ahead of the results with orthodox print.

The experiment continues . . . however the use of i.t.a. with retarded adolescents does work and does give remarkable results.

Red House Farm School,
Buxton,
Norfolk.

The last lines of this chapter are written by a Primary school teacher in Burton-upon-Trent with a remedial class whose I.Qs range from 62 or lower to 75—

. . . Children have made up to three times as much progress in reading on i.t.a. as children of equal ability on orthodox spelling. Their personal development, self-confidence, and even their handwork has also improved.

All the children in my class who have changed to orthodox spelling have done so without any pause or difficulty. Apart from the fact that they choose their book from a different shelf they hardly seem to notice any difference at all, and they do not come to me for help in reading individual words as much as children learning on orthodox spelling only.

I found an interesting illustration of the ease of transition only last month. I was testing (in orthodox spelling) children who were leaving my class after a two year course (the usual length of course here). For my own interest only I tested one boy who had only been with me for nine months and who has reached "ie nœ a story" in the *Janet and John* series. He has only read in i.t.a. during that time, yet on the Schonell Word Test he registered a reading age of 6·3 in orthodox spelling! When he joined the class in September his reading age was nil.

In the past, teaching in orthodox spelling, I have found that children would read a story, understand it, and be able to re-tell it either orally or in writing, but there they finished. The story was something separate and nothing to do with anything else in life. Time and time again since the children have been reading in i.t.a. they have broken off while reading to me, or come out to me when reading by themselves, to tell me something related both to their own lives and the story they are reading. They also remember more clearly what they have read. For example one boy suggested that he and a friend made their own snap cards for a game of snap. Given the cardboard, a group activity soon developed under the direction of the original boy. The cards were made in exactly the same way as that described in a book he had read at least three weeks before.

It is almost as if reading in i.t.a. is so easy that while reading the child also has time to think, whereas in orthodox spelling so much concentration went into the job of reading a word or sentence that there was neither time nor energy left to do anything else.

237

Since the children have been reading in i.t.a. they are more ready to hold a conversation with me, with other children, or with visitors who may be complete strangers to them. They are more ready to try to put things into writing too.

The reading period is much easier and more pleasant for me. When I was using the orthodox alphabet medium I often found it far too busy a time, hearing children read, helping those in difficulties (all the time), almost hanging over the children who were writing because most of them frankly did not want to do it at all, helping with many spelling difficulties, and always seeming to have a queue of children waiting for attention. Playtime has come as a welcome break, and yet I have often felt rather uncomfortably that some of the children should have had more attention.

Now, with i.t.a., the children read their books quickly by themselves, or write their news stories, or choose a work card or a reading game. I have time to hear every child read for a few minutes each day, and time to spare to go over their written work with them or to chat with a child who has a yarn to tell. The atmosphere is happier and more restful. My problem now is the child who "just wants to finish this, Miss," when he should be out to play; and the child who comes to me as the dinner bell rings begging to be heard for a second time because he has finished his book and wants to get another.

Such problems I can bear.

Christ Church Junior Mixed and Infants School,
Burton-upon-Trent.

12 Teaching the Deaf and the Blind with i.t.a.

For children who are partially or completely deaf the orthodox alphabet(s) and spelling create more than usually forbidding difficulties. These children are largely or even solely dependent on sight (and touch) for receiving communications and are deprived of the continuous reinforcement between sight and sound experienced by hearing children. Learning to read is not only more vital for deaf children's development but the skill is also far more difficult to acquire. The psychological frustrations that already flow from their handicap make it especially desirable that the initial stages in their attempts to read should be successful.

The deaf child[1] is subject to a special and severe form of linguistic impoverishment. He approaches the preliminary stages of reading with an infinitely smaller background of apprehended concepts and thus of meaningful words and language than the average hearing child. What little he has picked up comes from a restricted field of observation and from lip reading and his own attempts at forming words. By no means all the phonemes in English can be observed on a speaker's lips, though others can be felt by the deaf child's fingers on the speaker's throat or demonstrated by other means; opinions vary among the experts on how much can be observed by either method and it certainly changes from child

[1] For the purpose of this chapter it will be easier if it is written in terms of the completely deaf child; the same considerations affect the partially deaf child, depending on the degree of disability.

to child. Learning to say words and to read words on lips and in print go together, though frequently a deaf child possesses a larger vocabulary of words he can read than of words he is able to say or lip read. Printed words can be related to familiar objects (a chair, a dog) but even more than the hearing child his starting-point must be pictureable nouns (a dog, a man); demonstrable actions (giving, taking); directional motions (up, down); sensible qualities (hot, bitter, blue); and measurable quantities (one, two, three). Structural words (*a, and, for, is*) can follow later. It is surely simpler for the deaf child, dependent as he is on the visual element, if he can relate each of these concepts to a single, consistent printed form as provided by i.t.a.—if, for example, he can connect the classroom picture of a dog always to ɖog instead of to DOG, Dog, Dog, dog, dog, etc; and relate gœ to nœ and sœ, yet nevertheless dis-relate them in turn from ɖꝏ, tꝏ, and hꝏ.

Because the young deaf child's knowledge of speech is limited largely to other people's lip and mouth movements, it would surely make things easier for him if there were also a reliable relationship between printed words and the corresponding lip and mouth movements. The initial teaching alphabet can provide just such a reliable link between these two very different, but both visual, modes of communication. Similar factors apply when it comes to learning to form words that cannot be heard. The lip and mouth movements for the sound ie in *aisle, isle, I'll*, etc. are identical and therefore to link the sound common to these words with a common characterization in print—ie—must, by removing confusion and affording rational visual classification, assist with the learning of the relationship between (1) the concept; (2) the printed and/or written word; (3) the teacher's lip and mouth movements; (4) the child's own lip and mouth movements necessary to form the word in question.

As well as removing the dis-relationships suggested by the orthodox alphabet(s) and spelling, i.t.a. can also prevent the deaf child from making the mistake of thinking that visual pairs or groups of words like *go, do; have, save; live* (verb), *live* (adjective); *bone, done; gone, one*; etc., etc. require the same lip and mouth movements when spoken. It is of course essential that care be taken to ensure that the pronunciation of the teachers, the parents, and on highly amplified speech records or tapes used in special teaching apparatus is standardized. The lip and mouth movements in muɕh and mꝏɕh are entirely different and if people say the word differently to the young deaf child it can confuse him seriously. On the other hand he will relate the pronunciation of his own (unheard) lip movements and attempted speech to the standardized i.t.a. spelling with the same ease as does the hearing child (see pages 126–8).

The necessity of employing some form of phonetic medium when teaching the deaf is widely recognized, at any rate to the extent of supplementary whole word methods with phonic word analysis. What are known as the Northampton charts provide deaf children with some ninety symbols to denote sounds but, although this is more than twice the necessary number, they do not amount to a satisfactory phonemic code, several different symbols or character combinations being used for the same sound. It may be argued, on the other hand, that i.t.a. does not provide sufficiently detailed phonetic guidance to the deaf—as explained in Chapter 7, its objective would be defeated if it were chained to a rigid system of phonemic representation and had to convey every nuance of speech. Experience may show that i.t.a. should be supplemented with further symbolizing clues when it is used to teach the deaf to speak, as has been done in the case of "World i.t.a."—see Chapter 15.

There has been no lack of pioneers among teachers of the handicapped but it is understandable if they are more than usually hesitant to try out new teaching methods or a new medium such as i.t.a. A pioneering experiment with i.t.a. was however begun by Miss M. Beadsworth, head of the School for the Deaf and Partially Deaf at Beever Street, Oldham. As early as 1964 Miss Beadsworth had expressed undoubted, if cautious, satisfaction with the new medium and she is convinced that it can be of great help to the deaf child. To prove it, she demonstrated the results of using i.t.a. with a group of 6–12-year-old deaf children, in a talk given at Manchester University, during which she produced the following case histories—

. . . the little boy of 6, for instance, 90 I.Q., with 60–80 decibels (db) loss over the speech range, born deaf from Rhesus incompatibility. At 5 years 9 months he was a non-reader and began word-picture matching. A month later, January 1964, he began on the first i.t.a. book *Here We Go*. In February he went a step further to *My Little Books* 1–5; in the next two months through *Off to Play* and *My Little Books* 6–10, and in May 1964 the comparatively advanced *Out and About* from which he proudly read to the assembly.

A boy of 9½, deaf from causes unknown (but probably hereditary since his brother is also deaf) was a non-reader at 8½ but in 9 months, less 4–5 weeks' very poor school attendance, had progressed through all 10 of *My Little*

Books and was reading *Out and About*. He has an I.Q. of 90 on the W.I.S.C. scale but his deafness is profound as can be seen from his audiogram.

A little girl with 90–105 db loss in her right ear, total (unrecordable) in her left, from acute meningitis at 3 months, now 8½ years old, I.Q. 75, went from non-reader to the first *Janet and John* in 10 months. Another 75 I.Q. youngster, a non-reader at 11 years, was at *Through the Garden Gate* within 10 months. He went deaf from measles at 3 years of age, spent 4½ years, for better or worse, at a hearing school before he got to Beever Street. His hearing falls off steadily from 50 db at 500 c.p.s. to 75 db at 6,000. Between 2,000 and 4,000 the left ear is about 15 db better than the right.[1]

In my experience the Americans are more open-minded than the British and so prepared to welcome innovations in teaching the deaf— not only the teachers but also official bodies concerned with the deaf's welfare. For example, the Volta Bureau in Washington (Alexander Graham Bell Association for the Deaf) and Mr. George Fellendorf[2] have been particularly helpful in overcoming the initial inertia and in encouraging my own attempts to call attention to the potentialities of a medium for reading and writing that relates rather than conflicts with normal listening and speaking as well as lip-reading. Others who report satisfactory trials of i.t.a. in the teaching of lip-reading and speech have been Dr. John K. Duffy, Professor of Speech, Department of Speech & Theater of Brooklyn College, New York; Miss Bonnie Webster of the Acoustic Pre-School of The Bill Wilkerson Hearing and Speech Center, Nashville, Tennessee; Mrs. Margaret Withrow of the Illinois School for the Deaf, Jacksonville, Illinois; Mrs. Evelyn Stahlem of The Mary Bennett School for the Deaf, Los Angeles; and Mrs. Esther Larzalere of the Harold Upjohn School of Special Education, Kalamazoo, Michigan.

Mrs. Larzalere, for example, writes:

"i.t.a. is a tool through the use of which deaf students can read books. It is the first time that primary deaf children have given this teacher clues which indicated what they were ready to learn. Motivation has been easier to achieve and learning more rapid. Enthusiasm was high, attention span excellent and all the students were activated to learning. The use of natural language, made possible because of the static symbols, made for a

---

[1] *Hearing*, Vol. 19, No. 10, p. 305, October 1964.

[2] It was due to Mr. Fellendorf that I was invited to read a paper *Can i.t.a. help the Deaf Child, his Parents and his Teacher?* at the International Conference on Oral Education of the Deaf (Northampton School for the Deaf in Massachusetts and the Lexington School for the Deaf in New York City, June 1967). Reprints from the official proceedings are obtainable from the i.t.a. Foundation, 154 Southampton Row, London, W.C.1 or the i.t.a. Foundation, Inc., Hofstra University, Hempstead, Long Island, N.Y. 11550.

better understanding of self-feelings and a sensitiveness to the feelings of others. Transfer of learning, an area in which boys excel girls, is easier with the use of i.t.a, because of the constancy of the sound symbols. i.t.a. lends itself well to student active participation and involvement, so necessary for learning for deaf students."

As well as learning to read i.t.a., deaf children are able to write and express their thoughts in i.t.a. It would be quite wrong however to suggest that i.t.a. can enable deaf children to progress as fast as their hearing brothers and sisters; it is bound to take them longer and they will probably need to acquire an even greater fluency in i.t.a. before they are ready for the transition. Indeed some take the view that the complexities of orthodox print and writing should be delayed until the deaf child's communicative ability in lip-reading and speaking, as well as in reading and writing in i.t.a., is well established. But it is reasonable to conclude that if i.t.a. can benefit the hearing child, it should *a fortiori* benefit the deaf child.

In most U.K. schools for the deaf sign language and the finger alphabet are frowned upon because they are thought to inhibit the development of lip reading and attempts by the child himself at forming words—not so long ago at some schools for the deaf children caught making signs to each other were even punished! There are nevertheless strong differences among teachers of the deaf on this question—between the "pure" oralists and those who believe also in teaching the finger alphabet and/or signs (of which some 3,000 recognized ones exist). There is a resemblance to the phonic versus look-and-say controversy among normal teachers of reading; some advocates of finger spelling, for example, talk of a "global" approach and an expert finger speller is able to "write" so fast in the air that the "readers" are outpaced in some words and are able to understand only in so far as they can see the whole of a word rather than its constituent characters. It is difficult not to suspect that controversy among teachers of the deaf is similarly fomented by the deficiencies of the orthodox alphabet. It seems to me that the deaf child should be encouraged to make use of all means of communication open to him. Lip-reading and speaking are of the first importance, particularly because, if completely acquired, they enable communication to take place with the hearing, but signs and a finger alphabet (in addition to reading and writing), provided these are related to the actions and sounds of speech, will surely help to reinforce the more important skills.

As with children who can hear normally, the prime essential is to develop *language*, the two-way traffic in communication, by all means available. It is especially hard for the deaf child, for example, to generalize a single concept such as *dog* and to associate with it the apparently disparate shapes, sizes and colours that are included in the species. It is in the teaching of language (as well as reading) to the deaf that i.t.a. has, I believe, an important contribution to make. Of particular interest have been successful experiments to combine i.t.a. with Dr. R. Orin Cornett's "Cued Speech" (Gallaudet College, Kendall Green, Washington, D.C.). In this method each of the essential phonemes is represented by a combined configuration of the lips and of one hand. Since the lip configurations are those of normal speech and thus contribute what in the long run is more important, the function of the hand is supplemental only and is limited to giving twelve "cues." This method also has the advantage of providing sufficient distinct lip-hand combinations to match i.t.a. With the aid of film loops, it makes it possible to present the deaf child with a subtle but meaningful juxtaposition of (1) lip movements, supported by hand and finger movements; (2) immediately relatable printed i.t.a. characters and words; (3) amplification for whatever rudiments of hearing the child may possess. These three provide a valuable supportive triangle that is well suited to develop linguistic skills and generalization. It is possible that with an early start (at the age of two or even less) this will help the deaf child not only to become more proficient at reading lips and print and at speaking but also to learn how to read for enjoyment, an achievement as yet denied to most of those born deaf solely because of their lack of linguistic competence.

Once this triangular relationship is widely accepted, it may be possible to resolve the dispute among the teachers. At present the finger alphabet normally used consists of 26 signs to match the 26 characters in the roman alphabet[1] and the spellings used are orthodox. As the lip-hand combinations of Cued Speech match i.t.a., not only does it tie in with the characters and spellings the deaf child learns to read and write, but it also helps to reinforce his understanding of them and to form yet another (kinaesthetic) matching link with the movements of his own and other people's lips and mouths. Because for most words fewer characters are needed, it can also be a speedier method of communication. It would, I believe, be a

[1] The U.S. Standard Manual Alphabet has signs also for 7 digraphs: *oe*, *oi*, *ch*, *th*, *sh*, *ng*, *wh*.

mistake merely to add to the existing 26 finger characters new augmenting symbols related in appearance (as in i.t.a.) to the present orthodox version so as to facilitate an eventual transition; this could be done, but how much more satisfactory it has been to devise a new phonetic lip and finger code that can be used permanently! The initial teaching alphabet is purposely related to reading but a finger alphabet should be a substitute for and a supplement to speech, and there are no good reasons to relate it either to the roman alphabet or to the arbitrary symbols of the orthodox finger code; the latter could be learned in addition at a later age for the purpose of communicating with other deaf people who know no other.

Progress is also being made in perfecting a potentially important and parallel machine that presents the deaf child with electronically activated visual symbols related to the sounds of his own, unheard, speech—a modern version of Alexander Melville Bell's "visible speech" which gave written form to an elaborate set of symbols to represent diagramatically the positions of the speech organs and which at one time was in great vogue for teaching the deaf. The "celligraphone," for example, developed by G. W. and S. H. Barton of the Lawrence Radiation Laboratory, California, is an adaptation of the oscilloscope—widely used in laboratories to make electrical effects and sound vibrations visible. The sounds appear on a screen as variations of a circle or a closed curve, the size changing in accordance with the volume of the voice; the appearance of different people's voices varies at least no more than does their handwriting. An electronic device of this type could be very useful in helping the deaf speaker to learn when he is making the correct sounds at the right intensities, particularly if they are linked with the corresponding i.t.a. characters (and Cued Speech).

THE INITIAL TEACHING ALPHABET AND THE BLIND

Braille is based on a series of patterns of 6 dots corresponding, like the finger alphabet, to the 26 roman characters, though the normal "contracted" Braille also incorporates a few "augmentations" and some arbitrary word signs. The blind are thus hampered by the deficiencies of the orthodox alphabet(s) and spelling, in that there is a lack of consistency between what they hear and what they feel with the finger-tips when reading Braille. This makes it more difficult for the blind child to learn Braille and also means that for most words more Braille characters have to be employed than are phonetically necessary, thus making the signs slower to read and the already bulky volumes even bulkier.

To improve matters, there are, I believe, two possibilities: either (1) a new Braille code could be devised, based on the 40 essential phonemes in English, perhaps further augmented with some of the existing contractions; or (2) a phonetic Braille code similar to i.t.a. in that it would be a teaching medium only, closely related to the existing orthodox code and designed to pave the way for an effortless transition to it once fluency had been achieved. An objection to the first suggestion is that it would entail having two parallel systems and amount to a spelling reform, thus fomenting opposition; a Braille form of teaching medium also raises doubts because blind learners might run into difficulties when making the transition to orthodox Braille—with the sighted the ease of the transition is made possible in part by the reader being able to cast forward and to hark back and so recognize individual whole words as part of meaningful sentences. It is possible that an 8-dot system could overcome this problem, and I am sure that the principles on which i.t.a. is founded can be applied in some way or other for the benefit of the blind. But these questions can only be answered by means of well planned, systematic experiments. A potentially valuable start has been made by Dr. Randall Harley, of the George Peabody College for Teachers, Nashville, Tennessee, who, with financial help from the U.S. Office of Education, is trying out a digraphically augmented teaching medium for the blind. He hopes his system will facilitate a relatively effortless transition to standard Braille.

13   Future i.t.a. Research

So far the research has concentrated on investigating the validity of the basic claims made for the new medium but, in addition, the impact of i.t.a. on education suggests many other directions towards which research should be directed during the next few years; indeed it would seem that eventually many if not all researches into the teaching of reading which have hitherto been conducted with the orthodox alphabet(s) and spelling as the medium will need to be redone or at any rate revalidated.

Possible new lines of investigation include—

(1) The selection of the vocabulary used in i.t.a. primers, teaching apparatus, and supporting reading books needs to be reviewed if the fullest benefit is to be gained from the new medium. This is particularly true in the case of children who have been linguistically deprived. Research is required to discover what is the best selection of words, phrases and sentences that enable these children to obtain fullest advantage from the consistency and reliability provided by i.t.a. and which will help them to infer concepts that generate an increasing and corresponding vocabulary. In fact, any series of i.t.a. books should allow for a continuing and progressive growth of concepts and vocabulary (auditory as well as visual).

Children with adequate linguistic experience do so well so early with i.t.a. that their progress does not seem to be very seriously impeded by the traditional type of reading primer even though its vocabulary is restricted to make varying, if inadequate, allowances for the difficulties inherent in the orthodox alphabet(s) and spelling (e.g. stilted repetition or avoidance of "irregular" words). Nevertheless it is likely that they would do even better still if there were more copious supplies of reading material geared to their particular speech-levels and freshly arranged to suit any good teaching methods; this means that the books should cater for higher levels of content and maturity than is customary in orthodox classroom textbooks and supporting leisure reading matter. With i.t.a., children are soon able to read books fluently that approximate to their own level of general and linguistic maturity, provided they are based on experiences and situations that are meaningful to them. At five to six years old some are able to read *and comprehend* words normally only mastered at a reading age of ten to eleven years, because reading has widened their experience, multiplied and reinforced their concepts, and extended their vocabularies.[1]

Experience of using i.t.a. with different kinds of classes, as well as detailed research on specific elements of teaching technique, is necessary before we can give with complete assurance answers to such questions as: which features need to be emphasized in helping teachers to use i.t.a.? Which forms of teaching apparatus are best suited to i.t.a.? Are existing books suitable for children who have made the transition or is it necessary to devise more books in the orthodox alphabet that cater for a fluent reading skill and an appropriate progression to more complex concepts and vocabulary?

(2) Experience will also enable us to judge more precisely what is the optimum moment for the transition to orthodox print. My own expectation is that in time we shall come to regard i.t.a. and the orthodox medium

[1] A start has been made in compiling new types of reading material. The first to be published are the *Downing Readers*, by Dr. Downing who was head of the Reading Research Unit, University of London Institute of Education. (Initial Teaching Publishing Co., London, 1963.) This series takes advantage of the new freedom to compile stories that exploit to the full the child's experiences, knowledge and interests at the age of beginning school, unhampered by the vagaries of the orthodox alphabet(s) and spelling. The first books use a look-and-say approach with its proper emphasis on reading for meaning, but the regularities of i.t.a. quickly promote a readiness for phonics and thus each method supplements the other. The emphasis is on a high degree of repetition and the acquisition of skill in reading a number of common words which at an early stage cover the full range of sounds and characters.

The first i.t.a. primers to appear in the U.S.A. are those of the *Early to Read Program*. (Initial Teaching Alphabet Publications, Inc., New York, 1964–5.) This series was designed to exploit fully the capabilities of i.t.a. in the light of American approaches to reading; thus, it adopts a visual-auditory-kinaesthetic approach from the start in order to develop "language arts abilities" in speaking, reading, and writing. The formal vocabulary in the primers totals almost 2,000 words by the end of Book 7, which is reached in the first year of instruction.

Various i.t.a. series have been issued by some dozen other publishers in both countries.

as being readily and properly interchangeable in the same way as we slip effortlessly from orthodox lower case into orthodox upper case and back again in a happy parallelism; after all, laŋgwæj is much closer to *language* than the latter is to LANGUAGE. In the early stages of the i.t.a. experiment so much emphasis has been placed on the transition to orthodox print that the greater, more fundamental achievement of linguistic ability has been overlooked. Instead of encouraging the child to make the transition at the earliest possible moment why not continue with the simpler i.t.a. medium until reading has become indeed effortless and part-and-parcel of the child's life; until language really has been learnt and assimilated? It is language, not the transition that is the main goal. Wanting "to read grown-up" is a persuasive stimulus, but the moment for the transition should not be gauged too early as a result of the teacher's eagerness for the child's success; when first employing i.t.a. this is only too likely to happen, many teachers being unable to credit the feasibility of the transition until they see it with their own eyes, and therefore they tend to reach out for it anxiously. Regard must always be had for the child's background of linguistic experience and vocabulary, both of which will, in the case of many children, be developed only by deliberate teaching of communication by language, and be nurtured only by extensive reading which in turn is likely to take place only provided the simpler medium is retained. If regular reading is shirked, if it is not enjoyed and does not become effortless, the more difficult medium will remain a barrier. (A foreign language, though understood, presents a comparable barrier to many adults. Personally, though I can read French with, say, 99 per cent understanding, I do not in fact read French books because the process is less than 50 per cent enjoyable, because, for me, the medium is not fully habituated and therefore simple, and there will be "key words" whose meaning I cannot confidently guess from the context.)

(3) An investigation will, I hope, be carried out into the effect of using i.t.a. even with children in Secondary Schools who have not managed to gain a full measure of fluency when reading orthodox print—and I am not merely thinking of the C and D streams where the backward readers are concentrated. Every Secondary School pupil whose reading age is not at least one year in advance of his chronological age can potentially benefit from a specially organized i.t.a. course: this would last at least a term and consist of two to three sessions per day of reading practice and another one to two daily sessions devoted to studies and activities designed

to widen experiences in relation to concept formation and the acquisition of the corresponding vocabulary.

(4) It has so far been widely accepted that children are not ready to start learning to read until they have a mental age of six and a half (see page 26). This may be true when children are faced at the outset with words spelt in the orthodox manner but with i.t.a. it would seem that a lower mental age is sufficient for a start to be made—provided, as has been argued earlier, that pupils possess an adequate level of linguistic ability. This is borne out by the research findings in Oldham, an area in which children were eligible for the infants school in the school year during which they reach their fourth birthday; four-year-olds in Oldham were learning to read in i.t.a. with such ease that the whole question of reading readiness in relation to mental age demands to be reconsidered. This is not to assume that i.t.a. should necessarily be employed to push back the age of reading readiness as far as possible: the purpose of this research would be to discover the optimum age for starting to learn to read with i.t.a. as the medium, taking into account the corresponding effects on all the other factors involved in a child's intellectual and emotional development. The great quantity of variables that predispose or inhibit verbal competence may, admittedly, make it improbable that a research project could ever be designed capable of controlling and likely to provide a reliable answer.

(5) If the average child learns to read somewhere around one or two years earlier, it will necessitate a reconsideration of the remainder of the curriculum during the subsequent school years. It may well alter accepted views on children's rates of development and on the levels of attainment to be expected at various ages. Eventually it will be necessary to devise new tests of reading accuracy, speed, and comprehension because the existing tests are based on standards expected of children taught with all the frustrations of orthodox spelling. These tests are very suitable for attainments of children taught with the orthodox medium and have had to be used, by default, for the comparative research between it and i.t.a., but they do not reflect the higher norms to be expected when the use of i.t.a. becomes widespread, any more than recognized tests of human physical performance in famine areas can be expected to be adequate elsewhere.

(6) The employment of electric or very simply operated manual typewriters to help very young children to read and write, employed[1] by

---

[1] The earliest pioneer in the use of typewriters by very young children was Dr. Ben Wood of Columbia University. He was the first to appreciate the importance of the link between writing

Professor O. K. Moore of Yale University, also lends support to the view that the accepted criterion for reading readiness is mistaken. Moore has shown that electric typewriters built for the purpose can be used by a 2- to 3-year-old child who is not yet able to manipulate a pencil effectively. If the keys of such a typewriter were fitted with i.t.a. characters, the young child would at the outset have the simplest possible means of expressing visually and directly the words he has learned to speak. It would be interesting also if i.t.a. characters were added to the "talking typewriter," which not only utters the characters or words just typed by the child but also tells him which word to type and, when he has done so, throws on a screen simultaneously the word and a picture of the object the word represents, thus emphasizing the links between looking, speaking and writing, listening and reading. Experiments incorporating i.t.a. with both these typewriters could probably tell us a great deal about linguistic ability in the very young and enable us to discover whether the kinaesthetic processes employed in typing could be a sufficiently valuable forerunner of handwriting and an effective reinforcement of the perception of words through the visual channels.

The reliability of i.t.a. means that it can be very easily adapted for use in connection with teaching machines, and it lends itself to the logical sequence of steps which are such an essential part of the programmes fed through the machines. Thought is being given to the possibility not only of devising i.t.a. programmes but also of new machines that can take full advantage of the new medium.

(7) It is possible that colour could be effective in reinforcing even further the relationship between shape and sound provided by i.t.a. When colour is applied to the orthodox alphabet(s) and spelling there must

and reading and the need to overcome the difficulties experienced by the child in forming, much less emulating, the printed words he could already read. See *An Experimental Study of the Educational Influences of the Typewriter in the Elementary School Classroom* by Ben D. Wood and Frank N. Freeman (Macmillan, New York, 1932). Dr. Ben Wood was, not surprisingly, the first American educationist to cross the Atlantic in order to discover at first hand the potentialities of i.t.a. In an address given at Cleveland, Ohio, in 1963, he described the encouraging results of the first two years of the i.t.a. experiment in Britain, pointing out that the ". . . control children develop the habit of independent, self-propelled and success-motivated study and learning, attacking as a matter of course new words never before seen by them in print, by the strictly analogical reasoning method made possible by the Pitman transitional alphabet. . . . Successful practice in learning by analogical reasoning, as in learning to read through the medium of the Pitman Initial Teaching Alphabet, will almost surely 'carry over' to and be effective in exploiting more fully one of the most promising and dynamic elements of the educational revolution, that is, learning by discovery, which will probably turn out to be the long-sought breakthrough in the old, old problem of learning how to learn!"

inevitably be a residual conflict between shape and colour, but with i.t.a.—thanks to its consistency and invariability—colour and shape can always be in harmony. For most learners the shape is very probably sufficient in itself, but there would seem to be reason to justify some small-scale research to ascertain whether colour can be additionally helpful—in much the same way as singing is found to be helpful in the teaching of a foreign language.

(8) Throughout this book it has been stressed that i.t.a. is a teaching medium only, and that it does not necessitate any change of teaching method; that it can bring better results both with look-and-say and phonic methods, or with a mixture of the two. Teachers taking part in the research have also deliberately been asked to continue to use their normal methods. There are however already indications that minor adjustments to the mixture of existing methods may be advisable if the benefits of i.t.a. are to be exploited to the full. There have been reports, for example, of "spontaneous phonic building" among children taught by look-and-say methods, the visual/aural consistency of the syllables having caused the children to reach their own rational conclusions. My own belief is that i.t.a. will lead to the most satisfactory forms of eclectic integration of the two basic methods (see page 150) but the ideal integration can most convincingly be ascertained only by supplementing the teacher's own experience with comparative research in classes which all use i.t.a. In fact, the removal of the special difficulties of orthodox spelling not only enables both methods (and a *fortiori* a combination of the two) and indeed all methods to operate with maximum efficiency, but it also makes it possible for an accurate comparative assessment of the benefits of any particular mixture of methods to be made with reading material that, for the purpose of the test as well as for the benefit of the pupils, is constant. This research will need particularly careful design. Perhaps more experience with i.t.a. is desirable before it should be attempted.

(9) The Initial Teaching Alphabet can be adapted for use with other languages besides English. The same principles need to be applied and the first step must be to arrive at the number of essential phonemes upon which the particular language depends. The phonemes must then be considered in relation to the language's orthodox characters and spelling before a decision can be taken as to the number and forms of augmentations required. In addition, even digraphs which represent diphthongs accurately will need to be replaced by augmentations that stand for the two

phonemes in question (as does **oi**). The moment of transition to orthodox print should never be lost sight of, though, judging by the experience with English, this should cause no difficulties, provided the design of the characters and the choice of spellings be painstakingly made so as to harmonize as far as possible with orthodox forms of spelling.

For most languages, it is probably desirable to think of three tiers of special alphabets: (1) the first tier will be i.t.a., designed for learners of reading who already know how to *speak* the language; (2) the second tier will be for foreigners and will be a rather more elaborate form of i.t.a., providing extra signals for the learner to enable him to speak the strange language with reasonable efficiency and to listen to it with understanding as well as read and write it; for an indication of the kind of extra signals that should be given to the learner, see Chapter 15 on World i.t.a.; (3) the third tier will be a completely phonetic alphabet (such as the International Phonetic Alphabet or one even more discriminating), designed for foreigners who wish to speak the language so well and with such a perfect accent that they can pass as natives.

(10) When I originally proposed the research into an augmented alphabet I suggested that "the alphabet to be used would itself be on trial, and might as a result be modified." But now that i.t.a. has been proved to be effective and it is already being used widely I believe there is a very strong case for caution before tampering with it. I do not wish to follow the example of my grandfather who was rightly criticized for never leaving Fonotypy alone. At the risk of sounding smug, I must own to the belief that no changes or modifications in i.t.a. are necessary, though under certain conditions as explained below exploratory researches may possibly be justified. I think it would be wise to enforce a moratorium on changes in the i.t.a. characters and spellings during the next twenty years or so—until, say, 1990. For the moment the benefits likely to come from any future changes or additions to i.t.a. or in the principles by which it represents words (e.g. the extent to which it falls short of absolute phonetic truth) are likely to be more than offset by the dislocation and confusion any change would cause among teachers and by the outdating of the hundreds of i.t.a. books already in print. Further changes would, besides, have an unsettling effect both on teachers who use the alphabet and on those who are still hesitating. If the latter get the idea that i.t.a. is to be continuously tampered with, they will certainly be deterred from making a positive decision. The task of persuading the first teachers to

try the new medium was in all conscience difficult enough; even minor changes in a few of the i.t.a. characters would mean inflicting a further disturbance which could never be justified.

I do not wish to appear ungrateful to the experts such as Sir Cyril Burt, Dr. William J. Griffin, Dr. J. A. Downing, and others who have bothered to propose changes in the alphabet, but I feel it is reasonable to ask that a very strong *prima facie* case should first be made out in favour of each proposed modification before time and money is spent even on validating it in further research. It is not difficult to suggest changes and modifications that would make the transition even smoother than it is already, but they are self-defeating if at the same time they reduce the effectiveness of i.t.a. as a reading medium. Some experts, for example, have picked on ʃh and ŋ, maintaining that these characters cause particular difficulty at the transition, but they forget that they can be eliminated only at the expense of creating more *initial* difficulties: there would not, for example, be sufficient contrast between *mishap* and *bishop* (mishap: biʃhop) or between *finger*, *singer*, and *engaged* (fiŋger, siŋer, engæjed). In fact, since the transition is so effortless, it may be necessary to pose the question the other way round: could not the task of learning to read initially with i.t.a. be made even easier, albeit at the expense of the ease of the transition? Moreover the ascender and descender in ʃh and the idiosyncratic shape of ŋ make them easier to distinguish and remember.

The absolute copyright in the characters and spellings of i.t.a. has been retained for the i.t.a. Foundation. The alphabet is there for all to use (including authors and publishers) without payment of royalties or fees, but on the other hand I am determined to preserve the right to prevent ill-conceived research or tampering with the alphabet and, in particular, to prevent commercial concerns from taking my brain-child, introducing a few so-called "improvements," and then copyrighting the thus modified alphabet and establishing what could then be a profitable monopoly. It would however be quite unreasonable to attempt to hinder serious researchers; and I am on record that, subject to certain safeguards, *bona fide* research projects will be licensed.[1] Evidence must however be produced to show that there is at least a genuine hope that a significant improvement is likely to be substantiated. An undertaking must also be given that amended textbooks and other teaching materials will be

[1] *Phi Delta Kappan*, June 1967, p. 524. Bloomington, Indiana.

confined to the research classes; also that if the research findings fail to indicate the discovery of a significant improvement, the amended text-books, etc. will be destroyed; or, if the findings are positive, that the new or modified characters and/or spellings will be made generally available without charge. It is also insisted that the research must be carried out without publicity as this would disturb i.t.a. teachers; if improvements are to be researched, they must be researched by stealth.

Provided these conditions are adhered to, both the i.t.a. Foundation and I myself will favour issuing a licence and we shall help in any way we can, especially in discussing the *prima facie* case for the research being justifiable. But the incorporation in the near future of any modifications, even if they are validated, is another matter. In twenty years' time it is likely that we shall have a better understanding of the complex learning processes involved in acquiring speech and the ability to read and write. This plus the accumulation of experience of the practical use of i.t.a. will enable a surer assessment to be made of whether or not changes in i.t.a. can be justified. In the meantime I owe it to the publishers who have risked their capital in producing i.t.a. books, to the teachers who have taken the trouble to master the new medium, to the education authorities, and indeed to the alphabet itself, to leave it in peace.

* * *

The investigation of all these and many other questions needs to be co-ordinated on both sides of the Atlantic and throughout the English-speaking world. So much interest has been aroused by i.t.a. that there is a real danger of research being unnecessarily duplicated. It is hoped that the i.t.a. Foundations set up in London and at Hofstra University, U.S.A., will prevent this happening and will together act as a clearing house for research.

14   Why Wait any Longer?

THE TEACHING OF READING to children is a subject that stirs passion and emotion, and this is understandable because little children and their welfare rightly touch the deeper chords of genuine solicitude. Until very recently proposals to alter the alphabet(s) or spelling even for short-term teaching purposes have not so much been resisted as dismissed. The roman characters and spelling of the Authorized Version have virtually been "untouchable," sanctioned by centuries of use in church and classroom, immune from enquiry as any dogma; ". . . the traditional appearance of our language, its spelling, has become in our eyes a sacred shrine and cenotaph, which we are prepared to defend to the last drop of blue-black ink in our fountain pens."[1] In my own long campaign in Parliament and elsewhere to have the effect of our alphabet(s) and spelling on the learning processes involved in learning to read tested in a large-scale investigation, the worst obstacle has been the inability of many people to objectify, to depersonalize the problem. They assume that because *they*, personally, managed to learn to read without the alphabet being "tampered with," it must have been easy for them and therefore it must be equally simple for others to do likewise. If children fail to learn to read, the fault must lie elsewhere—in poor teaching, the wrong method, overcrowded classrooms. . . . As stated in the opening chapter of this book, all these and similar factors are of great relevance, but this is a poor reason for overlooking the medium in which reading is taught. Some of our

[1] Professor A. Lloyd James. *The Times*, 20 November 1937.

educational pundits are not unlike the surgeons when Lister first urged the advantages of asepsis. To us the necessity for sterilization appears to be self-evident, but it took Lister some twenty-five years before the surgical educationists of the day were prepared even to consider his simple remedy —and a further twenty-five for it to be generally applied. There was nothing, the pundits declared, wrong with their methods of operating; those who died shortly afterwards were as well served as those who lived —the fault must be lack of skill in the surgeon, or congenital weakness in the patient, or it was gangrene which was a *separate* matter altogether and impossible to cure . . . and so they continued to carry their instruments round in a velvet-lined morocco pocket-case and to sharpen their scalpels on the soles of their boots. Millions died needlessly just as, equally needlessly, millions of children have failed to read.

Among quite a few reading experts traditional practice (not to mention the orthodox alphabet(s) and spelling) is defended to the last ditch which, in the face of the challenge represented by i.t.a., is reached only after a phased withdrawal from previous defensive ditches—

DITCH 1. The Initial Teaching Alphabet is unnecessary and harmful, because children must find it equally difficult to learn to read in a medium whose bizarre novelty is its only feature and whose use is anyhow only provisional. If, however, the first research findings are mentioned and if one claims that scientific enquiry has already done much to substantiate the merits of i.t.a., it may or may not produce a concession, but too often it amounts merely to a falling-back, in an orderly withdrawal, to the next ditch.

DITCH 2. Even if it is admitted (but often it is not!) that it could be easier for a child to learn to read in the new medium, it is next argued that the child will then need to *unlearn* the new skill and to learn afresh to read orthodox texts; that the process of unlearning will be harmful and that in any case he will lose more time in the lengthy transitional processes of relearning than he could possibly have gained in the initial stages. Here again, it may eventually be conceded that *a priori* reasoning, plus existing and future evidence may together be capable of supplying the necessary proof. However the reservation is made that even should this proof (impossible as it may seem!) turn out to be to i.t.a.'s advantage, a series of four further defensive ditches are waiting to be occupied.

DITCH 3. Even if i.t.a.'s success at the transition is admitted, then the damage to the child's spelling will be devastating—and permanent.

DITCH 4. Even f good spelling, as well as reading, can be achieved with i.t.a., the child would anyhow and in due time have become literate and therefore gains nothing from learning to read and to write at an earlier age.

DITCH 5. Children who fail to learn to read are anyhow so unintelligent (for how otherwise have they failed?) that reading ability for them can make no real contribution to themselves or to the community sufficient to justify such a great disturbance to the more intelligent majority.

DITCH 6. When the ability to read orthodox print is acquired through i.t.a., it may recede at a later stage; i.t.a. children are unlikely to make the further progress which they would have made had they learned with the orthodox alphabet(s) and spelling from the beginning.

Even when all these ditches have been given up, there still are further ditches in reserve, such as—

DITCH 7. The evidence of i.t.a.'s success is not to be relied upon because it is merely the consequence of unusual pressure and enthusiasm of the teachers rather than the change of medium.

DITCH 8. Even if i.t.a. is admitted to be unassailable, its adoption should be postponed for a number of years until is has been established by a further series of researches that it cannot be further perfected.

The research results both in the UK and USA together with experience in numerous classrooms has now overwhelmed the first three of these eight objections. One is tempted to ask at what point does the onus of probability and proof change? At what point should an open-minded neutrality on the remaining points take the place of emotional opposition? Is even one of the remaining five lines of defence tenable? It cannot surely be held against i.t.a. that it enables children to read at an earlier age? This does in fact happen but it is certainly not its main justification. If it is considered preferable to learn to read at a later age (though this is at least debatable), the remedy is easy: the start of learning to read is postponed! The much lower rate of complete failures among i.t.a. classes makes the inhumanity of the occupants of Ditch 5 quite untenable. Again, is it really conceivable that the 67 per cent of the i.t.a. children who read and write in the orthodox alphabet(s) and spelling up to and beyond the standard of their chronological age (see Table XIV, page 183) will ever fall behind the 49 per cent of the corresponding control group children who were still reading at or below their chronological age? Is it likely that the i.t.a. children with their earlier skill in reading *orthodox* texts will be less, rather than more, amenable to improved comprehension, or faster reading, or both?

I believe that the findings of the research, if studied without prejudice, are more than sufficiently encouraging to justify a head teacher in deciding that it is in the best interests of his or her children to try out the new medium, and for the director of education and his local authority to approve and support the changeover.[1] The enthusiasm of the teachers and others concerned in the experiment confirms and reinforces the first conclusions from the research. They know from their own experience what the research results already indicate; they know—

(1) That the orthodox alphabet(s) and spelling are an important source of difficulty when learning to read.

(2) That with i.t.a. these difficulties are effectively removed and children learn to read in a much shorter time and with much less effort.

(3) That the transition to the orthodox alphabet(s) and spelling presents no important problems and is for the most part effortless and automatic.

(4) That after the transition the i.t.a. children read orthodox texts with greater accuracy and more comprehension.

(5) That both before and after the transition the i.t.a. children read far more books for their own enjoyment; there is a significant improvement in handwriting and in the ability to write creatively; their speech is improved; they show more self-confidence, are better behaved, and have a more positive attitude to school work—in short, they very quickly learn to learn.

This book is being published now rather than in a few years' time because I believe that the case for i.t.a. has been proved beyond reasonable doubt, and because the challenge that faces education is daunting. In the English-speaking world some six million children start school each year, of whom at least one million are likely to end up as backward readers and there are many more who, habitually, seldom or never read.

[1] Soon after the first intake had made the transition new i.t.a. classes began to be formed throughout the country on a completely voluntary basis. Classes were formed by teachers outside the research project as well as by teachers involved in it who elected to continue with i.t.a. despite the original agreement by the authorities that they might return to the orthodox medium once their research stint was concluded. Because of the shortage of i.t.a. books and organizational difficulties some educational authorities had even to be temporarily discouraged from joining in. Nevertheless by the end of the seventh year it was estimated that over 4,000 schools in the U.K. and a further 10,000 elsewhere were using i.t.a.

As we made clear at the outset, i.t.a. is not a cure-all, but it will, I believe, be at the very least a major element in a several-pronged attack, together with smaller classes, better teachers, better buildings, and other educational reforms. The introduction of i.t.a. can do more than any other single measure to save the majority of the million failures annually from a life in which the printed word brings neither light nor pleasure. Are we justified in waiting any longer?

Part III

15   World i.t.a. and the Spread of English

ENGLISH IS NOW the world's most popular choice as a second language. Whereas Chinese[1] can claim more adherents as a mother tongue, it is estimated that at least 250 million learn English as an auxiliary—though, dependent on the degree of proficiency taken as a criterion, it can be speculated that the total reaches 600 million. In many parts of the world a knowledge of English is essential if one is not to be debarred from communication with everyone except those who speak one's own very restricted, possibly tribal, tongue; without English or, dependent on the area, some other widely spoken and printed language, one's education is also likely to be gravely restricted because it is not economically feasible to write or translate many textbooks in a host of minor languages. It is true that there has been some reaction against English among Indian nationalists in favour of Hindi (against powerful resistance from the pro-English South), and that since the war the numbers learning Russian have increased greatly, but English is still way ahead of any competitors. No other language is more widely diffused throughout the five continents. The reasons for its success are partly historical: e.g. the far-flung character of the British Commonwealth, Britain's and,

---

[1] 650 million, compared with 255 million whose mother tongue is English—figures supplied by UNESCO (26 March 1965); certain assumptions had to be made as the available statistics were not uniform, covered different years, and referred to different definitions such as language currently spoken, race, or nationality. The written language has only one form, but spoken Chinese has several distinct forms, almost equal to separate languages, each with many dialects. The majority (c. 450 million) speak Mandarin Chinese.

above all, America's widespread commercial influence. The spread of a language is self-generating—the more people who speak it, the more programmes that broadcast in it, and the more literature that is published in it, the more there are who want to learn it—but the success of English can also be explained by its linguistic characteristics which make it, relatively, an easy language to acquire. No other major language possesses such a simple grammar and syntax or combines the following advantages—

For practical purposes there are no arbitrary genders (except in such rare instances as referring to a ship or a machine as "she").

Agreement between adjectives and nouns is unnecessary; nouns have no cases except for the possessive "'s" for the genitive.

The definite article has only one written form; verbs have very few inflexions and these tend to be regular.

Very few verbs are irregular.

Most words in common use have less than four syllables.

Exceptionally wide choice of vocabulary (though for beginners this can be a disadvantage) with which to achieve precise thought and expression, and to convey subtle overtones of association and feeling.

Few modern languages are capable of such precision, flexibility, and subtlety, allied with brevity.

Against these advantages have to be set the appalling difficulties of English spelling. Students, especially when they learn to read English before they can speak it, often complain of the difficulties of English pronunciation, but the spelling is what they really mean, because this fails to offer reliable clues to how words should sound and, worse, proffers countless false clues. The speech sounds of English do cause difficulty to some foreigners; the two *th*s do not exist in French, German, or Italian; the *r* usually becomes an *l* in the case of Chinese; and there are other difficulties peculiar to the individual mother tongues. Once these have been overcome it is the frequent impossibility of learning the pronunciation from the spelling that is the bugbear and makes foreigners despair. In addition, students whose mother tongues employ a non-romanic alphabet find the unnecessary variety of character forms (A, a, *a*, etc.) particularly perplexing.

Foreigners learning English are faced with the same conundrums and illogicality as face the English-speaking child learning to read and which have been outlined at length in Chapter 4, but with the additional difficulty that they possess no store of spoken words to which to relate the words they are given to read. Like the child, they can be helped in the early stages by the Initial Teaching Alphabet. Its unambiguous, one-for-one relationships between the printed symbols and the spoken sounds provide the foreigner with most of the guidance he needs. Above all, they eliminate all the false clues. The gap between what is read and spoken is closed and he is given a reliable guide to pronunciation. Once he has gained a certain degree of fluency and accuracy in speech, the necessity for close reliance on alphabeticism disappears and he can make the transition to orthodox spelling without conscious effort. Because i.t.a. has been designed solely in order to help people (whether English or not) to read English and therefore, as explained earlier, remains as near as practicable to the appearance of roman characters and to orthodox spelling, it is likely to be at least as beneficial as the International Phonetic Alphabet (IPA) to the average student of English who is not concerned with the minute differences between regional dialects. This point will be appreciated after comparing the following sentence printed (1) in IPA; (2) in i.t.a.; and (3) in the orthodox medium—

(1) ðə fənetik diskripʃənz prəvaidid bai ði intənæʃnəl fənetik ælfəbet ə prisais ənd cliə tə ði ekspəːt, bət ðei daivəːdʒ kənsidrəbli frəm ði əpiərəns əv ðə seim wəːdz printid in ɔːθədɔks roumən kæriktəz.

(2) ꝼhe fonetic descripʃhonſ provieded bie ꝼhe internaʃhonal fonetic alfabet ɑr presies and cleer tꝏ ꝼhe ekspert, but ꝼhæ diverj considerably from ꝼhe appeerans ov ꝼhe sæm wurdſ printed in orꝼhodoks rœman caracterſ.

(3) The phonetic descriptions provided by the International Phonetic Alphabet are precise and clear to the expert, but they diverge considerably from the appearance of the same words printed in orthodox roman characters.

By removing the spelling-pronunciation difficulty, i.t.a. can also help to make English even more widely known, to turn into a universal auxiliary language, the lingua franca man has always dreamed of. To my mind, its candidature is infinitely stronger than Esperanto, Ido, Volapük, or Novial. These synthetic languages, though contrived with great ingenuity, cannot hope to compete with a living organic language which has already put down so many roots in so many countries, which is already to some extent the common tongue of much of Asia, Africa, and elsewhere, and which is one of the world's chief storehouses of accumulated knowledge.

THE DIFFERENCES BETWEEN "WORLD" i.t.a. AND
"DOMESTIC" i.t.a.

The widespread adoption of i.t.a. as the medium for teaching English-speaking children to read is its best recommendation to the non-English-speaking student. It removes any possible suspicion that it is merely a debased form of the language, stigmatizing those who use it. Experience has however shown that it is desirable to provide additional information and clues for the student who has not grown up surrounded by the live language, who perhaps hears it only in "teaching situations," or who may even have no chance of hearing it at all. Stress, rhythm, and changes in vowel sounds are the worst obstacles. Students from all other countries have difficulty in knowing when a word or syllable is stressed or unstressed, in acquiring the subtleties of rhythm that are used unconsciously by the native speaker. To be more specific: the student needs to be given additional clues that provide—

A. Information about the degree of stress, or lack of it, on the vowel in certain words and syllables.

B. Information about the accompanying changes in vowel sounds that occur in unstressed syllables and words (which in other sentences may be stressed).

Fortunately this additional information can be supplied without changing any of the i.t.a. characters and spellings and without reducing the compatibility between the learning medium and what is eventually to be mastered. (The great disturbance to compatibility which would inevitably be introduced by representing the neutral vowel by its own special character has already been explained—see pages 135-7 (*h*). In the IPA passage of only 32 words quoted above the disturbing symbol for the neutral vowel occurs no less than 27 times.) The modifications are limited to printing selected syllables and words in semi-bold and others in smaller type. These smaller characters can be either raised or lowered so that they are aligned with the top or bottom level of the normal type line. The alphabet modified in this manner is now known as "World" i.t.a.

The differences between World i.t.a. and domestic i.t.a. can be summarized as follows—

(1) Whenever a syllable or word is to receive a primary stress, it is printed in semi-bold type but in the normal size, e.g. hek**sam**eter. Whenever the stress is only secondary, no change is made.

(2) Whenever the vowel in a syllable or word is to become unstressed (the relaxed vowel or *schwa*: see pages 135–7) and is to be spoken in its weak form, it is printed in smaller type[1] and aligned with the base of the main type line. Compare, for instance, the contrasting sizes and positions of the words for, hav, and, tω, wωd, woꭥ, in the following artificial sentences—

it iꭥ **not** for yω. yω ᴀulredy **hav** wun and tω hav

given mee **nun** wωd hav been **unfær. for,** yω

must ad**mit,** yω wωd œnly hav **wæst**ed it. **wωd**

yω hav **kept** it and **clœꭥd** ᴛhe dor tω in mie

fæs? and, for yet anuᴛher **ree**ꭥon it **woꭥ** ᴀfter

ᴀull mie turn **and,** if it woꭥ **not,** yω never

sed sœ.

(3) Whenever the vowel in a syllable or word is to be changed to the unstressed *i* (which it is convenient to call *schwi*), it is likewise printed in smaller type but it aligns with the top of the main type line. Contrast the treatment of words in the sentences overleaf—

[1] A ratio of 5 : 6 is recommended and is used in this chapter.

at ꭍhe ekwætor ꭍhe dæ iꭢ twelv ourꭢ loŋ. every

dæ from sundæ too saturdæ.   ꭍhe printed pæj iꭢ

reformd in œnly sum respects in ꭍhis æj ov ꭍhe

wuꭇld'ꭢ dœtæj.

These three modifications enable the student while reading to himself to hear in his imagination an acceptable rhythm of English speech as well as to practise it in his own efforts. It is of course impossible to be dogmatic over what rhythms are most acceptable. The subtleties of stress are infinitely individual and vary very considerably; the speech of no two individuals is identical, even though they be brothers, and it may even vary if the same words are immediately repeated by the same speaker. Although it is possible to talk of wrong and misleading stresses and changes in vowel sounds, a great many varieties are equally acceptable. The medium may therefore be adjusted to reflect the preferred varieties of stress and rhythm by means of the three types of modification (this licence does not extend, however, to changing i.t.a. characters or spellings—see pages 253–5). In choosing what are the best varieties of stress and rhythm the only advice one can give is (1) to avoid the really "bad" varieties for which the only guide is hesitant comprehensibility by someone whose mother tongue is English; and (2) to eliminate stresses and vowel sounds that would be rejected by a film or television director whose product is intended for distribution throughout the English-speaking world.

Apart from these three modifications, World i.t.a. is identical with domestic i.t.a. It is necessary to add only that it is advisable to exercise additional caution in deciding when a student is ready for the transition to orthodox print. This decision calls in each case for a careful assessment and trial of the student's progress. That i.t.a. merely approximates to pure phonetic truth is, as we have seen, of no import to anyone for whom English is the mother tongue, but for students who have no one continually at hand to correct them accurately the transition, if premature, can bed down bad speech habits (e.g. *gem* pronounced ǥem instead of jem). The rapid effectiveness of i.t.a. may in itself foster a phonetic confidence that will be dangerously mistaken, especially when the student is faced with unfamiliar words, if the transition occurs before he has acquired automatic, and reasonably accurate, habits of speech allied to a comprehensive vocabulary.

It is recommended therefore that the transition takes place in two stages: first, from World i.t.a. to domestic i.t.a.; only when the student has shown that he can manage without the extra clues to the language's rhythm should the transition be made from domestic i.t.a. to the orthodox alphabet(s) and spelling. It is anticipated that a student learning English in his own (non-English-speaking) country will require longer periods with both forms of i.t.a. compared with a student actually resident in an English-speaking country and thus surrounded by the live language and continuous opportunities for listening and self-correction.

RESEARCH INTO WORLD i.t.a.

Experience with immigrant children in the United Kingdom enables one to say with some confidence that, provided the transition is not rushed, it need cause no special problems. Records exist of children whose mother tongues are Italian, Hungarian, Polish, Pakistani, Hindi, or Chinese and who have learned to read and speak English with the help of i.t.a. without running into any noticeable difficulties at the transition. The proof of World i.t.a.'s effectiveness can however be provided, as in the case of domestic i.t.a., only by extensive trials in the classroom among different language groups, together with a carefully designed and lengthy research project, operated under the most respected academic auspices. My proposals to carry out this research were first mooted at the Commonwealth Education Conference at Ottawa in 1964, where they were well received by a number of Prime Ministers, Ministers of Education, or their representatives. The Kenya Government, and in particular Mr. Matiba, then Permanent Secretary of the Ministry of Education, was particularly receptive. My requests for co-operation were also directed to the Conference's Secretariat, to the British Council, and to the British Government's Department of Technical Co-operation (now the Ministry of Overseas Development). The upshot of all this was that the British

Government agreed to finance research in Western Nigeria, under the auspices of the University of Ibadan.

The research programme which, *mutatis mutandis*, is comparable to that designed for domestic i.t.a. in the United Kingdom was planned by Professor A. Taylor, a New Zealander, and was started early in 1966. The experiment involves about 1,200 children of whom at the outset 84 per cent were 5–6 year-olds and 16 per cent were 7 year-olds. They come from the mainland of Lagos and the rural areas to the North of Ibadan, and for the most part their mother tongue is Yoruba. Books and other materials have been printed in World i.t.a.; the children are divided into experimental and control groups, one being taught English with World i.t.a. and the other with the orthodox medium. At the time of going to press with this volume it is too early to draw any hard conclusions but, at the close of an interim report presented to the Commonwealth Education Conference in the Spring of 1968, J. O. O. Abiri felt able to say—

> This experiment has shown that the use of World i.t.a. influences the pronunciation of both the pupils and their teachers. Children who started to read English through World i.t.a. also progressed faster through their reading books and showed better word-recognition skill than those who use T.O. all the time. The permanent effects of World i.t.a. on pronunciation and other skills such as writing, spelling and reading comprehension are still to be investigated. It would appear, on the whole, that World i.t.a. has a lot to recommend it as a medium for the teaching of English as a foreign language. The children should begin to read as early as possible for maximum effect to be derived from the use of World i.t.a.

The books, etc., printed in World i.t.a. for the Nigerian experiment are now available for teachers of English in other areas. Until this material was ready and until the essential modifications that comprise World i.t.a. had been arrived at, I felt bound to discourage the adoption of i.t.a. for the teaching of English as an auxiliary language, but now I hope it will be possible for teachers and research units to test World i.t.a. in the widest possible variety of language areas. As well as testing the central proposition that the learning medium is a key factor in the improvement of teaching spoken and printed/written English, their experiences may well supply answers to some interesting questions. Recently, for instance, the tendency among language teachers has been to lay great initial emphasis on learning the spoken word and to postpone giving much attention to the printed word. Is this not perhaps a too radical and insufficiently thought-out reversal of the earlier tendency to learn from books first and to leave the sounds till later? How much validity is there in the idea that speech and print should be tackled almost *simultaneously right from the start*, that the auditory and visual capabilities of the students should be harnessed more closely together so that one reinforces the other? When teachers advocate that speech should antedate print—or vice versa—are they not in danger of being caught up in a pedagogic controversy as sterile as that between phonics and look-and-say? As I have argued earlier in this book, the differences between teachers of reading arise in the main from the handicaps of the orthodox medium. Will it be found that teachers of English are prey to a similar misunderstanding? If the research in Nigeria proves the worth of World i.t.a., my belief is that its ability largely to close the gap between the sound of the spoken word and its appearance in print will influence teaching practice so that even in the initial stages students will be enabled to see what they hear and hear what they see.

DANGERS OF "BABELIZATION"

A threat to the growth of English as a universal language is, paradoxically, inherent in its existing world-wide adoption. There are already signs that spoken English, in undergoing fairly considerable local changes, is becoming "Babelized," and this may lead to such a degree of diversification that a series of separate, though related languages may emerge. It has happened before in the case of Latin which became differentiated to form Italian, Spanish, Portuguese, French, Rumanian, and Romansch, and a similar fate was suffered by Greek in the Middle East, by Arabic, and the primitive Teutonic. It has happened most noticeably with Chinese whose written language and characters are understood perfectly by people whose spoken language diverges so considerably that they can share a newspaper yet cannot speak to each other. Distances and the variety of conditions and patterns of culture in the English-speaking world (cf. Jamaica and New Zealand) give rise to much of the diversification, particularly of idiom. In places where the original stock was not English-speaking the influence of local pronunciations are sometimes so persistent that it is difficult to believe that the inhabitants are speaking the same language as the inhabitants from another "English-speaking" region, with the result that the separate groups are in danger of becoming mutually incomprehensible (cf. an Ibo from Nigeria, an Indian, a West Indian, and a Malayan Chinese).

The process is vividly illustrated in this description of Jamaican Creole provided by Professor R. B. Le Page—[1]

> The bulk of the vocabulary of Jamaican Creole is English. Jamaican usage differs, however, from English usage, even among sophisticated speakers, much more frequently than most Jamaicans suspect, and the differences are a constant trap for the unwary visitor. They may be classified as follows—
> Words which have become obsolete in England.
> Words used in a sense which has become obsolete in England.
> Borrowings from dialect, non-standard English.
> Words adapted to a new sense in Jamaica.
> Words whose pronunciation has been changed so radically that they must be regarded as Jamaicanisms—e.g. busha < *overseer*.
> Words which may serve a greater number of grammatical functions than in England—e.g. as transitive verbs used only intransitively in England.
> Malapropisms.
> Compounds or iteratives formed on English stems, often by analogy with Africanisms.

Another, but rather different cause of Babelization is found in certain areas in which English has become the chief means of communication between non-English language groups. Here two levels of competence tend to appear: only the more ambitious and hard-working acquire a fluent knowledge both of spoken and written English (as can be understood in London or Washington), while the rest are content with being able to read and write it sufficiently well to hold down a job or win promotion; so far as speaking English is concerned, it is sufficient if they are understood by and understand others for whom spoken English is also merely a handy auxiliary. This leads to versions of English that are strongly influenced by local speech habits and move steadily away from the tongue that originated in these islands. The standard of reading and of expressing ideas on paper may be very high—enough to win a place or even a scholarship at a university in Britain—and yet the standard of speaking and listening may be so low—or diversified—that spoken communication with people whose mother tongue is English is very difficult. A student may even find he is unable to understand much of what his English or American lecturers are saying or be understood when he asks a question.

This tendency towards divergence in language is universal. When there

---

[1] *Jamaican Creole*, p. 119; in conjunction with David De Camp. Macmillan, London, 1960.

is no relationship between characters and sounds, as in Chinese, or where few can read and write, as was true of Latin, the forces of divergence operate without hindrance. Similarly, though to a lesser extent, the imperfect relationships between characters and sounds in English have speeded up the rate of divergence. Indeed, Babelization is not to be wondered at because people naturally tend to pronounce words as they appear and are further influenced by their own speech habits when the spelling gives them very little guidance; the lack of a reliable, unambiguous connection between print and speech is bound to lead to innumerable and pointless local variations in pronunciation. This is especially true of the thousands who learn to read English by eye from print without having the opportunity to hear it in any of its normally accepted forms and so learn it from teachers who in their day had learned it in this way themselves. It is said, for instance, that there are places where mothers start reading fairy stories to their children with something that sounds like "Onky upon a timmy . . ."

It is of course true that the printed word, despite its incomplete alphabeticism, nowadays does much in the case of many words to reduce the tendency towards Babelization. An even more powerful stabilizing force has come with the spread of sound films, radio, television, air navigation, and telecommunications generally, all of which help to make the English-speaking world one and, in the case of America and Britain, have fairly successfully preserved the similarity in the spoken language on both sides of the Atlantic and indeed increased its continuous renourishment with new words. The many forms of electronically transmitted speech may come to standardize speech in much the same way as the spread of printing standardized spelling.

Even so, despite these powerful new stabilizing forces, the root cause of Babelization—the imperfect relationship between print and speech—is still with us. There is an urgent need for a rational connection between the two during the formative learning phases, that is if spoken English is to be preserved in a form that is widely comprehensible and sufficiently conventional to suit the purposes of universal speech as well as of a universal written language. World i.t.a. is, I believe, potentially capable not merely of enabling many more to learn to read and speak English fluently; it can also help to preserve and standardize it as a practical means of world-wide spoken communication.

THE NEED FOR A COMMON STANDARD

Standardization in this context does not equate with dullness. Being permanent, the printed word tends to be pervasive and should be related to the language in one of its most widely used forms or in a form that is a common denominator of the most acceptable forms. World-wide agreement on which pronunciation of English should furnish the standard spelling could never be achieved—any more than i.t.a. can prevent people in the north of England saying pœblic and those in the south saying public or Americans and English saying tomæto and tomɑtœ respectively —but i.t.a. would tend to keep departures from the norm within reasonable bounds. Professor A. Lloyd James wrote—

> A rational phonetic spelling will do much to steady our language in the perilous seas upon which it is now embarked, for, in these days of universal literacy, the visual language exercises a remarkable influence on the spoken language. It is the one constant standard, common throughout the world: the more phonetic it is, the more uniform will pronunciation tend to be. When men first began to write, they wrote as they spoke; now they tend to speak as they write—and we cannot blame them.[1]

The new medium can lend to words the necessary standardization, and it is for this reason that, in giving the copyright freely in the use of it to the world, I have stipulated that its spellings as well as its characters must not be varied. World i.t.a. must be equally sacrosanct—apart from the right to indicate preferred variations in the incidence of stress and rhythm as outlined earlier in this chapter. Without standardization the new medium is more likely to reduce than promote the chances of English becoming the world's chief auxiliary language. The millions who use English now and the millions more who will learn it in the coming years will cause no confusion and are not going to worry if they learn to say ieʃher, fuetiel and sceɋuel instead of ɛɛʃher, fuetl, and ʃheɋuel. All will be able to understand each other.

[1] Introduction to *New Spelling*, p. 6, by Walter Ripman and William Archer. Sir Isaac Pitman & Sons, London, 1940.

Falsely Implied Relationships and Dis-relationships

To indicate pronunciation, use has been made of the characters and the names of the phonemes given on page 132.

CHOOSING which words to include in these tables involves the thorny, highly subjective problem of variations in pronunciation. A separate, very different list could be compiled for each regional speech area—and, to be strictly exact, for each individual in it! An objective criterion, however, is provided by the two standard dictionaries (*The Shorter Oxford English Dictionary* and Webster's *New Collegiate Dictionary*) and by the two pronouncing dictionaries compiled by Daniel Jones, and by J. S. Kenyon and T. A. Knott (see page 124). If a pronunciation(s) and spelling(s) merit indexing in one or more of these volumes it has been assumed that it is sufficiently prevalent to justify inclusion in the tables. Even so, this means that the selection of words is limited to pronunciations that are extensively used in some parts of the English-speaking world and that many well-known regional pronunciations have had to be excluded, e.g. *woif* for *wife* and *boidz* for *birds*.

Despite the objectivity of this criterion, the reader may feel, dependent on the particularities of his or her own pronunciation, that some examples have been forced in merely in order to strengthen the case against orthodox spelling. This suspicion is most likely to arise in the following three categories:

(i) *Rare words*: e.g. *studding-sail*, pronounced *stunsal*.
Anyone unfamiliar with this yachtsman's term may be forgiven for

thinking its inclusion unfair, yet the extraordinary lack of correspondence between its spelling and pronunciation has been established over many years of seafaring.

(ii) *Variations in pronunciations that are relatively unknown.*

Few readers can be expected to recognize the six recorded variations of the relatively familiar word *coyote*: two are American and four are British. There is an understandable, subjective reaction to assert that our own personal pronunciation is the only correct one, whereas the thousands of other English-speaking people who proclaim one or other of the rival versions provide the justification for the inclusion of all six versions in one or more of the dictionaries and so in this table.

(iii) *Proper names:* e.g. *Spokane* and *Leicester.*

Without the discipline provided by the pronouncing dictionaries the proliferation of similar oddities would be boundless.

Let me reiterate that the pronunciations of some of the words used as examples are in no sense "correct." Many of them differ from the pronunciations to which I am myself habituated. All that is claimed is that they are ones which are recorded as being widely used as cultivated speech in important speech areas.

TABLE IV
Falsely Implied Relationships between Characters and Phonemes

TABLE IV(i) consists of words in which the same single character represents a different phoneme: e.g., if the "a" in *man* is taken to represent one (the "normal") value of "a," then to employ "a" in *many, later, all*, etc. is misleading and an example of each type of trap merits inclusion in the table. It will be seen that in each "normal" case the example is shown in square brackets. Also included in the square brackets are examples in which the result is close enough to the normal to occasion no doubt about the identity of the word (e.g. *man: about*). The first figure against the entries indicates the total number of different phonemes represented by each character: the second figure indicates the total of phonemes close enough to the "normal."

The same system is adopted in Tables IV(ii) and (iii).

TABLE IV(ii) consists of: (1) words in which the same two consecutive characters (digraph) represent a different phoneme: e.g., if the *ai* in *aim* is taken to represent one (the "normal") value of *ai*, then to employ *ai* also in *said*, *plait*, *aisle*, etc. is misleading and an example of each type merits inclusion and is listed before the colon-and-dash; (2) words in which the two characters that make up a digraph also represent not one phoneme but two: thus the *ai* in *laity* and *naïve* is not a digraph and is listed separately after the colon-and-dash.

TABLE IV(iii) consists of words in which three consecutive characters are inconsistently and thus misleadingly used.

The compilation of TABLE IV(i) presented no special difficulties, but a list of all the possible permutations of the 26 characters in pairs or triplets, even if limited to examples that are misleading, would fill too many pages and therefore TABLE IV(ii) is confined not merely to the character *a* but to the 26 pairs in which *a* comes first; likewise TABLE IV(iii) is confined to the 26 triplets in which *ab* comes first. I make no claim to have included even in these much shortened lists all the possible falsely implied relationships. TABLE IV(i) is, I believe, reasonably complete.

TABLE IV(i)

Examples of words in which the same single character represents a different phoneme.

A, a, *a*

$$
\begin{bmatrix} /a/ & /\alpha/ \\ \text{man} & \text{about} \end{bmatrix} \quad \begin{matrix} /\alpha/ \\ \text{part} \end{matrix} \quad \begin{matrix} /e/ \\ \text{many} \end{matrix} \quad \begin{matrix} /æ/ \\ \text{making} \end{matrix} \quad \begin{matrix} /i/ \\ \text{imaging} \end{matrix} \quad \begin{matrix} /o/ \\ \text{was} \end{matrix}
$$

$$
\begin{matrix} /\text{au}/ \\ \text{fall} \end{matrix} \quad \begin{matrix} /u/ \\ \text{tam-tam} \end{matrix} \quad \begin{matrix} /\text{mute}/ \\ \text{Isaac} \end{matrix} \qquad\qquad 10\text{—}2
$$

B, b, (1 cursive)[1]

$$
\begin{bmatrix} /b/ \\ \text{by} \end{bmatrix} \quad \begin{matrix} /\text{mute}/ \\ \text{lamb} \end{matrix} \qquad\qquad 2\text{—}1
$$

[1] This indicates that there is in addition a cursive (hand-written) form of this character which is different from the typographical forms.

Appendix I

C

$$\begin{bmatrix} /c/ \\ can \end{bmatrix} \quad \begin{matrix} /s/ \\ cent \end{matrix} \quad \begin{matrix} /ʃh/ \\ ocean \end{matrix} \quad \begin{matrix} /ʤ/ \\ cello \end{matrix} \quad \begin{matrix} /z/ \\ sacrifice \end{matrix} \quad \begin{matrix} /g/ \\ eczema \end{matrix} \quad \begin{matrix} /mute/ \\ scent \end{matrix}$$ 7—1

D, d

$$\begin{bmatrix} /d/ & /j/ \\ did & soldier \end{bmatrix} \quad \begin{matrix} /t/ \\ dropped \end{matrix} \quad \begin{matrix} /mute/ \\ ribband \end{matrix}$$ 4—2

E, e (1 cursive)

$$\begin{bmatrix} /e/ & /ɑ/ & /ʊ/ \\ egg & open & fern \end{bmatrix} \quad \begin{matrix} /a/ \\ sergeant \end{matrix} \quad \begin{matrix} /a/ \\ femme \end{matrix} \quad \begin{matrix} /æ/ \\ feted \end{matrix} \quad \begin{matrix} /i/ \\ pretty \end{matrix}$$
$$\begin{matrix} /ɛɛ/ \\ be \end{matrix} \quad \begin{matrix} /y/ \\ azalea \end{matrix} \quad \begin{matrix} /mute/ \\ have \end{matrix}$$ 10—3

F, f (2 cursive)

$$\begin{bmatrix} /f/ \\ for \end{bmatrix} \quad \begin{matrix} /v/ \\ of \end{matrix}$$ 2—1

G, g (1 cursive)

$$\begin{bmatrix} /g/ \\ good \end{bmatrix} \quad \begin{matrix} /ʒ/ \\ rouge \end{matrix} \quad \begin{matrix} /j/ \\ large \end{matrix} \quad \begin{matrix} /mute/ \\ impugn \end{matrix}$$ 4—1

H, h

$$\begin{bmatrix} /h/ \\ his \end{bmatrix} \quad \begin{matrix} /w/ \\ when \end{matrix} \quad \begin{matrix} /mute/ \\ hour \end{matrix}$$ 3—1

I, i (3 cursive)

$$\begin{bmatrix} /i/ & /ɑ/ & /ʊ/ & /y/ & /ʒ/ \\ in & April & first & onion & soldier \end{bmatrix} \quad \begin{matrix} /a/ \\ meringue \end{matrix} \quad \begin{matrix} /ɛɛ/ \\ invalid \end{matrix} \quad \begin{matrix} /ie/ \\ hind \end{matrix}$$
$$\begin{matrix} /mute/ \\ business \end{matrix}$$ 9—5

J, j, ℐ (2 cursive)

$$\begin{bmatrix} /j/ \\ just \end{bmatrix} \quad \begin{matrix} /ʒ/ \\ jardiniere \end{matrix} \quad \begin{matrix} /y/ \\ hallelujah \end{matrix}$$ 3—1

K, k

$$\begin{bmatrix} /k/ \\ kind \end{bmatrix} \quad \begin{matrix} /mute/ \\ know \end{matrix}$$

2—1

L, l (2 cursive)

$$\begin{bmatrix} /l/ \\ like \end{bmatrix} \quad \begin{matrix} /r/ \\ colonel \end{matrix} \quad \begin{matrix} /y/ \\ tortilla \end{matrix} \quad \begin{matrix} /mute/ \\ psalm \end{matrix}$$

4—1

M, m

$$\begin{bmatrix} /m/ \\ me \end{bmatrix} \begin{matrix} /\alpha m/ \\ spasm \end{matrix} \quad \begin{matrix} /mute/ \\ mnemonics \end{matrix}$$

3—2

N, n

$$\begin{bmatrix} /n/ \\ no \end{bmatrix} \quad \begin{matrix} /ŋ/ \\ think \end{matrix} \quad \begin{matrix} /m/ \\ Banff \end{matrix} \quad \begin{matrix} /ny/ \\ canon \end{matrix} \quad \begin{matrix} /mute/ \\ hymn \end{matrix}$$

5—1

O

$$\begin{bmatrix} /o/ \\ on \end{bmatrix} \begin{matrix} /au/ \\ orb \end{matrix} \begin{matrix} /\alpha/ \\ atom \end{matrix} \begin{matrix} /mute/ \\ reason \end{matrix} \quad \begin{matrix} /i/ \\ women \end{matrix} \quad \begin{matrix} /u/ \\ mother \end{matrix} \quad \begin{matrix} /œ/ \\ over \end{matrix}$$

/ω/ /ω/ /w/
woman do choir

10—4

P (1 cursive)

$$\begin{bmatrix} /p/ \\ pay \end{bmatrix} \quad \begin{matrix} /mute/ \\ pneumatics \end{matrix}$$

2—1

Qu, qu (2 cursive)

/kw/ /k/ /mute/
quite quay lacquer

3—0

R, r (1 cursive)

$$\begin{bmatrix} /r/ \\ very \end{bmatrix} \begin{matrix} /ɾ/ \\ vernal \end{matrix} \quad \begin{matrix} /mute/ \\ car \end{matrix}$$

3—2

S, s (1 cursive)

$$\begin{bmatrix} /s/ \\ this \end{bmatrix} \begin{matrix} /z/ \\ is \end{matrix} \begin{matrix} /ʃh/ \\ sure \end{matrix} \begin{matrix} /ʒ/ \\ measure \end{matrix} \begin{matrix} /mute/ \\ isle \end{matrix}$$

5—1

T, t (2 cursive)

$\begin{bmatrix} /t/ \\ \text{to} \end{bmatrix}$ /ʃh/   /ʒ/   /ʤ/   /ʧh/
     nation   equation   question   Southampton

/mute/
whistle   6—1

U

$\begin{bmatrix} /u/ & /ʊ/ & /ɑ/ \\ \text{cut} & \text{turn} & \text{upon} \end{bmatrix}$ /e/   /i/   /w/   /ω/   /ꭤ/
     bury   busy   persuade   full   truly

/ue/   /mute/
during   built   10—3

V (4 cursive)

$\begin{bmatrix} /v/ \\ \text{view} \end{bmatrix}$ /mute/
     sevennight   2—1

W (1 cursive)

$\begin{bmatrix} /w/ \\ \text{war} \end{bmatrix}$ /h/   /v/   /mute/
     when   wagnerian   write   4—1

X (1 cursive)

/k/   /ks/   /kʃh/   /gs/   /gʒ/   /z/
except   vex   anxious   exact   luxurious   beaux arts

/mute/
billet doux   7—0

Y (1 cursive)

$\begin{bmatrix} /y/ & /i/ & /ʊ/ & /ɑ/ \\ \text{yet} & \text{any} & \text{myrrh} & \text{methyl} \end{bmatrix}$ /ʃh/   /ie/
     ye   by   6—4

Z (1 cursive)

$\begin{bmatrix} /z/ \\ \text{zoo} \end{bmatrix}$ /d/   /s/   /t/   /ʒ/
     mezzo   waltz   pizzicato   azure   5—1

                                             131—42

TABLE IV(ii)

Examples of words in which (1) the same digraph beginning with "a" represents a different phoneme; or (2) the same two characters represent not a single phoneme but two separate and different phonemes.

aa   ma'am   bazaar   Isaac   Aaron :—   Baal
/a/   /ɑ/   /ɑ/   /æ/   /æɑ/   5—0

ab ⎡cab   about⎤   cable   squab   Kabul
      ⎣/ab/   /ɑb/ ⎦   /æb/   /ob/   /aub/   5—2

ac ⎡act   acute⎤   acorn   acid   facade   face   facia
      ⎣/ac/   /ɑc/ ⎦   /æc/   /as/   /ɑs/   /æs/   /æʃh/   7—2

ad ⎡/Adam   ado⎤   lady   Padre   adieu   squad
      ⎣/ad/   /ɑd/ ⎦   /æd/   /ad/   /ɑj/   /od/   6—2

ae ⎡brae ⎤   diaeresis   aegis :—   Israel   aerated
      ⎣ /æ/ ⎦   /e/   /ɛɛ/   /æe/   /æɑ/   5—1

af ⎡gaffe   after   afoot⎤   wafer   quaff
      ⎣/af/   /af/   /ɑf/ ⎦   /æf/   /of/   5—3

ag ⎡ Agatha   again⎤   sago   agent   saga   magic   image
      ⎣/ag/   /ɑg/ ⎦   /æg/   /æj/   /ag/   /aj/   /ij/
      agenda
      /ɑj/   8—2

ah sahib   rajah   dahlia :—   ⎡ ahead   yahoo⎤   yahoo   yahoo
      /a/   /ɑ/   /æ/   ⎣/ɑh/   /ah/ ⎦   /ah/   /ɑh/
      Cahill
      /æh/   8—3

ai aim   aisle   plait   said   Saint John :—   laity   naive
      /æ/   /ie/   /a/   /e/   /i/   /æi/   /aɛɛ/
      naive   naivety
      /iɛɛ/   /æɛɛ/   9—0

aj ⎡Hajji   ajar⎤   major   rajah
      ⎣/aj/   /ɑj/ ⎦   /æj/   /ɑj/   4—2

ak ⎡kayak   akin⎤   khaki
    ⎣/ak/   /ɑk/⎦   /ɑk/   3—1

al   talk   palm :—   ⎡Alice   alone⎤   gala   alien   scald   7—2
    /au/   /ɑ/   ⎣/al/   /ɑl/⎦   /ɑl/   /æl/   /aul/

am ⎡amber   among⎤   famous   drama   swamp
    ⎣/am/   /ɑm/⎦   /æm/   /am/   /om/   5—2

an ⎡ban   canoe⎤   dance   mania   anger   wand   any
    ⎣/an/   /ɑn/⎦   /ɑn/   /æn/   /aŋ/   /on/   /en/   7—2

ao   gaol   Pharaoh :—   ⎡extraordinary⎤   aorta   Maori   chaos
    /æ/   /œ/   ⎣   /ɑo/   ⎦   /æau/   /ao/   /æo/
    Aonian
    /æœ/   7—1

ap ⎡chapel   appeal⎤   apron   swap   graph   graph
    ⎣/ap/   /ɑp/⎦   /æp/   /op/   /af/   /ɑf/
    seraph
    /ɑf/   7—2

aq ⎡aquamarine   aquatic   aqueous⎤
    ⎣/ak/   /ɑk/   /æk/⎦   3—3

ar ⎡Arab   arise⎤   barber   canary   warm
    ⎣/ar/   /ɑr/⎦   /ɑr/   /ær/   /aur/   5—2

as ⎡asterisk   asleep⎤   as   laser   vast   waste   casual
    ⎣/as/   /ɑs/⎦   /aʐ/   /æʐ/   /ɑs/   /æs/   /aʒ/
    wash   passion
    /oʃh/   /aʃh/

at ⎡atlas   atone⎤   fatal   squat   water   ate   scathe
    ⎣/at/   /ɑt/⎦   /æt/   /ot/   /aut/   /et/   /æth/
    athlete   athirst   atheist   bath
    /ath/   /ɑth/   /æth/   /ath/   11—2

au	author	laurel	aunt	aunt	gauge	gauche	gaucho	
	/au/	/o/	/a/	/ɑ/	/æ/	/œ/	/ou/	
	meerschaum :—		Menelaus					
	/ɑ/		/æɑ/					9—2

av	cavil	avoid	gravy	lava	octave	
	/av/	/ɑv/	/æv/	/ɑv/	/iv/	5—2

aw	awful	lawyer :—	awake	
	/au/	/o/	/ɑw/	3—1

ax	axe	coax	
	/aks/	/ks/	2—0

ay	play	aye	Rothesay	says :—	Bayeux	Bayeux	
	/æ/	/ie/	/i/	/e/	/æy/	/iey/	6—0

az	topaz	bazaar	razor	plaza	piazza	
	/az/	/ɑz/	/æz/	/ɑz/	/at/	5—2

147—40

TABLE IV(iii)

Examples of words in which (1) the same trigraph beginning with "ab" represents a different phoneme: or (2) the same three characters represent two or three different phonemes.

aba	aback	abacus	abaft	abase	
	/ɑba/	/abɑ/	/ɑba/	/ɑbæ/	4—2

abb	rabble	abbreviate	wabbly	
	/ab/	/ɑb/	/ob/	3—2

abe	abet	aberrance	aberration	label	babe	
	/ɑbe/	/abe/	/abɑ/	/æbɑ/	/æb/	5—3

abi	Abigail	ability	abide	labial	labile	
	/abi/	/ɑbi/	/ɑbie/	/æbi/	/æbie/	5—2

abl	tablet	ablaze	able	
	/abl/	/ɑbl/	/æbl/	3—2

283

abo $\begin{bmatrix} \text{abort} \\ \text{/ɑbo/} \end{bmatrix}$ abort   abode   about   above   caboose
              /ɑbau/   /ɑbœ/   /ɑbou/   /ɑbu/   /ɑbω/

     /aboil   Nabob   tabor
     ɑbɔi/   /æbo/   /æbɑ/   9—1

abr $\begin{bmatrix} \text{abrogate} & \text{abrade} \\ \text{/abr/} & \text{/ɑbr/} \end{bmatrix}$ Abram   sabre
                            /æbr/   /æbɑ/   4—2

abs $\begin{bmatrix} \text{absent} & \text{absorb} \\ \text{/abs/} & \text{/ɑbs} \end{bmatrix}$ absorb
                            /ɑbʒ/   3—2

abu $\begin{bmatrix} \text{abut} \\ \text{/ɑbu/} \end{bmatrix}$ abuse   Abukir   Abukir   Abukir   Kabul
              /ɑbue/   /abω/   /abω/   /ɑbω/   /aubω/

     Abu   Kabul
     /abω/   /abω/   8—1

aby $\begin{bmatrix} \text{Abyssinia} & \text{abyss} \\ \text{/abi/} & \text{/ɑbi/} \end{bmatrix}$ Kabyle   baby
                            /ɑbie/   /æbi/   4—2
                                                     48—19

TABLE V

Falsely Implied Dis-relationships between Phonemes and Characters

The names of the phonemes on the left-hand side are to be found in Table XII, page 132.

1. /puh/

(*p*) p   pp   ppe   pe   ph   (*g*)   gh
     put   happy   flapped   rope   shepherd: hiccough:
(*l*)   lfp
    halfpenny: 7

2. /buh/

(*b*) b   bb   bbe   be   bh   (*c*)   ckb
     bad   hobby   ebbed   babe   bhang: Cockburn
(*p*)   pb   (*t*)   tb
    cupboard: hautboy: 8

3. /tuh/

(*t*) t   tt   te   th   tw   (*b*)   bt   (*c*) cht
tap better mete thyme two: debt: yacht

    ct   (*d*) dt   (*e*)   ed   (*g*) ght   (*p*) phth
indict: veldt: picked: might: phthisis

    pt   (*z*) z
receipt: pizzicato: 14

4. /duh/

(*d*) d   dd   de   dh   ddh   (*b*) bd
dog muddy made dhow Buddhist: bdellium

(*e*)   ed   (*l*)   ld   (*t*)   th   (*z*) z
moved: would: burthen: mezzo: 10

5. /cuh/

(*k*) k   ke kh   kk   (*c*) c   cc   cch
kill bake khaki Habakkuk: can account bacchanal

    ch   che   ck   cke   cqu   (*g*) gh   (*l*) lc
school ache back hacked lacquer: lough: falcon

    lk   (*q*) q   qu   que   quh   (*s*) sc
walk: quack quay antique Urquhart: viscount:

(*t*) tch   (*x*) x   xh
nut-hatch:[1]   next exhibition: 23

6. /guh/

(*g*) g   gg   gge gh   gu   gue   (*c*) c
girl foggy begged ghost guessed plague: eczema

    ckg   (*x*) x   xh
blackguard: example: exhibit: 10

7. /fuh/

(*f*) f   ff   fe   ffe   ffh   fl   ft
fun muff safe stuffed Swaffham flugelman often

---

[1] The /cuh/ pronunciation is supported by *The Random House Dictionary of the English Language* and by *Birds of the World*: Oliver L. Austin (Paul Hamlyn). The O.E.D. states that *hatch* is "connected with *hack. v.,* ... bird ... so named from the way it breaks nuts to feed on the kernel."

(*g*) gh   lf (*p*) ph   pph   (*u*) u
    laugh: half: photo sapphire: lieutenant: 12

8. /vuh/

(*v*) v   vv   ve (*f*) f   (*l*) lv   lve
   van   navvy   have: of: Belvoir   halve:

(*p*) ph   (*s*)   sv   (*z*)   zv
  nephew: Grosvenor: rendezvous: 9

9. /thuh/

(*th*) th   the (*h*)   h (*g*)   gh   (*p*)   phth
    thing blithe: eighth: Keighley: apophthegm:

  (*t*)   t   tth
   Southampton   Matthew: 7

10. /then/

(*th*) th   the (*y*) y
   that   breathe: ye: 3

11. /suh/

(*s*) s   ss   sse   sc   sce   sch   se   sh
   sit   hiss   kissed   scene   coalesce   schism   case   dishonest

     sp   st   sth   str   sw   (*c*) c   ce
  raspberry   thistle   isthmus   mistress   sword: cell   ace

      ces   (*p*) ps   (*r*)   renc   rces
  Gloucester: psalm: Cirencester   Worcester

     rs   (*t*) tsw   tz   tzs   (*x*) x   xc
  worsted: boatswain waltz britzska: next   except

    xh   (*z*)   zs   z
  exhibition: britzska   pizzicato: 28

12. /zuh/

(*z*) z   zz   zze   ze   (*c*)   c   cz
  zoo   buzz   whizzed   freeze: sacrifice   czar:

(*d*)   ds   (*i*)   is   (*s*) s   sc   se   sew
   Windsor: Salisbury: as   discern   ease   housewife

sh	si	sp	ss	sth
dishonour	business	raspberry	scissors	asthma

sw	(*w*)	ws	(*x*)	x	xh	
Keswick:		bellows:		beaux	exhibit:	21

13. /shuh/

(*c*) c   ch   chs   (*p*) psh   (*s*) s
special machine fuchsia: pshaw!:   sugar

      sci   sh sk ss   sshe   ssi
conscience fish ski issue Assheton passion:

(*t*) ti   (*x*) xi
nation: noxious: 13

14. /zhuh/

(*g*)   g   ge   (*j*) j   (*s*) s   si
rouging rouge: jabot: pleasure division

      ssi   (*t*) ti   (*z*) z
scission: equation: azure: 8

15. /chuh/

(*c*) c   ch   che   chi   (*g*) ght
cello each arched chioppine: righteous:

(*j*)   jori   (*t*) t   ti   tch   tche
Marjoribanks: Mantua question match matched

      th
posthumous: 11

16. /juh/

(j) j   jj   (*c*) ch   (*d*) d   dg
jug Hajji: spinach: soldier judgment

      dge   dj   (*g*) g   ge   gg
knowledge adjust: gem age exaggerate

      gh
Bellingham: 11

17. /muh/

(*m*) m   mm   mme   mb   me   mn   mp
man rummy shammed lamb lame hymn Campbell:

287

(*c*) chm　(*g*)　gm　(*l*) lm　　lmonde　(*n*) n
drachm:　　phlegm:　　palm Cholmondeley:　　Banff

nd　　nte
sandwich Pontefract:　　　　　　　　　　　　　14

18. /nuh/

(*n*) n　nn　nne　nd　ne　nh
not funny planned handsome line ipecacuanha

nt　　nw　(*d*) dding　(*e*) en
Saint Clair gunwale:　　studding sail:　opening:

(*g*) gn　(*h*) hn　(*k*) kn　(*l*) ln　　lne
gnaw:　John:　know:　Colnbrook　Calne:

(*m*) mn　　mp　　mpt　(*o*) on
mnemonic comptroller compter:　reasoning:

(*p*) pn　　(*s*)　sn　(*w*) wn
pneumatic:　demesne:　known:　　　　　　22

19. /ung/

(*n*) n　nd　　ng　nge　ngue　ngh
bank handkerchief sing winged tongue gingham

nz
Menzies:　　　　　　　　　　　　　　　　7

20. /luh/

(*l*) l　ld　ll　lle　le　lh　　ln
lad Guildford holly travelled ale silhouette kiln:

(*a*)　al　(*c*)　cle　(*g*)　gl　(*h*) hl　(*s*) sl
magdalen:　muscle:　intaglio:　buhl:　island:

sle　(*t*)　tl　(*u*) ual　　uall　(*w*) wl
aisle:　nestle:　victuals victualler:　knowledge:　17

21. /ruh/

(*r*) r　rr　rre　re rh　rhe　　rps
run hurry referred fire rhyme rheumatism corps

rrh　rs　　rt　(*l*) l　(*w*) wr　　12
myrrh hors d'oeuvre mortgage:　colonel:　write:

22. /huh/

(*h*) h   gh   (*j*)   j   (*l*) lquh   (*w*) w   wh
hot   Callaghan: Navajo: Colquhoun: when   who: 6

23. /wuh/

(*w*) w   wh   (*h*) h   (*o*) o   oi   ou   (*u*)   u
wet   when: when: one   memoir   bivouac: persuade: 7

24. /yuh/

(*y*) y   (*e*)   e   eo   (*g*) gn   (*i*)   i
yes: azalea   courteous: vignette: onion:

(*j*)   j   (*l*)   ll   (*n*)   n
halleluja: tortilla: manana: 8

25. /ak/

(*a*)   a   a'a   ac   ach   ack   a-e   a--e
man   ma'am   Mackay   drachm   blackguard   have   lapse

      ag   ah   ai   al   a--ue   au   au-e
seraglio   Messiah   plaid   salmon   harangue   laugh   laughed:

       ha   (*i*)   ia   i--ue   (*u*)   ua   ui
(*h*) Clapham: special   meringue: guarantee   guimp: 19

25/26. /aft/

(*a*) a   a   a'a   a—e   au   au--e
ask   wigwam[1]   ma'am   passed   laugh   laughed:

26. /ahm/

(*a*) a   aa   a-e   a—e   ag   agh   ah   al
father   bazaar   are   passed   seraglio   Armagh   ah   alms

    al-e   at   au   a--ue   (*e*) e   ea
Malmesbury   eclat   aunt   barque: sergeant   heart:

(*h*) ha   (*o*)   oi   ois   (*u*) ua
habitant: memoir   patois: guard: 18

---

[1] It is curious that those who pronounce *ask* with the /ahm/ vowel pronounce the *wam* with the /ak/ vowel, while those who pronounce *ask* with the /ak/ vowel pronounce *wam* with the /ahm/ vowel. The sub-total of 6 has been excluded from the total because these spellings have been counted under /ak/ and /ahm/.

27. /ek/

(*a*) a   ac   a-e   ae   a-e   ai   ay
any   Pontefract   separate (adj.)   diaeresis   Thames   said   says

        ave   (*e*)   e   ea   eb   ed   e-e
Abergavenny: pen head debt Wednesday allege

e--e   ee   e--e   e--es   eg   eh   ehea
edge keelson parterre belles lettres phlegm eh! forehead

ei   eice   eo   e-ue   eve   ez
heifer Leicester leopard cheque sevennight rendezvous:

(*h*) he   (*i*) ie   ie--e (*o*) oe
rhetoric: friend conscience   foetid

    oi   (*u*) u   ue   ue--e
connoisseur: bury guess guessed: 34

28. /aim/

(*a*) a   aa   a-e   ae   ag-e   ah
making Aaron made maelstrom champagne dahlia

  ai   ai-e   aig   aigh   ait   alf   ao
maim raise campaign straight trait halfpenny gaol

ao-e   au   a-u   au-e   ay   aye
gaoled gauging plaguing gauged may played

  ayo (*e*) e   e-e   ea   e   e-e e'e   ee
mayor: re there great feted fete e'er matinee

  eh   ei   er   ei-e   eig   eig-e   eigh
eh! veil dossier Seine reign reigned eight

  eighe   et   ey   eye   ey-e eyo   (*h*) hei
weighed ballet they conveyed eyre eyot: heir:

(*u*)   ue   uet
applique bouquet: 43

29. /ip/

(*a*) a   ae   ai-t   a-e   ai
imaging caesura Saint John village mountain

    agh   ai-e   au   ay (*e*) e
shillelagh captained Jervaulx Sunday: pretty

ea   eau   e-e   ee   ehea   ei
guinea   beaufin   college   breeches   forehead   forfeit

eig   eo   et   ewi-e   ey   ez
foreign   pigeon   billet doux   housewife   money   rendezvous:

(*h*)   hi   hy   (*i*) i   ia   ia-e   ic
exhibit   rhythm: it   marriages   carriage   victuals

i-e   ie   ie-e   ieu   igh   is
give   carried   sieve   Beaulieu   sevennight   chassis

i--ue   ive   (*o*) o   oe   oi   ois
bisque   fivepence: women   felloe   Jervois   chamois:

(*t*)   tre   (*u*) u   u-e   uey   ui   uy
mistress: busy   minute   plaguey   build   plaguy:

(*w*)   whi   wi   (*y*)   y   y--e   ymo
Tyrrwhit   Chiswick: very   apocalypse   Wymondham: 51

30. /eem/

(*a*) ae   aiu   (*e*) e   ea   eae   ea-e   eau
aeon   Caius: be   each   Fleaed   leave   Beauchamp

ea-ue   ee   e-e   e'e   ee-e   eg   egh
league   feet   these   e'en   seemed   impregn   Legh

eh   ei   eip   ei-e   eig   eigh   eip
vehicle   either   receipt   receive   Seignory   Leigh   receipt

el   eo   es   ey   eye   e-y
Belvoir   people   demesne   key   keyed   Wemyss:

(*h*)   hoe   (*i*)   i   ie   i-e   ie-e   ig
diarrhoea: albino   grief   marine   believe   signor

il   is   i-ue   (*o*)   oe   (*u*)   uay   ui
fusil   debris   intrigue: amoeba: quay   mosquito:

(*y*)   y
Chypres: 40

31. /ok/

(*a*)   a   ach   au   au-e   (*e*) e   eo
was   yacht   laurel   because: rendezvous   George:

(*h*) ho   (*o*)   o   o-e   o--e   og   oh
honour: not   gone   conned   cognitive   John

oi-e   ou   ou--e   o-ue   ow
scrutoire   trough   coughed   pedagogue   knowledge:

(*w*)   wo
sword: 18

32. /aub/

(*a*) a   ag   ah   al   a-e   ao
all   Magdalen   hurrah   talk   false   extraordinary

            as   au   au-e   augh   augha   aul
Arkansas   autumn   Maude   naughty   Vaughan   aulner

   aw   awe   (*e*)   eo--e   (*o*)   o   oa   o-e   oi-e
saw   awe: George: lost   broad   gone   turquoise

  ol   ors   ough   (*w*)   wo
solder   hors d'oeuvre   sought: sword: 23

33. /uk/

(*a*)   a   au   (*e*)   eo   (*h*) hu
riband   meershaum: escutcheon: humble:

(*i*)   io   iou   (*o*)   o   oe   o-e   oi-e   oo
motion   conscious: son   does   some   tortoise   blood

   ou   ou--e   ow   (*u*)   u   u--e   u--ue
country   touched   bellows: cut   rubbed   brusque: 17

34. /ome/

(*a*)   aoh   au   au-e   aut   (*e*) eau   eaux
Pharaoh   chauffeur   mauve   hautboy: beau   Bordeaux

   eo   ew   ewe   (*h*) ho   (*i*)   io   (*o*) o
yeoman   sew   sewed: ghost: mustachio: no

  oa   oa-e   oat   ock   oe   o-e   o'e
coal   Soames   boatswain   Cockburn   toe   stove   o'er

     og   og   og-e   oh   ol   oo   os
inbroglio   oglio   Cologne   oh!   yolk   brooch   a propos

    os-e   ot   ou   o-ue   ough   oug   ow
Grosvenor   depot   soul   rogue   though   youghall   know

   owa   owe   ow-e   (*u*)   uo   (*w*)   wo
toward   owe   Knowles: quoth: sword: 37

35. /oop/

(*o*) o   o-e   oo   ooh   or   or-e
woman   Bolingbroke   good   pooh!   worsted   Worcester

   oul   ouc   (*u*) u   u-e   u--ue
  would   caoutchouc: full   sure   brusque:

36. /oob/

(*a*) aou   (*e*) eew   eo   eu   eugh
   caoutchouc: leeward   galleon   pleurisy   Buccleugh

   ew   ewe   (*h*) heu   hu   (*i*) ieu   (*o*) o
  crew   brewed: rheumatic   rhubarb: lieu: do

   oe   o-e   oeu   oo   ooe   oo-e   ooh   ou
  shoe   move   manoeuvre   too   wooed   loose   pooh!   soup

   ou-e   ou--e   oue   ough   ougha   oup
  route   douched   denouement   through   brougham   coup

      ous   ouse   out   ow   oux
  rendezvous   rendezvoused   ragout   Cowper   billet doux:

(*u*) u   ue   u-e   ugh   ui   ui-e   ul   uo
  truly   true   rule   pugh!   fruit   bruise   Hulme   buoy:

(*w*) wo   w-o   w-o-e
  two   who   whose:

37. /ibe/

(*a*)   ai   ais-e   ay   aye   (*e*) ei   eigh   ey
  assegai   aisle   McKay   aye: either   height   eying

   eye   (*h*) hei   hi   hi-e   hy   hy-e
  eye: rheinberry   rhino   rhinestone   rhyolite   rhyme:

(*i*)   i   ia   ic   ie   i-e   ig   ig-e   igh
  child   diamond   indict   die   knife   sign   signed   high

   ighe   i-ue   is   is-e   (*o*) oi   oy
  sighed   oblique   island   lisle: choir   coyote:

(*u*) ui   ui-e   uy   uye   (*y*) y   ye   y-e
  guiding   guide   buys   guyed: my   dye   type

38. /oum/

(*a*) aou   au   (*e*)   eo   (*h*) hou   (*i*) iaou
  caoutchouc   kraut: Macleod: hour: giaour:

(*o*) o   ou   ou--e   oub   ough   oughe   ow
compter noun renounce doubt bough ploughed cow
owe
allowed: 13

39. /oim/

(*e*)   eoi   (*o*) oi   oi-e   oig   oig-e   oy
bourgeois: boil noise poignant coigne boy

oye   oy-e   (*u*) uoi   uoi-e   uoy   uoye
employed gargoyle: quoit turquoise buoy buoyed: 12

40. /ume/

(*e*) eau   eo   eu   eu-e   ev   ew   ewe
beauty feod feud deuce Leveson-Gower few ewe:

(*h*) hu   (*i*) ieu   iew   iewe   (*l*) lu
humour: lieu view viewed: flugleman:

(*u*) u   ua   uch   u-e   ue   ueue   ug
during mantuamaker fuchsia use due queue impugn

ug   ughe   uh   ui   uis-e   u-ue   (*y*) yew you
Hugh Hughes buhl suit puisne fugue: yew you

yu-e
yule: 28
                                                          ―――
                                                          727

The "central" or "relaxed" vowel may be read from many different spellings. Of these that follow, the different spellings have been classified according to their spellings in i.t.a.[1] Those marked with an asterisk are normally pronounced with the "strong" or "stressed" form /uhr/; the rest are normally pronounced with the unstressed form /uh/; *amateur* is pronounced with either—as well as with a vowel /ume/.

(*a*) a   ae   a--e   agh   ah   ai
about Michael nuisance Shelagh sirrah Britain

anc   ar   ea   ia--e   ua
blancmange pillar ocean allegiance piquant   11

[1] These 66 spellings of the relaxed vowel have been included in the final total of 793 (on page 296). Thus in effect the number of phonemes represented in this Table is not 40 but 40 + 1.

e (e)	e	ea	ear	ear-e	er	ere			
	open	sergeant	earth*	hearse*	over	were			
	er-e	eu	her	ie	uer				
	concerned*	pleurisy*	herb*	patience	lacquer				
	uere	wer							
	lacquered	answer							13

i	i	ir	irre				
	pencil	bird*	stirred*				3

o	o	oar	or	ough	our		oure	
	reason	cupboard	for	thorough	labour		clamoured	
	uor							
	liquor							7

u	or	oi-e	olo	or-e	our	u	
	work*	tortoise	colonel*	worked*	journey*	upon	
	uhr	ur	ur-e				
	buhr*	turn*	turned*				9

y	y	yr	yrrh	
	methyl	martyr	myrrh*	3

ω	o	u	oul	
	to	-ful	could	3

ꞷ	ou	our	
	your	your	2

ɑ	are	
	are	I

æ	a		ai	ai-e	eir	ere	
	a (the indefinite article)	captain	captained	their	there		5

au	au	
	restaurant	I

ie	i-e	ire	
	futile	Shropshire	2

œ o
   so   I

ue   eur   u-e   ure   ueur
   amateur* ferrule picture liqueur   4

ou   ou
   Dartmouth   I

Total number of dis-relationships 793

296

APPENDIX II

Comparison of Phonetic Alphabets and Spellings

TABLE VIII(i–v)

T HE MOST EFFECTIVE WAY of demonstrating the aims and merits of the alphabets described in Chapter 6 is to arrange a selection of them side by side in relation to a constant set of phonemes. For this purpose I have employed the 40 phonemes which are the basis of Pitman's shorthand (see p. 42) and of my own alphabet, i.t.a., whose structure is described at length in Chapter 7. Without a common phonetic framework such as this it would be difficult not only to make comparisons between the alphabets but also to comprehend the different frameworks on which each was constructed. Again, as in TABLE V, the phonemes are identified by the numbers for them given on page 132.

To marshal all these alphabets in this manner does however give rise to difficulties: their creators held widely differing opinions on the number of phonemes that ought to be included and on the consequent number of characters. Moreover there have always been disputes over borderline cases, particularly where two or more phonemes are not as sharply discrete as are, for instance, /puh/ or /buh/. Each of these phonemes is exceptional in that it gives rise to no recognized varieties. With /tuh/ or /duh/, on the other hand, some experts detect at least two distinct phonemes —those in *ten* and *postman*; and those in *dog* and *handcuff*. A particularly complex group of borderline cases is to be found in words which may be said to contain the phoneme /ip/, represented in our orthodox spelling by the characters *i* or *y* (see phoneme No. 29).

In an attempt to categorize these complications, TABLE VIII(i) provides the symbols used in the pronouncing dictionaries compiled by Daniel

Jones, and by Kenyon and Knott (see p. 124 *ante*), in Webster's *New Collegiate Dictionary*, and in *The Shorter Oxford English Dictionary*. The function of these four is to depict phonetic niceties, whereas most of the other alphabets in TABLE VIII were designed to make the task of reading easier; the latter, while essaying to provide a practicable and unambiguous relationship between character and phoneme, therefore made less elaborate discriminations between phonemes, and there tended to be fewer characters.

The pronouncing dictionaries demonstrate that the unstressed neutral vowel is intractable within any framework, because when stressed it changes to another phoneme altogether (cf. *metal, metallic*); this is why the character ə appears in items 21, 27, 29, 31, 33, 35, 38, and 40.

Another major difficulty in compiling this table has been the manifold differences in regional pronunciations. It will be noted that Kenyon and Knott specifically provide for several regions. This explains why they often report a number of pronunciations for a particular word (e.g. the word *were* in phoneme No. 27). With the early alphabets the analysis has been made even more difficult by the changes in pronunciation that occur with the lapse of centuries and by the uncertainty of how words used to be pronounced. At times one also suspects that the printer has not always faithfully carried out the designer's intentions or that the proofs were not adequately corrected.

The alphabet designed by Richard Hodges (1644) bristles with examples of this kind of difficulty. For instance, he employs five different characters for words which we now pronounce with the single sound /vuh/ as in *of*. Did he intend one or two sounds as might be implied by his employment of two distinct characters in the words we now spell *of* and *whereof*? Similarly, did he pronounce the *k* as /kuh/ in the word *known*? Did he pronounce the *w* in *writing* but not in *Southwark*, though it is certain that he pronounced *Authority* as *Autority* as in the modern *Anthony*? But how can we tell if his use of the same "a" in *any*, *gate*, *that*, and *garden* was a misprint in one or more of these cases; or whether, as I have recorded in the table, four different phonemes were intended to be represented by this single character?

The alphabets which employ diacritical marks cause another type of special difficulty. If a look-and-say view of learning to read in the new medium is adopted, every difference of characterization could, strictly speaking, be included—for instance, all the 51 characterizations of the phoneme /ip/. If a phonic view is taken all those forms in which the alphabetic principle has been met merely by marking the misleading characters as mute can be eliminated from the table: for instance in the word *ploughed*, Hodges indicates mute characters by a line beneath the *h* and *e*, and above the *g*; Fry, who adds a line beneath the *ou*, puts slash marks through the *g*, *h*, and *e*. I decided it would be wiser therefore to adopt the phonic and less accurate alternative and to refer the reader to Table V with a reminder that even those 51 characterizations for /ip/ do not exhaust the visual forms in which this phoneme is represented. To cater for all these, as would be necessary with the look-and-say approach, would entail an immense quantity of different visual patterns and make the table even more complex than it is already.

I hope I have done no injustice to past reformers who sought, as I have done, to make the achievement of literacy easier. In some instances I have intentionally disregarded their attachment of characters to what appear to be inappropriate phonemes on the assumption that they were intended to convey pronunciations that are now forgotten. Though great care has been taken, there are, I am sure, errors of commission as well as errors of omission. I hope that others will help me to achieve a more accurate analysis in any future edition.

TABLE VIII is divided for convenience into five parts as follows:

[1] In this table the phonemes (1) /puh/; (2) /buh/; (7) fuh/; (8) /vuh/; and (11) /suh/ are omitted because the characters—*p*, *b*, *f*, *v*, and *s*—that represent them in each alphabet, and also in i.t.a., are the same.

TABLE VIII (i) PHONETIC ALPHABETS

No.	i.t.a.	Example	Daniel Jones	Kenyon and Knott	Webster	Shorter Oxford
φ3	t	ten	t	t	t	t t
		postman	*t*	"	"	
4	d	dog	d	d	d	d
		handcuff	*d*	"	"	"
5	k	kitten	k	k	k	k
	c	cat	"	"	"	"
	ch	loch	x|k	x|k	"	χ
6	g	gag	g	g	g	g
9	th	thin	θ	θ	th	þ
10	th	then	ð	ð	~~th~~	ð
12	z	zero	z	z	z	z
	z	used	"	"	"	"
13	ʃh	shop	ʃ	ʃ	sh	ʃ
14	ʒ	vision	ʒ	ʒ	zh	ʒ
15	ch	chest	tʃ	tʃ	ch	tʃ
	tch	match	"	"	"	"
16	j	jam	dʒ	dʒ	j	dʒ
	dʒ	edge	"	"	"	"
	dj	adjust	"	"	"	"

300

No.	i.t.a.	Example	Daniel Jones	Kenyon and Knott	Webster	Shorter Oxford
17	m	custom	m	m	m	m
		chasm	m̩	əm|m̩	"	"
		comfort	m|m̩	m	"	"
18	n	no	n	n	n	n
		buttoning	n̩	n̩	"	"
19	ŋ	long	ŋ	ŋ	ng	ŋ
20	l	full	l	l	l	l
		cradling	l|l̩	l|l̩	"	"
21	r	run	r	r	r	r
	r	her	*	˞|(r	r	ɹ
22	h	how	h	h	h	h
22/23	wh	when	hw	hw	hw	hw
23	w	watch	w	w	w	w
24	y	yes	j	j	y	y
	i	million	"	"	"	"
		idiot	ĭ|j	ɪ	ĭ	"
25	a	cat	æ	æ	ă	æ
		account	ə	ə	ȧ	ă
		accept	"	"	ă	æ̆
		sofa	"	"	ȧ	ă
		metal	—	—|(l̩)	'	"|'

301

No.	i.t.a.	Example	Daniel Jones	Kenyon and Knott	Webster	Shorter Oxford
25 (cont.)	ar	arid	ær	ær	ăr	ær
		polar	ə*	ɚ	ēr	ăɹ
25/26	ɑ	bath	ɑ:	æ|a|ɑ	à	ɑ
26	ɑ	alms	ɑ:	ɑ	ä	ā
	ar	far	ɑ:*	ar|a:(r	är	āɹ
27	e	get	e	ɛ	ĕ	e
		the	i:|i|ə|—	ə|ɪ|i	ē|ė|ĭ|ē	ē|ə|i̇|ī
		continent	ə	ə	ĕ	ĕ
		added	i	ɪ	ē|ĭ	ė
		remain	i|ə	"	ĕ	ĭ
		react	i(:)	i	"	ī
	er	Eric	er	ɛr	ĕr	er
	er	her	ə:*|ə*	ɝ|ɜ(r|ɚ ə(r	ûr	ə̄ɹ|əɹ|ĕɹ
		mother	ə*	ɚ|ə(r	ēr	əɹ
		were	ə:*|ɛə* ə*	ɝ|ɛr|ær ɜ(r|ɛə(r æə(r|ɚ ə(r	û|â	eɹ|ĕr əɹ
28	æ	day	ei	e	ā	ēⁱ
		Sunday	i|ei	ɪ	ĭ	eⁱ|i
		separate (adj.)	i	"	"	ĕ
	ær	there	ɛə*|ə* r	ɛr|ær ɛə(r|æə(r ɚ|ə(r|	âr	ēᵊɹ|ĕr əɹ

No.	i.t.a.	Example	Daniel Jones	Kenyon and Knott	Webster	Shorter Oxford
29	i	it	i	ɪ	ī	i
	y	yttrium	"	"	"	"
	i	charity	"	ə	ĭ	ī
	y	very	"	ɪ	ĭ	i
	i	April	ə|i	ə|ɪ	ĭ	"
	y	Beryl	i	"|"	"	"
	ir	virile	ir|aiər	ɪr|aɪr	ĭr|īr	ir|əiᵊr
	yr	myriad	ir	ɪr	ĭr	ir
	ir,yr	bird	ə:	ɝ|ɜ	ûr	ə·ɹ
		myrtle	"	"	"	ə·ɹ
		elixir	ə*	ɚ|ə(r	ēr	əɹ
		martyr	"	"|"	"	"
30	ɛɛ	see	i:	i	ē	ī
	ɛɛr	here	iə*|jə:*ei ə:*	ɪr|ɪə(r jɛə(r|jɪə(r ɛə(r	ēᵣ	ī³ɹ
31	o	got	ɔ	a|ɒ	ŏ	ǫ
		what	"	e|ʌ|ə	"	ǫ
		soft	"|ɔ:	ɔ|ɑ	ộ	ǫ̀
		vitriol	ə	ə	ŭ	ǫ̆
		violet	"	"	ȯ	ǭ
		connect	"	"	ŏ	ǫ̆
		altogether	"	"	ōō	ŭ
	or	forest	ɔr	ɔr|ar|ɒr	ŏr	ǫr
		theory	ər	ər	ŏr	ŏr
		story	ɔ:r	or|ɔr	ōr	ō³ᵣ
		ichor	ɔ:*	ɔr|ɚ|ɔə(r ɹe(r	ôr|ēr	ǫ̆ɹ
		orb	ɔ:	ɔr|ə	ôr	ǭɹ
		order	"	ɔr	"	ǭ·ɹ

303

No.	i.t.a.	Example	Daniel Jones	Kenyon and Knott	Webster	Shorter Oxford
32	au	fought	ɔː	ɔ	ô	ọ̄
		authority	″|o|ə″	ə	″	ọ|ọ̄|ọ̄
	aur	aural	ɔːr	ɔr	ôr	ọ̄r
33	u	up	ʌ	ʌ	ŭ	ɒ
		circus	ə	ə	ŭ̄	ɒ̄
	ur	hurry	ʌr	ɝ|ɝr|ʌr-ʼ	ŭr	ɒr
	ur	curl	əː	ɝʼ|ɝ	ûr	ɒ̄ɹ
		femur	ə*	ɚ|ə(r	ēr	ɒ̄ɹ
34	œ	old	ou	o	ō	ōͧ
		hero	″	″	″	o
		Noah	ou|ɔ	o	″	ōͧ
35	ω	put	u	ʊ	o͞o	u
		to	uː|u|ə|–	ʊ|u|ə	o͞o|o͝o|ū̆	ū|u|u|ū̆|ə
		unto	u|uː|ə	ʊ|ə|u	o͞o|o͝o	u|ū̆
	ωr	poor	oə*|ɔə*|uə*	ur|uə(r	o͞or	ū̆ʼ|ʼʴū̆ʼ
			ɔː*	oə(r|ɔə(r		
36	ω	food	uː	u	o͞o	ū̄
		you	uː|u	u|u|ə	o͞o	ū̄|ū̆
	ωr	your	ɔː*|ɔə*|oə*	ur|uə(r	o͞or	ʼʴọ̄r|ʼʴū̆ɹʼʴọ̄ɹ
			uə*|o*|ə*	oə(r|ɔə(r		
				ɚ|ə(r		
37	ie	ice	ai	aɪ	ī	əi
		futile	″	–|ɪ	ĭ|ʼ	″
	ier	shire	aiə*	aɪr|aɪə(r	īr	əiʼʴ
		–shire	iə*|ə*	ɪr|ɚ|ɪə(r	ĭr|ēr	əɹ|iʼʴə
				ə(r		

304

No.	i.t.a.	Example	Daniel Jones	Kenyon and Knott	Webster	Shorter Oxford
38	ou	out	aʊ	aʊ	ou	aʊ
		Dartmouth	ə	ə	ū̃	ŏ̃
	our	our	aʊə*	aʊr|ar	our	auˠʃ
				aʊə(r		
				ɑ:(r		
39	oi	oil	ɔi	ɔɪ	oi	oi
		boy	"	"	"	"
	oir	coir	ɔiə*	ɔɪr|ɔɪɪc(r	oir	oiˠʃ
40	ue	cube	ju:	jʊ|ɪʊ	ū	iū̃
	yω	Matthew	"	jʊ	"	iu
		unite	ju:|ju	"	u̇	yu
		June	u:	u|ɪu	o͞o	u
		lute	u:|ju	" "	ū	ˡū̃
		circular	ju|jə	jə	u̇	iū̃
		ferrule	u:|ju|ə	ə	ū|o͞o	ə
	uer	fury	juər|jɔər	jur|ɪur	ūr	iū̃ˠr
			jʊər|jɔ:r			
		pure	juə*|jɔə*	jur|ɪur	ūr	iū̃ˠʃ
			jɔə*|jɔ:*	ɪuə(r		
				juə(r		
		lure	juə*|uə*	ur	ūr	ˡū̃ˠʃ
			jʊə*|jɔə*	ɪur		
			jɔ:*			
		measure	ə	ɚ|ə(r	ēr	ˡū̃ʃ
	tuer	nature	tʃə*	tʃɚ	tū̇r	tiū̃ʃ
				tʃə(r		tʃū̃r

305

No.	i.t.a	Example	Daniel Jones	Kenyon and Knott	Webster	Shorter Oxford
40 (cont.)	duer	duration	djuər djoər djɔər djɔːr	djur dɪur dur	dŭr	diur
		verdure	dʒə* djə* djuə* djoə*	dʒɚ dʒur dʒə(r dʒuə(r	dŭr	dɪŭɹ dʒəɹ

Table VIII (ii)—Augmented Alphabets
starts on page 308 overleaf

TABLE VIII(ii) AUGMENTED ALPHABETS

Number	i.t.a.	Smith 1568	Hart 1569	Franklin 1768	I. Pitman June 1846 version	Leigh 1866	Bridges 1933	S.S.A. Fonetic Alfabet 1962	Shaw–Malone Unifon 1962
1	p	p	p	p	p	p	p	p	P
2	b	b	b	b	b	b	b	b	B
3	t	t	t	t	t	t,đ	t,tw,ht	t	T
4	d	d	d	d	d	d	d	d	D
5	c,k	k,q,x,x	k	k	c	k,c,q,x	c,k,ch,q,x	k	K
6	g	g	g	g	g	g	g	g	G
7	f	f	f	f	f	f,fh	f,lf	f	F
8	v	▽	v	v	v	v,f	v,f	v	V
9	th	ð	đ	ħ	t	th	th	ħ	Θ
10	th	◿	ƀ	ħ	đ	th	ch	ħ	⊥
11	s	ſ	s	f,s	s	s,c	s,c,sw	s	C
12	z,ƨ	z	s,z	s,z,ſ	z	s,z	z,ʂ	z	Z
13	ſh	ƨ	ʃ	ħ	ʃ	s,sh	sh,si,ʂ,ci,ti	ſ	S
14	ʒ	–	"	z,ħ	ʒ	s	ʂ	ʒ	Ƨ
15	ch	c	Ɠ	tħ	ç	ch	ch	ç	C
16	j	ʓ	ʒ	dħ	j	j,g	j,g	j	J
17	m	m	m	m	m	m	m	m	M
18	n	n	n	n	n	n	n,kn	n	N
19	ŋ	–	ng	ɲ	ŋ	ŋ	ŋ	ŋ	Ͷ
20	l	l	l	l	l	l	l	l	L
21	r,ɾ	r	r	r	r	r,r	r,wr	r	R

Number	i.t.a.	Smith 1568	Hart 1569	Franklin 1768	I. Pitman June 1846 version	Leigh 1866	Bridges 1933	S.S.A. Fonetic Alfabet 1962	Shaw–Malone Unifon 1962
22	h	*h*	ɦ	ɦ	h	h	*h,wh*	h	H
22/23	wh	*hw*	ɦu	ɦu	w	wh	*wh*	hw	–
23	w	*w*	u	u	w	w,ɵ,ɯ,ɯ	*w*	w	W
24	y,i	*i,y*	i,ị	*i*	y	y	*y,i*	y	Y
25	a	*a*	a,ạ,e	*a,e*	a	a,a	*a,ɲ*	a	A
25/26	ɑ	–	–	–	–	a	–	–	–
26	ɑ	–	a	*a,e*	ɑ	ɑ	*a*	ɑ	–
27	e	*e*	e,ẹ,ė	*e,y*	e	e,a	*ɛ,e*	e	E
28	æ	{â,ä,a-, ê,ë,ē,e-}	aẹ,aẹẹ	*êẹ,ee*	ɛ	ɜ,a,e,ɛ	*a,ɠ*	ɐ	Δ
29	i,y	*i,y*	i,ị	*i*	i	i,y,ėu	*i,y,ie*	i	Ⴙ
30	ɛɛ	*ė*	i,ịẹ	*ii,i,ı*	i	ė,ẹ,i	*ɯ,ɪ,ɪ-e*	ɛ	I
31	o	*o*	o,a	*ɑ*	o	o,ɵa	*o-e,o,a*	ɒ	O
32	au	"	ou	*ɑɑ,ɑ*	ɵ	ɐ,a,ɵ	*ɐ*	ɔ	Λ
33	u	*u*	ʋ,u,ʋ	*ʏ*	u	u,u,ɒ	*ʋ,v-e*	ʋ	U
34	œ	*ô,õ,ö,o*	o,ʋ	*o*	ʘ	ʘ,ʘ	*o,ow*	o	Ω
35	ω	*u*	u,ủ	*u*	ɯ	ω,ɵ,ɯ	*u,∞*	u	Φ
36	ω	*ʋ,p,ủ,w̄*	u,ụ	*u*	ɯ	ɯ,ɥ,ɵ	*∞,ʮ*	ɯ	"
37	ie	*ī,ï,i-*	ei	*ʏi*	i̧	i,y	*i̧*	ɑ̇	Ⴤ
38	ou	–	ou	*ɑu*	ɤ	oɥ,oɯ	*av*	ɑu	Ɵ
39	oi	–	oi	*ɑi*	ɵ̇	ʘi,oy	*oi*	ɑ̇i	Ɠ
40	ue	*ẏ*	iu	*iu,eu,u*	ʮ	ɐ,ɐ	*ʮ,ɹɯ,ʮe*	iu	Ʊ,ɰ

TABLE VIII (iii)   DIACRITICAL   ALPHABETS

No.	i.t.a.	Hodges 1644	No.	i.t.a.	Hodges 1644
1	p	p,g̈	22	h	h,ḥ
2	b	b	22/23	wh	wh
3	t	t,ḑ,z̧	23	w	w,ŭ
4	d	d	24	y,i	y,i̧,ȩ
5	c,k	c,k,q̧,x,ĝ	25	a	a,â,i
6	g	g,x̂	25/26	ɑ	–
7	f	f,p̦h,g̦h,û	26	ɑ	a,ȩ
8	v	v,f̦,f̧,p̦h,g̦h	27	e	e,a,ȩ,u̧
9	ʈh	th,g̦h	28	æ	ai,a,ä,ë,ay,ȩi,ey,e
10	ɟh	tḩ,th	29	i,y	i,i̧,i̧ȩ,eȩ,y,êy,o̧,u̧,y
11	s	s,ʃ,č,z̧,x	30	ɛɛ	ê,ee,ë,êy
12	z,ᴢ	z,ş,ʃ,ç,x̂	31	o	o
13	ʃh	ʃh,ʃi,ʃʃi,ci̧,ti,x̧	32	au	â,ó̦
14	ȝ	ʃ,ẑ	33	u	u,o̧,i̧
15	ʤh	ch,ç,ṭ	34	œ	ô, e᷄w
16	j	j,ǧ	35	ω	o̧,ọ̈,oo,u̧
17	m	m	36	ω	e᷄w,o̦o,ô,û
18	n	n,kn,ĝn	37	ie	î,ŷ,ei,ey
19	ŋ	ň	38	ou	ou,ow
20	l	l	39	oi	o̧i,oy,o̧î,o̧ŷ
21	r,ɾ	r,wr	40	ᵾe	û,e᷄w,ieu,eu,ew,eau

No.	i.t.a.	Fry 1964	No.	i.t.a.	Fry 1964
1	p	p, g̊	22	h	h, j̊
2	b	b	22/23	wh	wh
3	t	t, d, z̊	23	w	w, qu, o̊, u̇
4	d	d	24	y, i	y, e̊, i, j̊
5	c, k	c, k, qu, x, g̊	25	a	a, ȧ, i
6	g	g, x̊	25/26	ɑ	–
7	f	f, ph, g̊, u̇	26	ɑ	a, e̊, i̊
8	v	v, f̊, p̊h	27	e	e, å, u, ė
9	th	th, g̊, t	28	æ	ā, ė
10	th	th	29	i, y	i, y, å, ė, u̇
11	s	s, c, z̊	30	ɛɛ	ē, ẙ, å, i
12	z, ʒ	z, s, x̊	31	o	o, ȯ, ä, ė
13	ʃh	sh, c̊, s̊, t̊, x̊	32	au	a, o̊
14	ʒ	z̊, g̊, j̊, s̊, t̊	33	u	u, o̊, u̇
15	ch	ch, c̊, t̊	34	œ	ō, ä, ė
16	j	j, g̊, c̊, d	35	ω	oo, o̊, u̇
17	m	m, n̊	36	ꞷ	oo, u, o̊, ė
18	n	n, m̊	37	ie	i, ȳ
19	ŋ	ng, n̊	38	ou	ow, ou, ů, o̊
20	l	l	39	oi	oi, oy
21	r, r	r̊, , l	40	ue	ū, ė

TABLE VIII (iii) *continued*

WILLIAM BULLOKAR[1]

The extensive variety of Bullokar's characterizations makes it impossible to arrange them in columns as with the other alphabets. In the character "e," for example, not only are there five black-letter variants but also two Caroline variants (shown in the extracts reproduced here), making a total of seven. When marked with accents these seven variants can represent a total of four sounds. Use is also made of doubling the consonant and, finally, each of them can be joined in a ligature with *A*, a, or *a*, to give a digraphic version. Despite their multiplicity all these variants represent no more than those four sounds, their purpose being to achieve not so much a more perfect phonetic relationship as his important objective of "joining perfect conference of the olde use and new together" and to improve upon "Sir Thomas Smithes and Maister Chesters" (Hart, the Chester Herald) whose "workes did take no place, for their figures and letters differed so greatly from the olde writing and printing" and who "left some letters out of use, that in time to come there might appeere two languages for one."

These quotations and the extracts reproduced on the page opposite come from Bullokar's *A Short Introduction or guiding, to print, write, and reade Inglish Speech: conferred with the olde printing and writing*, printed in 1581 by Henrie Denham, London (see also the extract from *Bullokar's Booke at Large*, 1580; *Plate VII*). The extracts are taken from the only extant copy of the second edition (1581), one of the treasures in Isaac Pitman's library. It was Bullokar's personal copy, annotated in his own hand. The mark in the top line of the second section of the upper extract refers to an instruction on the previous page to place the three variant characters resembling *G*, *g*, and *I* (designed exclusively for the sound *juh* which at that date did not possess a discrete character) between *I*, *i*; *y*; and *K*, *k*; in the same order of rote as is employed today.

Finally—from his title page:
>"Euen as printing, to the world brought light:
>"So vnto Inglifh, this, ftarre fhineth bright.
>"And as fpeech was caufe, letters were deuized,
>"So let them not, from right fpeech be difguized."

---

[1] See pages 89–91.

ꜳ.ᷓ c.c.ch.d.e.æ.e.f.g.g.h.i.k.l.l.m.ḿ.n.ń.o.ꝏ.
p.ph.q.r.ŕ.ſ.ſh.t.th.ꞇh.v.y.v́.w.wh.x.y.z.&.ꝶ

ꜳ.a.B.b.C.ć.C.c.Ꜧ.ch.D.d.E.e.æ.E.é.F.f.G.g.G.g. (
I.i.H.h.I.i.y.K.k.L.l.l.M.m.ḿ.N.n.ń.O.o.ꝏ.P.p.
Ꝕ.ph.f.Q.q.R.r.ŕ.S.ſ.s.ʒ.Ꞩ.ſh.ſh.T.t.Ꞇh.th.Ꞇh.ꞇh.ꞇh.
V.v.u.V.y.u.o.ꝏ.ꝏ.V.v.u.W.w.WH.wh.X.x.Y.y.z.z.

Ꞇhe lýk adicionʒ ár vʒed, in this new amendment,
With lýk ſtrykʒ, prikʒ, & nótʒ alſo, with lýk ve of accent,
In wrýtñ hãd, aʒ in the print, no-thing wantiꞇh, but cõſent.

Bullokar's suggestion for handwriting "in the Romaine, Italian and
Chauncerie handes." He showed also "the Secretarie hande." (". . . fower
written hands easie to be followed of all writers")

Queſtion.
What vowelʒ be of ſhoʒt ſound?
Anſwer.

Ꞇhæʒ fiu vowelʒ: a: e, caḽed e, flat and ſhoʒt: i, caḽed
i, ſhoʒt: o: and, y, caḽed fó, y: be of ſhoʒt ſound: alſo y,
caḽed crꝏked, y: u, caḽed minum, u: and, o, caḽed round
o: ꝏ, caḽed dobḽ, ꝏ: and, ꝏ, caḽed, ꝏ, deryuatiu, be of
ſhoʒt ſound: except ón of ꞇhæʒ accentʒ (´) caḽed ſingḽ accent: (^) caḽed foʒked accent: (˝) caḽed dobḽ accent be ſett
ouer: a: e: y: oʒ o: thus: áá́a̋: éé́e̋: ýý́y̋: óó́ő: oʒ
that: a: e: oʒ: y: be dobḽed, thus, aa: ee: yi: oʒ: iy: foʒ
then any of ꞇhóʒ accentʒ, ouer any ſuch ſhoʒt vowel, oʒ the do-
bḽing of ſuch ſhoʒt vowel, cauʒeth the ſám vowel tꝏ be ſounded long, excepting aḽway, that whær any conſonant iʒ dobḽed,
the vowel oʒ dobḽ vowel going next befóʒ, iʒ aḽway of ſhoʒt
ſound: and tꝏ this end cheflý, a conſonant iʒ dobḽed at the end
of a ſillabḽ, yet ſounded aʒ ſingḽ: aʒ of the verb, tꝏ hýd: hýdd,
oʒ hýddñ: of tꝏ ſlýd: ſlýdd, oʒ ſlýddñ: of tꝏ být: býttñ: And
if: ea: e: oʒ æ, be the next vowel oʒ dipꞇhꝏng befóʒ ſuch dobḽ
conſo-

His Maximilian (black) letter type in which his text was printed. This
lower extract is from page 4 of *A Short Introduction* . . .

TABLE VIII (iv) DIGRAPHIC ALPHABETS

Number	i.t.a.	Ellis (Glossic) 1870	I. Pitman 1897	Zachrisson (Anglic) 1932	Follick 1934	Simplified Spelling Society U.K. 1938	New Spelling (U.S. and U.K.) 1955	Laubach 1966	World English Spelling USA 1968
1	p	p	p	p	p	p	p	p	p
2	b	b	b	b	b	b	b	b	b
3	t	t	t	t	t	t	t	t	t
4	ḍ	d	d	d	d,t	d	d	d	d
5	c,k	k	k	k,x,qu	c,k	k	k	c,k,ck,x,q	k
6	g	g	g	g	g	g	g	g	g
7	f	f	f	f	f	f	f	f,ph	f
8	v	v	v	v	v	v	v	v	v
9	ţh	th	th	th	th	th	th	tth	thh
10	ţħ	dh	th	dh	dh	dh	dh	th	th
11	s	s	s	s	s	s	s	s	s
12	z,ℨ	z	z	z	z	z	z	z	z
13	ʃh	sh	sh	sh	sh	sh	sh	sh	sh
14	ʒ	zh	zh	zh	zh	zh	zh	zh	zh
15	ȼh	ch	ch	ch	tsh	ch	ch	ch	ch
16	j	j	j	j	j	j	j	j	j
17	m	m	m	m	m	m	m	m	m
18	n	n	n	n	n	n	n	n	n
19	ŋ	ng	ng,n	ng,n	ng	ng,n	ng,n	ng	ng,n
20	l	l	l	l	l	l	l	l	l
21	r,ɾ	r,'r	r	r	r	r	r	r	r

Number	i.t.a.	Ellis (Glossic) 1870	I. Pitman 1897	Zachrisson (Anglic) 1932	Follick 1934	Simplified Spelling Society U.K. 1938	New Spelling (U.S. and U.K.) 1955	Laubach 1966	World English Spelling USA 1968
22	h	h	h	h	h	h	h	h	h
22/23	wh	wh	wh	wh	hu	wh	wh	wh	wh
23	w	w	w	w	w	w	w	w	w
24	y,i	y	y	y	_i	y	y	y	y
25	a	a	a	a	a	a	a	a	a
25/26	ɑ	aa	aa,a	aa	a	aa,a	aa,a	a	aa,a
26	ɑ	aa	a,aa	aa,a	aa	aa,a	aa,a	aa,ah,a	aa,a
27	e	e	e	e	e	e	e	e	e
28	æ	ai	a,ai,ay	ae,a	ei	ae,a	ae	ā,ae,ai,ay,a-e,a	ae
29	i,y	i	i	i	i	i,y	i	i,y	i
30	ϵϵ	ee	e,ee	ee,e	ie	ee,e	ee	ē,ee,ey,e-e,ea	ee
31	o	o	o	o		o	o	aa,o,ōu,ōo,o-e	o
32	au	au	au,aw,o	au	oa	au	au	aw,au,ong	au
33	u	u	u	u		u	u	u	u
34	œ	oa	o,oa	oe,o	ou	oe,o	oe	o,oe,oa,ōw,o-e	oe
35	ω	uo	u	oo	uu	oo	oo	uu	uu
36	ω	oo	oo,ú	uu	"	uu,u	uu	oo,ww,w	oo
37	ie	ei	ei	ie,i	ai	ie,i	ie	ī,ie,ȳ,igh,i-e	ie
38	ou	ou	ou,ow	ou	au	ou	ou	ow,ou	ou
39	oi	oi	oi,oy	oi	oi	oi	oi	oi,oy	oi
40	ue	eu	iu,yu	ue,u	iu	ue	ue	ū,ue,ew,yoo,u-e	ue

TABLE VIII(iv) *continued*

DR. AXEL WIJK'S REGULARIZED ENGLISH[1]

This system appears to be aimed primarily at someone who is able to speak English but is ignorant of its spelling. It is remarkable for the number of alternative sounds catered for by a given character as well as for the number of rules that govern the sounds it represents. Much depends on a character's position in relation to the characters on either side of it: for instance in *cat, cent, cello, check, ocean, chalet*, and *scene* the sounds represented by the character *c* vary widely: thus *ce* represents no less than three sounds in *cent, cello, ocean*, and is mute in *scene;* at the same time not only does *cc* represent a variety of sounds in *occur* and in *accent*, but the spelling of *soccer* is regarded as such an intolerable irregularity that it needs to be changed to *socker*, in order that it may conform to the new rules and become "regularized." His rules require the re-spelling of *suggest* as *sugest* because the *gg* preceding *e* would indicate the hard *g* as in *nugget*. But this is different from the change of *soccer* to *socker* in relation to *accent*, although the circumstances are the same—and although it will be seen that no effort is made to retain the basic principle (with *e* following *g*) in differentiating the spelling of *gelatine* from that of *gelding*.

Dr. Wijk's rules occupy over 100 pages of a 361-page book—*An Investigation in the English Spelling Reform Problem with a new detailed plan for a possible solution* (Almquist and Wiksell, Stockholm, 1959). Rather than attempt to list his rules (his own "summary" takes up ten pages) I have tried to tabulate their effect upon an (incomplete) selection of well-known English words, set out in the order of phonemes as in the other tables. In *round* brackets will be found other words in which the same character, even in an identical series of characters, represents a different sound. Square brackets identify words that may be dubious.

It would seem that the true purpose of the multiplicity of rules is to conserve as much as possible of our present orthography for reading rather than to reduce the load upon the memory. In fact, Dr Wijk limits his changes to only the 10 per cent of words which he judges to be now so misleadingly spelled that they cannot be tolerated.

3   t   –   *t*ake, bak*e*d, (wic*k*ed)
4   d   –   *d*og, dol*e*d, (knowle*d*ge) (*editor*)
5   k   –   *c*at, ba*c*k, ac*c*ount, (ac*c*ent), *k*ing, e*x*tra, (e*x*alt)
6   g   –   *g*ain, *gu*arantee, e*x*amine, (e*x*change)

[1] See pages 48 and 101.

9	þh –	*th*in, (*th*ine)
10	ħh –	*th*an, (*th*ank), ba*the*, (ma*th*ematics), faa*dh*er
11	s –	*s*ay, *sc*ene, (*sc*ratch), chint*se*, (po*se*), cha*s*ten, (pla*s*tic), *c*ell, (*c*ello), a*x*e, (an*x*ious)
12	z –	*z*eal, di*ss*olve, (pa*ss*ion, mi*ss*), ladie*s*
13	ʃh –	o*ce*an, (*ce*aseless), *ch*alet, (*ch*at), suspi*ci*on, (*ci*rcular), pa*ss*ion (pa*ss*ing), bi*sh*op, (mi*sh*ap), educa*ti*on, (o*ti*ose), musi*ci*an, *su*gar, (*su*rrender) (ab*s*urd)
14	ʒ –	gara*ge*, (a*ge*), *j*abot, (*j*ab), a*z*ure, (a*z*imuth), deri*si*on, abscis*si*on, (permis*si*ve), equa*ti*on, (na*ti*on, ha*t*ing), lin*ger*ie, (*G*ertrude, *g*erm)
15	ʧh –	*ch*eck, (*sch*ool, *ch*alet), cat*ch*
16	j –	*j*am, *g*elatine, (*g*elding), ba*dge*, fi*dg*et, *d*anger, (*d*anger),
18	n –	*n*o, *kn*ow, *gn*at, (a*gn*ostic)
19	ŋ –	le*ng*th, (i*ng*ress), li*nk*
21	r –	*r*ight, *Rh*ine, io*r*n, (re-spelling i*r*on)
23	w –	*w*ait, *wr*eck, g*u*ano
24	y –	*y*et, span*i*el, (n*i*ece)
25	a –	*a*rid, (c*a*r, p*a*rent)
26	ɑ –	faa*dh*er, c*a*r, (*a*rid, p*a*rent)
27	e –	v*e*ry, (*e*rth)
28	æ –	f*a*ce, p*a*per, (*pap*), m*ai*d, *ai*led, str*aigh*t gr*ei*t, *eigh*tth (sic), gr*ey*, gr*ey*ed ball*et*, *ae*rial
29	i –	g*i*v, (h*i*ving), pract*i*ce, lad*ie*s, (d*ie*s), m*y*th, (m*y*), surf*a*ce, (*a*cetone), vall*ey*, theory
30	ee –	*se*cret, (*se*cure), the*ze*, *se*e, n*ee*dle m*ea*t, (cr*ea*te), br*ie*f, (den*ie*d), bel*ie*ve, alb*i*no, (b*i*n)
31	o –	dr*o*p, s*o*lve, qu*o*rrel, f*o*rti, f*o*arteen, bur*eau*cracy
32	au–	w*au*ked, c*au*ze, l*aw*, (*aw*ay), h*aw*se, c*augh*t
34	œ –	g*o*, (g*o*t), h*o*me, t*oe*, *oa*k, bur*eau*
35	ω –	p*oo*ll, [p*u*ll], t*o*
36	ꙍ–	r*u*by, (r*u*b), r*u*le, (d*u*ly), p*oo*l, sn*oo*ze
37	ie –	f*i*nd, (*i*ndex), l*ie*, (lil*ie*s) m*y*, (mum*my*), d*ye*, *y*le, [*ai*sle], h*igh*, sl*ygh*t
38	ou–	*ou*t, n*ow*, pl*ough*, pl*ough*ed
39	oi –	*oi*l, t*oy*, b*oye*, [b*uoy*]
40	ue-	d*u*ly, (*J*uly), t*u*be, (r*u*de), s*ue*, (purs*ue*r)

317

TABLE VIII (v) NON-ROMANIC ALPHABETS

Number	i.t.a.	I. Pitman 1843	Deseret (Mormon) 1855	Bell 1870	Jones and Passy 1907	Kingsley Read (G.B. Shaw) 1962	Number	i.t.a.	I. Pitman 1843	Deseret (Mormon) 1855	Bell 1870	Jones and Passy 1907	Kingsley Read (G.B. Shaw) 1962
1	p						22	h					
2	b						22/23	wh					
3	t						23	w					
4	ḍ						24	y,i					
5	c,k						25	a					
6	g						25/26	ə					
7	f						26	ɑ					
8	v						27	e					
9	th						28	æ					
10	ŧh						29	i,y					
11	s						30	ɛɛ					
12	z,ʒ						31	o					
13	ʃh						32	au					
14	3						33	u					
15	ch						34	œ					
16	j						35	ω					
17	m						36	ω					
18	n						37	ie					
19	ŋ						38	ou					
20	l						39	oi					
21	r,ʀ						40	ue					

318

APPENDIX III

i.t.a. Research in the United States

Compiled by Dr. H. J. TANYZER, i.t.a.
Research Center, and Dr. J. R. BLOCK,
i.t.a. Foundation of Hofstra University,
New York

BEFORE i.t.a. RESEARCH in the United States can be discussed, it is necessary to review some important differences between reading instruction practices in the United States and in the United Kingdom. In the United States, reading usually is not formally taught to children until they are at least six years of age. At this point, they enter the first grade of what is called "elementary" school. Prior to this, almost all of them have spent a year in kindergarten. Here the curriculum usually involves developing readiness for reading through a relatively informal program which stresses experiences and activities of a linguistic, perceptual, and conceptual nature. As a result, the age for beginning reading in the United States is usually delayed until the child is a year older than he would be if he were attending school in the United Kingdom. Partly because the child is older, the use of i.t.a. in the United States has taken on a somewhat different character from that generally encountered in the United Kingdom. For the most part, the majority of schools experimenting with i.t.a. in England have been using traditional basal readers, such as the JANET AND JOHN reading scheme, transliterated into the new medium. As such, the instructional material in i.t.a. is considered to be almost identical in content, structure, and methodology to that used in the teaching of reading with our conventional alphabet. The fact that the British i.t.a. studies demonstrated that children instructed in this medium learn to read more easily than those who have been taught to read in the orthodox alphabet encouraged American educators to initiate their own projects. The approach toward teaching reading with the i.t.a. medium, however, has taken on a quite different character in the United States. The vast majority of American children in the i.t.a. classrooms are being taught to read with instructional materials specifically developed to take advantage of

319

certain properties of the new medium. The materials most frequently used are the *Early-to-Read* i/t/a series, published by i/t/a Publications, Inc., of New York, although other i.t.a. materials have been developed in the United States.[1] This is a basal reading scheme constructed quite differently from those generally employing traditional orthography. In an attempt to exploit the advantages of i.t.a.'s phonemic regularity, the authors of the *Early-to-Read* series introduce a significantly greater number of words than is customarily introduced in more conventional series. They also considerably increase the rate of introduction of new words to running words so that vocabulary control is significantly less restrictive and the frequency of word repetitions is reduced sharply. Teachers' manuals recommend an instructional approach which emphasizes a language-experience procedure and an earlier and more intensive teaching of word recognition and word analysis skills than is commonly taught in beginning T.O. basal reader series in the United States. The accelerated word analysis program of the *Early-to-Read* series stresses character-sound associations and the structural characteristics of words. In addition, writing is used as an aid to developing word analysis skills and a means through which the child can communicate and express his ideas in written composition. Finally, to capitalize on the new medium and take advantage of the accelerated pace of the instructional approach, the selections in the readers are considerably more mature in content and interest level and of a higher level of reading difficulty than those appearing in most basal readers; and, hence, approximate more nearly to the intellectual and comprehension capabilities of the children being taught.

The essential difference, then, between the most common approach being used to teach reading with i.t.a. in the United States and that being used in England is with respect to the content and methodology employed in the instructional material. In England, the methodological approach is eclectic, using both "look-say" and phonic approaches, which is essentially the same procedure used in a typical T.O. series. Phonic skills are introduced at later levels and at a relatively slower pace of presentation than in the American approach, and greater control is exercised over the language factor with the word count significantly lower and the frequency of word repetitions considerably higher. The other important difference to be considered is the age at which formal reading instruction begins.

The question of which approach or combination of approaches is most effective for teaching reading to a particular type of child has not been systematically investigated thus far. The fact that i.t.a. has been shown to work successfully with different teaching practices and methodologies is consistent with Sir James Pitman's original contention that all accepted methods and procedures of teaching reading can be used effectively and in conjunction with the new medium. It is to be hoped that investigators interested in i.t.a. will study the relative effectiveness of different approaches to teaching reading and writing with i.t.a. to deter-

[1] The i.t.a. Foundation at Hofstra University, Hempstead, N.Y. 11550, publishes a complete catalog of all i.t.a. materials available in the United States, Great Britain and Canada. The catalog is arranged alphabetically by publishers.

mine the relative strengths and weaknesses of each with children differing in levels of intelligence, experiential and socio-economic backgrounds, interests, and linguistic capability.

Development of i.t.a. in the United States

The Initial Teaching Alphabet appeared as a formal approach to reading in American public schools (state schools) in the fall of 1963. Its first large-scale use was in Bethlehem, Pennsylvania, in a study of its effectiveness sponsored by the Ford Foundation. This investigation was not designed to be a copy of the research in Great Britain. The aim of the study was to compare the achievement of approximately 400 children using the *Early-to-Read* series with a control group using one or more of the popular basal reader series available in traditional orthography.

By the fall of 1966, i.t.a. had grown from these small beginnings to the point where it was being used in almost every state in the United States. Further, it was being used in applications as widely varied (perhaps even more widely varied) as those in the United Kingdom. For example, within these three years, the American use of i.t.a. involved the remedial student (backward reader), the adult illiterate, the deaf, the mentally retarded, the emotionally disturbed, the dyslexic child, the culturally disadvantaged, the non-English speaking as well as normal children for initial teaching purposes. Indeed, it was also being used to teach literate adults the properties of English poetry.

While the geographical spread of i.t.a. in the United States is virtually complete, it is found most frequently in suburban areas known for their support of educational innovations, and for the support of education generally. These are almost invariably "high support" centers providing a per pupil expenditure significantly greater than the United States average. This should not be construed, however, to mean that it is not being extensively used with "deprived" children. In most cases, the usual pattern of adoption of i.t.a. is for a school system to initiate a "pilot" class and then (depending upon the success of the program) to increase it. At present, there are a score of United States cities scattered throughout the country that use i.t.a. exclusively to teach beginning reading, including the original starting city, Bethlehem, Pennsylvania, and school systems in communities in Pennyslvania, New York, New Jersey, Minnesota, Missouri, Wisconsin, Kentucky, and California. By 1968, i.t.a. had become well known not only to professional educators, but to the general public as well.

It is possible that the wide-spread interest and use of i.t.a. and its rapid dissemination with its unique approach in the United States is due to the surge of national interest in education generally. Coincident with this great interest in education, the curricular changes that America has learned to call "post Sputnik," there has been a great influx of funds from federal programs, and to a lesser extent from private foundations, making educational innovation generally easier to accomplish.

Despite the great interest in i.t.a. and its remarkable dissemination, it should

321

be pointed out that traditional basal readers, similar to the British JANET AND JOHN reading scheme, are predominantly used in the vast majority of reading programs in the United States. Most children learning to read in the United States are still taught to read with the orthodox alphabet and in conventional materials, with ten per cent or less using i.t.a. or other innovative approaches. Despite this, the impact of i.t.a. has been extraordinary. At this time, it may be the most widely used, most intensively and heatedly discussed and researched innovation in reading in the recent history of education in the United States.

i.t.a. Research in the United States

As noted earlier, the studies of the effectiveness of i.t.a. in the United States have taken on a very different character from those in England. Studies conducted in Great Britain have attempted to vary only the alphabet while holding materials and methods constant. Implicitly, it appears that American investigators have accepted, more or less, the validity of these studies and have elected to pursue more complex issues. Exceptions to this are the work of Dr. Helen Robinson, at the University of Chicago, and a study by Dr. Miriam Goldberg, of Teachers College, Columbia University, in New York. Dr. Robinson is attempting to replicate the United Kingdom studies using a transliterated basal reader series compared with the same series in T.O. Dr. Goldberg's three-year project is an evaluation of various approaches to beginning reading for disadvantaged children. Three of the programs to be tested use the i.t.a. medium. One aspect of the New York City study is to determine the relative effectiveness of an urban oriented T.O. basal series, relevant to the experiences of children, compared with the same series in the i.t.a. medium (Goldberg, 1966). Both studies are currently in progress, and, at the time of writing, there has been no published report of results. Virtually all of the studies in the United States have attempted to evaluate the effectiveness of complex reading packages differing simultaneously in alphabet, method, and content.

As is true for most research in education in general, i.t.a. studies in the United States have tended to suffer from several methodological weaknesses. Block (1966) has presented an extensive critique of research in i.t.a. elsewhere. At least two of the most critical points he makes may be discussed here. First, most studies have tended to use standardized measures of reading achievement, raising serious problems for the adequate evaluation of i.t.a. Second, most studies have been limited to one academic year.

With regard to the first point, Block notes that most standardized measures of reading achievement have been constructed within the framework of the assumptions made when existing basal reader series are used to teach reading. Thus, such measures may be totally inappropriate for use with the new medium of instruction making widely different assumptions. Further, he points out that most of the sub-tests of these instruments are highly intercorrelated. As a result, they do not provide independent evaluation of various dimensions of a child's reading ability. Thus, if the study suggests no significant difference between the experimental and control groups, it will tend to appear that there is absolutely no effect. Conversely, if the i.t.a. group scores significantly higher, it will appear to be effective for all aspects of reading.

With regard to the one-year duration of the study, it has been suggested by some investigators that results favoring i.t.a. may be a function of the well-known Hawthorne effect. Many investigators in the United States have attempted to control for this problem, using a wide range of techniques. How successful they have been cannot be determined. Other investigators have pointed out that the newness of the approach may put teachers at a disadvantage resulting from a general lack of experience and general confidence with the medium. Eichel (1966), for example, notes that "it was observed that occasionally unnecessary time was spent on some of the workbook pages, even though it was evident that the children did not need the additional practice provided by these pages." Thus, it would appear that a one-year study would exert a complex influence on teachers, on the one hand making i.t.a. appear more effective than it really was, and, on the other hand, obscuring successful aspects.

More important perhaps is the question of the level of reading proficiency achieved by children instructed in the i.t.a. at the end of one year. While many investigators have failed to report the percentage of children having made the transition to T.O. at the conclusion of a one-year period, the average seems to be approximately 50 per cent. At this point in time, evaluation instruments are conventionally administered in traditional orthography since this is the ultimate goal of most studies. Parenthetically, it may be noted that in almost every study, when children are tested in the medium in which they were initially instructed (i.e., i.t.a. or T.O.) the i.t.a.-taught children show a marked superiority in reading over the T.O. control. Despite the fact that many children are tested in the medium with which they have not been instructed, it can be generalized that no study suggests the children taught with traditional orthography perform at a significantly higher level than children taught with the Initial Teaching Alphabet on most measures of reading ability. The contrary, in fact, seems to be the case. Most studies seem to show an advantage for the i.t.a. group over the T.O. controls, even though a sizeable percentage have not completed the transition at the end of one year.

The issue of the one-year's duration raises still another point with regard to research methodology, i.e., the definition of "transition" implied by most investigators is that children have completed all of the existing books in a particular i.t.a. series. In no case are data presented concerning the amount of experience children have had of reading in traditional orthography as of this particular point in time if they have made the transition. Further, investigators seldom indicate the extent to which transition may have been "forced" by a teacher who believed her class *should* make the transition by the end of first grade. Finally, complete transition obviously would involve not only the passive activity of reading, but also of spelling and writing in traditional orthography as well. These issues are seldom dealt with in i.t.a. studies on either side of the Atlantic.

Despite these and other methodological shortcomings (most typical and unavoidable in educational research in general), several generalizations may be made. The most important of these is that *the majority of i.t.a. studies conducted in America indicate that children in the i.t.a. classes perform at a higher level than those in the control group, and that no study thus far has shown the i.t.a. children to be generally inferior to the control populations.* Studies which have reported positive results include Alden and Manning (1965); Bosma and Farrow (1965); Canfield (1967); Clark (1966); Dunn, Mueller, and Neely (1966); Henning and Hayenga (1967); Jameson (1965); Kidd and Horn (1967), Kirkland (1966); Mazurkiewicz (1964); Monson (1967); Montesi (1965, 1966); Myers (1965); Regan (1965); Shapiro (1966); Sloan (1966); Stewart (1965); and Wapner (1967). Studies which show no significant difference between i.t.a. and control groups using standardized reading measures at the end of the first year include Chasnoff (1967); Eichel (1966); Hahn (1966); Mountain (1966); Nemeth and Hayes (1966); Tanyzer and Alpert (1965); and Tanyzer, Alpert, and Sandel (1965). Although there are seldom objective measures, most investigators report an unusually high degree of acceptance of i.t.a. on the part of teachers, administrators, and parents. Subjective impressions of experienced teachers usually indicate a marked superiority of the i.t.a.-taught children over the T.O. controls. This superiority appears not only in formal reading situations, but perhaps more importantly in children's behavior and attitude in class in general.

In addition to this generalization, however, it is important to discuss several major issues in i.t.a. research conducted in America which tend to be controversial. The first of these deals with spelling in traditional orthography for i.t.a.-taught children. Studies conducted in the United States tend to show that at the conclusion of the first year of instruction, the i.t.a. group spelling scores (including a large percentage of children who have not completed the transition to T.O.) are significantly lower when standardized measures of spelling achievement are used. These studies include Fry (1966); Hahn (1966); Mazurkiewicz (1966); Tanyzer and Alpert (1965); and Tanyzer, Alpert, and Sandel (1965). On the other hand, Shapiro (1966) reports no significant difference in spelling between the i.t.a. and control groups at the end of the first year, while Jameson (1965); Montesi (1965); and Stewart (1966) all indicate that children in the i.t.a. group score significantly higher in spelling achievement than the T.O. control group after one year of instruction. The advantage of the i.t.a. children shows up most clearly when spelling is evaluated through the use of children's writing rather than through the use of standardized measures of spelling achievement based upon existing curricula. These studies include those by Jameson, Montesi, and Stewart cited above, although it should be noted that Stewart's study also included measures of spelling achievement using a standardized instrument.

Another interesting and controversial issue deals with the extent to which children in i.t.a. groups write more effectively than children in a T.O. control group. Few, if any, effective measures of children's writing ability are available in the United States. Nonetheless, Fry (1966) has noted that children in the i.t.a. groups write longer stories than their T.O. controls, and Stewart (1966) and Montesi (1965) both report that children in i.t.a. groups write more effectively than children in the control groups. Most of these studies tend to use simple measures such as number of words, number of different words, number of polysyllabic words, etc. Fry has cautioned that instruction in writing has not been controlled in most i.t.a. studies.

The transition process is another highly controversial issue and an area in which relatively little controlled and systematic research has been conducted. One exception is an unpublished study by Tanyzer, Alpert, and Sandel (1967) which investigated the effect of transition upon the child's reading level in the orthodox alphabet: (1) to determine whether children maintain their i.t.a. reading skill in the traditional alphabet when transition is made—whether there is a loss in reading proficiency, and if so, is the loss negligible or serious; (2) to determine whether differences in the time at which transition is made produce any differences in reading level in i.t.a. and in traditional orthography; (3) to evaluate the effect of intelligence upon the ease or difficulty of transition in order to determine whether the transition is more difficult for children of low intelligence or high I.Q. children. Transition was defined by the investigators as the point at which the child completed the *Early-to-Read* i/t/a series and was no longer being instructed in the i.t.a. medium in the classroom. Equivalent forms of the Stanford Achievement Test, one printed in the traditional alphabet and the other transliterated into i.t.a., were administered at the time of transition to a sample of 104 children.

To facilitate analyses of the data, three points of transition were utilized: (i) the group which made the transition during the period May to June of the first year, approximately eight to nine months after the start of the instructional program; (ii) the period from October to November of the second year; and (iii) those children who were last to make the transition, during the period from January through March of the second year.

Results of the study of transition show that for each of the groups making transition at a different time and for the total sample, there were virtually no differences of statistical significance or practical significance between i.t.a. and T.O. performances of children in the areas of word recognition, comprehension and spelling ability. This was true regardless of the time at which transition occurred or whether the children had high I.Q.s (greater than 100) or low I.Q.s (less than or equal to 100). Exceptions to these results were noted in the November–December transition group in which the sample was extremely small (N=16). There was statistical significance and practical significance in comprehension and in spelling with the T.O. level being higher than the i.t.a. level for this group and for the high I.Q. children (N=9); for the November–December low I.Q. group (N=7) there was a significant difference in comprehension with the T.O. level being higher.

In the area of word analysis, there were significant differences between the i.t.a. and T.O. levels, with the i.t.a. performance consistently higher—in most instances by an average of approximately one grade level or one year—for the total transition sample and for each of the transition groups, except for two very small sub-samples, each with an N of seven. This was true regardless of

I.Q. level—high I.Q. or low I.Q. This finding suggests that the i.t.a. medium is easier than the orthodox alphabet for learning to decode. For the low and high I.Q. groups, there was no significant difference between their i.t.a. levels in word analysis, but there was a significant difference in their word analysis levels in T.O., with the high I.Q. group attaining a higher level. This is further verification of the ease and consistency of the i.t.a. medium. In the i.t.a. medium, intelligence does not seem to be a crucial factor in developing skill in word analysis; but in T.O., the higher I.Q. children are better able to deal with the inconsistencies of traditional orthography than are the low I.Q. children. Disregarding the time at which transition occurred, comparisons between the levels attained in i.t.a. and in T.O. for the high I.Q. children and low I.Q. children indicate no significant differences in the areas of word recognition, comprehension, and spelling. In other words, when children complete *Book 7* of the *Early-to-Read* series and are no longer instructed in the i.t.a. medium, children of low I.Q.s attain the same level of reading proficiency both in i.t.a. and in T.O. as that attained by children of high intelligence, but at a later time. It should be noted that in the high I.Q. group, 45 of the 61 children made the transition during the first year in which they were instructed in i.t.a., whereas only 18 of the 43 children in the low I.Q. group made the transition within the first year with results equal to that achieved by children who did not make the transition until the second year, and that 16 high I.Q. children did not make the transition until the second year. These results suggest that factors other than intelligence were influencing progress in learning to read.

To summarize these results, it would appear that children generally maintain their reading i.t.a. skill in the orthodox alphabet when transition occurs, and that there is no loss, or relatively little loss of practical significance, in word recognition, comprehension, and spelling. Also, regardless of the time at which transition is made or level of intelligence, children generally attain a comparable reading level in both i.t.a. and T.O., although the time of transition is generally later for the low I.Q. children. Only in the area of word analysis is the i.t.a. level generally higher than the T.O. level regardless of the intelligence level or time at which transition occurs. This further testifies to the phonemic consistency of the i.t.a. medium and the ease with which the child can learn to read by it.

Another important issue in i.t.a. research in America deals with the effectiveness of this medium with children who are of below average ability. While little research has been completed thus far, Dunn, Mueller, and Neely (1965) indicate that Negro children from disadvantaged backgrounds perform significantly better when i.t.a. is used, as compared with T.O. Hayes (1966) noted that, "For the low I.Q. third, the i.t.a. score was generally highest in both silent and oral achievement." Tanyzer and Alpert (1965) analyzed data by I.Q. level and found no significant difference in favour of low I.Q. children in i.t.a., as compared with one T.O. low I.Q. treatment group; but a difference was observed in favour of the low I.Q. i.t.a. group when compared to another T.O. control of low intelligence.

Although i.t.a. is relatively newer in America than in England, a limited number of two-year studies have been conducted. These include Montesi (1966); Stewart (1965); and Tanyzer, Alpert, and Sandel (1966). These studies tend to be generally more favorable with regard to i.t.a. than the one-year studies. Tanyzer, Alpert, and Sandel investigated the longitudinal effects of i.t.a. and T.O. on the reading and spelling achievement of approximately 1,900 children, differing in levels of intelligence and living in suburban communities adjacent to New York City, who were introduced to formal reading instruction at a kindergarten level or first grade in i.t.a. or T.O. At the end of two years of the study, the following results were reported: (1) i.t.a. is an easier and more effective medium for developing word recognition and analysis skills regardless of whether reading is initiated in kindergarten or grade one; (2) comprehension does not appear to be affected by the medium of instruction, as no significant differences were found in comprehension; (3) at the end of grade one, i.t.a.-taught children are poorer in spelling ability regardless of when reading instruction is introduced in kindergarten or first grade; (4) at the conclusion of second grade, the i.t.a. group that was initially taught to read in first grade was significantly better in spelling than the T.O. group that began reading instruction in first grade; (5) in comparing children who began i.t.a. in kindergarten with those who were not formally instructed in reading i.t.a. until first grade, both groups did equally well in reading and spelling achievement when tested at the end of first grade. Somewhat similar results were found in comparing the T.O. groups with and without kindergarten reading instruction, with neither group significantly better than the other in reading and spelling ability. Regarding the formal teaching of reading at the kindergarten level, the investigators concluded that the data did not warrant such a practice with all children, "and that the present practice of initiating formal reading instruction at first grade is preferred."

Stewart (1965) has reported a study using over 1,300 children in the Bethlehem, Pennsylvania, area. At the end of two years of instruction with i.t.a., teachers were asked to determine the instructional levels of the pupils in their group. She reported that over 26 per cent of the i.t.a. group were reading in T.O. at a reader level rated as 3–2 or higher while no children in the control group were reading at that level. Using the California Reading Test, no significant differences were obtained either for Vocabulary or Comprehension measures for the total group, but the i.t.a. groups scored significantly higher on the Spelling sub-test of the Stanford Achievement Test. Since the i.t.a. group was reported to have had a higher proportion of lower socio-economic status children, matched groups of 196 children were used for further analysis. These groups were matched to within one point in terms of I.Q. and also matched with regard to sex and socio-economic status. When the matched groups of 196 children were studied, the i.t.a. group scored significantly higher on the Vocabulary sub-test of the California Reading Test. No significant difference was found using the Comprehension sub-test. The i.t.a. children in the matched group comparisons continued to score significantly higher on the Spelling sub-test of the Stanford Achievement Test.

In addition to these results, Stewart obtained writing samples from 144 children in the matched pairs group. The writing samples were analyzed according to a number of criteria. The i.t.a. children received higher scores in terms of number of running words, number of polysyllabic words, and spelling (when judged by T.O. standards). The T.O. group scored significantly higher on a measure of the ability to use capitals. There was no difference in the two groups in the use of correct punctuation.

In addition to these relatively objective data, Stewart reports, "i.t.a. . . . provided a learning environment which made observable differences in reading achievement; in independent learning; in motivation; in perseverance; in the ability to observe; and, in the ability to write."

In another investigation, Montesi (1966) studied 242 children living in Simsbury, Connecticut. Children in the i.t.a. and control groups were matched according to age, I.Q., and reading readiness. At the end of the second grade, children taught with i.t.a. were found to have scored significantly higher on the Stanford Achievement Test sub-tests of Word Meaning, Word Study Skills and Spelling. No significant difference was found between the two groups on the Paragraph Meaning sub-test.

Although research with i.t.a. has had a relatively short history, it has, in a brief period of six years, stimulated considerable enthusiasm and interest in education circles and generated a phenomenal amount of research on both sides of the Atlantic. Thus far, the majority of studies have been comparative investigations to determine the differential effects of teaching reading by the Roman alphabet and the new augmented alphabet. Since i.t.a. was originally designed as a medium for simplifying the decoding act involved in learning to read, there was a need to test the hypotheses of whether or not it was an easier medium than traditional orthography and whether children could successfully transfer their i.t.a. reading skill to T.O. Also, since reading is generally acknowledged as the most important school subject (as witnessed by the fact that more time is spent in the primary grades on the teaching of reading than any other subject), and because reading achievement can be objectively measured, there may have been other reasons why investigators have concentrated their attention on reading. Up to the present time, there are no studies evaluating the attitudinal and psychological effects of an i.t.a. programme. There is a need for investigators to determine adequately what effects i.t.a. has on a child's taste and interest in literature and enjoyment of reading. Also, what effects does i.t.a. have on the young learner's self-concept and attitudes toward himself as a result of learning in a more consistent and reliable medium. Is he more highly motivated? Does he develop greater self-confidence? These are difficult areas to evaluate adequately because of the inadequacy of our present instrumentation and the complexity of the factors involved. It is hoped that in the future, researchers of i.t.a. will begin to address themselves to investigating these thorny problems. The greatest contribution of i.t.a. may eventually prove to be not so much in its effectiveness as an easier and more rational learning and teaching medium, but instead in the positive psychological and motivational effects it may have on the learner's personality and behavior.

i.t.a. Research in the United States

REFERENCES

ALDEN, C. E. & MANNING, R. *The use of the initial teaching alphabet in reading instruction—a report on the pilot study conducted at Broadway School during the school year 1964-1965.* Unpublished manuscript, Maple Heights, Ohio, 1965.

BLOCK, J. R. "A critique of research with the initial teaching alphabet and some recommendations." *The i.t.a. Foundation Report*, Vol. 1, Nos. 2 & 3 (Combined Issue), Summer-Fall 1966, pp. 32-42.

BOSMA, R. L. & FARROW, V. L. "Teaching Reading with i.t.a.: A Research Report." *Reading Horizons*, 6, 1, 6-19, Fall 1965.

CANFIELD, Robert. *An experimental study of the effectiveness of the use of the augmented Roman alphabet (i.t.a.) on the reading development of beginning readers.* Unpublished manuscript, State University College at Oswego, New York, 1967.

CHASNOFF, R. E. "Two alphabets." *Elem. School Journal*, Vol. 67, February 1967, pp. 257-264.

CLARK, G. E., Jr. "An adult basic education program." In A. J. Mazurkiewicz (Ed.), *i.t.a. and the World of English.* Hempstead, N.Y.: i.t.a. Foundation, 1966.

DUNN, L. M., MUELLER, M. W. & NEELY, M. D. "An Interim Report on the Efficacy of the Initial Teaching Alphabet and the Peabody Language Development Kit with Grade One Disadvantaged Children." In A. J. Mazurkiewicz (Ed.), *i.t.a. and the World of English*, Hempstead, N.Y., i.t.a. Foundation, 1966, pp. 91-100.

EICHEL, A. J. *A study of the effect of the initial teaching alphabet on reading achievement.* Unpublished doctoral dissertation, New York University, 1966.

FRY, E. B. "Comparing the diacritical marking system, ITA, and a basal reading series." *Elementary English*, Vol. XLIII, pp. 6, 607-611, 1966.

GOLDBERG, Miriam L. *The effects of various approaches to beginning reading for disadvantaged children.* Teachers College, Columbia University, New York (Unpublished proposal), February 1966.

HAHN, H. T. "Three Approaches to Teaching Reading in Grade One." In A. J. Mazurkiewicz (Ed.), *i.t.a. and the World of English*, Hempstead, N.Y., i.t.a. Foundation, 1966, pp. 268-272.

HENNING, J. & HAYENGA, J. *Evaluation of first grade reading achievement in i.t.a., programmed reading, and Scott-Foresman programs.* Unpublished preliminary report, St. Cloud Public Schools, St. Cloud, Minnesota, 1967.

JAMESON, M. C. *An experimental study of the effects of the initial teaching alphabet on reading achievement in the primary grades, with emphasis on grade one. A report on a primary reading experiment.* N.D.E.A. Title III, No. S7591X. Unpublished manuscript, Waterford Township School System, Pontiac, Mich., June 7, 1965.

KIDD, J. W. & HORN, C. J. *i.t.a. with E.M.R.* Unpublished manuscript, Special School District of St. Louis County, Missouri, 1967.

KIRKLAND, Eleanor. *The effect of two different orthographies on beginning reading.* Unpublished manuscript, San Juan Unified School District, Carmichael, California, December 1966.

MAZURKIEWICZ, A. J. "A Comparison of i.t.a. and t.o. Reading Achievement when Methodology is Controlled." In A. J. Mazurkiewicz (Ed.), *i.t.a. and the World of English*, Hempstead, N.Y., i.t.a. Foundation, 1966, pp. 289-292.

MAZURKIEWICZ, A. J. "A Tiger by the Tail." *Proceedings of the 29th Educational Conference of the Educational Records Bureau.* New York: Educational Records Bureau, 1964.

MONSON, H. *The i.t.a. key and the doors it unlocks.* Unpublished manuscript, City School District of Newburgh, Newburgh, N.Y., 1967.

MONTESI, Richard L. *The Initial Teaching Alphabet Experiment September 1964–June 1965.* Unpublished manuscript, Simsbury Public Schools, Simsbury, Connecticut, August 1965.

MONTESI, R L. *The initial teaching alphabet experiment, research report No. II.* Unpublished manuscript, Simsbury Public Schools, Simsbury, Conn., August 1966.

MOUNTAIN, Lee H. "A Comparison of i.t.a., Diacritical Marking System, and Basal Reader Programmes." In A. J. Mazurkiewicz (Ed.), *i.t.a. and the World of English*, Hempstead, N.Y., i.t.a. Foundation, 1966, pp. 280–288.

MYERS, Nancy Joanne. *A comparison of the achievement of children using traditional orthography with that of children using the Initial Teaching Alphabet in the Greater Johnstown School District, Grade One.* Unpublished master's thesis, Indiana State College, 1965.

NEMETH, J. S. & HAYES, R. B. "The New Castle Beginning Reading Study—A Preliminary Report." In A. J. Mazurkiewicz (Ed.), *i.t.a. and the World of English*, Hempstead, N.Y., i.t.a. Foundation, 1966, pp. 258–267.

REGAN, J. F. *An experimental study of the effectiveness of the i.t.a. method of teaching reading in year one.* Unpublished manuscript, North Syracuse Central Schools, North Syracuse, N.Y., 1965.

SHAPIRO, B. J. *A comparison of the Reading Achievement of i.t.a. and T.O. Groups in the First Grade, 1964–65.* Cleveland, Educational Research Council of Greater Cleveland, February 1966.

SLOAN, C. A. *A Comparative Study of Matched Pairs, i.t.a.—T.O. in Beginning Reading Instruction.* Unpublished manuscript, Board of Education of the Owatonna, Minnesota Public School System, 1966.

STEWART, Rebecca. "i.t.a.—After two years." *Elementary English*, November 1965, pp. 660–665.

STEWART, Rebecca. "Two Years with i.t.a.—An Interim Report of the Bethlehem-Lehigh Research Project." In A. J. Mazurkiewicz (Ed.), *i.t.a. and the World of English*, Hempstead, N.Y., i.t.a. Foundation, 1966, pp. 121–124.

TANYZER, H. J. & ALPERT, H. *Effectiveness of Three Different Basal Reading Systems on First Grade Reading Achievement.* Hempstead, N.Y.: Hofstra Univ., Cooperative Research Project no. 2720, 1965.

TANYZER, H. J. & ALPERT, H. "The effects of transition from i.t.a. to T.O. on reading and spelling achievement." Hofstra University, Hempstead, N.Y. (Unpublished paper), 1967.

TANYZER, H. J., ALPERT, H. & SANDEL, LENORE. *Beginning Reading—The Effectiveness of Different Media.* Mineola, N.Y., Nassau School Development Council, 1965.

TANYZER, H. J., ALPERT, H. & SANDEL, LENORE. *Beginning Reading—The effectiveness of i.t.a. and T.O.* Hofstra University, Hempstead, N.Y., 1966.

WAPNER, I. *The initial teaching alphabet in a non-experimental setting: a preliminary report.* Unpublished manuscript, Lompoc Unified School District, California, 1967.

Selected Bibliography

ABERCROMBIE, David. "Augmenting the Roman Alphabet." *The Monotype Recorder*, Vol. 42, no. 3, pp. 2–17, London, Winter 1962–3.
  Studies in Phonetics & Linguistics. Oxford University Press, London, 1965.
  Elements of General Phonetics. Edinburgh University Press, Edinburgh, 1967.
ALSTON, R. C. *See* DANIELSON, B.
ARCHER, Walter. *See* RIPMAN, Walter.

BAKER, Alfred. *The Life of Sir Isaac Pitman*. Pitman, London, 1908.
BARKLEY, William. *The Two Englishes*. Pitman, London, 1941.
  A Last Word. Pitman, London, 1961.
BARNHARDT, C. L. *Let's Read: A Linguistic Approach*. Appleton–Century–Crofts, New York, 1961.
BEADSWORTH, M. "augmented rœman agæn." *Hearing*, Vol. 19, no. 10, pp. 303–305, London, October 1964.
BERNSTEIN, B. "Some Sociological Determinants of Perception—An Enquiry into Sub-cultural Differences." *British Journal of Sociology*, Vol. 9, no. 2, pp. 159–174, London, June 1958.
Best Method of Teaching Children to Read and Write, The. Simplified Spelling Society and Pitman, London, 1924.
BETTS, Emmett Albert and BETTS, Thelma Marshall. *An Index to Professional Literature on Reading and Related Topics*. American Book Co., New York, 1945.
BLADES, William. *The Life and Typography of William Caxton*. Joseph Lilly, London, 1861.
BLOOMFIELD, Leonard. "Linguistics and Reading." *Elementary English Review*, Vols. 19 and 20, London, 1942.
  See also BARNHARDT, C. L.

331

BONNEMA, Helen. "Writing by Sound: a New Method of Teaching Reading." *Spelling Progress Bulletin*, Hollywood, California, March 1961.

BRIDGES, Robert. *English Pronunciation*. Clarendon Press, Oxford, 1913.

BROWN, A. L. "The Work of the Reading Research Unit." *Bulletin of Institute of Education*, University of London; new series, no. 5, pp. 3–10, 1965.

BULLOKAR, William. *Bullokar's Booke at Large, for the Amendment of Orthographie for English Speech*. Henrie Denham, London, 1580. *See also* DANIELSON, B.

BURROUGHS, G. E. R. *A Study of the Vocabulary of Young Children*. Oliver and Boyd, Edinburgh, 1957.

BUTLER, Charles. *The English Grammar or the Institution of Letters, Syllables, and Words in the English Tung*. Oxford, 1633.

CRAIGIE, William. *The Pronunciation of English*. Oxford University Press, 1917. *English Reading Made Easy*. Oxford University Press, 1922.

CROUCH, Elsie and LEEDHAM, John. *i.t.a. Teachers' Instruction Pack*. Initial Teaching Publishing Co., London, 1964.

DALE, N. *On the Teaching of English Reading*. Dent, London, 1898.

DANIELS, J. C. and DIACK, H. *Progress in Reading*. University of Nottingham Institute of Education, 1956.

DANIELSON, B. and ALSTON, R. C. *The Works of William Bullokar. A Short Introduction or Guiding, 1580 and 1581*. University of Leeds, 1966.

DAVIS, Frederick B. *See* TENSUAN, Emperatriz S.

DEWEY, Godfrey. *English heterografy or How we Spel!* Lake Placid Club Education Foundation, N.Y. *World English Spelling*. (U.S.) Simpler Spelling Association, New York, 1964.

DIACK, Hunter. *In Spite of the Alphabet*. Chatto and Windus, London, 1965. *See also* DANIELS, J. C.

DIRINGER, David. *The Alphabet*. Hutchinson, London, 1948.

DOMAN, Glenn J. *Teach Your Baby to Read*. Cape, London, 1965.

DOWNING, J. A. *How Your Children are being Taught by the Augmented Roman Alphabet Method*. University of London Institute of Education, 1961. (Revised edition 1964.)

The Augmented Roman Alphabet : a New Two-stage Method to Help Children Learning to Read. University of London Institute of Education, 1961.

"Experiments with an Augmented Alphabet for Beginning Readers in British Schools." *Frontiers of Education*: report of twenty-seventh Educational Conference. New York, 1962.

and GARDNER, Keith. "New Experimental Evidence on the Role of the Unsystematic Spelling of English in Reading Failure." *Educational Research*, Vol. 5, no. 1, pp. 69–76, Newnes (for the National Foundation for Educational Research in England and Wales), London, 1962.

The Initial Teaching Alphabet. Cassell, London, 1964. (Originally published as tꞷ bεε or not to be, 1962.)

"The Relationship Between Reading Attainment and the Inconsistency of English Spelling at the Infants' School Stage." *British Journal of Educational Psychology*, Vol. 32, pp. 166–177, Birmingham, 1962.

Experiments with Pitman's Initial Teaching Alphabet in British Schools. Paper delivered to International Reading Association, Miami, May 1963. i/t/a Publications, New York, 1963.

"The Augmented Roman Alphabet for Learning to Read." *The Reading Teacher*, Vol. 16, no. 5, pp. 325–336, International Reading Association, Newark, Delaware, March 1963.

The i.t.a. Reading Experiment. Evans (for University of London Institute of Education), London, 1964.

and HALLIWELL, Stanley. "The i.t.a. Reading Experiment in Britain." Paper delivered to International Reading Association, 1964. *Improvement of Reading through Classroom Practice*, pp. 260–265. International Reading Association, Newark, Delaware, 1964.

"The Initial Teaching Alphabet." *New Society*, Vol. 5, no. 124, pp. 12–15, London, 11th February, 1965.

Examples of Children's Creative Writing from Schools Using i.t.a. Reading Research Document, No. 4, University of London, Institute of Education, 1965.

THE i.t.a. SYMPOSIUM. RESEARCH REPORT ON THE BRITISH EXPERIMENT WITH i.t.a., by John Downing. With contributions by H. L. Elvin, A. Sterl Artley, Sir Cyril Burt, Hunter Diack, R. Gulliford, James Hemming, Jack A. Holmes, A. R. MacKinnon, A. H. Morgan and M. Procter, Marie D. Neale, Jessie F. Reid, M. D. Vernon, W. D. Wall. The National Foundation for Educational Research in England and Wales, Slough, 1967.

DUNCAN, John. *Backwardness in Reading.* Harrap, London, 1953.

ELLIS, A. J. *A Plea for Phonetic Spelling.* Fred Pitman, Phonetic Depôt, London, 1848

Transactions of the Philological Society, pp. 89–118, London, 1870.

Dimid'iun Spel'ing or Haaf ov Whot is needed. Lundun, 1880.

ELVIN, H. L. and others. *Some reasons why we are initiating an investigation into the early stages of learning to read.* . . . University of London Institute of Education in association with the National Foundation for Educational Research in England and Wales, London, 1960.

EVANS, W. R. *A Plea for Spelling Reform*, F. Pitman, London, and Isaac Pitman, Bath, 1877.

FAIRBANK, Alfred. *A Book of Scripts.* Penguin Books, Harmondsworth, 1949.

Five Rules for the Improvement of English Spelling without the Addition of New Signs. American Spelling Reform Association and the American Philological Society, c.1882.

FLESCH, R. *Why Johnny Can't Read.* Harper, New York, 1955.

FOLLICK, Mont. *The Influence of English*. Williams and Norgate, London, 1934.
See PITMAN, Sir James. *Inaugural Mont Follick Lecture*. Manchester University, 7th February 1964.
The Case for Spelling Reform. Pitman, London, 1965.
Fonotypic Bible, The. Isaac Pitman, Bath; Samuel Bagster, London; Andrew and Boyle, Boston, 1845.
FRANKLIN, Benjamin. *A Reformed Mode of Spelling. A Scheme for a new Alphabet and reformed mode of Spelling; with Remarks and Examples concerning the same; and an Enquiry into its Uses, in a Correspondence between Miss S——n and Dr. Franklin, written in the Characters of the Alphabet*. 1768.
FRIES, C. C. *Linguistics and Reading*. Holt, Rinehart and Winston, New York, 1962–3.
FRY, Edward. "A Diacritical Marking System to Aid Beginning Reading Instruction." *Elementary English*, Vol. 41, no. 5, Illinois, May 1964.
"The Diacritical Marking System and a Preliminary Comparison with the Initial Teaching Alphabet." *The Journal of Typographic Research*, Vol. 1, no. 1, Cleveland, Ohio, January 1967.

GARDNER, Keith. "Pitmans Initial Teaching Alphabet Applied to Remedial Teaching." *Forward Trends*, Vol. 8, no. 1, pp. 7–11. The Guild of Teachers of Backward Children, London, 1964.
See DOWNING, J. A.
GATES, Arthur I. "The Role of Personality Maladjustment in Reading Ability." *The Journal of Genetic Psychology*, Vol. 59, pp. 77–83, Provincetown, Massachusetts, U.S.A., 1941.
GATTEGNO, Caleb. "Words in Colour System." *Forward Trends*, Vol. 7, no. 4, pp. 141–144. The Guild of Teachers of Backward Children, London, 1964.
GEORGIADES, N. J. *Report on i.t.a. in Remedial Reading Classes*. Reading Research Unit, University of London, Institute of Education, 1964.
GRAY, William S. *The Teaching of Reading and Writing*. UNESCO and Evans, London, 1956.

Half Our Future ("The Newsom Report"). H.M.S.O., London, 1963.
HALLIWELL, Stanley, *see* DOWNING, J. A.
Hansard.

1961	1st August	Question in House of Lords by Lord Douglas of Barloch (about 43-letter alphabet).
1962	1st March	Question by Sir Richard Pilkington (about Spelling Reform).
1963	11th July	Question by Mr. Alan Fitch.
1964	19th March	2 Questions by Dr. King.
	26th March	Debate.
1965	18th March	2 Questions by Mr. Tam Dalyell.
	7th April	Question by Mr. Tam Dalyell (to Sec. of State for Scotland).

20th May	2 Questions (Nos. 80 & 81) by Mr. Tam Dalyell.
3rd August	Question by Mr. James Tinn.
1967 20th April	Mr. Barnes, Mr. Crosland.
21st April	Debate—Mr. Richard Hornby, The Minister of State, Department of Education and Science (Mrs. Shirley Williams).
11th May	Mr. Barnes, Mr. Roberts.

HARRISON, Maurice. *The Use of Simplified Spelling in Teaching Infants to Read and Write.* Pitman (for Simplified Spelling Society), London, 1946.

Instant Reading : the Story of the Initial Teaching Alphabet. Pitman, London, 1964.

"Reading through the i.t.a. 1–9." *The Teacher*, Vol. 3, nos. 3–13, London, 1964.

HART, John. *A Methode or comfortable beginning for all unlearned, whereby they may bee taught to read English, in a very short time, vvith pleasure.* Henrie Denham, London, 1570.

An Orthographie, conteyning the due order and reason, howe to write or painte thimage of manne's voice, moste like to the life or nature. W. Serres, London, 1569. Reprinted by Isaac Pitman in 1850.

HODGES, Richard. *A Special Help to Orthographie or the True-Writing of English.* London, 1643.

The English Primrose. Richard Cotes, London, 1644.

HUEY, E. B. *The Psychology and Pedagogy of Reading.* Macmillan, New York, 1908.

i/t/a Bulletin, Vol. 1, no. 1. Pitman's i/t/a Publications, New York, 1963.

ita jurnal No. 4. Pitman, London, April 1963. Previously Augmented Roman News, No. 1. November 1961.

i.t.a. spelliŋ gied and nœts. Initial Teaching Publishing Co., London, 1964.

i.t.a. Word List. Initial Teaching Publishing Co., London, 1964.

JACKSON, R. "Phonetics and Phonetic Texts in the Teaching of Reading." *Miscellanea Phonetica*, Vol. 1, pp. 33–7, 1914.

JONES, Daniel. *English Pronouncing Dictionary.* Dent, London (eleventh edition), 1957.

KENYON, J. S. and KNOTT, T. A. *A Pronouncing Dictionary of American English.* G. and C. Merriam, Springfield, Massachusetts, 1943.

KNOTT, T. A. *See* KENYON, J. S.

LAUBACH, Frank C. *Learn English the New Way.* Book 1, New English in Twenty Lessons, New Readers Press, New York, 1960 (revised edition 1962).

Let's Reform Spelling—Why and How. New Readers Press, New York, 1966.

LEE, W. R. *Spelling Irregularity and Reading Difficulty in English.* National Foundation for Educational Research in England and Wales, London, 1960.

LEEDHAM, John. *See* CROUCH, Elsie.

Le PARE, R. B. (in conjunction with David De Camp). *Jamaican Creole*. Macmillan, London, 1960.

MACKINNON, A. R. *How DO Children Learn to Read?* Copp Clark Publishing Co., Toronto, 1959.

MALONE, John R. "The Larger Aspects of Spelling Reform." *Elementary English*, Vol. 39, pp. 435–445, Illinois, May 1962.

MORRIS, Joyce. *Reading in the Primary School*. Newnes (for the National Foundation for Educational Research in England and Wales), London, 1959.

How Far can Reading Backwardness be Attributed to School Conditions? A paper read to a conference on Recent Research and Development in the Teaching of Reading, St. Hilda's, Oxford, 1964.

Standards and Progress in Reading. National Foundation for Educational Research in England and Wales, London, 1966.

MORRISON, Stanley. *Note on the Development of Latin Script from Early to Modern Times*. Cambridge University Press, 1949.

MOUNTFORD, John. *Short Notes for Reference on i.t.a. Transliteration*. Reading Research Document, No. 3, Institute of Education, University of London, 1965.

MULCASTER, Richard. *The Elementarie*. 1582.

MULLER, Max. "On Spelling." *Fortnightly Review*. Vol. 25, pp. 556–579, London, April 1876.

NEALE, M. D. *Neale Analysis of Reading Ability*. Macmillan, London, 1963.

OGG, Oscar. *The 26 Letters*. Crowell, New York, 1948.

Phonetic Journal. 1848–1905.

Phonotypic Journal. Vol. 1. 1842–1847.

PITMAN, Benn. *Life and Labors of Sir Isaac Pitman*. Cincinnati, 1902.

PITMAN, Sir Isaac. *A Plea for Spelling Reform*. Series of tracts compiled from *The Phonetic Journal* and other periodicals. Fred Pitman, London, and Isaac Pitman, Bath, 1878.

See also BAKER, Alfred.

PITMAN, Sir James, and SMITH, Charles M. *Phonetic Orthography*. Pitman, London, 1937.

PITMAN, Sir James, "Learning to Read: a Suggested Experiment." *The Times Educational Supplement*, London, 29th May 1959.

The Ehrhardt Augmented Roman Alphabet. 39 Parker Street, London, 1959.

"A Phonetic Alphabet." Letter to editor of *Print in Britain*, Vol. 8, no. 4, Southampton, August 1960.

"Learning to Read: an Experiment." Paper delivered to the Royal Society of Arts, 23rd November 1960. *The Journal of the Royal Society of Arts*, Vol. 109, no. 5055, pp. 149–180, London, February 1961.

The Future of the Teaching of Reading. Paper delivered to the Twenty-eighth

Educational Conference, arranged by Educational Records Bureau, New York, 1963.

The Late Dr. Mont Follick—an Appraisal : The Assault on the Conventional Alphabets and Spelling. Paper delivered at Manchester University, 7th February 1964, Pitman and University of Manchester, London and Manchester, 1965.

"New Alphabets." *Book of Knowledge.* Grolier Society of Canada Ltd., Toronto, 1964.

"Communication by Signs." *New Scientist*, Vol. 25, no. 433, pp. 580–1, London, March 1965.

An Appreciation of "The i.t.a. Symposium." Initial Teaching Alphabet Foundation, London, 1967.

Pitman's Journal: 1906–1929 September.

Pitman's Journal of Commercial Education: 1929 October–1935 September.

Progress in Reading 1948–1964. H.M.S.O., London, 1966.

RAVEN, J. C. *Guide to Using the Crichton Vocabulary Scale with Progressive Matrices* (1947), *Sets A, Ab, B.* Harrap, London, 1950.

Reading Ability. H.M.S.O., London, 1950.

REED, T. A. *A Biography of Isaac Pitman.* Griffith, Farran, Okeden, and Welsh, London, 1890.

RIPMAN, Walter and ARCHER, Walter. *New Spelling.* Pitman, London, 1910. (New edition, revised by Professor Lloyd Jones, Professor Daniel Jones, Walter Ripman, Harold Orton, and I. J. Pitman, 1940 and 1948.)

SCHONELL, F. J. *Backwardness in the Basic Subjects.* Oliver and Boyd, London, 1949.

The Psychology and Teaching of Reading. Oliver and Boyd, London (fourth edition), 1961.

SHAW, George Bernard. *Androcles and the Lion.* The Shaw Alphabet Edition. Penguin Books, Harmondsworth, 1962.

On Language. Edited by Abraham Tauber; Foreword by Sir James Pitman. Philosophical Library, New York, 1963. Peter Owen Ltd., London, 1965.

SILBERMAN, Charles E. "Give Slum Children a Chance." *Harper's Magazine*, Vol. 228, pp. 82–84, pp. 89–92, New York, May 1964.

SIMPSON, Percy. *Proof-Reading in the Sixteenth, Seventeenth, and Eighteenth Centuries.* Oxford University Press, 1935.

SKEAT, Walter W. *Principles of English Etymology.* Clarendon Press, Oxford, 1892.

SMITH, Charles M. *See* PITMAN, Sir James.

SMITH, Sir Thomas. *De recta et emendata Linguae Anglicae Scriptione.* Paris, 1568.

SOFFIETTI, James P. "Why Children Fail to Read: A Linguistic Analysis." *The Harvard Educational Review*, Vol. 25, no. 2, pp. 63–84, Cambridge, Massachusetts, Spring 1955.

SOUTHGATE, Vera. "Augmented Roman Alphabet Experiment: an Outsider's Report." *Educational Review*, Vol. 16, no. 1, pp. 32–41, Institute of Education, Birmingham, November 1963.
"Approaching i.t.a. Results with Caution." *Educational Research*, Vol. 7, no. 2, pp. 83–95, Newnes (for National Foundation for Educational Research in England and Wales), London, February 1965.
Spelling Reform, Report of a Public Meeting on, 29th May 1878. Isaac Pitman, Phonetic Institute, Bath, 1878.
The S.S.A. Fonetic Alfabet. U.S. Simpler Spelling Association, Lake Placid Club, New York, final edition, 1959.
Standards of Reading 1948–1956. H.M.S.O., London, 1957.

TENSUAN, Emperatriz S. and DAVIS, Frederick B. "An Experiment with Two Methods of Teaching Reading." *The Reading Teacher*. Vol. 18, no. 1, pp. 8–15, International Reading Association, Newark, Delaware, October 1964.
THORNTON, William. *Cadmus, or a Treatise on the Elements of Written Language.* Philadelphia, 1793.
TRAXLER, A. E. *Ten Years of Reading Research.* Educational Records Bureau, New York, 1941.
Another Five Years of Research in Reading. Educational Records Bureau, New York, 1946.
Eight More Years of Research in Reading. Education Records Bureau, New York, 1955.
Research in Reading during another Four Years. Educational Records Bureau, New York, 1960.

VALLINS, G. H. *Spelling.* André Deutsch, London, 1954.
VERNON, M. D. *The Experimental Study of Reading.* Cambridge University Press, 1931.
Backwardness in Reading. Cambridge University Press, 1960.
"Specific Dyslexia." *The British Journal of Educational Psychology*, Vol. 32, pp. 143–150, London, 1962.

WEEKLEY, Ernest. *The English Language.* André Deutsch, London, 1952.
WIJK, Axel. *Regularized English.* Almqvist and Wiksell, Stockholm, 1959.
WILKINS, John. *An Essay towards a Real Character and a Philosophical Language.* London, 1668.
WILSON, R. A. *The Miraculous Birth of Language.* Dent, London, 1942.
WINGFIELD, Frederick S. Fonetik Crthqgrafi. Northwest Printery, Chicago, 1942.
WRENN, C. L. *The English Language.* Methuen, London, 1949.

ZACHRISSON, R. E. *Anglic, an International Language.* Almqvist and Wiksell, Upsala and Stockholm, 1932.

Index

Index

Index

Greek, 66, 271; alphabet, 60; words derived from, 62
Gregory, Dr. William, his "Lebtor," 46
Griffin, Dr. William J., 254
Gulliford, R., 163n.

HAHN, H. T., 324
Handicapped children: and reading backwardness, 8, 34–9; taught with i.t.a., 228–38
Handwriting of i.t.a. pupils, teachers' reports on, 205–7
Hanna, P. R., 48
Harley, Dr. Randall, 246
Harrington, Sir John, translation of *Orlando Furioso*, 65–6
Harris, William, on Leigh's alphabet, 87
Harrison, Maurice, *Instant Reading*, 217n.
Hart, John, 91; his alphabet, 76–7, 90
Hawthorne Effect, 165–6 *and n.*, 323
Hayenga, J., 324
Hayes, R. B., 324, 326
Hearing defects, and reading backwardness, 35, 36. *See also* Deaf children
Hemming, James, 163n.; on the Hawthorne Effect, 167n.
Henning, J., 324
Herbert, Sir Alan, "A Criminal Type," quoted 143
Heterotypic homophones, 45
Hildreth, G. H., 32
Hindi, 263, 269
H.M.S.O. publications: *Standards of Reading*, 3n.; *Reading Ability*, 3n.; *Progress in Reading*, 3n.; *Half Our Future*, 5n.
Hodges, Richard, his alphabet, 91–2, 298–9
Hofstra University, U.S.A., i.t.a. Foundation at, 255, 319
Hogben, Lancelot, *Interglossa*, 78n.
Holmes, Jack A., 163n.
Home background, and reading backwardness 27, 35, 151
Homotypic heterophones, 44n.
Horn, C. J., 324
Horsburgh, Miss Florence, 100
How Far can Reading Backwardness be Attributed to School Conditions?, quoted 6–7
Hungarian language, 269
Hunter, 32

i, i.t.a. characterization for, 134–5
Ibadan, University of, 270
Ido, 265
Ilg, F. L., 32
Illinois, 87

Illiteracy, in England and Wales, 3–5, 7, 12
Indefinite article, variants of, 51
Initial Teaching Alphabet: founded on Fonotypy, 79; first steps towards, 111–14; easy to read, 117; typographical description and design, 117–18; printed form and names of characters, 118–19; function of the additional characters, 119–20; digraphic characters, 120–1; freedom from ambiguity, 121; abolition of misleading differences, 122; use of lower-case only, 122–3; replacement of multiple variants of Roman alphabet, 123; two main stages of learning, 123–4; and pronunciation, 126–30; avoidance of pedantic phonemic purity, 130–1; character-to-sound relationships, 131–8; i.t.a. by phonemes, 132; reduces the task of learning, 138–9; a medium for teaching reading, 139–40; divergences from orthodox spelling, 140–1; transition to T.O., 140–6, 152, 159, 164; emotional antagonism to, 147; adaptable to any method of teaching, 147–8; and question of child's age when starting to read, 151; reading primers and supplementary books, 152; and learning to write, 153–8; common doubts about, 158–61; and the deaf, 241–5; and the blind, 246; adaptable for other languages, 252; question of copyright, 254–5; objections to, and answers, 256–60. *See also* Remedial teaching; Research into i.t.a.; Teachers; World i.t.a.; United States
Institute of Education (University of London), 100, 162, 163; Reading Research Unit, 163, 248n.
Intelligence. *See* Low intelligence
International Phonetic Alphabet (IPA), 88, 253, 265
International Phonetic Association, 89
Investigation in the English Spelling Reform Problem with a new detailed plan for a possible solution, An, 316
IPA. *See* International Phonetic Alphabet
Ireland, pronunciation in, 125, 128
i.t.a. *See* Initial Teaching Alphabet
i.t.a. Foundation, 254, 255
i.t.a. Research in the United States, 319–28
i.t.a. Symposium, The. See Downing, Dr. John
Italian language, 40, 55–6, 61, 88, 264, 269, 271

j, i.t.a. characterization for, 133
Jackson, R., "Phonetics and Phonetic Texts in the Teaching of Reading," quoted 89

342

Index

Marion County Public Schools, West Virginia, 201

Mill Hall, Pennsylvania: Bald Eagle-Nittany Schools, 224

Mineville, New York: Central School District # 1, Town of Moriah, 218

Mogadore, Ohio: O.H. Somers Elementary, 209

Nashville, Tennessee: The Bill Wilkerson Hearing and Speech Center, 242

New Riegel School, Ohio: 191

Newburgh Public School, New York, 204-5

Oak Park, Michigan, 191

Old Tappan, New Jersey, 195

Orangeburg, New York: Rockland State Hospital, 229-30

Piscataway Township, New Brunswick, N.J.: Holmes Marshall School, 205

Pontiac, Michigan: Oakland School, 195

Princeton, New Jersey: Miss Mason's School, 192

Rensselaer, New York: Fort Crailo School, 232

St. Cloud Public Schools, Minnesota, 207

Schronn Lake and Moriah Central Schools, New York, 219-20

Uniondale, New York: Union Free School District No. 2, 218

Union Free School District, No. 13, Valley Stream, New York, 191

University City Public Schools, Missouri, 209

Ventnor City, New Jersey: The Anita Metzger School, 195, 206

Warren Township Public Schools, New Jersey, 191-2

Singapore: Pasir Panjang Junior School, 220-1; Alexander Junior School, 222

Scotland, pronunciation in, 125, 128, 129, 136-7

Secondary schools, i.t.a. suggested for, 249-50

Semi-literacy, in England and Wales, 3-7, 12

Shakespeare, variants of his name, 65

Shapiro, B. J., 324

Short Introduction or guiding, to print, write, and read Inglish Speech, A, 312

Shorter Oxford English Dictionary, 275, 298

Sign language, 243

Silberman, Charles E., on the home background, 27

Shaw, Bernard, 111-12; on Dr. Johnson, 73; advocates rejection of Roman alphabet, 102-3; alphabet based on his ideas, 103-4, 112-13; on variations in vowel pronunciation, 124-5

Simpler Spelling Association (U.S.A.), 96, 98, 110; its Fonetic Alfabet, 88

Simplified Spelling Board (U.S.A.), 95-6, 105

Simplified Spelling Society (U.K.), 95-6, 110

Skeat, Walter W.: *Principles of English Etymology*, 60*n*.; on changes in spelling, 67

Sloan, C. A., 324

Smith, Charles M., his colour system, 101-2

Smith, Henry Lee, (Jr)., 89*n*.

Smith, Sir Thomas, 91; his Alphabetum Anglicum, 76, 77, 90

Soffietti, James P., 50; on children's reading difficulties, 54-5

Spanish language, 40, 55, 61, 88, 271

Special schools, i.t.a. in, 228-38

Speech: defects of, and reading backwardness, 36; connection with reading, 54, 232; effect of i.t.a. on, 159-60; imperfect relationship with written word, 273

Speler, The, 95

Spelling: relationship to pronunciation, 75; insistence on accuracy undesirable with i.t.a., 156-7; i.t.a. research results, 180-1; alleged damage to, with i.t.a., 257-8. *See also* Spelling reform; Traditional orthography

Spelling reform: number of systems, 59; five groups of proposals, 75-6; in U.S.A., 105-6; small advance in, 106-7; objections to, 107-11; mistaken tactics, 111; steps towards i.t.a., 111-14

Spence, Thomas, 89

Stahlem, Mrs. Evelyn, 242

Stanford Achievement Test, 325, 327

Stewart, Rebecca, 324, 327-8

Story method of teaching, 22

Sweet, Henry, his Romic characters, 89

Swift, Jonathan, 73

Synthetic languages, 265

Tanyzer, Dr. H. J., 168, 319-28

Taylor, Professor A., 270

tch, i.t.a. characterization for, 133

Teach Your Baby to Read (Glenn J. Doman), 151

Teach Yourself to Spell, 48

Teachers: and backwardness in reading, 12; quality of, 29; and patience, 26; and choice of teaching method, 147-52; and children's facility in writing in i.t.a., 153, 155; and spelling, 156-7; and their own ability to write in i.t.a., 157; doubts about, and objections to i.t.a., 158-61, 256-60; general comments on i.t.a., 189-92

347

Index

Teachers—*cont.*
REPORTS FROM, ABOUT i.t.a.
the transition to T.O., 192–5; keenness to read, 195–6; creative writing, 196–201; problem solving and concept forming, 201–5; handwriting, 205–7; morale and behaviour, 207–10; remedial teaching (children), 216–24, (adults), 224–7 (special schools), 228–38

Teachers' Instruction Pack (Elsie Crouch and John Leedham), 157

Television, 12

Teutonic language, 271

th, i.t.a. characterization for, 120

Thai language, 41

Thomas, Mrs. Marie, 223

Thorndike-Barnhart Dictionary, 98

Thornton, Dr. William, his Universal Alphabet, 79

Times, The, 109

Traditional Orthography (T.O.): structure of, 40*ff.*, 264; evolution of, 60*ff.*; i.t.a. divergences from, 140–1; transition from i.t.a. to, 124, 140–6, 152, 159, 164, 171–8, 192–5, 257, 259; reading in, compared with i.t.a., 168–71, 322–8

Trager, George L., 89*n.*

Transition from i.t.a. to T.O.: teachers' comments on, 192–5; question of optimum moment for, 248–9, 323; criticisms of, 257; ease of, 259

Transition from World i.t.a. to domestic i.t.a., 269

Truancy, among backward readers, 10, 11

Turkish language, 88

Tyndale's Bible, 68–9, 71–2

Typewriters, as aid to reading and writing, 250–1

UNDERDEVELOPMENT. *See* Handicapped children

UNESCO, 263*n.*; *Current School Enrolment Figures*, 7*n.*

Unifon, 88

United States: backward readers in, 7; and achievement of reading readiness, 26*n.*; and shortage of good teachers, 29 *and n.*; and inadequacies of reading failure research, 31; spelling reform in, 105–6, 147; remedial teaching in penal institutions, 226–7; use of i.t.a. with deaf children, 242–3; i.t.a. primers, 248*n.*; pronunciation in, 125, 128, 137, 274; use of i.t.a. in, 152, 158, 188; teachers' reports on i.t.a., 191–2, 195–6, 200–1, 204–7, 209–10; teachers' reports on remedial teaching with i.t.a., 218–20, 223–4, 226–7, 229–32; i.t.a. research, 319–28

U.S. National Council of Teachers. *See* National Council

U.S. Simpler Spelling Association. *See* Simpler Spelling Association

VALLINS, G. H., *Spelling*, 60*n.*

Vernon, Professor M. D., 32; on early and later stages of learning to read, 24; on inadequacies of reading failure research, 31; on the basic characteristic of reading disability, 37–8; on the Hawthorne Effect, 166*n.*

Vernon, Professor P. E., 3, 30, 32, 163

"Visible" speech, 102, 103, 245

Visual-auditory element, 15–16

Visual perception. *See* Ocular defects

Visual-to-sound relationship, 40

Volapük, 265

Volta Bureau (Alexander Graham Bell Association for the Deaf), 242

Vowels: variations in pronunciation, 124–5; neutral vowels in i.t.a., 135–7

WALES: literacy and illiteracy in, 3–7, 12; pronunciation in, 125, 128

Wall, Dr. W. D., 162, 163; on the Hawthorne Effect, 166*n.*–7*n.*

Waltham, Massachusetts, 85

Wapner, I., 324

Watts, Dr. A. F., 3, 30

Watts-Vernon literacy test, 3–5

Webster, Miss Bonnie, 242

Webster, Noah, his spelling reforms, 105–6

Webster's *New Collegiate Dictionary*, 275, 298

West Africa, 125

West Indies, 125

Whole sentence method of teaching, 22

Whole word methods of teaching. *See* Look-and-say

Wijk, Dr. Axel, 100; on irregular spellings, 48–9; his Regularized English, 101, 111, 316–17

Wilkins, John: his augmented alphabet, 78; his shorthand system, 78*n.*, 103

Wilson, R. A., on oral and written language, 14

Wingfield, Frederick S., his fonetic crthqgrafi, 100

Withrow, Mrs. Margaret, 242

Wood, Dr. Ben, 250*n.*; (with Frank N. Freeman), *An Experimental Study of the Educational Influences of the Typewriter . . .*), 251*n.*